Object-Oriented Analysis and Design for Information Systems

Object-Oriented Analysis and Design for Information Systems

Agile Modeling with BPMN, OCL, IFML, and Python

Second Edition

Raul Sidnei Wazlawick

Department of Informatics and Statistics Technological Center,
Federal University of Santa Catarina, Florianópolis, SC, Brazil

MORGAN KAUFMANN PUBLISHERS

AN IMPRINT OF ELSEVIER

Morgan Kaufmann is an imprint of Elsevier
50 Hampshire Street, 5th Floor, Cambridge, MA 02139, United States

Notices

Knowledge and best practice in this field are constantly changing. As new research and experience broaden our understanding, changes in research methods, professional practices, or medical treatment may become necessary.

Practitioners and researchers must always rely on their own experience and knowledge in evaluating and using any information, methods, compounds, or experiments described herein. In using such information or methods they should be mindful of their own safety and the safety of others, including parties for whom they have a professional responsibility.

To the fullest extent of the law, neither the Publisher nor the authors, contributors, or editors, assume any liability for any injury and/or damage to persons or property as a matter of products liability, negligence or otherwise, or from any use or operation of any methods, products, instructions, or ideas contained in the material herein.

ISBN: 978-0-443-13739-6

For Information on all Morgan Kaufmann publications
visit our website at https://www.elsevier.com/books-and-journals

Publisher: Mara Conner
Acquisitions Editor: Chris Kasarapoulos
Editorial Project Manager: Toni Louise Jackson
Production Project Manager: Prasanna Kalyanaraman
Cover Designer: Matthew Limbert

Typeset by MPS Limited, Chennai, India

Working together
to grow libraries in
developing countries

www.elsevier.com • www.bookaid.org

Contents

1

Introduction

Key topics in this chapter

- Object-Oriented Systems Development
- Agile Software Development

1.1 This book

There is a vast literature that aims at presenting UML (Unified Modeling Language)[1] and other diagrams by using a syntactical approach, such as Miles and Hamilton (2006). There are also a significant number of books about development processes and management activities, such as Satzinger et al. (2011). However, there are relatively few books that go deep into the presentation of best practices that allow the effective application of object-oriented techniques in software development in the real world, especially if we consider the new generation of agile methods. This means that despite the vast literature in this area, many questions faced by developers are still left unanswered.

In our approach, agile principles and rules adopted by *Scrum*[2] are largely accepted. As Scrum does not explicitly explain how to develop software, but how to manage the software development process, this book shows how to use object-oriented techniques to improve the team's ability to understand and communicate aspects of the problem and solution.

Furthermore, this book presents some original concepts and other details on topics as follows:

- Objective criteria to identify use cases and decide when to subdivide them or not.
- A technique to systematically derive system use cases from BPMN (Business Process Modeling and Notation) and machine-state diagrams.
- A technique to expand use cases that reduces the disparity among descriptions created by different analysts.
- System sequence diagrams built with actor, interface, and control (instead of actor and system only) to help realize a clear difference between system events and system operations.
- An original approach for writing system commands and queries contracts with the use of the Object Constraint Language (OCL) (Object Management Group, 2010) that allows for automatic generation of running code and not only postcondition checking.

---

[1] http://www.uml.org/
[2] https://www.scrum.org/resources/scrum-guide

Object-Oriented Analysis and Design for Information Systems. DOI: https://doi.org/10.1016/B978-0-443-13739-6.00015-0

- An adaptation of Fowler's (2003) analysis patterns to UML and restructuring and evolving some of those patterns to simplify their identification and application in practice.
- A systematic technique to generate dynamic object models from OCL contracts, which follows good design patterns and significantly reduces the amount of code necessary for running an application, avoiding, for example, redundant verifications.
- An interface tier design presented with the use of IFML (Interaction Flow Modeling Language).

The aforementioned features are useful for producing high-quality software that is well organized, based on a multitiered architecture, and able to change or accommodate new requirements.

1.2 Object-oriented systems development

What is object-oriented systems development? By observing the way object-oriented analysis and design are taught and practiced in some places, it can be concluded that many professionals simply adopt an object-oriented programming language or use fragments of an object-oriented-based development process without exploring the approach in full. Thus very often, they are not as effective as could be expected.

It is not sufficient to organize the system architecture in tiers and modules if the code implemented inside of it is disorganized. Some programmers organize the system adequately in classes and packages, but they still write *spaghetti code* inside the methods of these classes and packages. In addition, other developers still use top-down functional decomposition inside methods, which is not appropriate when using object-oriented programming. Top-down decomposition is adequate if *structured programming* is used instead.

In order to build code that is really object-oriented, developers should learn the techniques of *delegation* and *responsibility assignment*, which can lead to reusable code and low coupling. Those techniques are explained in this book.

It is useless to invest heavily in object-oriented CASE (computer-aided software engineering) tools without learning the way to *think* in terms of object-oriented modeling. The use of diagrams will not necessarily improve the quality of the software, although it may help.

1.3 Agile software development

In relation to the development process, it can be observed that throughout the 20th century several models were proposed. These processes usually mention different stages of development, such as the so-called Waterfall Model of the 1970s (Royce, 1970). In the Waterfall Model, each stage is dedicated to one discipline, such as system requirements, software requirements, analysis, program design, coding, testing, and operation. At the end of each stage, several documents needed to be finalized, including some diagrams. In his original paper, Royce also described why this simplified staged model would not work in practice, and he proposed some other features to improve the process, as shown in the left part of

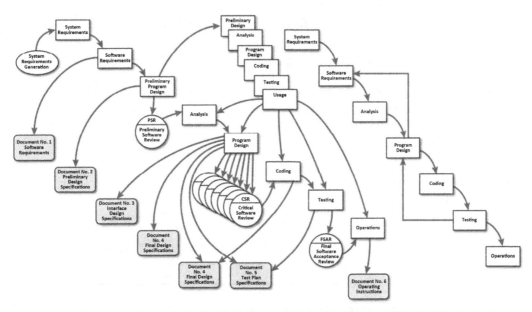

FIGURE 1–1 Final version of Royce's Waterfall Model. *By Winston W. Royce - IEEE WESCON, Public Domain, https://commons.wikimedia.org/w/index.php?curid = 88212953.*

Fig. 1—1. Unfortunately, it seems that many people liked the simpler waterfall version seen in the right part of Fig. 1—1 and adopted it without reading the rest of the paper.

The Unified Process, which arose in the 1990s, disassociated the concept of "stage" from the concept of "discipline" (correlated activities). It placed stages and disciplines in two orthogonal dimensions, indicating that all disciplines can be exercised during all stages of the project, but with different intensities: requirements more intensely at the beginning and more tests at the end, for example (Fig. 1—2).

Still, despite its agile versions, the Unified Process remained basically an artifact-oriented model, requiring, in many cases, the construction of diagrams and other documents.

The agile revolution, from the beginning of the 21st century changed the focus of software development models, which went from processes and artifacts to people and communication.

The difference between those methods can be clarified by a metaphor. In this metaphor, the *prescriptive* process-based bakery of the 20th century would have at the disposal of bakers the best recipes of breads and other delicacies, and that the rule is that bakers should follow the recipes. If something didn't work well, the recipe is corrected or complemented so that the same problem would not happen again. But with this process, the recipes become increasingly complex and difficult to follow. Also, the bakers often could spend more time discussing the recipe than effectively making bread.

With the *agile* bakery, something different would happen. At first, the bakery would hire experienced bakers capable of working as a team, give them an ideal working environment with the best tools and ingredients. They know how to make bread. They can develop their

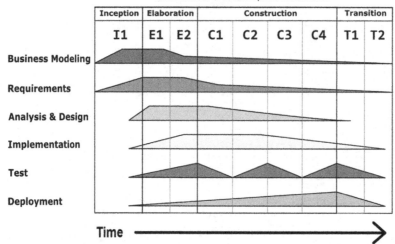

FIGURE 1–2 A simplified view of the Unified Process. *By Jakob Farian Krarup - Own work, CC0, https://commons. wikimedia.org/w/index.php?curid = 93364952.*

own recipes, based on their experiences and knowledge about the taste of the customers, which they consult frequently. Frequently they would be exchanging information about what was going on, about the best and worst recipes and thus would jointly evolve a development model based on their skills and intense communication among them and clients. That way, they would spend more time actually making breads and still experimenting with new and original recipes, quickly solving among them any problems that arise and improving their experience even more.

Bringing this metaphor to the software industry, we see that it is increasingly less important to think in terms of stages and procedures and increasing focus on the human beings who produce software and who use that same software (the user) and the quality of their communications.

As the agile manifesto says[3], there may be documentation, contracts, processes, tools, plans, and customer negotiation, but *more important* is to have motivated individuals, easy interactions, collaboration, working software, and the ability to accommodate change.

1.4 Discussion

Agile models have not changed, however, the way software is programmed. The object-oriented paradigm is still dominant today in the software industry. Most agile models also deal more with management aspects than software modeling and programming. Thus the

[3] https://agilemanifesto.org/

software produced in an agile way does not rule out the construction of good models. Maybe XP—eXtreme Programming (Beck and Andres, 2004) one day has given the impression that agile development should consist of "go and program fast" without any planning. But that's a myth. Before we start developing lines of code, we need to understand the user's needs and pains, their context, their journey, and their obstacles. Some diagrams can help a lot in this. After understanding the problem and prioritizing features, we need to draw one or more solutions to the prioritized features. Again, diagrams can help in crafting, refining, and communicating these ideas.

Thus this book will go through several activities of software development assuming they are conducted by an agile model such as Scrum, and presenting several notations, diagrams, and languages that can be used as tools of thought so that agile teams can represent and evolve their ideas.

Questions

1. What differentiates a process-based software development from an agile one?
2. What is UML?
3. What is Scrum?
4. Do agile methods hinder object-oriented programming? Why?
5. What is the agile manifesto and how should it be interpreted?

2

General view of the system

Key topics in this chapter

- General view of the system
- Early effort estimation
- Product backlog
- Business use case diagram

2.1 Introduction to general view of the system

The activities related to the definition of the scope of a project should usually take a relatively small fraction of the time of the whole project, although variations may exist depending on the kind of the project: projects with simple and well-defined requirements (e.g., a vaccination app) may demand no more than a couple of days of business modeling while complex and large projects (e.g., a hospital management system) may demand weeks or months. At the time of scope definition, all information about the organization can be explored by interviewing users, clients, and domain specialists, as well as by the examination of documents, reports, existing systems (desk research), and related bibliography.

For most projects, the first question the team should answer is the following: What is the vision of the organization for the project? In other words, what does the organization want with the project? Why is it being proposed, and why is the organization going to spend money with it? What are the pains of the users in their daily journey? What bothers them? At that moment, another question, often forgotten, may be raised: Buying or developing? Sometimes, the product the client wants is available for purchase.

These questions must be answered in a relatively short time, because, at this time, the client and the development team usually do not have an idea of the real extension of the project and it is, from the point of view of both, an investment on the future and, therefore, a risk.

The general view of the system or executive summary is a free format document, where the team may report the relevant items they discovered about the system after the initial interviews with the stakeholders.

This book does not intend to propose rules for writing that document. But it is suggested that it should not be too long. A few pages of text and some diagrams may be sufficient to describe in a summarized way the scope of most systems. More than that could mean that too much detail was included in the summary.

Object-Oriented Analysis and Design for Information Systems. DOI: https://doi.org/10.1016/B978-0-443-13739-6.00002-2

The scope declaration in the general view should present the products that must be developed, what must be included, and eventually, what could be included but would not. This information may be obtained initially by interviewing the stakeholders and may be refined later with the use of the tools presented in this book.

If possible, the main deliverables of the project should be also defined in the general view as well as the time frame when the client is going to receive some kind of delivery from the development team. Normally, this list of deliverables consists of implemented versions of the software, but the list can also include other items, such as design, manuals, media, training, and documentation.

2.2 Early effort estimation

It can be difficult to establish deadlines for deliveries before doing the requirements analysis of the system, because estimation effort techniques such as *function points* (Albrecht and Gaffney, 1983), *use case points* (Karner, 1993), or *COCOMO II* (Boehm, 2000) can generally be applied after a good deal of the requirements is known. Thus the information about deadlines at this early stage can be more a guess than a formal strong commitment for development.

At the Bridge Laboratory, a technique that is obtaining success in early development cost estimation is a variation of the technique known as "expert opinion." A senior systems specialist known as CXO (Chief Experience Officer) conducts the first contacts with the client to understand the project's goals and products. This is outlined in a report with three levels, as shown in the UML Object Diagram in Fig. 2−1.

Then, each product, usually an epic, is presented and discussed by an experienced agile team. More than one team may be consulted for the same product if necessary. The team will try to understand the extension, complexity, and risks of each product and produce an effort estimation for each one. This divide-and-conquer technique helps in obtaining a more precise estimation than trying to estimate the whole project at once. In soccer, one probably would miss the goal if trying to kick the ball from the center of the field (neither Pelé could do it). However, with small kicks, one can approach the goal more precisely and convert.

2.3 Acceptance criteria

The general view document may also contain some acceptance criteria for the product, that is, quantifiable items that will be used to decide whether the project was a success or not. The product acceptance criteria should at least include metrics for deadlines, budget, and quality.

If subjective criteria such as "customer satisfied," "system easy to use," or "state-of-the-art technology" are used, they should be quantified, that is, it should be defined how to measure "customer satisfaction," "ease of use," "state of the art," and so on. Examples of quantifiable acceptance criteria are "the system must support up to 50,000 simultaneous accesses without degrading performance," "the system must eliminate the need to use paper for performing

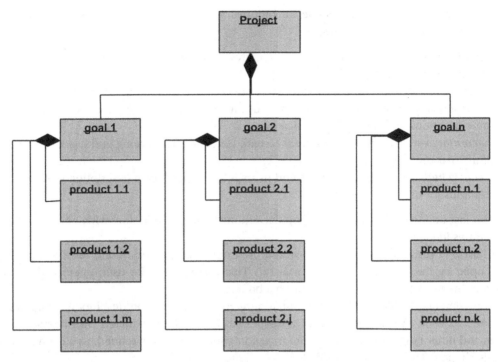

FIGURE 2–1 Object diagram with the initial three-level structure of a project.

processes x and y," "the system must allow any user to send pictures taken from their own smartphone," and "the system must allow the management of 20,000 works of construction simultaneously."

2.4 Completing the general view of the system

More information may be added to the general view document if needed (e.g., main risks, technologies to be used). The general view of the system is the base agreement document for the client and the developer. It will be taken as a basis for planning the rest of the project.

It is important to mention that when the general view is being built, the requirements analysis has not yet been completed, and therefore, the information mentioned in the general view consists of early commitments. It is expected that the requirements analysis will detail the scope in depth, but not augment its extension. For example, in requirements analysis, the process of managing construction works may be detailed with propositions, authorizations, assessments, and so on (considering that "managing construction works" is mentioned in the scope declaration), but if the payment roll of the building company was not mentioned in the scope declaration, then the inclusion of that item in the project would require a renegotiation of the scope declaration.

Pressman (2008) proposes some techniques to communicate with stakeholders to discover business goals, for example:

- *Traditional focus groups*, where a trained analyst meets with a group of end users or people representing their roles.
- *Electronic focus groups*, where the meetings are conducted using electronic media.
- *Iterative surveys*, where a few surveys are conducted among end users, presenting them some questions and asking for clarification.
- *Exploratory surveys*, where exploratory research is conducted among end users that use a similar existing product.
- *Scenario building*, where a group of end users is led to produce a description of some scenarios for using the system.

The last option seems to be very popular among agile practitioners, where scenarios are sometimes identified as *user stories*.

Chart 2−1 presents a general view with a preliminary scope declaration for a real project developed by the Bridge Laboratory in 2017[1]. This example will be used often to illustrate some of the modeling techniques within this book.

The contents of this chart are the initial agreement between the development organization and its client. Using it as a basis, a deeper study may be conducted with business use cases and other diagrams, so that the information contained in it is refined, as shown further in this chapter. The document is divided into 10 parts:

- A short *summary*, as this is the third phase of the project, and many modules were already developed for the other two versions and are known by the client.
- A short *presentation* of the developing organization.
- The *public* intended to be using this system.
- The *justification* for this project and the investment.
- The *objective* of the project.
- The *methodology* (agile development) to be used in this project.
- The *success indicators* used to assess whether the project has achieved its goals.
- A concern about the *sustainability* of the project.
- The *work plan*, built in accordance to Fig. 2−1.
- The *schedule*, considering possible parallelism that can be obtained by using four agile teams for Web (Teams A, B, C, and D), two agile teams for mobile (Teams iOS and Android), one Quality Assurance team, one team specialized in producing media, and three specialized teams at the end of the project.
- A preliminary *risk list*.
- The *lead time* of the project.

---

[1] This 18-month project was the third phase of a project named SISMOB—Sistema de Monitoramento de Obras (Construction Works Monitoring System) that was developed having the Brazilian Ministry of Health as client and federal, state, and municipal managers, professionals of control organizations, and society in general as users.

UNIVERSIDADE FEDERAL
DE SANTA CATARINA

Bridge Lab

Project Proposal
19/10/2017

Construction Works Monitoring System (SISMOB) Phase 3

Summary

This project will conduct research, development, and implementation of technologies for the evolution of the Construction Works Monitoring System (SISMOB), as well as, the updating of existing modules, implementation of new modules, updating of business rules, updating of the current flow and database in the Web system and apps for mobile devices.

The Construction Works Monitoring System - SISMOB aims to monitor all engineering works and infrastructure of Primary Health Care Units, Emergency Care Units, Health Academies, among other health facilities that are financed with federal resources.

It should allow comparisons of the planned and executed activities of each work, as well as its phases and stages, allowing the manager to compare the predefined schedule of the work, carried out by a specialized professional, with the actual progress, providing a financial and executive view of the entire work. The entire history of the work along with the images can be viewed in the historical series available in the system.

It should also allow the manager to receive alerts when some stage of the work is critical or overdue, thus facilitating feedback and improving the quality of information.

SISMOB also contributes to the structuring and strengthening of the National Health System (SUS). In addition, it contributes to the continuity of change in the health care model in the country by proposing that the improvement of the physical structure of health is a facilitator for changing practices.

Presentation

The Bridge Laboratory of Research and Technological Innovation was created in 2013 with the proposal of producing knowledge in health information technology. Thus, based on its know-how in the development of systems for public health management, it proposes the implementation of the SISMOB evolution project for the Ministry of Health (MS).

Public

The public for this project is composed by federal, state, and municipal managers, professionals of control organizations, and society in general.

bridge.ufsc.br | contato@bridge.ufsc.br | 48 3721 6190   UNIVERSIDADE FEDERAL DE SANTA CATARINA   **bridge_**

CHART 2–1 Example of a general view of the system with its scope declaration.

Justification

The Construction Works Monitoring System (SISMOB) has the mission of contributing to the strengthening of the SUS (National Health System), through the improvement of the physical structure of public health facilities in the country.

Developed by a partnership signed between the Ministry of Health (MS) and the Federal University of Santa Catarina (UFSC), SISMOB has as main objective the monitoring of all engineering and infrastructure construction financed by the Ministry of Health.

Its main characteristics are transparency, data security, integration with systems of the National Health Fund (FNS) and National Registry of Health Establishments (CNES), agility in the evaluation of proposals and works in progress, greater efficiency, and quality in the preparation of reports, greater agility in the release of financial resources until the completion of the work.

It also allows greater support to public management, access to control organizations, decision support, essential information to sign agreements, transfer contracts, and carry out money transfers and qualitative evaluations on investments and monitoring the execution of the financed object.

Objective

The main objective of this project is to ensure the evolution of SISMOB by the research, development, and implementation of new features and the updating of its modules, as well as the functionalities already developed, incorporating into the Web system and applications for mobile devices, rules, improvements, and optimization of source code and operation processes.

Methodology

The products of this proposal will be developed using agile software engineering techniques considering individuals and interactions more important than processes and tools, the proper functioning of the software, collaboration between those involved, and immediate responses to changes.

Success Indicators

The levels of customer and users' satisfaction are the main indicators for evaluating the delivered products. However, it is important to highlight that if any diagnostic tool is used by the client, it should also be available to the Bridge Laboratory to perform the respective analyses to compare the results and identify any non-conformity.

Project Sustainability

To ensure the sustainable development of the project it is essential that all schedules are respected and fulfilled, i.e., development, deliveries, and payments.

CHART 2–1 *(Continued).*

Work Plan

PROJECT NAME	Construction Works Monitoring System (SISMOB) Phase 3			
GENERAL OBJECTIVE	Research, develop, and implement technologies for the evolution of SISMOB			
GOAL	PRODUCT	DESCRIPTION	EFFORT[1]	COST[2]
1 - Management Panel	1 - Consolidated information module for the federal profile	This module will enable the generation and display of consolidated information regarding the deadlines and situations of all works under construction	1 AT x 4 Months	M$210,341
	2 - Consolidated information module for State and municipal profiles	This module will enable the generation and display of consolidated information regarding the situation of the works under construction for the states and municipalities	1 AT x 4 Months	M$210,341
2 - Integration with external systems	3 - File generation module with records for payments	This module will enable the generation and export of proposals information that enable the releasing of payments	1 AT x 3 Months	M$157,755
3 - Evolution and Maintenance	4 - Adaptation and improvement of functionalities in the system	The activities relevant to this goal are specifically in the modules and functionalities already developed in the software	1 AT x 18 Months	M$946,535
4 - Mobile apps	5 - Module with the evaluation form in the SISMOB Android App	Implementation in the Android version of the Module SISMOB App to record the evaluation report information	1 AT x 4 Months	M$210,341
	6 - Module with the evaluation form in the SISMOB iOS App	Implementation of the iOS version of the Module SISMOB App to record the evaluation report information	1 AT x 4 Months	M$210,341
	7 - Citizen App for Android Platform	Application to enable the citizen to monitor the execution of works, and make and forward complaints to the MS	1 AT x 6 Months	M$315,511

[1] AT stands for "Agile Team" and "months" is linear time. Thus, for example, "1 AT × 4 months" means one agile team working for four months.
[2] M$ stands for "Mira", a fictional currency used in the "Legend of Heroes" series of games. The cost is the product of the effort by the average cost of the agile team allocated to the task. Different teams may have different average costs depending on the number of members and their experience, among other factors.

CHART 2–1 *(Continued).*

	8 - Citizen App for iOS platform	Application to enable the citizen to monitor the execution of works, and make and forward complaints to the MS	1 AT x 6 months	M$315,511
5 - New Modules and Features	9 - Proposal reactivation module	This module will enable the federal manager to reactivate canceled proposals	1 AT x 3 Months	M$157,755
	10 - Address change module by federal manager	This module will allow the federal manager to change the address of the works	1 AT x 3 Months	M$157,755
	11 - Module Size Change	This module will enable the proponent to request changing the size of the work and the reviewer to issue a report about this request	1 AT x 5 Months	M$262,926
	12 - Module Revocation of Opinions	This module will enable the federal manager to revoke opinions issued	1 AT x 3 Months	M$157,755
6 - Technological Research for Recognition of patterns in images	13 - Technical Research Report	Conduct a study on available, accessible, and applicable technologies regarding the identification of images	1 AT x 4 Months	M$210,341
7 - Update Technology of the Framework Vaadin	14 - Framework Vaadin version 8	Upgrade the Vaadin Framework from version 7 to version 8	1 AT x 5 Months	M$262,926
8 - Digital tutorials for system use	15 - Tutorial videos about system use	Guided navigation videos about system operation totaling 60 minutes	1 AT x 10 Months	M$525,852
9 - Internalization of the system in the environment of the MS	16 - Documentation of functional requirements and business rules	Prepare documentation containing the functional requirements and business rules of the software (Web and mobile applications)	3 AT x 2 Month	M$105,170
	17 - Software source code (Web and mobile applications)	Provide software source code (web and mobile applications)		M$105,170
	18 - Database modeling	Make conceptual model for databases (Web and mobile applications) available		M$105,170

CHART 2–1 *(Continued)*.

Schedule

GOAL	PRODUCT	1	2	3	4	5	6	7	8	9	10	11	12	13	14	15	16	17	18
1	1 - Consolidated information module for the federal profile. Agile Team A	█	█	█	█														
1	2 - Consolidated information module for state and municipal profiles. Agile Team A					█	█	█	█										
2	3 - File generation module with records for payments. Agile Team B	█	█	█	█														
3	4 - Adaptation and correction of functionalities already in the system. QA Team				█	█	█	█	█	█	█	█	█	█	█	█	█	█	█
4	5 - Module with the evaluation form of works in the APP SISMOB Android. Agile Team Android	█	█	█	█														
4	6 - Module with the evaluation form of works in the APP SISMOB iOS. Agile Team iOS	█	█	█	█														
4	7 - Citizen App for Android Platform. Agile Team Android					█	█	█	█										
4	8 - Citizen App for iOS platform. Agile Team iOS					█	█	█	█										
5	9 - Proposal reactivation module. Agile Team D		█	█															
5	10 - Address change module for the federal manager. Agile Team B					█	█	█	█										
5	11 - Size Change Module. Agile Team D						█	█	█										
5	12 - Module for Revocation of Opinions. Agile Team B							█	█										
6	13 - Technical Research Report. Agile Team C													█	█	█			
7	14 - Framework Vaadin Version 8. Agile Team B												█	█	█	█			
8	15 - Tutorial videos about system usage. Media team				█	█	█	█	█	█	█	█	█	█					

bridge.ufsc.br | contato@bridge.ufsc.br | 48 3721 6190   UNIVERSIDADE FEDERAL DE SANTA CATARINA   bridge_

CHART 2–1 *(Continued).*

9	16 - Documentation of functional requirements and business rules. Analysts team																
9	17 - Software source code. Programmers team																
9	18 - Database modeling. Database team																

Risks Identification

Some occurrences may directly or indirectly impair the execution of the project and its level of overall satisfaction, as follows:

- Scope changes.
- Delay in defining business rules.
- Changes in the prioritization of deliveries.
- Changes to Datasus (final installation environment) infrastructure without notice.
- Delays in installment payments.
- Adverse situations at UFSC such as lack of workforce.

Total Lead Time

Eighteen (18) months from the date of signing the contract.

CHART 2–1 *(Continued)*.

After agreeing to this summary with the client, the team may start deepening the knowledge about the client/user needs. In the Bridge case, this document was used to build a contract with the client in order to start the development.

2.5 Product backlog

Product backlog is one of the most cherished tools in agile development. It may have different configurations, though. For example, in Kanban (Anderson, 2010), its columns or cells have limits in the number of tasks than can be contained; this happens to avoid many tasks being initiated but not concluded, which could happen because Kanban does not use the concept of *sprint* as in Scrum and other methods, but continuous development without timeboxes. In Scrum, only a limited number of tasks are selected and must be concluded within the sprint. This avoids the problem of having many unfinished tasks in the backlog.

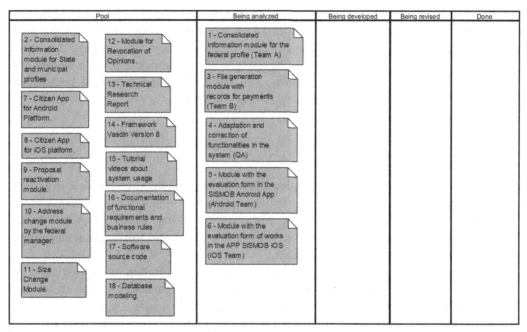

FIGURE 2–2 A product backlog with epics.

Scrum divides the Kanban board into two boards: the product backlog and the sprint backlog. The sprint backlog is used to manage one single sprint (usually 2 weeks of work), while the product backlog is used to manage the whole project (usually several months). This chapter concentrates on the product backlog.

The product backlog may have a different number of columns depending on the team's needs. One possible and useful configuration is to have the following columns.

- Pool of epics (initialized with all 18 products in the example shown in Chart 2–1).
- Epics being analyzed (epics from the first column are moved here when the team starts studying them—the team may use a schedule, as in the SISMOB example, or deciding on priorities along the project with the client).
- Epics being developed (in this case, the epics may be broken in shorter activities using the 100% rule, that is, the sum of the products of the shorter activities corresponds to 100% of the product of the epic).
- Epics being revised (all work is revised!—after developing the products of the epic, they will be revised as well, preferably by people more experienced).
- Epics done (after revision and acceptance of the products, the epic is considered done).

The 18 products shown in Chart 2–1 may be considered as the epics that will populate the product backlog for the SISMOB project. Fig. 2–2 shows how the product backlog for SISMOB would look a few days after the project started. Notice that different teams are working on different epics, and some epics that will be started later are still in the first column.

Notice also that not every epic in this project consists of the implementation of new features for the system. For example, Product 15 is about producing videos, not software. Product 14 is about upgrading the framework used in the software, and although it is about developing and revising software, it does not imply in the implementation of new features. Those kinds of activities will not be addressed in this book. Instead, we will continue to explore the epics that mean features development or modification.

2.6 Business use cases

Jacobson (1994) presents in detail techniques for business modeling with business use cases. In general, in business models, there are entities (people or organizations) external to the target organization, called *business actors*, and internal entities, called *business workers*. Business use cases are the processes performed by those actors and workers that allow them to reach some of the company business goals.

The business use case model considers the entire target organization as a system, and the actors may be people, companies, government, or other organizations that create and maintain relationships with the target organization (Kroll and Kruchten, 2003).

The first thing the team must think about when doing business modeling is that what is being modeled is *not* a software system. An *organization* is being modeled. Business information is sought from higher-level management people and specialists because they know and sometimes create the organization's goals.

Most agile teams may prefer to use *epic user stories* instead of business use cases. In this book, we consider that user stories are written by users while use cases are usually the same stories but refined by analysts. Thus the team may first hear the client and users and identify the important stories and then work on them to refine, obtain more details, correct imperfections, and improve optimization. After that, the user story may be considered as a use case.

The quantity of business use cases that will be identified may be small relatively to the size of the project. A business process is a long-range process that is performed by the organization; think, for example, of one of the main objectives of the SISMOB system that is to manage the development of construction works. Some relatively simpler processes may compose the stages of that larger process, for example, "registering a proposal," "publish a proposal," "assess a proposal," and "deliver money". The larger process consists of a business use case while the smaller component processes are *system use cases*, which will be introduced later.

Although UML officially does not have a standard symbol to differentiate business use cases from system use cases, it is usual to represent business use cases with the stereotype ≪*business*≫, or by cutting the use case ellipse with an edge as shown in Fig. 2–3.

In this example, "Manage work" is a business use case because it involves a relationship between the organization (the Ministry of Health) and external entities (such as municipal proponents, external reviewers, citizens), producing a perceptible and consistent result: one

FIGURE 2–3 Business use case.

construction work is managed from its proposal to its conclusion. This use case possibly will be performed by the external users with the collaboration of some workers inside the organization.

Use case names must be chosen carefully, because at this stage they will summarize critical information about the system, and wrong choices may prevent the team and stakeholders from sharing comprehension about the real intention of business actors and workers. Blain[2] presents some best practices collected from many sources:

- *Good use case names reflect user goals.* Names such as "Access system" or "Open main window" must be avoided because they reflect technology and not a business goal. Also, names without verbs such as "Invoice" must be avoided because it is not clear what is going to happen to the invoice. Better names might be "Generate invoice," "Cancel invoice," "Pay invoice," etc.
- *Good use case names are as short as possible.* Although some people may propose that a use case name should not have more than two or three words (or any other number), it is unfeasible to define such a limit because there is a risk of losing clarity on the business goal if the name is too short. As Blain points out, which word could be removed from the name "Collect late payment" without obscuring its meaning? However, that name is better than "Collect late payment from customers that are past due."
- *Good use case names use meaningful verbs.* Use case names not only should have *strong* verbs, but they must be meaningful. A meaningless verb is one that does not make clear what the use case accomplishes; for example, what does a use case such as "Process order" accomplish? What result does it produce? A name such as "Separate ordered items for dispatch" would be more meaningful in that case.
- *Good use case names use active voice.* As in general writing, active voice is preferable to passive voice. "Pay for order" is better than "Order is paid."
- *Good use case names use present tense.* The present tense indicates what the user is trying to do. Past and future tense may sound confusing and unnecessary.
- *Good use case names do not identify the actor.* As use cases are linked to actors, actors must not be part of their names. Thus a use case name must not identify the actor as in "Manager creates sales report." Just name the use case as "Create sales report" and link it to a manager and other actors if necessary.
- *Good use case names are consistent.* The same naming rules and naming conventions should be applied along a project or group of projects. Avoid, for example, naming one use case "Generate sales report" and another "Produce reservations report." Choose one verb for that meaning and use it consistently.

---

[2] http://tynerblain.com/blog/2007/01/22/how-to-write-good-use-case-names/

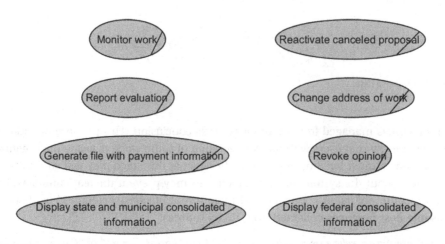

FIGURE 2–4 Some business use cases found in the example.

Additionally, Probasco (2001) proposes that the list of use case names should resemble a *to-do* list. Thus instead of writing "Cash withdrawal," "Funds transfer," and "ATM service," it would be better to write "Withdraw cash," "Transfer funds," and "Service the ATM," respectively.

Probasco also insists that the meaning of a use case name must be precise. For example, is "Auction" a good use case name? Is it a verb or a noun? If you consider that it is a noun and that a verb must be added, is "Execute auction" a good name? The verb "Execute" would probably be a programmer's choice, but it probably has no meaning for an auctioneer (Is the auction going to be shot to death?). In this case, an idea would be to hear the user or a domain specialist in order to discover a better name. On the other hand, even if "auction" is indeed a verb, it is not sufficiently clear. Is it the auction of a single item? Is it the auction of a complete set of items? Is it simply an auction participant placing a bid? In that case, names such as "Auction items," "Auction single item," or "Place bid" would be clearer.

Fig. 2–4 presents some business use cases that were detected among the 18 products of the SISMOB Phase 3 project. Considering the more general use case of this project that is to manage works from proposal to conclusion, we can observe that some of those use cases are in fact extensions or used by the main use case. The arrows with stereotypes ≪ *extend* ≫ and ≪ *use* ≫ may be used to represent extensions and uses, respectively. The difference between them is the following:

- An *extension* is a use case that can be performed while the main use case is performed, but not mandatorily. The arrow flows from the extension to the main use case.
- A use case *includes* another if it is a mandatory part of the former. The arrow flows from the main use case to the included use case.

Fig. 2–5 presents the structure of extensions and inclusions of the business use cases for the SISMOB project. As use cases "Display state and municipal consolidated information" and "Display federal consolidated information" are not necessarily performed during the management of a single work, they are not related to "Manage work" by those criteria.

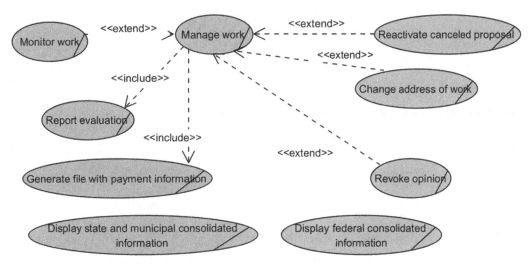

FIGURE 2–5 Examples of the use of «extend» and «include».

On the other side, "Report evaluation," and "Generate file with payment information" are mandatory parts of the use case "Manage work." Finally, "Monitor works" (by a citizen), "Reactivate cancelled proposal," "Change address of work," and "Revoke opinion" are use cases considered as optional regarding the management of a single work, that is, they can happen or not.

2.6.1 Business actors and business workers

During business modeling, there are two kinds of actors that must be addressed:

- *Business actors*: People, organizations, or even systems that perform some activities belonging to the process, but which are not part of the target organization. That is, they are not under the organization's control. Business actors could be, for instance, customers, publishers, external reviewers, partner companies, or even other automatic systems that the target organization could interact with.
- *Business workers*:[3] People, organizations, or even systems that perform some activities belonging to the process and that are part of the target organization. They could be the organization's employees, its departments, or even existing software systems belonging to the organization. Graphically, they are distinguished from business actors by the use of the stereotype «*worker*».

Examples are shown in Fig. 2–6.

[3] If we are modeling an organization as a whole, usually business workers do not appear, as they are internal to the company's system. But if connections between different subsystems of the company are shown, then business workers must appear.

FIGURE 2–6 Business actor and business worker.

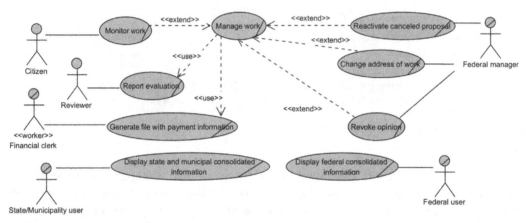

FIGURE 2–7 Business actors and business use cases.

This differentiation is important because business actors usually cannot be automated, that is, they will not be replaced by computational systems. However, business workers' roles can possibly be replaced by automatic systems (English, 2007).

Business actors and business workers are linked to the business use cases they participate in by connecting lines without arrows,[4] as shown in Fig. 2−7.

2.6.2 Automation opportunities

SISMOB is a system that is operated by several actors through the Internet. Before its existence, works funded by the Ministry were managed by using paper and spreadsheets. Considering this situation, the original system had business workers that were basically real people. Some of these workers' roles were automated. For example, the role of the clerk that sends email to stakeholders after the identification of delays or irregularities was replaced by an automatic messaging system. However, the role of the analysts that assess the works and

---

[4] Some approaches suggest the use of arrows to indicate whether the actor only receives or sends information to the system. But that practice, besides not being supported by UML 2, brings practically no useful information at this point of the business analysis, because now it is only important to know which use cases really exist, and which actors are involved with them. The details on the interaction will be given later with the activity diagrams that will describe how a business use case is performed.

decide if it is going well or not was not automated. Maybe only artificial intelligence may fill this role in the future.

Not every business worker role will usually be replaced. It depends on the scope of the project and the technology available. A nurse role to measure a patient's temperature could be replaced by an automatic device, for example.

An advantage in making the business use case diagram, then, is to help in visualizing and making decisions on automation. With the diagram, it is possible to visualize what must stay inside and outside the automation scope, depending on the project's goals.

Normally, during an automation process within an organization, it is useful to replace at least the workers' roles that correspond to mere proxies, that is, the ones that simply perform actions in the place of an external actor. In the case of SISMOB, for example, the clerk that only receives an email, prints it, and stores it in the appropriate physical file could be replaced by a system that allows the reviewers to type their own texts on the system.

The association of the business use cases with the organization's major business goals helps to identify the scope of the system, that is, the activities that will be effectively automated in the project that is being initiated.

The system boundary can be used to identify the set of business use cases and business workers that will be automated, as shown in Fig. 2−8.

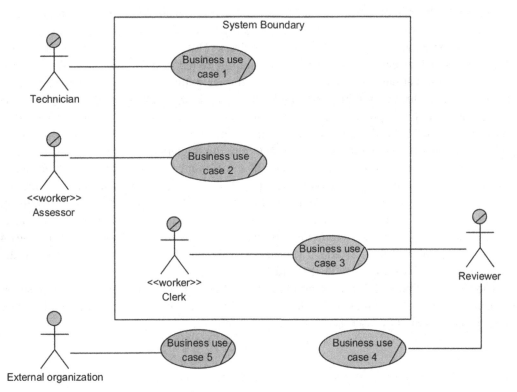

FIGURE 2–8 System boundary.

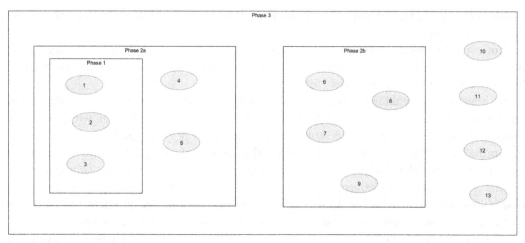

FIGURE 2–9 Using system boundaries to represent a project with many phases.

The business use case diagram shows that the automation project will include use cases 1, 2, and 3 and the role of "Clerk." It also shows that use cases 4 and 5 are not meant to be automated at least for the moment.

Regarding the actors, it can be said that only actors outside the system boundary that own at least one connection to a use case that is inside the boundary are meant to continue to be system actors in the next steps of analysis. This is the case with "Technician," "Assessor," and "Reviewer." The last one will continue to perform business use case 4 as it is done today and will have business use case 3 routines implemented in the new system. As for actor "Clerk," its role will be automated, and no such actor will exist when the new version of the system is implemented. Finally, actor "External organization" is not associated to any use case that is inside the system boundary, meaning, that this actor will continue to perform business use case 5 the same way as before the implementation of the new system.

If the project, on the other hand, consists of some subprojects or stages, in which different parts of the it would be automated, that could also be indicated by the use of different system boundaries in the diagram: one for each subproject or stage. Fig. 2–9, for example, shows a project that starts with phase 1, by the implementation of use cases 1, 2, and 3. Then, it has two parallel developments: phases 2a and 2b, which will develop use cases 4 and 5 (Phase 2a) and 6, 7, 8, and 9 (Phase 2b). Finally, Phase 3 can be executed by the implementation of use cases 10, 11, 12, and 13.

The next step that leads to the requirements analysis is the detailed study of the business use cases that will be automated. The level of precision and detail depends on the objectives of the project, as already discussed early in this chapter.

2.7 Discussion

It is important to remember that the goal of business modeling is usually to find a general view of the business and not a detailed specification of its processes. Thus in most cases, the team's goal is to concentrate on discovering information about the business and not on formally specifying how the business works as if it was a machine.

Business modeling is not just about building diagrams, however. The purpose of diagrams is to help understand the context and the initial general requirements of a project and a system. Business modeling is one of the key activities that help a team to identify and prepare for project risks. Other risk mitigation activities may also be performed, such as proof-of-concept, workshops, prototyping, and early tests. Any strategy that helps in understanding the big picture and identifying the major risks and complexities of a project is valid.

Questions

1. Why effort estimation is less precise at the beginning of a project?
2. What is the public for a general view of a system; who would be interested in reading it?
3. Why are acceptance criteria important in a software project?
4. Why the business use case diagram may be useful for a general view of the system?
5. How to represent in a business use case diagram a project with many phases?
6. What is the difference between a business worker and a business actor?

Business modeling

Key topics in this chapter

- BPMN—Business Process Modeling and Notation
- State Machine Diagram

3.1 Introduction to business modeling

In the beginning of the analysis process, the team must understand not only what is going to be developed but also the environment where this system is going to work. For example, a team that is going to develop a vaccination app could think about registering the name of the patient, some identification number, address, allergies, age, etc. However, why to register all that information if it is already available in other health record systems that the app could eventually interact with? Thus the team cannot start by focusing only on the system they are going to develop, they must understand the surroundings of the system, and business analysis is what they can use to accomplish it.

In the beginning of this process, it is assumed that the knowledge that the team has about the business is minimal, and that the interaction with the stakeholders will be intense. One of the goals in this stage is to discover if it is worth to do the analysis without dwelling too deep into the project.

Business modeling is, therefore, an activity that supports the discovery of user needs by helping the team to perceive the wider business context where the future system will operate. Different text or diagram artifacts can support it, as this chapter presents.

The artifacts in this phase usually do not need to be too detailed. Meetings with stakeholders could produce a record (minutes) that probably can register several ideas about the goals of the organization and the automation opportunities.

Business modeling starts with business use case diagrams, as seen in Chapter 2. Some business use cases would be very simple to understand, but others may be complex and need a deeper analysis to be completely understood. As business use cases are processes, diagrams such as the UML activity diagram and fluxograms could be used. However, the *Business Process Model and Notation*[1], BPMN[2], became dominant as a language for modeling processes, and for this reason, it will be introduced in this chapter.

---

[1] Formerly known as "Business Process Modeling Notation."
[2] http://www.bpmn.org/

Object-Oriented Analysis and Design for Information Systems. DOI: https://doi.org/10.1016/B978-0-443-13739-6.00019-8

Business modeling consists of studying and understanding the organization and its context, because usually the system to be developed will not be an isolated product, but an organic part of the organization environment. The goals of this discipline are to:

- Understand the *structure and dynamics* of the target organization in which the software will be used.
- Understand the *current problems* of the target organization and identify *potential improvements* that can be obtained with the software.
- Assure that clients, users, and the development team share a *consistent understanding* of the target organization.
- Derive the *requirements* that will lead to the desired improvements.

Another important aspect of business modeling is to bring the business team and the software engineering team closer, so that the actual problems of the users and their needs are understood, analyzed, and solved using information technology.

Business modeling is more important when significant behavioral changes are introduced to a group of people. In this case, business context and the consequences of installing a new system must be acknowledged and studied. It may be less important when such behavioral changes are not expected.

Thus business modeling may have different levels of importance depending on the project's needs. Kruchten (2003) identifies six scenarios of growing complexity in terms of the need for business modeling:

- *Organizational chart*: It may be necessary only to build an organizational chart to know the sectors and responsibilities related to the area in which the system is inserted. In this case, business modeling, in general, is very simple. The organizational chart will help analysts to locate the people that are responsible for the different aspects related to the future system, and what degree of authority is assigned to each one when deciding the requirements.
- *Domain modeling*: If the goal of the project is to build applications to manage and present information, then business modeling may be performed during domain analysis, that is, when a static model of the information (conceptual model) is produced.
- *One organization, many systems*: It may be the case that the team is developing a whole family of systems for an organization. In this case, business modeling is not only about one system, but spreads along many projects, and could even be a separated project of its own. It will help to discover individual system's requirements as well as to determine a common architecture for the whole family.
- *Generic business model*: If the goal is to build one or more systems that will serve a pool of organizations, then business modeling is useful in order to align the different organizations to a common business view, or, if that is not possible, to obtain a business view in which the specifics of the organizations are visible.
- *New business*: If an organization decides to start a new business, and a whole set of systems must be developed to give support to it, then a significant business modeling

effort must be undertaken. In this case, the goal of business modeling is not only to help finding system requirements but also to verify the effective viability of the new business. Thus business modeling, in that situation, could be an independent project.

- *Renewal*: If an organization decides to completely renew its way of business, then business modeling will be a separate project, performed in several steps: vision of the new business, reverse engineering of the existing business, direct engineering of the new business, and installation of the new business.

Other factors that increase or decrease the need for business modeling in a project are:

- Well-defined and stable requirements at the beginning of the project (e.g., creating a substitute for an existing system) reduce the need to perform intense business modeling.
- If the new system is going to change the way people do their work, then special attention must be paid to business modeling, especially when the business model is going to be changed or rebuilt after the automation of some business use cases.
- If the project has important risks, especially business risks, then business modeling must be more detailed and intense.
- If the user community is large and heterogeneous, then business modeling probably will be more difficult.
- If it is necessary to integrate the new system with hardware and legacy systems, then the comprehension of those elements must be included in business modeling, generating more work.
- More uncertainty about requirements means more attention to business modeling.

No matter the level of detail and effort to be put into business modeling, every project must begin with preliminary documentation that allows for an understanding of its scope. A project with poorly defined scope may give rise to discomfort or even fights between the client and development team, regarding the inclusion (or lack of inclusion) of certain features.

3.2 Business Process Modeling and Notation

The Business Process Modeling and Notation (BPMN) is a very popular option for studying the details of a business use case. With this diagram, the different tasks performed by business actors and workers to reach the general goal of the use case can be specified.

For a better understanding of the way the organization works through its use cases, it is possible to create a BPMN diagram for the nontrivial business use cases that are going to be developed. This is especially important when the team and even the users are not very sure about how the different activities are performed by the actors involved.

BPMN is a notation similar to fluxograms and UML activity diagrams, in the sense that it represents tasks by nodes and dependencies by arrows. But it introduces several new elements that help to improve the understanding on how the tasks are really performed and what kind of dependency exists among them.

3.2.1 Tasks

Before introducing a first example of business use case modeling with BPMN, let's look at the basic types of BPMN nodes, which represent different kinds of tasks. First, a *task* is an atomic activity, that is, a task cannot be broken into smaller complete activities—by *complete* it is meant that the task must start, happen, and finish without being allowed to be interrupted and resumed later. A task is usually performed by a human or a system. BPMN defines seven types of tasks:

- *Service task*: a task that is performed by an automated system. For example, an automated credit card paying system registering payment.
- *Send task*: a task that sends a message from an actor to another. For example, a reviewer informing the manager of a project that she has completed a review.
- *Receive task*: a task that indicates that the process must wait until a message arrives. For example, a manager that must wait until all expected reviews have come before deciding on funding or not a project.
- *User task*: a task that is performed by a human user using an application. For example, a proponent registering her project in the system.
- *Manual task*: a task that is performed by a human without the use of an application. For example, a municipal manager monitoring the works under her jurisdiction.
- *Business task*: a task that provides data to a business rule engine (BRE) and receives output from it. A BRE is an application that runs a logic program that takes decisions based on previously defined rules written in an appropriate language.
- *Script task*: a task that corresponds to a script that a business engine may interpret and execute.

A task may also be left as generic if there is doubt about its kind. Fig. 3−1 summarizes the representation of the task types in BPMN.

Fig. 3−2[3] presents a simplified version of one of the core processes of SISMOB. It uses three kinds of tasks: manual, user, and service, and aims to explain the initial understanding of the flow of activities for proposing and executing a construction work.

Besides the already mentioned tasks, other elements appear in the diagram of Fig. 3−2, such as the start and end events, a gateway (decision node) and flows (labeled or not). Fig. 3−3 shows their respective representations.

3.2.2 Gateways

BPMN introduces a series of different kinds of gateways. In Fig. 3−2, two *exclusive* gateways were used: "Decision" and "Assessment." Gateways can be used, as in this example, to allow

---

[3] Syntactically, a task node in BPMN should not receive more than one incoming flow such as happens with "Register proposal" and "Monitoring" and a merge gateway should be used instead of two flows as seen in the figure. However, as the purpose of this diagram is to discover and document and not automatically generate systems, this syntactic flaw may be acceptable.

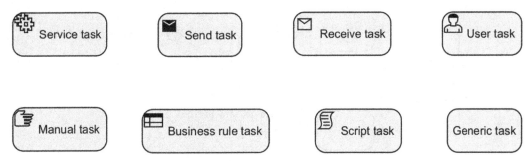

FIGURE 3–1 Different types of tasks in BPMN. *BPMN*, Business Process Modeling and Notation.

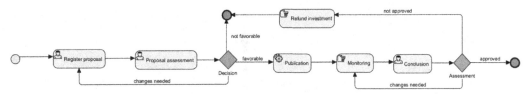

FIGURE 3–2 An initial BPMN diagram for use case "Manage work." *BPMN*, Business Process Modeling and Notation.

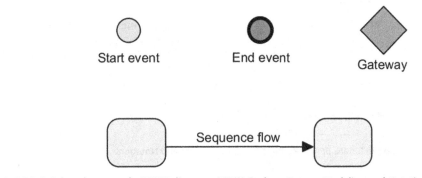

FIGURE 3–3 Other elements of a BPMN diagram. *BPMN*, Business Process Modeling and Notation.

the process to follow different paths depending on one or more conditions. Gateways may also be used to allow parallel paths, or even a combination of decision and parallelism as necessary. Each kind of gateway is explained below:

• *Exclusive gateway*: when a process comes to this gateway, a decision is taken and only one of the flows out of the gateway may be followed. In Fig. 3–2, the exclusive gateway "Decision" has three flows out of it: "favorable," "not favorable," and "changes needed," meaning that only one of those paths may be followed after the decision represented in the gateway. In this case, it can be said that the gateway *splits* the flow of the process. Optionally, another exclusive gateway can be used to represent the *merge* of the paths,

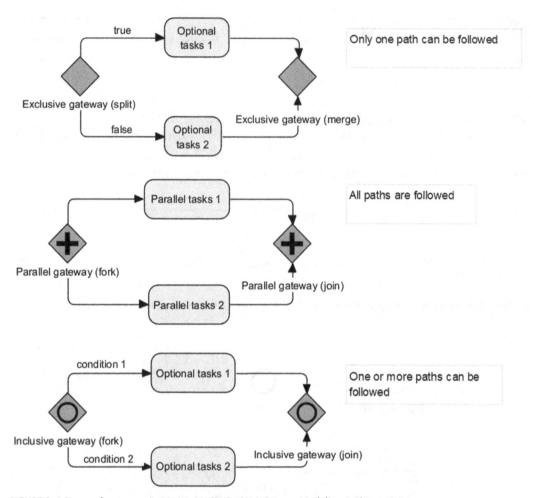

FIGURE 3–4 Types of gateways in BPMN. *BPMN*, Business Process Modeling and Notation.

as seen in Fig. 3–4 (upper part). In this case, the paths that enter the gateway may be the same that have left the gateway used to split the process and only one flow may leave the gateway. There is no decision being made in a merge gateway; this is only a notation that serves to represent that after following different flows, the process proceeds in a reunified flow.

- *Parallel gateway*: it can be used to define parallel paths, that is, different sequences of tasks that may be executed at the same time or, at least, without any dependency among them. As seen in Fig. 3–4 (middle), when a process comes to a parallel gateway, a *fork* happens, that is, all the flows out of the gateway may be executed in parallel (usually by different actors). The parallel gateway is also used to *join* the parallel paths back into a single flow. In the case of merging, the flow that goes out of the gateway can only be followed when all the incoming flows reach it. That means that if a path is completed before another, the gateway will hold the execution until the other process is also complete.

- *Inclusive gateway*: it is a combination of decision and parallelism. In this case, one or more decisions are taken, and one or more outgoing paths may be executed. The condition must be true for at least one of the outgoing flows. If it is true for more than one flow, then each flow for which it is true is executed in parallel from this point.

BPMN has other types of gateways, but they are used only in more advanced cases and will not be described here. For more information, see Shapiro et al. (2012).

3.2.3 Pools and lanes

Sometimes, BPMN diagrams represent activities that are performed by more than one actor. This situation can be described using pools and lanes. Just like in the case of a swimming pool, each lane is reserved for one actor; the tasks performed by each actor are represented inside her respective lane. Fig. 3–5 presents the first part of a complete diagram for the SISMOB project indicating the final understanding of the flow of the business use case "Manage work." Three actors are participating in this use case: the municipal manager (who asks for money to build/reform a health facility), the federal manager (who assess and approves or denies proposals and reports), and an organization, the National Health Fund (FNS), which allocates money to the projects.

The flow of the process initiates with the municipal manager registering a proposal for a construction or reformation of a municipal healthcare building (user task "Register proposal"). After finishing registering all the information necessary (it can take days), she sends the proposal to the federal manager (sending task "Send proposal").

Then, the federal manager will read and evaluate the proposal (user task "Produce assessment"). After that, there is an exclusive gateway that splits the flow into three possibilities:

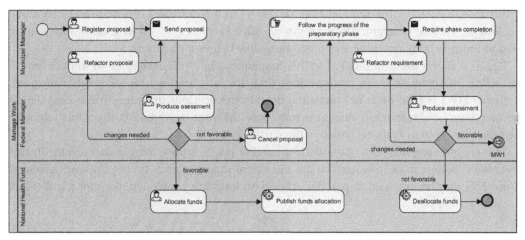

FIGURE 3–5 First part of a complete BPMN diagram for "Manage work." *BPMN*, Business Process Modeling and Notation.

1. If the decision is "not favorable," the federal manager cancels the proposal (user task "Cancel proposal") and the process is finished.
2. If the decision is "changes needed," the federal manager will return the flow to the municipal manager who, based on the information reported in the system by the federal manager in the task "Produce assessment," will try to refactor the initial proposal (task "refactor proposal"). The refactored proposal is then sent back to the federal manager, and this decision cycle may be repeated one or more times.
3. If the decision is "favorable," then the National Health Fund may allocate funds to the project (user task "Allocate funds"), and the official legal publication must be generated (automatic task "Publish funds allocation").

Notice that in case (1), the process is finished; in case (2), the process enters a cycle and returns to this decision point; and in case (3), the process proceeds further.

If the process proceeds further, the municipal manager must follow the preparations for the beginning of the construction works (manual task "Follow the progress of the preparatory phase"). When she decides that all necessary prerequisites are in order, she requires from the federal manager the completion of the preparatory phase (user task "Require phase completion"). That starts a decision cycle very similar to the last one. However, this time, instead of assessing the initial project, the federal manager will evaluate the completion of the preparatory phase as informed by the municipal manager.

The federal manager then produces an assessment on the preparation phase and decides:

1. If "not favorable," then the FNS deallocates money and the process is canceled.
2. If "changes needed," then the municipal manager refactors the requirement and restarts the decision cycle.
3. If "favorable," the process moves forward.

There is no space in Fig. 3–5 to conclude the diagram and keep a good visualization size. In this case, a continuation link (labeled as "MW1" in the example) can be used to continue the flow in another diagram. The *link intermediate event* (Fig. 3–6) is a node that can be used to indicate both incoming and outcoming flow between diagrams.

Fig. 3–7 shows the continuation of the diagram in Fig. 3–5. Instead of an initial event, it has a link intermediate event that specifies that this is a continuation of another diagram. The label MW1 is (and must be) the same used in the previous diagram. In this case, labels are mandatory because many diagrams may have different continuation diagrams and only the labels can help in knowing which is the correct one.

The second diagram then starts with a parallel node, representing a fork event. In this case, tasks "Follow work" allocated to the municipal manager and "Issue payment" allocated to the FNS may be executed in parallel. After both tasks are concluded, another parallel link

link intermediate event

FIGURE 3–6 Link intermediate event.

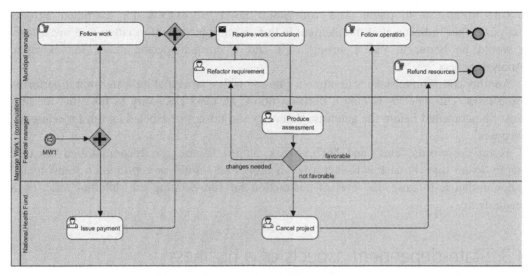

FIGURE 3–7 Second part of a complete BPMN diagram for "Manage work." *BPMN,* Business Process Modeling and Notation.

will join both paths and the municipal manager may perform the task "Require work conclusion" when she seems convenient. Notice that the last task can only be initiated after "Issue payment" and "Follow work" are both completed.

A third decision cycle is then initiated with the following differences from the previous others:

1. If "not favorable," then the FNS cancels the project (user task "Cancel project"), and the municipal manager must return the funds received (manual task "Refund resources"). This is a failure ending for this process.
2. If "changes needed," then the municipal manager refactors the requirement and restarts the decision cycle.
3. If "favorable," then the project has been completed with success and the municipal manager can follow the operation of the healthcare unit until a reform or deactivation of the unit is necessary.

Other elements exist in BPMN. If the reader is looking for a more profound view of the language, Shapiro et al. (2012) is a recommended reference.

3.2.4 General recommendations

Although BNPN seems to be a clear and understandable notation, as many other, modelers must take care not to violate some syntactic and sematic rules that may render the diagram obscure. D. Silingas and E. Milleviciene[4] present some antipatterns that would be avoided.

[4] https://www.modernanalyst.com/Resources/Articles/tabid/115/ID/2438/Efficient-BPMN-from-Anti-Patterns-to-Best-Practices.aspx

One mistake is to name tasks with noun-based expressions, for example, "Project analysis." That indicates that the element is in fact an object of information and not a task. It would be better to use a strong verb and a domain-specific noun, for example, "Analyze project."

Another common mistake is to name a gateway with a label that indicates that it performs some tasks. The gateway is only a decision point. All tasks necessary to take the decision must be performed before the gateway. Gateways should not be labeled except for reference purposes.

Using the words "and" and "or" in task names is also not recommended because this indicates that the task is in fact a set of tasks that should be represented individually. Other option is to raise the level of abstraction for representing the different tasks by a single name.

3.3 State-dependent aspects of a business

Besides business use cases, which may be detailed by BPMN diagrams, it may be important to understand other aspects of a business that do not always appear clearly in those diagrams, such as some key business objects that change state during their life cycle.

A UML diagram that can help the team to understand the organization's business objects is the *state machine diagram*. It is a behavioral diagram, but, instead of modeling *activities* in processes, it represents a set of *states* in which a system, actor, or entity could be at a given instant.

The state machine diagram specifies *events* in its flows. An event triggers the flow that takes the entity from one state to another. That is, the flows are labeled with events that, if they occur, make the entity change from one state to another.

Those occurrences may be, however, restricted by *guard conditions*. For example, the *login* event may only send the system to a *logged* state if the password is correct.

Graphically, the events are represented in the flows by simple expressions, and guard conditions are represented between brackets as, shown in Fig. 3–8. In it, the entity goes from "State 1" to "State 2" when the event "login" happens, but only if the guard condition "password is correct" is true.

The transitions in a state machine diagram can also include *effects* that are performed in response to a state transition. For example, the transition activated by the event "login" and guarded by the condition "password is correct" can activate the action "grant access," which is an effect of the transition (not its cause). Actions associated to transitions are represented by expressions initiated by a slash (/) as shown in Fig. 3–9.

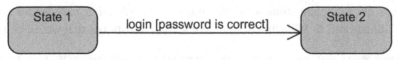

FIGURE 3–8 An event and guard transition between two states.

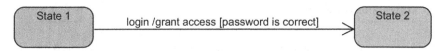

FIGURE 3–9 An event, action, and guard condition between two states.

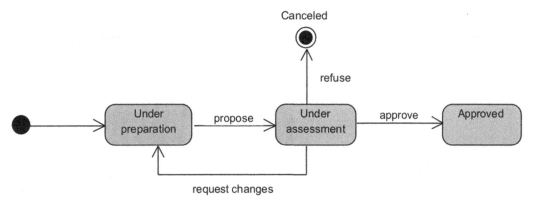

FIGURE 3–10 Initial (incomplete) state machine diagram for a construction work.

As an example on how that diagram can be useful during business analysis, we can imagine that a team is interested in understanding the life cycle of a construction work in the SISMOB project. Examining the different states of a key business object such as a work for this project may reduce the risk of underestimating the complexity of the system requirements.

Using the BPMN diagram of Figs. 3−5 and 3−7 as a basis, some different states of a work and some different events can be identified. Initially, a proposal for a work is in state "Under preparation," meaning that it is being written or modified by a municipal manager. After the event "propose," it changes to the state "Under assessment" meaning that it is being assessed by a federal manager and cannot be further modified unless another event occurs changing state again to "Under preparation." After assessment, three possibilities can happen. If modifications are needed, the state returns to "Under preparation." If the project is rejected, a final state is reached. If the proposal is approved, then the state changes to "Approved."

The team could continue to complete this state machine diagram with information taken from the BPMN diagrams. But the question now is "Why?": Why taking information from one diagram and represent it in another diagram? The answer is that the state machine diagram can help the team to see events that are not so easily seen in the BPMN diagram. At this point, the team would ask: "What other events and transitions could be possible between states that are not yet represented." In Fig. 3−10, there are four states to consider. Some pairs have a transition between them and others not as seen in Table 3.1.

The question that the team now must clarify with the client/user is if there is a possibility of new events/transitions that are not represented in the state diagram. For example, may an approved project return to the assessment phase? If the answer is "yes," which event allows this?

Table 3.1   States and transitions.

From: To:	Under preparation	Under assessment	Approved	Canceled
Under preparation		Request changes		
Under assessment	Propose			
Approved		Approve		
Canceled		Refuse		

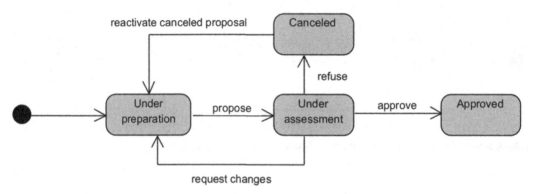

FIGURE 3–11 A state machine diagram with new transition/event.

In the case of the SISMOB project, for example, Phase 3 introduced a new feature that allows a canceled project to be reactivated. In the state diagram, it would be a transition from state "Canceled" that is not anymore a final state, to the state "Under preparation." The event that triggers this transition is "reactivate canceled proposal," which corresponds to a business new use case to be added to the set in Figure 2–4. Fig. 3–11 shows the state machine diagram updated with this transition. Notice that this new event is not necessarily part of the "Manage work" business use case, but a different use case. In this sense, the state machine diagram is important to help the team to discover different effects on a business object that may occur in different business use cases.

3.4 Discussion

It is important to remember that the goal of business modeling is usually to find a general view of the business and not a detailed specification of its processes. Thus in most cases, the team's goal is to concentrate on discovering information about the business and not on formally specifying how the business works as if it was a machine.

A question still may be asked: Which business use cases and objects deserve the production of a BPMN or state machine diagram? Unless stated to the contrary, it is not advisable to prepare a diagram for every business element, because some of them would be trivial. What is usually needed at this point is a model for some key elements, so that their behavior can be better understood, and their requirements derived later.

A clue to identify those key elements is to ask what the business objects are. In the case of a bookstore, they are books, in the case of a hotel, lodging, in the case of a court, criminal processes, and so on. Thus those are the key elements that must be modeled in greater detail to help in understanding the business.

A second question could be the following: Which diagram should we use—BPMN or state machine? The answer depends on the nature of the element to be modeled. BPMN models processes, that is, a set of tasks, while state machine diagrams model states of an object, not tasks.

In order to perceive that a state is different from a task, try to imagine a TV set. It may be in state "Off" and during it, it is not performing any task.

If the business object is active, then it *may* be executing some action during a state. For example, an elevator that is going up (task) and is in the state "Ascending." However, many business objects may be passive and not active. Those kinds of objects cannot perform any action. They only can suffer the effects of actions done by others. For example, a book is incapable of performing any task. But it can have states, such as "Available," "Sold," "Damaged," and "Lost."

A BPMN diagram is useful when modeling people, organizations, or systems doing things. On the other hand, the state machine diagram is useful when a single entity passes through different states in which it is not necessarily doing something. Furthermore, the activity diagram usually details a business use case (i.e., a process such as selling, buying, checking), while the state machine diagram is usually associated with a business object (such as books, people, orders).

Business modeling is not just about building diagrams, however. The purpose of diagrams is to help understand the context and the initial general requirements of a project and a system. Business modeling is one of the key activities that help a team to identify and prepare for project risks. Other risk mitigation activities may also be performed during analysis, such as proof-of-concept, workshops, prototyping, and early tests. Any strategy that helps in understanding the big picture and identifying the major risks and complexities of a project is valid.

Questions

1. What is the purpose of business modeling?
2. Business modeling can occur with different levels of intensity for different kinds of projects. Explain and give examples!
3. Which aspects of a business may be detailed by a BPMN diagram? Which may be detailed by a state machine diagram?
4. Which kind of gateways does BPMN have, and which are their purpose?
5. Can active objects have a state in which they are not performing any task? Give an example.

4

High-level requirements

Key topics in this chapter

- System Actors
- System Use Cases
- How to Find System Use Cases in the Business Diagrams
- Types of Requirements
- Preliminary Conceptual Model

4.1 Introduction to high-level requirements

Once the business has been reasonably understood and modeled, the requirements analysis may be deepened. Although there are several approaches to represent requirements, this book presents a technique based on system use cases.

The *system use case* is an individual process that may be derived from the business diagrams. A *high-level* (or *brief*) system use case represents the more abstract *functional requirements* of a system. The *annotations* on those use cases represent the *nonfunctional requirements* or *business rules*, that is, the constraints related to those functions. The *supplementary requirements* are nonfunctional requirements that apply to the system as a whole—not only to an individual system use case. Table 4−1 explains the differences among the three types of requirements and their associations to use cases.

System use cases are useful for many activities related to systems development, such as:

- *Definition and validation of the system architecture*: In general, classes, associations, and attributes that form part of the system architecture are obtained from the detailed use case[1] texts.
- *Creation of test cases*: Use cases can be seen as a basis for system and acceptance tests, where the functionality is tested from the point of view of the user. In agile development, it is useful to have a test analyst working with a use case analyst for developing testing units while use cases are being defined.
- *Planning sprints*: For each use case, it may be assigned a priority, and an effort estimation to develop it, so that the team can decide on which use cases to develop at each sprint.
- *Basis for user documentation*: Use cases are descriptions of the system's normal operation flows, as well as alternate flows that represent how to deal with eventual exceptional conditions. These descriptions are an excellent basis for starting the user manual because all possible functionalities are described there in a structured and complete way.

---

[1] From now on, system use cases will be referred as *use cases* for simplicity, except when they are compared to business use cases.

Object-Oriented Analysis and Design for Information Systems. DOI: https://doi.org/10.1016/B978-0-443-13739-6.00006-X

Table 4–1   Classification of requirements.

Type	Explanation
Functional requirements	Things that the system should do—may be represented by system use cases
Nonfunctional requirements	Constraints about how a functional requirement may work—may be represented by annotations to a system use case
Supplementary requirements	Constraints about the whole system, not necessarily a single requirement or use case—usually represented in an appropriate table or list

Each use case represents a coherent set of functional system requirements. Usually, more than one function is related to a single use case, especially if it is a complex one. Some functions, on the other hand, may be associated to more than one use case. In some situations, it may also happen that a function corresponds to a single use case and vice versa. This usually occurs with very simple use cases such as reports and entity management.

As use cases are requirements, then the activities of requirements elicitation and analysis correspond to the discovery and study of use cases and their properties.

4.2 System actors

A *system actor* represents an entity of the real world that interacts with the system through a use case. Actors may be roles performed by people such as customers, publishers, sellers, and operators. Actors can also be external systems, that is, systems that are outside the scope of the project being developed.

Human actors or external systems interact with the target system by sending and receiving information through an interface. In the case of human actors, the information is usually exchanged through data entry devices such as keyboards, mice, or other special devices. Those actors receive information from the system through interfaces such as screens, printers, or other special devices.

Communication with actors that are external systems usually happens through a computer network. In this case, the communication interface consists of the network and its protocols.

The idea of external systems as actors must not be confused with internal ones that are components of the system under development. For instance, a database management system, used to implement data persistence for the system under development, is not an actor but a component of the inner architecture of the system. The following rules may help to appropriately identify external systems that could be actors:

- System actors are *complete information systems,* and not only libraries of classes or procedures. These systems store their own data, which can be exchanged with the system being developed. That data may change independently from the system being implemented.
- System actors are *out of the scope of development,* that is, the team will not necessarily have access to the internal design of these systems or the ability to change them. The team must communicate with a system actor using the system actor's own interfaces, and they usually cannot be modified by the team.

Some approaches consider that there are two kinds of actors: *primary* and *secondary*. Primary actors are the ones whose goal the use case is trying to satisfy, while secondary actors are actors that just provide some help to the process under study. Examples of secondary actors are a clerk (secondary actor) that confirms that the client (primary actor) has paid in cash. In this book, we do not follow that distinction: we distinguish use case actors into *human* or *system* actors only.

A recurrent question is that if actors correspond to security profiles. This is not necessarily the case. The goal behind the identification and modeling of actors is more related to the process of finding and organizing requirements than to the process of granting access to the system. A good software design will treat access permission in a dynamic way, allowing user profiles to be created, and permissions to be associated to the different profiles of individual users. As that aspect of the system is not domain-dependent, it is not adequate to model it within the domain. In other words, use case actors may not be necessarily considered as security profiles. Those profiles will be created dynamically with the use of a generic domain-independent mechanism. Although, the use cases may be a hint in order to define such profiles.

4.3 System use cases

System use cases differ from business use cases in some respects. For example, business actors may spend days or even weeks performing a business use case, while system use cases are often performed in a short period of time, usually seconds or minutes, with one or a few actors interacting with a system and obtaining a consistent and complete result for at least one of their goals. System use cases must also usually be performed without interruptions while business use cases are not restricted in that respect.

Another fundamental difference between a business use case and a system use case is that the business use case is usually performed by many human actors, while a system use case is normally performed by a few (sometimes just one) human actors. The fact is that if a system use case is going to be performed by more than one human actor, then they should be interacting at the same time with the system, and that is not a common situation. Usually, each human actor accesses the system at a time of her convenience, accessing necessary data and performing the necessary actions. For example, a municipal manager registers and sends a proposal on Monday, but the federal manager will read it only on Wednesday. Thus those two activities may belong to the same business use case but not to the same system use case.

As said above, sometimes more than one human actor should be available online for a system use case. For example, at a supermarket when a customer is buying goods, a supervisor may be summoned to perform actions that the cashier is not allowed to do (e.g., cancel a sale). The point is that the supervisor must be available online and the other actors must wait for her to show up before proceeding.

On the other hand, external computational systems may be considered *online* actors, because they are available continuously. For example, it can be assumed that a credit card operator is available online 24/7. When a customer decides to make a payment with her credit card, the system actor "Credit card operator" should be available.

A high-level system use case is represented only by a name inside an ellipse. It is usually associated to one or more actors as seen in Fig. 4–1. Notice that the stereotype for business use cases and business actors is no longer used.

In the diagram in Fig. 4–1, the ellipses represent system use cases. By default, an actor is a role performed by a human. Other kinds of actors may be represented using stereotypes, as shown in Fig. 4–1, where the stereotype «*system*» indicates that "Publication system" is an external system, not a human.

The use case diagram is a very popular UML diagram, but it is also frequently misunderstood. It is usual to see these diagrams with dozens of use cases and some of their *fragments* attached. A fragment is an incomplete activity, that is, an activity that does not produce an actor's business goal. For example, "Register a proposal" may be considered as a use case because it produces a record that can be evaluated by a third part. One of its first steps could be "Open registering page." Although this is something that must be done if the user is going to fill in this page, just opening the page does not produce a business goal. Consider, for example, that if the user turns the system off just after opening the page, no result will be available for using when the system is again turned on.

The presence of fragments in the use case diagram and the use of the *include* and *extend* relationships between use cases (which sometimes reveal part of their internal structure)

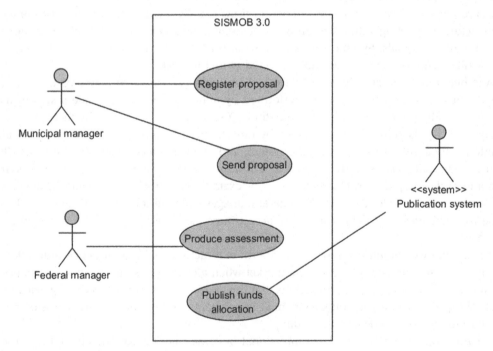

FIGURE 4–1 System use cases and system actors.

should be made with some concerns. Not every possible piece of a use case must be represented in this diagram, as there is a better structure (yet to be shown in this book) to show use case details. Sometimes, a use case really includes another complete use case, for example, "Register new user" that may be part of many other use cases that demand a registered user.

Thus there is a need for strong criteria to decide which use cases should be maintained in the diagram to avoid, on the one hand, many excessively detailed processes, and on the other hand, too few processes that could lack important features of the system.

The rule is to consider as a use case only those processes that can be performed not only as part of a bigger process (this affirmation is only valid for system use cases, not business ones). Partial processes that must *necessarily* be performed during other processes should not be represented in the system use case diagram, except if they are a part that is shared by two or more use cases.

However, even following this guide, the number of use cases in a real-world system may still be too high, so that dealing with them may become difficult. To reduce the number without losing information and precision, a second rule may be used. It consists of grouping use cases that are somewhat related, especially if that may be done more than once, like a pattern. For example, there could be four use cases such as "Create user," "Retrieve user," "Update user," "Delete user," and "List users," or just one use case called "Manage user" that includes the five single processes. This is a pattern, because it may be repeated for other concepts: "Manage reviewer" may be used instead of Create, Retrieve, Update, Delete reviewer. This pattern is known as CRUDL, which is an acronym for Create, Retrieve, Update, Delete, and List.

Other example is a screen where a user may update some data about herself such as date of birth, document number, name, and address. After updating one information (such as "document"), she could decide to save the register and resume updating other fields later. Thinking like this, we could decide that there are use cases named "Update date of birth," "Update document number," "Update name," "Update address," etc., that can be performed one after the other in any order. However, this is too verbose and not useful for understanding the user activities. It is preferable that the use case represented is "Update user" that allows the user to update one or more fields and save the record. Later we will see also that there are fields that can never be updated in normal conditions (date of birth, for example).

The next subsections present other criteria for achieving the best use case granularity.

4.3.1 Single session

A good system use case must be performed in a single session.[2] This means that it should begin and finish without long interruptions. For example, the registration of a project is made during a single session of the system, involving the identification of the municipal manager, type of construction work, justification, cost, etc.

---

[2] That idea follows Larman's (2004) definition of an *EBP* (*Elementary Business Process*) *use case*. The EBP definition comes from the business process engineering field: "a task performed by one person in one place at one time, in response to a business event, which adds measurable business value and leaves the data in a consistent state."

This process may terminate in two ways: even it is finished and submitted, or it is saved to be continued later. In the second case, the business value obtained is a project partially registered in the system. For now, consider that a use case such as "Register proposal" (Fig. 4–2 left) is better than having one use case for each field composing the proposal as in Fig. 4–2 (right).

On the other hand, a proposal is not automatically evaluated when it is registered: the federal manager is responsible for verifying, from time to time, which proposals have been registered; and only after that she decides on which one to assess.

If the municipal manager is lucky, the assessment can start just a few seconds after it is registered; on the other side, it can take weeks.

This fact indicates that the use case "Produce assessment" is not part of the use case "Register proposal" or "Send proposal"; it should be considered as a different system use case.

4.3.2 Interactive

A use case must also be interactive, meaning that an actor must exist to interact with the system. The internal processes of the system are not use cases no matter how complex they are. On the other side, a simple query on some information may be a (very simple) use case if there is an actor that starts it.

A system actor, such as a clock, for example, may also start a use case by sending some information to the system.

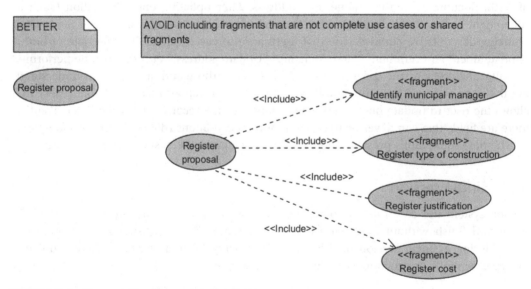

FIGURE 4–2 Avoid representing fragments in the diagram.

4.3.3 Consistent result

A use case must produce a consistent result, be it a complete entry or transformation on a piece of information, or simply a query where relevant information is passed to a user. A use case cannot leave the information at an inconsistent state at its end. For instance, the registering of an project cannot be concluded without the identification of the municipal manager that is responsible for it, or else the information about the proposal would be incomplete regarding the business rules. If the author of the proposal is not known and the proposal is registered, who would be able to gain access to proceed with it? Usually, allowing data registration only for logged users may cope with this issue.

To decide if a use case has a consistent result, one could think like this: only a complete process is a system use case, in the sense that a user could go to the computer, turn it on, perform the process, and at its end, turn off the computer, because some business goal was obtained (some relevant information was received or updated by the user).

This excludes from the use case definition fragments such as "Login," because it is not an isolated process that produces palpable change in data or user information. Considering that the computer could be turned off immediately after that operation, no business goal would have been produced. "Login" usually is part of so many use cases that it is omitted from diagrams in order to not pollute them.

4.3.4 Essential and concrete

Regarding abstraction level, at least two styles for writing use cases may be identified:

- *Essential use cases*, which do not mention interface technology.
- *Concrete* (or *real*) *use cases*, which are specifically written for a given interface technology.

During requirements elicitation and analysis, system use cases are considered requirements, not design. It is a mistake to include among these use case actions that are purely related to an interface technology, such as *Open main window*, *Print report*, or *Login*. People prepared to handle that facet of design will decide on those actions later, after the real user needs are better understood.

Ambler (2000) points out that essential models are more flexible, leaving more options open and more readily accommodating changes in technology. He also says that essential models are more robust than concrete representations because they are more likely to remain valid in the face of changing implementation technology.

A team that uses the UX technique may try to test different approaches to the same interface. They could initiate with an essential use case and then produce one or more possible interfaces for the user. The different designs may be evaluated, and the best may be chosen for finally producing real (concrete) use cases that indicate which buttons or menus may be activated by the user.

Thus essential use cases can be chosen as the best option during requirements elicitation before a study on the best interfaces has not yet been made. After decisions about technology are taken, real use cases may be produced, usually by just adding notes to the essential use case. This is detailed later in the book.

4.3.5 Brief

During analysis, use cases usually are brief, meaning that they are described just by their name or, in some cases, by one or two sentences. However, this is not the only way a use case may be described. Later they will be extended and contain more details. Cockburn (2001) identifies three types of use cases regarding the level of detail:

- *Brief*: A one-paragraph synopsis of the use case.
- *Casual*: Written in simple, paragraph, prose style. It is likely to be less rigorous in its description than a fully dressed use case.
- *Fully Dressed* or *Detailed*: Expanded to include a main flow and alternate flows, as well as other sections such as postconditions, preconditions, stakeholders, and technological variations.

In this book, we expect that use cases considered during the initial phases will be brief. This means that usually their name is sufficient to explain their meaning. However, additional explanation is allowed for the sake of requirements comprehension. Also, if some key use cases must be expanded to identify risks regarding their inherent complexity, this is also acceptable. Usually, fully dressed or detailed use cases will be useful only when requirements must be understood in their most complete details.

4.3.6 System boundary

One of the decisions a team must make when designing system use cases is where to place the system boundary. Graphically, the boundary is only a rectangle that is placed on the diagram. Inside it are the use cases and outside are the actors. In business use case diagrams, the system boundary represents the limits of the organization (company, department, etc.). But now, at the system level, it represents the limits of a computational system.

A decision was made earlier on which workers to include in the automation border. One example is the clerk that helps the reviewers entering their reviews. If this assignment is to be performed directly by the reviewer using an information system, then the worker clerk role disappears, and the reviewer is connected directly to the use case (Fig. 4−3).

4.4 How to find system use cases in the business use case model?

To discover system use cases and actors, the team may examine the business use case diagram with the defined automation boundary (scope of automation).

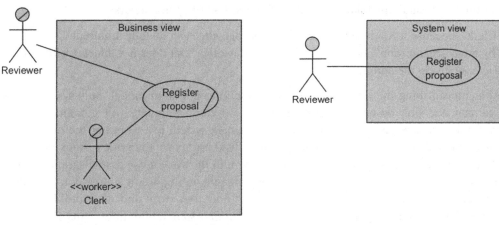

FIGURE 4–3 From business to system use cases diagram.

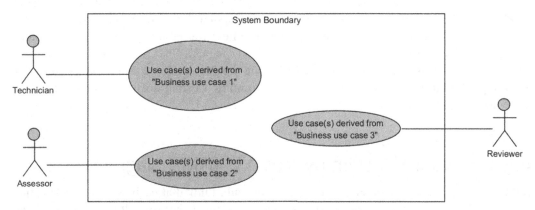

FIGURE 4–4 Login must not be considered a complete use case.

First, the actors that are really interested in the process to be automated should be identified. These are the business actors that interact with the business use cases inside the automation scope, and the business workers that interact with such use cases but that are not themselves inside the automation scope. Let's go back to Chapter 2 and look at Fig. 2−8. Applying the above rules to the actors and use cases in that figure, the following system actors could be identified (Fig. 4−4):

- "Technician" and "Reviewer": because they are business actors that interact with use cases that will be automated.
- "Assessor": because it is a business worker that will not be automated and that interacts with a use case that will be (business use case 2).

On the other hand, the following will not be considered system actors:

- "Clerk": because it is a business worker whose activities will be fully automated.
- "External organization": because it is a business worker that does not interact with any use case inside the automation scope.

After transforming the business use case model into a system model, only system users will remain and only system use cases inside the system boundary will remain. In many cases, a business use case can be derived into a single system use case, but the most interesting business use cases are those that will be derived into more than one system use case.

Despite some business workers being not present in the system use case diagram because their tasks will be automated or reassigned, they are still an important source of information during the initial steps of analysis, when knowing how they work and what problems they face may be useful for designing the new system. Another source of requirements is the business actors that will become system actors.

However, business actors and workers would not always be available for requirements elicitation, and in that case, the team should try to find other domain specialists. For example, it may not be possible to interview the user of a system for a business that does not yet exist. Thus someone that knows about the new business will be a key person for obtaining the right requirements.

If some business actors are not available but the knowledge about their business is already published, then it would be possible to examine existing documentation instead of interviewing them.

4.5 How to find system use cases in BPMN diagrams?

BPMN is a good source for system use cases. One could think that each task in a BPMN diagram could correspond to a system use case. However, this is not true all the time. If two or more tasks in a path *must* be executed without, say, a long interruption, then they are to be considered as parts of the same use case. For example, in Fig. 3–5 in the previous chapter, the municipal manager may perform the task "Register proposal," but as soon as the registration is concluded, it is not mandatory to perform "Send proposal." She may wait hours or even days before sending the proposal. This situation characterizes "Register proposal" and "Send proposal" as two separate use cases.

On the other hand, as soon as the FNS has performed the task "Allocate funds," it may (or even *must*) perform "Publish funds allocation" immediately. There is no need to wait to make this publication and even postponing the publication could create concurrency problems, for example, with other projects trying to allocate the same funds. This situation indicates that the tasks "Allocate funds" and "Publish funds allocation" both belong to the same system use case, meaning that there is no situation where you can allocate funds and not immediately publish it.

4.6 How to find system use cases in machine state diagrams?

A machine state diagram is also particularly helpful in terms of finding system use cases. Each event that changes the state of a business object may be done by someone or some system. Usually, that someone or some system is an actor performing a system use case.

Let's consider, as an example, the initial machine state diagram for a work in the SISMOB system (Fig. 3−11). Notice that the nodes in this case are not tasks such as in BPMN diagrams, but states in which the object may exist (e.g., "Under preparation," "Canceled"). If a task is executed in this diagram, it occurs in the flows between the nodes. For example, when a proposal is finished and sent to evaluation, the event "propose" indicates that the proposal goes from state "Under preparation" to "Under assessment." Therefore the system use case that occurs here is "Propose Project." It would be preferable to use "Propose project" instead of simply "Propose" because other things may be proposed in the context of this diagram, for example, and ongoing project and a concluded project. Thus from the diagram in Fig. 3−11, the following system use cases could be identified:

- *Register project*: from the start node to "Under preparation."
- *Propose project*: from "Under preparation" to "Under assessment."
- *Approve project*: from "Under assessment" to "Approved."
- *Request changes in project*: from "Under assessment" to "Under preparation."
- *Approve*: from "Under assessment" to "Approved."

Here, we do not consider that approval or cancelation of a project must be made just after the assessment of the project. The federal manager could produce an assessment, record it, and only take her decision later. This is symmetrical with the situation between "Under assessment" and "Under preparation" because the municipal manager is not forced to modify the project as soon as she receives the changes request.

4.7 Requirements

As seen up to this point, requirements are represented in use cases: business use cases are the more abstract, and organization-related requirements and system use cases are more user oriented. The team can and must use every available source to identify requirements (specialists, users, documents, interfaces, literature, etc.), and for each source, a set of functions that the system must perform may be identified.

Requirements elicitation, in this case, is the activity that involves studying business models and interacting with clients, users, and other stakeholders in order to discover which are their needs. For now, we have identified the existence of system use cases, that are, *per se*, a set of user stories. Let's first discuss their nature and properties, and later we could manage to start detailing them and producing the user journey that corresponds to the possible paths of the detailed use case.

Remember always that a requirement does not establish how the constraint will be implemented, it just demands a solution to a problem. The design and implementation of the system must meet the requirement in one way or another, or otherwise, the analyst should negotiate with the client for some requirement flexibility.

4.7.1 Requirements challenges

So, why to describe and draw so many diagrams at this point of the analysis? Why do not start programming yet? Well, before starting to build the more concrete and more expensive parts of the software, a good common understanding about requirements is necessary, because refactoring code is expensive (although sometimes necessary). This is true even in the agile culture. The challenges regarding requirements are, at least, the following (Pressman, 2010):

- How to *discover* requirements.
- How to *communicate* requirements to the other phases and teams of the project.
- How to *recall* requirements during development to verify if they have all been implemented.
- How to *manage* requirements change.

It would be useless to develop a nice use case diagram and later not be able to know if the requirements incorporated there were included in the design. The existence of automatic mechanisms to conduct this verification is crucial. Therefore it is important to maintain traceability relations between use cases and other parts of the design. The following chapters show how those relations among design artifacts are obtained.

It is necessary to keep in mind that requirements necessarily change during the development of a project. In the case of SISMOB Phase 3, more than 30% of the products were changed after the project started. Thus the change must be managed, not avoided. However, this is not only an inspirational coach quote: you must be prepared to that. In special, keep the user close and check with her about any doubts you have about requirements.

The changing nature of requirements incentives the software industry to avoid the requirements-driven analysis (Alford, 1991), because it would be inadequately time-consuming for most systems. Using requirements as a base to support system architecture is like building a house over moving sand; when requirements change, the structure suffers. However, we can use a much more stable basis for the system architecture, which is the set of classes and components that encapsulate information and behavior, the so-called "object-oriented" development.

These classes implement functionalities that combined allow the implementation of the requirements. If requirements change, the combinations change, but not the basic structure. This kind of architecture follows the *open-close principle* (Meyer, 1988), in the sense that the system components are always closed for modification (they work), but open for extension (they may accommodate new functionalities).

It is important to trace the origin of each requirement (e.g., a business actor, a business worker, the client itself, or even a domain specialist), because it is necessary to validate requirements with those sources, verifying if they are well written, complete, and sound.

Sometimes it may also occur that different people or departments present different specifications for the same requirement. In that case, it is necessary to produce an agreement among them, or identify who has the highest authority to determine the acceptable form for the requirement.

4.7.2 Evident and hidden functional requirements

Functional requirements can be optionally identified as *evident* or *hidden* (Gause and Weinberg, 1989):

* *Evident* functional requirements are functions that are performed with the user's knowledge. These requirements usually correspond to information exchange between the user and the system, such as queries and data entry, which flows through the system interface.
* *Hidden* functional requirements are functions performed by the system without explicit knowledge of the user. Usually, these functions are math operations and data updating performed by the system without explicit user knowledge, but because of other functions performed by the user.

Hidden requirements are performed internally by the system. Thus although they do not appear explicitly as use cases, they must be adequately associated to them to be recalled at the time of design and implementation. Thus they could also be added as annotations to a use case.

An example of an *evident* requirement is the task "Allocate funds" in Fig. 3−5 because, the employee at the FNS must know that she is approving those funds. However, the task "Publish funds allocation" is performed automatically by the system. Although the user may know that this is going to happen, she must not take any action to initiate it. Thus "Publish funds allocation" can be considered here as a hidden requirement and part of the "Allocate funds" use case.

4.7.3 Nonfunctional and supplementary requirements

Nonfunctional requirements are not tasks neither use cases, but constraints that may be linked to specific use cases of a system (e.g., "a description of a project must not exceed 4000 words."), and therefore, they can be treated as annotations on those use cases.

Sometimes, however, nonfunctional requirements may be generic, that is, not necessarily attached to a function (e.g., "the application must work on a smartphone with 32GB"), and in that case, they will appear in the *supplementary specifications document*, not attached to any use case.

Constraints that are specifically related to a use case are called *nonfunctional requirements*, and generic constraints are called *supplementary requirements*.

4.7.4 Logical and technological nonfunctional requirements

There are two kinds of nonfunctional requirements:

- *Logical*: Business rules attached to a use case. For example, the date in the project registration must be the same date or before the project was submitted.
- *Technological*: Constraints and qualities related to the technology used to perform the function, such as the user interface, the kind of communication protocol, security constraints, and fault tolerance. The second type is mostly related to the software qualities, such as security, usability, and configurability. Please refer to ISO 25010 for a complete set of possible software qualities.

4.7.5 Permanent and transient nonfunctional requirements

One of the most fundamental features of a requirement is whether a given nonfunctional or supplementary requirement is *permanent* or *transient.*

Nonfunctional and supplementary requirements can be considered permanent (they are not expected to change) or transient (they are expected to change) depending on a decision made by the team and the client. Permanence or transience is not an intrinsic feature of a requirement: the requirement may change or not independently of our will, but we can decide if we are going to be prepared for the change or not. The criteria to consider a requirement as permanent or transient depends on the cost of the change if we are prepared, the cost of the change if we are not prepared, and the cost of the preparation itself.

It is like deciding on buying insurance. If your car is expensive and you drive poorly, maybe you should buy insurance to avoid losing a large quantity of money if an accident happens. Otherwise, maybe it is not wise to pay insurance for a car that has little value and is kept on the garage most of the time (you better count on luck).

However, an accident may happen whether or not you buy an insurance. In the first scenario, you spend more before the accident and save money after it, and in the second scenario, you save money before the accident but spend more after. The first scenario is the one with transient requirements because you bet something (an accident) may produce high cost in the future. The second scenario is the one with permanent requirement because you bet that even if a cost happens in the future, it would be too low to compensate the investment in insurance.

If a software team invests in flexible design, so that most requirements are transient, less effort will be spent during maintenance to accommodate changes. However, the cost of that flexible design during development may become prohibitive for some projects. It will always be a good idea to ponder which constraints should really be treated as transient requirements.

For example, a supplementary requirement could establish that the SISMOB system must deal with a single currency: the Mira. If that requirement is considered permanent, then the system will be designed for a single currency ("Mira" could even be a primitive data type used to define variables and attributes). However, if the requirement is considered transient, then even if there is no other currency being used today, the whole system must be prepared to accommodate future currency, or even more than one currency at a time.

The consequences of deciding that a requirement is *permanent* are the following:

- It is cheaper and quicker to develop the system.
- It is more expensive and difficult to change the system if, by any chance, the requirements change in the future.

On the other hand, deciding that the requirement is *transient* has the following consequences:

- It is more expensive and complex to develop the system (it should accommodate functionalities for changing the currency, for example).
- It is easier and quicker to maintain the system (if the currency changes, the system is already prepared to accommodate that with a simple reconfiguration).

Thus it is not the nature of the nonfunctional requirement that will decide whether it is permanent or transient. It is the client, with the help of the team, that must make the decision. The ideal situation would be to list the requirements of greater importance (those that are really expected to change soon with a bigger impact on the system) and consider them transient, while leaving the others as permanent.

4.7.6 Mandatory and desired requirements

Requirements (especially nonfunctional ones) may also be considered *mandatory* or *desired*,[3] that is, those that must be obtained by any means and those that could be obtained if no bigger issue hinders the development process.

In the case of functional requirements, that classification indicates development priorities. If there is flexibility in the contract such that only the most important use cases are implemented if there is no time to implement them all, then the team must know which ones are mandatory for they have bigger priority.

However, if the team can make a good estimate of the effort needed to develop the system, and if they have a good history of accurate estimation, there will be less motivation for such distinction regarding functional requirements, because all requirements are expected to be implemented in time.

On the other hand, nonfunctional and supplementary requirements are much more unpredictable than functional ones regarding effort estimation. Thus in some cases, it may be necessary to consider those requirements with some flexibility.

In this case, some restrictions are defined such that they must be obtained by any means and others may be considered simply desirable, and some time is allocated to pursue them.

---

[3] Another option is to use the MoSCoW scale: Must, Should, Could, and Would.

For example (real Bridge case), in the case of the vaccination app, a mandatory requisite is that a patient must be identified by the number of her document. One could suggest also that a camera on a smartphone could be used to read the document number avoiding the need to type it and the possible errors that come with this kind of entry. As the team had no experience with text extraction from image, they decided to consider this feature as desired, not mandatory. After developing the more important features and study about text extraction, they decided with the client that the effort to develop and perfect this feature would not compensate the cost and time necessary to do it and also the urgency to have the system available during the pandemics.

4.7.7 Supplementary requirements

Supplementary requirements are all types of constraints and qualities related to the system as a whole and not only to individual functions. For example, a supplementary requirement may establish that the system must be compatible with a given legacy database, or be implemented with a given programming language, or even follow a given *look and feel.*

Care must be taken when supplementary requirements are defined. A requirement such as "the system must be easy to use" is not sufficiently clear. It would be better to say something like "novice users must be able to complete tasks without errors in their first attempt." That gives a more precise idea of what must be designed to accomplish the requirement.

Nonfunctional and supplementary requirements may also be identified with different groups such as interface, implementation, performance, and fault tolerance. The goal of making such distinctions is to allow for better organization.

Although most teams would choose to use the *FURPS +* classification system (Grady, 1992) for organizing supplementary requirements, the newest source to decide on supplementary requirements classification is ISO/IEC 25010,[4] as shown in Table 4−2.

Although this list is extensive, the team must keep in mind that it is only a classification to improve the ability to identify which requirements are important. There is no need to seek nonexistent requirements only to fill a box, for example, establishing complicated packaging requirements for a client that does not care about the way the software will be packaged.

It is also advisable not to lose time discussing if a given requirement belongs to this or that type. More important than deciding on its type is to know that it exists: long discussions on requirements classification do not add significant knowledge to the project.

Not every feature must have a requirement generation question. Thus usually there are not requirements in all categories. The questions that generate requirements mentioned in Table 4−2 are a good basis for finding eventual needs in meetings with the client. But it is not mandatory to have an answer to all those questions.

[4] http://www.iso.org/iso/catalogue_detail?csnumber = 35733

Table 4–2 Supplementary requirements classification based in the norm ISO/IEC 25010:2011 and requirement generating questions.

25010 Feature	25010 Sub feature	Requirements generating questions
Functional suitability	Functional completeness	Must all necessary functions be implemented? May some of them be left outside the system scope? May some functions be implemented by a further project?
	Functional appropriateness	In which degree the user activities must be made easier by the system?
	Functional correctness (accuracy)	Are there accuracy specifications, that is, a desirable precision for data? Are there limits for tolerating imprecision?
Reliability	Maturity	Must special care be taken to avoid the system to present defects during use? Must critical parts be defined by formal specification? What is the intensity and type of tests that must be performed to assure the system is free from bugs?
	Availability	Which is the degree of availability required for the system? How many simultaneous accesses must be supported? How many hours by day? How many days by year?
	Fault tolerance	How should the system react in the case of anomalies externally provoked, such as communication interruption?
	Recoverability	Must the system recover automatically in the case of a disaster? Lost data and aborted processes can be recovered under which circumstances?
Usability	Appropriateness recognizability	In which way should the software present itself to a potential user so that she may recognize its applicability? How should the software be packaged?
	Learnability	How are the concepts inherent to the software being presented to the user so that she can become competent on its use?
	Operability	In which degree must the product be easy to use and control? What kind of help must the system provide? What forms of documentation and manuals should be available? How are they going to be produced? What kind of information should they present?
	User error protection	What kind of protection against user error is necessary?
	User interface esthetics	Which design patterns will be used for the interface to provide visual pleasure and satisfactory interaction?
	Accessibility	In which degree must the product be designed to attend people with special needs?
Performance efficiency	Time behavior	Which time restrictions exist related to the software processes and functions?
	Resource utilization	Are there data storage space restrictions? Energy limitations? Communication network limitations?
	Capacity	Regarding processing capacity, which are the nominal values expected and which are the critical values? For example, the software may be designed to support up to 2000 simultaneous accesses but assured to keep working when up to 10,000 simultaneous accesses happen.
Security	Confidentiality	In which degree must the information and functions of the system be available only to those authorized to access them?
	Integrity	In which degree data and functions must be protected against unauthorized modification by people and systems?
	Nonrepudiation	In which degree must the system guarantee that the records kept by it are effectively true so that their authors cannot deny them?
	Accountability	In which degree user actions are recorded by the system? Which information is kept?
	Authenticity	In which degree it must be guaranteed that a logged user is really who she is supposed to be?

(Continued)

Table 4–2 (Continued)

25010 Feature	25010 Sub feature	Requirements generating questions
Compatibility	Coexistence	With which products must the software potentially coexist? Which tools and programming languages must be used? Is it necessary to run the system with legacy systems?
	Interoperability	Which other products must communicate with the system? To which systems must it send data? From which systems must it receive data?
Maintainability	Modularity	What kind of architecture will be used? Layers? Partitions? Components? Web services?
	Reusability	Will the system be produced from parts of other systems? Must the system de designed so that its parts could be reused in future projects?
	Analyzability	Will special techniques or tools be used to ease debugging the code?
	Modifiability	Will special techniques or tools be used to guarantee that changes introduced in the system will not produce new defects?
	Testability	Will special techniques and tools be used to ease regression tests? Automated test tools will be used? TDD (Test-Driven Development) will be used? How are test assets produced during development going to be kept?
Portability	Adaptability	In which degree must the software adapt itself to other contexts besides the ones it was originally designed? Must it be recompiled or just reconfigured? What can be configured in the system? Examples of configurable items are printers, currency, company policies, interface fonts and colors, language, etc. Transient requirements would probably be related to configurable items.
	Installability	What installation resources will be provided? Should installation be automatic? Is data migration automatic?
	Replaceability	What resources must the system provide when it replaces other systems with the same goals? What resources must the system provide when it is going to be replaced by other system with the same goals? Should it generate data and configuration in formats widely understood such as XML?
Effectiveness	Effectiveness	Which business goals on the real use environment must the system help to obtain? In which degree must the system be responsible for obtaining those goals in a complete and correct way?
Efficiency	Efficiency	What kind of return of investment (ROI) must the system produce to the client?
Satisfaction	Utility	In which way must the software be designed to help the user to perceive the consequences of its use?
	Pleasure	In which degree must the system provide pleasure to its users?
	Comfort	In which degree must the system preserve or improve physical and mental user comfort?
	Trust	In which way must the system be designed so that the stakeholders trust it will do the work?
Freedom from risk	Economic risk mitigation	What kind of financial risk (including property and moral damage) must the system reduce?
	Health and safety risk mitigation	What kind of physical risk to people must the system reduce?
	Environmental risk mitigation	What kind of environmental and property risks must the system reduce?
Context coverage	Context completeness	In which degree must the system be used effectively, efficiently, without risks, and with user satisfaction in its use contexts? Which are those use contexts? Are there legal requirements related to the use of the software?
	Flexibility	In which degree must the system be used effectively, efficiently, without risks, and with user satisfaction in use contexts other than the ones it was originally designed? Which are those use contexts?

4.8 Preliminary conceptual model

Although further chapters present conceptual modeling techniques in detail, it is interesting to mention here that a *preliminary conceptual model* (Larman, 2004) can be derived from the high-level system use cases.

4.8.1 Finding concepts by examining system use cases

The preliminary conceptual model consists of a class diagram that represents the main information units of the system. Usually, only classes are used to represent the concepts the user has about the information managed by the system. Associations between classes may be added too if possible, but not necessarily detailed, and attributes are not necessarily used at this time.

One of the main utilities for this diagram at this point is to discover which are the concepts derived from the high-level use cases and then, use this class diagram to discover which use cases may be lacking from the use case diagram. That allows the team to discover new use cases and complete the use case list for the system.

For exemplifying this technique, let's consider again our SISMOB example. From Fig. 3–5, we identified a series of system use cases that are listed in the center of Table 4–3. Just to remember, we consider that activities that must be executed immediately after another are part of the same use case, automatic tasks just after user tasks are part of the same use case, and activities that are simply manual ones are not use cases.

Below, the reasoning for each choice of identifying a concept from a high-level use case is explained:

- *Register proposal*: A Proposal is a central concept. Registering is merely the fact of recording it in the system and therefore, not a concept.
- *Send proposal*: A Proposal was already identified. Now it can be associated with a Sending event.

Table 4–3 System use cases and concepts derived from them.

Actor	High-level system use case	Concepts
Municipal manager	Register proposal	Proposal
Municipal manager	Send proposal	Sending
Municipal manager	Refactor proposal	
Federal manager	Produce assessment about proposal	Proposal Assessment
Federal manager	Cancel proposal	Cancellation
FNS	Allocate funds	Funds Allocation, Publication
Municipal manager	Require phase completion	Phase Completion Requisition
Federal manager	Produce assessment about phase	Phase Assessment, Funds Deallocation

- *Refactor proposal*: As is consists only of adjustments in the proposal and its new submission, there is no new concept here.
- *Produce assessment about proposal*: Here, a new concept is Assessment that will be associated to Proposal.
- *Cancel proposal*: To cancel an event or object is not usually just erasing it from the system. That is why a "Cancelation" concept is identified here and would be associated to a proposal if the last one is canceled.
- *Allocate funds*: this use case has an included fragment that is the task "Publish funds allocation." Then, two new concepts appear: "Funds Allocation" and "Publication."
- *Require phase completion*: at this point, a Proposal (if approved) will be transformed into an ongoing project. For that to happen, it is necessary that a "Phase Completion Requisition" concept to be associated to the Proposal.
- *Produce assessment about phase*: This use case has an extension fragment that is the "Deallocate funds" task, which will be performed if the evaluation is not good. Thus it completes our model with concepts Phase Assessment and Funds Deallocation.

Fig. 4–5 shows a possible configuration of the class diagram that represents a preliminary conceptual model. Many doubts remain, however, and the diagram will possibly change after analysis is deepened. Since we use multiplicity annotations in the diagram, notice that:

- "0..1" represents an optional single role. For example, a Proposal *may* have a Cancelation.

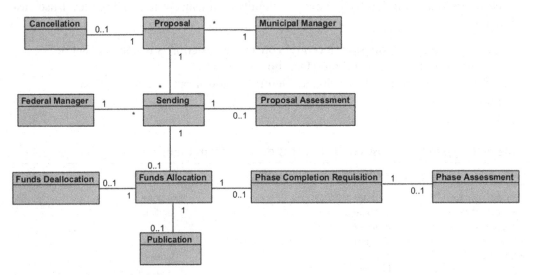

FIGURE 4–5 Preliminary conceptual model.

- "1" represents a mandatory single role. For example, a Proposal *must* have a Municipal Manager.
- "*" represents an optional multiple role. For example, a Proposal may be associated to a set of "Sending" objects depending on how many times it is refactored and resent.

4.8.2 Finding new use cases using the CRUDL pattern

A next step in analysis could be to verify if the set of use cases is minimally complete. This can be done by comparing each concept discovered with the four operations of the CRUDL patterns. Remember that "C" stands for "create," "R" for "retrieve," "U" for "update," "D" for "delete," and "L" for list.

If you look at the use case diagram or list, you could see that there are already use cases that create certain concepts, use cases that retrieve information about concepts, use cases that update information about concepts instances, and use cases that delete instances of concepts.

The set would be incomplete, however, if there are use cases that create information, but no use case retrieves or consumes that information, or if there are use cases that consume information that is nor created neither updated by any other use case. These gaps in the Concept/CRUDL matrix should be filled with new use cases.

However, before proceeding, we must remember that there are concepts that not necessarily implement all four CRUDL operations. For example, the list of weekdays has seven elements. We cannot delete, create, or update new weekdays. Thus the only operation that it implements is Retrieve.

Moreover, in many cases there are concepts which instances cannot be deleted. For example, a product once sold in a store may not be deleted from the catalog, or older sales would be inconsistent. This product may be marked as "out of sale" or something else. Then, this concept only implements the concepts of Creating, Retrieving, Updating, and Listing.

Other concepts can even be created and deleted but not updated. A sale, after completed, may not be changed anymore. Thus it implements only Create, Retrieve, Delete, and Listing.

Our first attempt to complete the use case list will populate the Concept/CRUDL table (Table 4−4) with the concepts discovered so far, the use cases that we know that operate at least one of the CRUDL operations on them and a mark "X" indicating a CRUDL operation that this concept must not implement.

Finally, we can complete the table with a set of use cases that appear to be missing. This may be just a guess unless the client is present with the team at this point. But it is a good exercise to think about the completion of the operations necessary to the system. Table 4−5 shows the complete set of use cases.

Those in italic are new use cases that should be implemented in order to the information to complete its life cycle of being created, used, and disposed, when it is the case. Cells marked with "X" continue to be operations possible but not acceptable by the business rules.

Table 4–4 Concepts versus CRUDL operations: before completion.

Concept	Create	Retrieve	Update	Delete	Listing
Proposal	Register proposal	Refactor proposal	Send Proposal	X	Refactor proposal, Send Proposal
Sending	Send proposal		X		Send Proposal
Proposal assessment	Produce assessment about proposal	Refactor proposal	X		Produce assessment about proposal
Cancellation	Cancel proposal		X	X	
Funds Allocation	Allocate funds	Require phase completion	X	X	
Publication	Allocate funds	Require phase completion	X	X	
Phase Completion	Require phase completion		X		Require phase completion
Requisition	Require phase completion		X		
Phase Assessment	Produce assessment about phase		X		
Funds Deallocation	Produce assessment about phase		X	X	

Table 4–5 Concepts versus CRUD operations: before completion.

Concept	Create	Retrieve	Update	Delete	Listing
Proposal	Register proposal	Refactor proposal	Send Proposal	X	Refactor proposal, Send Proposal
Sending	Send proposal	Report on sent proposals	X	Delete proposal	Send Proposal
Proposal assessment	Produce assessment about proposal	Refactor proposal	X	Delete assessment	Produce assessment about proposal
Cancelation	Cancel proposal	Report on cancelations	X	X	Report on cancelations
Funds Allocation	Allocate funds	Require phase completion	X	X	Report on funds allocation
Publication	Allocate funds	Require phase completion	X	X	Report on publications
Phase Completion	Require phase completion	Report on phase requirements	X	Delete phase requirement	Require phase completion
Requisition	Require phase completion	Report on requisitions	X	Delete requisition	Report on requisitions
Phase Assessment	Produce assessment about phase	(Would appear in the continuation of the diagram in Fig. 3–7)	X	Delete phase assessment	Report on assessments
Funds Deallocation	Produce assessment about phase	Report on funds deallocation	X	X	Report on funds deallocation

4.9 Discussion

The identification of that preliminary conceptual model is especially useful to ease the visualization of the structure of the information that is going to be managed by the system; this helps in unifying the vocabulary among the team members and other stakeholders. The decisions about changing use case names to clean the vocabulary should be used in the tables and diagrams every time it seems reasonable to do.

Also, the conceptual model at this point helps in identifying possible missing use cases, which can then be identified and introduced in the diagram.

Questions

1. Explain the differences between a business use case and a system use case.
2. What is the utility of a system use case through the software development process?
3. Which business actors and business workers are converted into system actors?
4. What are functional, nonfunctional, and supplementary requirements and what features might they have?
5. Why must a preliminary conceptual model be made during the Inception phase?

Use case-based project planning

Key topics in this chapter

- Effort Estimation
- Risk Assessment
- Ideal and Minimum Development Times
- Prioritizing Use Cases

5.1 Introduction to effort estimation

The motivation for effort estimation in software projects comes from the fact that historically most software development projects:

- Take more time to complete than expected.
- Cost much more than expected.
- Generate a product that does not have the quality expected.
- Generate a product that does not have the scope expected.

Thus the point is that software development teams and clients must learn to expect the right time, cost, quality, and scope regarding their project. Effort estimation techniques are used to accomplish these goals.

Effort estimation may be divided into two big groups: parametric and nonparametric. In the following subsections, both will be presented and discussed.

5.2 Ad hoc techniques

Several techniques for effort estimation have been proposed and used in the last several decades. One that is very popular is the *Smith* technique, which may be summarized as "Smith, tell us how much time you need to develop that system!" A variation of the Smith technique is the *Constrained Smith*, which may be summarized as "Smith, you have three months to develop that system!." Although popular (and known by other names, such as Susan, Peter, Mary, etc.), this approach may not be very accurate and depends strongly on the person experience on estimating software effort.

Another ad-hoc technique that is used is the *Six Months* technique. It consists of estimating "six months" for any software project at the beginning of its negotiation with the client and then adjusting it up or down as the real scope and requirements are discovered.

Object-Oriented Analysis and Design for Information Systems. DOI: https://doi.org/10.1016/B978-0-443-13739-6.00018-6

Variations of that technique are virtually infinite, including the *One Year* technique and the *Eighteen Months* technique, among others.

Somerville (2006) identifies some other *ad hoc* techniques:

- *Expert judgment.* The expert judgment technique proposes that one or more experts on the project domain and software development should meet and use their experience to produce an estimate. The Smith technique is a potentially bad scenario for the expert judgment technique: the technique may be very inaccurate, depending on the expertise of the estimators. However, if the experts really have wide experience in similar projects, it is a feasible, quick, and relatively effortless technique.
- *Estimation by analogy.* That technique is in fact the pragmatic basis for the expert judgment technique. It is assumed that the effort for developing a new system will be like the effort for developing other similar systems. The technique is not feasible if similar projects are not available for comparison. It can make good use of one or more experts to determine what qualifies as a *similar* system and how the time spent to develop it may be used as a basis to estimate the effort for the current project. Thus this technique usually may evolve to expert judgment.
- *Parkinson's Law.* That technique is not usually adopted openly, but it is recurrent in software projects and in other areas: *the project costs whatever resources are available.* The advantage is that the project will not cost more than expected, but eventually the scope of the system will not be completely covered. This technique is explained by the dialog: "How much will the system cost?" answered by the question "How much do you have?."
- *Pricing to win.* The cost of the project is equal to the price that is believed to win the contract. The disadvantage of this method is that the system the client gets may not be what she expected, because as costs must usually be reduced, this may impact on quality and scope.

These kinds of techniques are known as *nonparametric estimation* because they are not based on measures on the project to be developed.

5.3 Parametric techniques

Another class of estimation techniques includes the parametric ones, which aim to present an effort estimation based on the estimated *size of the system*, the technical difficulty to develop it, and the capacity of the team, among other features. The size of the system may be measured in terms of:

- *Lines of code.* Techniques such as COCOMO II—COnstructive COst MOdel II (Boehm, 2000) start estimating how many *source lines of code* the system will have. In fact, as most systems have thousands of lines of code, the usual measure is *kilo source lines of code* (KSLOC).

- *Function points.* Techniques based on function point analysis (FPA) (Albrecht, 1979) and its variations are not concerned about lines of code. They estimate that the effort to develop a system depends on the *apparent functionality* that is going to be implemented. Thus usually these techniques count the number of functional requirements and evaluate their complexity by asking about how many elements and functions the interfaces have and about the number and size of database tables.
- *Use case points.* That is a variation of the FPA technique that is based on use cases instead of functional requirements for estimation.

Although COCOMO II is the most detailed technique, it has a disadvantage compared with function points and use case points: the number of KSLOC must be estimated by specialists before applying the method, and this is a significant source of uncertainty.[1] In the end, COCOMO II is like a variation of specialist opinion with a lot of technical adjustments made based on statistics about real projects. However, the first kick problem remains: will the system have 20K, 30K, or 70K lines of code?

5.4 User story points

The agile community usually adopts an estimation strategy that is based on story points. As we discussed before, a *user story* is a scenario of use of a system, and it is somewhat like a use case. However, use cases are more structured and formal; they are produced by a team of analysts. User stories, on the other hand, must be written by the users themselves. They must represent a scenario where the users see themselves using the system that is going to be produced. The idea behind this is that the users present the needs that are most important for them first; the details would be recalled later.

This book measures the size of use cases with story points, because a use case can be in fact the evolution of a user story.

One story point is one ideal working day (6–8 hours focused and dedicated to a project). The estimation effort is then calculated for each user story or use case in terms of story points. The question to be answered by the team is, "How many ideal days x people would take to develop a given user story?" If the answer is x people would take y days, then the number of story points is $x \times y$. Story points assignment is subjective, and this is why it is considered a nonparametric technique.

5.4.1 Two ways to estimate story points

We have seen that the Bridge Laboratory uses an estimation technique that is a variation of user expert. The difference is that the expert does not estimate alone, the estimation is made together with one or more agile teams. The agile teams are free to use the estimation

---

[1] To minimize this uncertainty, *backfire tables* that convert function points into KSLOC may be used for some classes of systems (Boehm, 2000).

technique they prefer given that they deliver the result in story points. Two of those techniques are presented in the following subsections.

5.4.1.1 Selecting from the whole set of stories

When this technique is used, all histories (or use cases) have their names written in stickers and placed on a table or a wall where all the team may see them. The first step of the algorithm is to remove the stories or use cases considered to be feasible by one developer in less than one day, that is, a user story or use case with less than one story point. Those stories are left separated for being joined later with one of themselves or another related but more complex story.

The second step is to remove stories that are feasible in more or less one day by one developer. Those stories are attributed one story point and will be separated from the other more complex stories that remain in the table or wall.

The third step, you may have guessed yet, is to separate user stories with two story points and make a new group with them. This algorithm proceeds by separating stories that are similar in size until no story is left on the table or wall.

However, the increasing scale used is not the natural numbers, but a kind of rounded Fibonacci numbers, as seen in Table 5–1.

The team may use other scales, such as 1, 2, 4, 8, 16, ... The important thing is that they understand that the idea here is not to hit the value but to identify which stories are similar in terms of effort to be developed. This idea is based on the fact that a human usually does not know how much an adult horse weighs, but she knows that it weighs more than a dog and less than an elephant.

5.4.1.2 Planning poker

Another way to estimate the effort for a user story or use case is to give each team member a set of cards representing the numbers in the rounded Fibonacci scale and voting. The voting process happens as follows: one user story or use case is selected from the stack or list and presented and discussed by the team. Then, each team member places one card on the table with the number hidden to the other members. When all have placed their cards, they are all open. If they agreed more or less, for example, 3, 5, 3, 3, 3, 2, 3, their rounded average is assigned as their user points; in the example: 3. If one or more disagree a lot, for example, 3, 2, 3, 20, 3, 5, 2, where the "20" is far from the average of the other numbers, then the member that disagreed must explain why she has done so, and the team will discuss if the reasons are valid or not. Then a second round is done and values more similar are expected.

Table 5–1   Natural, Fibonacci, and rounded Fibonacci numbers.

Natural	1	2	3	4	5	6	7	8	9	10	11	12
Fibonacci	1	2	3	5	8	13	21	34	55	89	144	233
Rounded Fibonacci	1	2	3	5	10	15	20	35	50	90	150	250

If the disagreement happens again, the team may discuss and vote again. Continuing the discussion after a second round may be frustrating and useless. Then, if a quasi-agreement is not obtained, the number of user points may be calculated as:

$$UP = \left(W_{\text{max}} + W_{\text{min}} + 4 \times W_{\text{average}}\right)/6$$

where *UP* is the number of user points assigned to the user story or use case, W_{max} is the value of the maximum guess by the team, W_{min} is the value of the minimum guess by the team, and W_{average} is the average of the other guesses by the team.

5.4.2 What to consider when estimating story points

The team usually evaluates the effort of a system component based on their experience on similar past projects. The assignment is made based on effort, complexity, and risk:

- *Effort*: How many lines of code or function points must be considered?
- *Complexity*: How difficult is to analyze, implement, and test the component?
- *Risk*: How much does the team understand the component?

In the following subsections, we will discuss those criteria in more detail.

5.4.2.1 Effort

Effort may be associated with the "brute force" involved in programming. In the case of user stories, the length of the story and the quantity of scenario variations may be a clue to estimate the user story effort.

In the case of use cases, usually the team must estimate or develop the detailed version of the use case to know how many transactions it has. A transaction is a pair of input and output to and from the system. For example, if a user requires the balance of her account and the system informs the value, that was a complete transaction. If, after that the user asks to withdraw some money and receives the money, that was a second complete transaction.

Karner initially proposed the t-shirt[2] scale for use cases:

- Use cases with up to three transactions are small.
- Use cases with four to seven transactions are medium.
- Use cases with more than seven transactions are large.

However, Karner did not show how to convert those values into developing time, such as story points. Thus we suggest that the team should use the estimated number of transactions together with complexity and risk for helping to decide on the number of story points of the use case.

---

[2] Sizes: small, medium, and large.

5.4.2.2 Complexity

Complexity is related to the difficulty to analyze, implement, and test the story or use case. The Use Case Point Technique of Karner adapted the Technical Complexity Factor from Function Points technique and introduced a new set of Environmental Complexity Factors that were later adapted to the Function Point Technique too.

We can use the technical complexity factors to understand the complexity of the component and the environmental complexity factors to understand its risks.

Each factor receives a rating from 0 to 5, where 0 means no influence on the project, 2.5 is nominal influence, and 5 is maximum influence on the project.

There are 13 technical factors, each one with a specific weight, as shown in Table 5–2.

Tables 5.3–5.17 show the interpretation of each of those complexity factors and how the rank should be assigned.

For the Function Points and Use Case Points Analysis those ranks would be used to reach a value that would be used in the calculations to produce a number known as "Adjusted Function/Use Case Points" that number is used to calculate the time to develop the system by multiplying it by the productivity index of the team. However, here we are not making this conversion so fast.

Those thirteen complexity factors usually apply to the system as a whole, but looking at the parts of the system, we can see that they are not usually homogeneous. For example, one use case may demand high-level security, but others do not. Thus the team can use this tables as a reference to analyze the relative complexity of each part of the system.

Table 5–16 shows an example of a comparative table with some use cases belonging to the same application being analyzed individually. The last row is the average that allows to compare use cases among them in terms of complexity. Ranks closer to 0 mean easy use cases, ranks closer to 5 means very complex use cases and 2.5 is the nominal or average complexity use case.

Table 5–2 Technical factors used by function points estimation technique.

Factor	Description	Weight
T1	Distributed system	2.0
T2	Response time/performance objectives	1.0
T3	End-user efficiency	1.0
T4	Internal processing complexity	1.0
T5	Code reusability	1.0
T6	Easy to install	0.5
T7	Easy to use	0.5
T8	Portability to other platforms	2.0
T9	System maintenance	1.0
T10	Concurrent/parallel processing	1.0
T11	Security features	1.0
T12	Access for third parties	1.0
T13	End user training	1.0

Table 5–3   Distributed system.

Is the system architecture centralized or distributed?

Rank	Scenario
0	The application ignores any aspect related to distributed processing.
1	The application generates data that will be processed by other computers with human intervention (e.g., spreadsheets or preformatted files sent by media or email).
2	Application data are prepared and transferred automatically for processing in other computers.
3	Application processing is distributed, and data are transferred in just one direction.
4	Application processing is distributed, and data are transferred in both directions.
5	Application processes must be executed in the most appropriate processing core or computer, which is dynamically determined.

Table 5–4   Response time/performance objectives.

What is the importance of the application response time to its users?

Rank	Scenario
0	No special performance requirement was defined by the client.
1	Performance requirements were established and revised, but no special action must be taken.
2	Response time and transfer rates are critical during peak hours. No special design for processor core use is necessary. The deadline for most processes is the next day.
3	Response time and transfer rates are critical during commercial hours. No special design for processor core use is necessary. Requirements regarding deadlines for communication with interfaced systems are restrictive.
4	In addition to 3, performance requirements are sufficiently restrictive for requiring performance analysis tasks during design.
5	In addition to 4, performance analysis tools must be used during design, development, and/or implementation, in order to meet the client's performance requirements.

In this table, we considered that UC1 is a mathematical related module, with less human interaction, but high internal processing. UC2 is a user-oriented module with less internal complexity but a lot of user specific resources. UC3 is a module that deals with sensitive data and demands special security but has no other important features.

The averages resulting indicate that UC1 and UC2 have similar complexity while UC3 is relatively simpler.

5.4.2.3 Risk

The last important factor that determines the relative size of a use case or user story is *risk*. Risks are variable and volatile, and many risks tables can be found in literature. In this book we decided to work with risks in order to calculate effort in developing and thus it seemed natural to use the environmental complexity factors of use case points in order to help understanding relative use case sizes based on risks.

Table 5–5 End-user efficiency.

Is the application designed to allow final users just to do their job or is it designed to improve their efficiency?

Rank	Scenario
0	The application does not need any of the items below.
1	The application needs one to three of the items below.
2	The application needs four to five of the items below.
3	The application needs six or more of the items below, but there is no requirement related to user efficiency.
4	The application needs six or more of the items below, and the user efficiency requirements are so strong that the design must include features to minimize typing, maximize defaults, use templates, etc.
5	The application needs six or more of the items below, and the user efficiency requirements are so strong that the design activities must include tools and special processes to demonstrate that the performance goals are obtained.

The following items must be considered for the assessment of the end-user efficiency item:
- Navigational help (e.g., dynamically generated menus and adaptive hypermedia).
- Online help and documentation.
- Automated cursor movement.
- Predefined function keys.
- Batch tasks submitted from online transactions.
- High use of colors and visual highlights in screens.
- Minimizing the number of screens to reach the business goals.
- Bilingual support (counts as four items).
- Multilingual support (counts as six items).

Table 5–6 Internal processing complexity.

Does the application need complex algorithms?

Rank	Scenario
0	None of the options below.
1	One of the options below.
2	Two of the options below.
3	Three of the options below.
4	Four of the options below.
5	All five options below.

The following options need to be considered for assessing internal processing complexity:
- Careful control (e.g., special audit processing) and/or secure processing specific to the application.
- Extensive logical processing.
- Extensive mathematical processing.
- Lots of exception processing resulting from incomplete transactions that needs to be reprocessed, such as incomplete automated teller machine transactions caused by interruption of communication, missing data values, or failed data change.
- Complex processing to manage multiple inputs and output possibilities, such as multimedia or device independency.

Table 5–7   Design aiming for code reusability.

Is the application designed so that its code and artifacts will be highly reusable?

Rank	Scenario
0	There is no concern about producing reusable code.
1	Reusable code is generated for use inside the same project.
2	Less than 10% of the application must consider more than the user needs.
3	10% or more of the application must consider more than the user needs.
4	The application must be specifically packaged and/or documented for facilitating reuse, and the application must be customizable by the user at the level of source code.
5	The application must be specifically packaged and/or documented for facilitating reuse, and the application must be customizable by the user with the use of parameters.

Table 5–8   Easy to install.

Will the application be designed so that its installation is automatic (e.g., in the case of users with low or unknown technical capacity), or is there no special concern about it?

Rank	Scenario
0	The client established no special consideration, and no special setup is necessary for installation.
1	The client established no special consideration, but a special setup is required for installation.
2	The client established requirements for data conversion and installation, and conversion and installation guides must be provided and tested. The impact of conversion in the project is not considered important.
3	The client established requirements for data conversion and installation, and conversion and installation guides must be provided and tested. The impact of conversion on the project is considerable.
4	In addition to 2, tools for automatic conversion and installation must be provided and tested.
5	In addition to 3, tools for automatic conversion and installation must be provided and tested.

There are eight environmental factors that assess the working environment. Each one has its own weight and two of them have negative weights. Again, ratings range from 0 to 5, but their meaning is a little different from those of the ratings attributed to the technical factors. While the ratings of the technical factors evaluate the *influence* of those factors on the project, the ratings of the environmental factors evaluate the *quality* of those factors in the working environment. For example, a 0 rating for the "motivation" factor means that the team is not motivated, a 2 or 3 rating means that motivation is about average, and a 5 rating means that the team is highly motivated. The environmental factors are defined in Table 5–17.

Ribu (2001) presents a reference for assigning ratings to the environmental factors, which is described in Tables 5–18 to 5–25 with some adaptation.

Those environment factors are applied to a team, not to parts of the system. However, as a project may have many teams, their respective risks can be calculated individually. Then, the risk associated to the team may be associated to the use cases they are developing in case of an estimation.

Table 5–9   Easy to operate[3].

Are there special requirements regarding the operation of the system?

Rank	Scenario
0	No special considerations about the operation of the system besides normal backup procedures were established by the user.
1	One of the items below applies to the system.
2	Two of the items below apply to the system.
3	Three of the items below apply to the system.
4	Four of the items below apply to the system.
5	The application is designed to operate in nonsupervised manner. "Nonsupervised" means that human intervention is not necessary for keeping the system operational, even if crashes occur, except maybe for the first startup and final turn off. One of the application features is automatic error recovery.

For the evaluation of the easy to operate factor, the following items must be considered:
- Effective processes for initialization, backup, and recovery must be provided, but operator intervention is still necessary.
- Effective processes for initialization, backup, and recovery must be provided, and no operator intervention is necessary (counts as two items).
- The application must minimize the need for data store in offline media (e.g., tapes).
- The application must minimize the need for dealing with paper.

Table 5–10   Portability.

Is the application or parts of it designed to work on more than one platform?

Rank	Scenario
0	There is no user requirement to consider the need for installing the application in more than one platform.
1	The design must consider the need for the system to operate in different platforms, but the application must be designed to operate only in identical hardware and software environments.
2	The design must consider the need for the system to operate in different platforms, but the application must be designed to operate only in similar hardware and software environments.
3	The design must consider the need for the system to operate in different platforms, but the application must be designed to operate in heterogeneous hardware and software environments.
4	In addition to 1 or 2, a documentation and maintenance plan must be elaborated and tested to support operation in multiple platforms.
5	In addition to 3, a documentation and maintenance plan must be elaborated and tested to support operation in multiple platforms.

Let's, for example, consider two teams. Team 1 is a group of five professionals recently graduated in Computer Science that studied object-oriented techniques, but without significant professional experience. Three of them are fully dedicated to the project, while the other

[3] Occasionally, this item is referred to as "usability," but the original concept of usability was already considered in factor T3, "end-user efficiency." We prefer to interpret this factor as "easy to operate" to avoid confusion and redundancy with the end-user efficiency factor.

Table 5–11 Design aiming for easy maintenance.

Does the client require that the application must be easy to change in future?

Rank	Scenario
0	None of the items below.
1	One of the items below.
2	Two of the items below.
3	Three of the items below.
4	Four of the items below.
5	Five or more of the items below.

To evaluate this factor, the following items are considered:

- A flexible report structure must be provided to deal with simple queries such as logical binary operators applied to just one logical archive (count as one item).
- A flexible report structure must be provided to deal with medium complexity queries such as logical binary operators applied to more than one logical archive (count as two items).
- A flexible report structure must be provided to deal with high complexity queries such as combinations of logical binary operators applied to one or more logical archives (count as three items).
- Business control data are kept in tables managed by the user with interactive online access, but changes must only be effective on the next day (count as one item).

Business control data are kept in tables managed by the user with interactive online access, and changes are effective immediately (count as two items).

Table 5–12 Concurrent/parallel processing.

Must the application be designed in order to deal with problems related to concurrency such as data and resource sharing?

Rank	Scenario
0	No concurrent access to data is expected.
1	Concurrent access to data is expected sometimes.
2	Concurrent access to data is expected frequently.
3	Concurrent access to data is expected all the time.
4	In addition to 3, the user indicates that a lot of multiple accesses are going to happen, forcing performance analysis tasks and deadlock resolution during design.
5	In addition to 4, the design requires the use of special tools to control access.

two have other activities. This will be the first project they are going to work professionally together. Despite having little experience in software industry, they are highly motivated, and their lead analyst has a little more than 1 year of experience as such.

On the other hand, Team 2 is a dream team as they have experienced people (more than 3 years) in Scrum, object-oriented processes, knowledge of application, and programming language. The team is highly motivated, and all workers are full-time. The different ranks for teams 1 and 2 are shown in Table 5–26.

Table 5–13   Security.

Are the security needs just nominal or are a special design and additional specifications required?	
Rank	**Scenario**
0	There are no special requirements regarding security.
1	The need for security must be taken into account in design.
2	In addition to 1, the application must be designed so that it can be accessed only by authorized users.
3	In addition to 2, access to the system will be controlled and audited.
4	In addition to 3, a security plan must be elaborated and tested to support access control to the application.
5	In addition to 4, a security plan must be elaborated and tested to support auditory.

Table 5–14   Access to/for third-party code.

Is the application going to use code already developed, such as commercial off-the-shelf (COTS) components, frameworks or libraries? High reuse of good quality software reduces the value of this item as it implies less development effort.	
Rank	**Scenario**
0	Highly reliable preexistent code will be used extensively for developing the application.
1	Highly reliable preexistent code will be used in small parts of the application.
2	Preexistent code that eventually needs to be adjusted will be used extensively for developing the application.
3	Preexistent code that eventually needs to be adjusted will be used in small parts of the application.
4	Preexistent code that needs to be fixed or is hard to understand will be used in the application.
5	No preexistent code will be used in the application or questionable quality code will be used in the application.

Table 5–15   User training needs.

Will the application be easy to use, or must extensive training be given to future users?	
Rank	**Scenario**
0	There are no specific requirements for user training.
1	Specific user training requirements have been mentioned.
2	There are formal specific user training requirements, and the application must be designed to facilitate training.
3	There are formal specific user training requirements, and the application must be designed to support users with different levels of training.
4	A detailed training plan must be elaborated for the transition phase and executed.
5	In addition to 4, the users are geographically distributed.

The difference between the two teams shows that the first team may face a lot of problems if they start a nontrivial project without trying to improve some of their ranks. On the other side, the dream team may face the project risks with more competence. In the end, Team 1 would take much longer to develop the same project as Team 2, and that may be reflected to every use case assigned to them.

Table 5–16   Some use cases and their complexity comparison.

Factor	Description	Weight	UC1	UC2	UC3
T1	Distributed system	2.0	0	0	3
T2	Response time/performance objectives	1.0	3	4	2
T3	End-user efficiency	1.0	2	5	1
T4	Internal processing complexity	1.0	5	1	2
T5	Code reusability	1.0	3	2	2
T6	Easy to install	0.5	0	5	0
T7	Easy to use	0.5	1	5	1
T8	Portability to other platforms	2.0	0	0	0
T9	System maintenance	1.0	3	3	3
T10	Concurrent/parallel processing	1.0	5	2	0
T11	Security features	1.0	2	2	5
T12	Access for third parties	1.0	4	0	5
T13	End user training	1.0	1	5	4
	Weighted average		2.03	2.07	1.75

Table 5–17   Environmental complexity factors.

Factor	Description	Weight
E1	Familiarity with development process used	1.5
E2	Application experience	0.5
E3	Object-oriented experience of team	1.0
E4	Lead analysis capability	0.5
E5	Motivation of the Team	1.0
E6	Stability of Requirements	2.0
E7	Part-time staff	− 1.0
E8	Difficulty with programming language	− 1.0

5.5 Linear time

There are many ways to address the issue of the linear or calendar time to run a project. One is based on the number of agile teams available. As we know the size of each team, we know how many story points each team can develop each working day. We also know the number of story points attributed to each product of the project that is the sum of the story points of each use case or user story. Then, it would be possible to allocate each team to different products until all products are allocated. As the teams can work in parallel, they can use the same calendar days to perform their work.

For example, consider a project with seven products, the size of which (number of story points) is depicted in Table 5−27.

Then, we can allocate products to the three agile teams considering if they are idle or not.

Table 5–18   Familiarity with the development process used[4].

This factor assesses the team's experience with the development process they are using.

Rank	Scenario
0	The team does not have experience with the development process or does not use any process.
1	The team has theoretical knowledge about the development process, but no experience.
2	A few members of the team have already used the process in one project.
3	A few members of the team have used the process in more than one project.
4	Up to half the team has used the process in many projects.
5	More than half the team has used the process in many projects.

Table 5–19   Experience in the application.

This factor assesses the familiarity of the team with the application area or domain. For example, if the application is about e-commerce, have the team already worked with systems in the same area?

Rank	Scenario
0	No team member has any experience in projects in the same area.
1	Some team members have 6–12 months of experience in projects in the same area.
2	Some team members have 12–18 months of experience in projects in the same area.
3	Some team members have 18–24 months of experience in projects in the same area.
4	Most team members have 18–24 months of experience in the same area.
5	Most team members have more than 24 months of experience in the same area.

The agile teams may have different sizes. Thus let's consider that Team 1 has five members, Team 2 has seven members, and Team 3 has four members (Table 5–28). Each time we allocate a team in the calendar (this calendar considers only working days, not holydays), we allocate a number of days that is the number of story points of the project divided by the size of the team.

First, we allocate project P1 with 220 story points to Team 1 that has five members. So, we must allocate 220/5 = 44 working days. Then, we allocate P2 to Team 2. As P2 has 630 story points and Team 2 has seven members, we should allocate 630/7 = 90 working days. Then, Team 3 with four members will have allocated P3 with 400 story points. Thus we allocate 400/4 = 100 working days. Notice that even if P3 has less effort than P2, it takes more time because the team is smaller. The linear time each team would use to develop each product is depicted in Table 5–29.

The results up to now may be seen in Fig. 5–1.

We see then that the first team to terminate a product is Team 1. Thus they can take over P4. As P4 has 240 story points and Team 1 five members, we should allocate 240/5 = 48 working days. As Fig. 5–2 shows, the next team to terminate a product is Team 2. We

---

[4] Originally the factor mentioned the Unified Process, and some authors even mention UML here. But this has been adjusted to reflect the fact that other processes and modeling languages could be used instead.

Table 5-20   Object-oriented experience of the team.

This factor must not be confused with either familiarity with the development process (E1) or experience in the application (E2): this is about the experience of the team in doing object-oriented analysis, modeling, design, and programming, independently of the application area and the development process used.

Rank	Scenario
0	No team member has any experience in projects in object-oriented techniques.
1	Some team members have 6–12 months of experience in object-oriented techniques.
2	Some team members have 12–18 months of experience in object-oriented techniques.
3	Some team members have 18–24 months of experience in object-oriented techniques.
4	Most team members have 18–24 months of experience in object-oriented techniques.
5	Most team members have more than 24 months of experience in object-oriented techniques.

Table 5-21   Lead analyst experience.

This factor measures the experience of the lead analyst with requirement analysis and object-oriented modeling, that is, typical analysis tasks.

Rank	Scenario
0	The lead analyst has no experience.
1	The lead analyst has up to 6 months of experience.
2	The lead analyst has 6–12 months of experience.
3	The lead analyst has 12–18 months of experience.
4	The lead analyst has 18–24 months of experience.
5	The lead analyst has more than 2 years of experience.

allocate P5 to them: $80/7 = 11.5 \cong 12$ working days (we should probably always "round" up in these cases).

As the process continues, we allocate P6 to Team 1 with $120/5 = 24$ working days and P7 to Team 3 with $70/4 = 17.5 \cong 18$ working days. The final allocation is depicted in Fig. 5–3.

Notice that if teams with different sizes would have been used, the allocation could be very different from this one. Notice also that if we have allocated P7 or P6 to Team 2 and P5 to Team 3 or Team 1, we could finish all the project a couple of days earlier. This can be considered before deciding on the final allocation (unless you need Team 2 to be free before the others, of course). But, considering the allocation of Fig. 5–3 we have:

- P1 starts at day 1 and finishes at day 44.
- P2 starts at day 1 and finishes at day 90.
- P3 starts at day 1 and finishes at day 100.
- P4 starts at day 45 and finishes at day $45 + 48 - 1 = 92$
- P5 starts at day 91 and finishes at day $91 + 12 - 1 = 102$
- P6 starts at day 93 and finishes at day $93 + 24 - 1 = 116$
- P7 starts at day 101 and finished at day $101 + 18 - 1 = 118$

Table 5–22   Motivation of the team[5].

This factor describes the team's motivation.

Rank	Scenario
0	The team is not motivated at all. Without constant supervision the team becomes unproductive. The team only does what is strictly asked.
1	The team has very little motivation. Constant supervision is necessary to keep productivity at acceptable levels.
2	The team has little motivation. Management interventions are necessary from time to time to maintain productivity.
3	The team has some motivation. Usually the team has initiative, but management intervention is still necessary sporadically to keep productivity.
4	The team is well motivated. The team is self-managed usually, but the existence of supervision is still necessary because productivity can be lost without it.
5	The team is highly motivated. Even without supervision everyone knows what has to be done, and pace is maintained indefinitely. The team is proactive and addresses almost all problems by themselves.

Table 5–23   Stability of requirements.

This factor evaluates if the team has been able to keep requirements stable in past projects, minimizing their change during the project. This factor may vary from project to project, and from client to client, because there are domains where requirements change often independently of the capacity of the analysts.

Rank	Scenario
0	There is no historic data about requirement stability or, in the past, poor analysis caused big changes in requirements after the project started.
1	Requirements were predominantly unstable in the past. Clients asked for many changes caused mainly by incomplete or incorrect requirements.
2	Requirements were unstable in the past. Clients asked for some changes caused by incomplete or incorrect requirements.
3	Requirements were relatively stable in the past. Clients asked for changes in secondary functionalities with some regularity. Changes to main functionalities were seldomly asked.
4	Requirements were mostly stable in the past. Users asked for little changes, especially cosmetic ones. Changes in main or secondary functionalities were unusual.
5	Requirements were practically stable in the past. Little changes, if any, had no impact on projects.

Here, we can see that the project as a whole takes 118 days and that P3 and P7 assigned to Team 3 belong to the *critical path*, meaning that if they are delayed, the whole project is delayed. The other projects have some space to delays: 2 days for Team 1 and 16 days for Team 2.

In the example above, we allocate projects to teams without considering any special features. But that could be the case. For example, just one of the teams may be specialized in

---

[5] Surely that is one of the hardest environmental factors to assess, because the real motivation of the team may be masked. Ribu's (2001) suggestion seemed to help very little in rating this factor, and we took the liberty of reinterpreting the reference.

Table 5-24   Part-time workers.

This is a negative factor, that is, contrary to the first six environmental factors, higher values here represent more risk, not less. A team with many members involved in other projects or activities tend to be less productive than a dedicated team.

Rank	Scenario
0	No team member is part time on the project.
1	Up to 10% of the team is part time.
2	Up to 20% of the team is part time.
3	Up to 40% of the team is part time.
4	Up to 60% of the team is part time.
5	More than 60% of the team is part time.

Table 5-25   Difficulty with programming language.

This is another negative factor, meaning that high values here are bad for the development time. It measures the experience of the team with the language to be used in the project.

Rank	Scenario
0	Most team members have more than 24 moths of experience with the programming language.
1	Most team members have 18–24 months of experience with the programming language.
2	Some team members have 18–24 months of experience with the programming language.
3	Some team members have 12–18 months of experience with the programming language.
4	Some team members have 6–12 months of experience with the programming language.
5	Team members have up to 6 months of experience with the programming language.

Table 5-26   Ranks for two different teams.

Factor	Description	Weight	Team 1	Team 2
E1	Familiarity with development process used	1.5	1	5
E2	Application experience	0.5	0	5
E3	Object-oriented experience of team	1.0	3	5
E4	Lead analysis capability	0.5	3	5
E5	Motivation of the team	1.0	4	5
E6	Stability of requirements	2.0	0	5
E7	Part-time staff	−1.0	3	0
E8	Difficult programming language	−1.0	4	0
	Average ranks		0.30	5.00

mobile applications. If that kind of issue exists, it must be considered when the project is being planned.

We have allocated random products to random teams without worrying about team size or product size. But what if we allocated the bigger product to the smaller team and they

Table 5–27   Seven products and their story points.

Product	Story points
P1	220
P2	630
P3	400
P4	240
P5	80
P6	120
P7	70
TOTAL	1760

Table 5–28   Teams size.

Team	#Members
1	5
2	7
3	4

Table 5–29   Linear time for each team to develop each project.

Product	Story points	Team	#Members	Linear time
P1	220	1	5	44
P2	630	2	7	90
P3	400	3	4	100
P4	240	1	5	48
P5	80	2	7	12
P6	120	1	5	24
P7	70	3	4	18

take much more time than the other teams to complete the product, delaying so the project? That would not be good for sure. For example, if we allocate P2 (630 story point) to Team 3 (four members), they would take 630/4 = 158 working days to conclude P2 and the project would be delayed considering that it could be concluded in 118 days with the previous allocation that we found.

Other important issue is that projects cannot be accelerated indefinitely. If a team with two people can do it in 4 weeks, it does not mean that a team with eight people can do it in one week, neither that 16 people could do it in half a week.

Although there are formulae that dictate the ideal relation between total effort and linear time, their application in practice is very relative. First, they do not work for small projects and second, depending on the type of the project, the numbers would be very different. We suggest here that the team should use common sense and experience to decide if a project can be

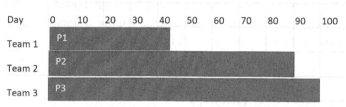

FIGURE 5–1 Three products assigned to three different teams.

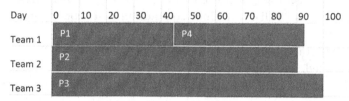

FIGURE 5–2 Four projects assigned to three teams.

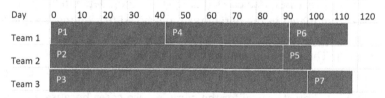

FIGURE 5–3 All seven projects assigned to three teams.

done with the number of people allocated. Unless you work with projects that last for less than 1 or 2 months, agile teams with less than 10 members usually would do the work in time.

In any case, always allocate bigger project to bigger teams and smaller projects to smaller teams.

5.6 Estimating the duration of the sprints

An sprint begins with planning and finishes with a new version of the system being released internally and/or delivered to the client. The duration of a sprint in Scrum and most agile methods usually ranges from 1 to 8 weeks,[6] and it depends, among other factors, on the complexity of the project and the size of the team.

---

[6] Agile methods prefer the shortest duration possible. Some methods such as XP are more radical by forbidding iterations with more than 3 weeks, but other methods are more relaxed on that.

Our experience in the Bridge Laboratory was to initiate with 4-week sprints and after a couple of years of experience changing to 2-week sprints aiming to finally reach 1-week sprints. Nowadays, about half the agile teams work with one and the other half with 2-week sprints.

5.7 Defining use case priority

One of the main techniques for reducing risk in a project is dealing first with the most complex use cases, especially if they are those that represent the most critical business processes, because with them the team may learn more about the system than with other use cases. Pattern use cases such as CRUDL (medium complexity) and reports (smallest complexity) can be addressed later.

Planning meetings at the beginning of the sprint may indicate which use cases are going to be analyzed, designed, and implemented.

When planning a sprint, the following aspects must be considered when choosing which use cases to address:

- *Use case complexity*: Use cases of higher risk and complexity or less understood should be addressed first in most cases.
- *Dependencies among use cases*: Use cases that have a strong dependence to the ones that were already accommodated in the iteration should be addressed together, if possible, because it avoids fragmenting the work on the classes.
- *Team load capacity*: The development work must be assigned to team members based on their capacity in story points (number of members $\times$ number of days of the sprint).

The order of this list is most critical for the complex use cases because a wrong choice in terms of their priorities could lead to otherwise unnecessary refactoring in subsequent iterations. However, the order of use cases with lower risk such as CRUDLs and reports is not so critical.

Have in mind also that use cases are not the only elements that would be allocated to a sprint. If this is not the first sprint, the user would have already asked for some modifications in the system, and they take time to be done and this time must be allocated to the team. Also, project risks that are of high expositions should be treated, and sometimes they need several days to be analyzed and dealt with.

Then, for each element (use case, risk, or change requested), there must be effort estimation or allocation. Estimating effort to develop or change use cases usually is more feasible that estimating time to mitigate a risk. Thus usually a risk has time allocated to it instead of estimated. For example, the team allocates 2 days for three members to mitigate the risk and at the end of this schedule analyzes if the risk was mitigated or not. If not, they decide if it is worthy to start a new mitigation cycle with the same or a different duration or involving other people.

The elements will be selected for inclusion in one sprint or another depending on their priority. Higher priority must be given to the more complex and risky elements, which are the ones with greater potential for learning about the system. The suggestion is to pick first:

- Use cases that represent the most critical business processes, for example, those that help the company achieve its organizational goals, such as obtaining profit.
- High-importance (or high-exposure) risks, that is, those with high impact and a high probability of becoming problems.
- Urgent change requests, for example, those that demand architecture refactoring.

When considering the elements of highest priority, other elements with lower priorities, but closely related to the higher priority ones, may be added to the same sprint for convenience. The important thing is that the total effort assigned to the sprint does not surpass the team capacity.

5.8 Monitoring a project

Now that we have a project divided into products with each product divided into use cases, the size of which is known we can use a system to monitor whether the project is running in schedule or not. First, take the total story points of the project and divide it by the number of linear days of the complete project. In our example, it would be a total of Table 5−27, 1760 divided by the duration of the project, which is 118 days. The total is 14.9 story points. This is the number of story points expected to be delivered each day, and it is compatible with the total size of all teams that is 16 people.

In Bridge, we usually use a monthly report to allow the team and other stakeholders to watch the pace of the project. We could be very accurate by observing how many business days there is in each month, but in this example, we simply consider that a month have 20 working days.

Then the project would take $118/20 = 5.9$ months (ok, 6!) and should deliver in average $14.9 \times 20 = 298$ story points per month. That would allow us to draw a burn up chart to monitor this project as in Fig. 5−4.

The "Estimated" line is easy to obtain. It starts in 0 and each month we add the number of expected story points to be delivered (298 in our example) until the last position that must correspond to the total number of story points of the project.

For the "Obtained" line, data are captured from the agile teams. Each time a team finishes a use case, the number of story points of that use case is added to the delivered story points of that team in that month. At the end of the month, we simply sum the number of delivered story points by each team.

In Fig. 5−4, we can see that the team did not deliver as expected in the first and second months (this is usually the case, as the project is initiating, and all the team is learning about it). In the third and fourth months, they accelerated and not only returned to the expected productivity but surpassed it. With only 2 months lasting until the end of the project, there is a good chance that this team would meet the schedule at the end of the sixth month.

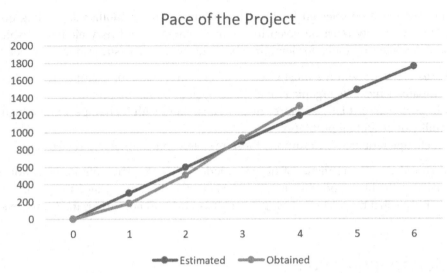

FIGURE 5–4 Burn-up chart of a project that seem to be going well.

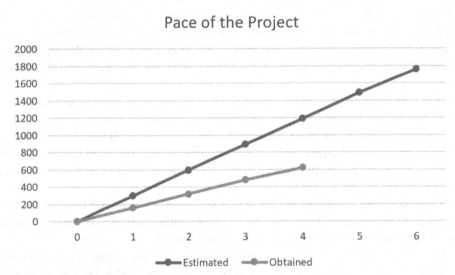

FIGURE 5–5 Burn-up of a project that is dangerously delayed.

In Fig. 5—5, we see a team (or set of teams that is not able to deliver the story points as planned). That project probably will not be fully delivered at its end. The teams should have taken some correction to path after perceiving that they could not reach the expected results after month 1 and 2. However, it seems that nothing was done, and that is moving the project to failure or delay.

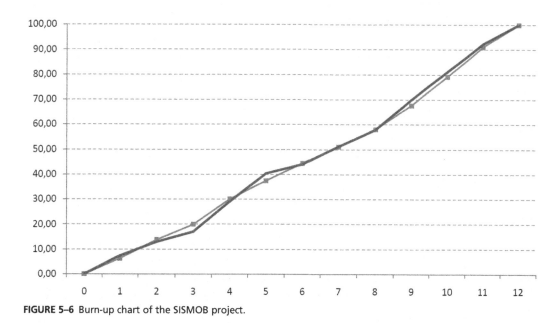

FIGURE 5–6 Burn-up chart of the SISMOB project.

In Fig. 5–6, we see the real burn-up chart for project SISMOB Phase 3 during all its 18 months of development.

Questions

1. How do you establish a list of priorities for use cases?
2. Why estimating software development effort is so difficult? Which are the obstacles?
3. Which elements an agile software team must consider in order to attribute effort for a product?
4. Why is the rounded Fibonacci series used to assign story points instead of the natural numbers?
5. How a duration of a sprint can be decided?

6

Expanded use cases

Key topics in this chapter

- Main flow of a use case
- Alternate flows: exception handlers and variants
- Use case fragments
- Writing recommendations
- Essential and real use cases

6.1 Introduction to expanded use cases

As seen before, use cases may be used to represent system requirements, among other things. They are useful for requirements because they allow the building of a structure that is easy to understand, communicate, and manage. They allow the representation of the system processes and actors in different levels of abstraction. Ivar Jacobson identifies some reasons why use cases are so useful:[1]

- A use case model is a picture that allows a team to describe even a complex system. It tells in simple terms what the system is going to do for its users.
- A use case produces value to a particular user, not to an unidentifiable community of them.
- Use cases are also test cases; when the team finishes organizing requirements in use cases, they have also produced the structure needed for test cases.
- Use cases are the starting point to design effective user experiences or stories.
- Use cases drive development from analysis to design, from design to code, and from code to testing.

In the beginning of a sprint, the team performs a *Sprint Planning Meeting*, which consists, among other things, in choosing the user stories or use cases from the Product Backlog accordingly to their priority and the capacity of the team.

The next task is to find scenarios inside the more complex use cases, which could be a way to divide the more complex use cases into manageable fragments. Here, there is an agile principle that states that the tasks allocated to a sprint should not be too big neither too small. From the point of view of XP, the ideal task must have from one to three story points, while the PMBOK[2] accepts 1–10 story points or 8–80 hours. Thus the team must evaluate

---

[1] http://blog.ivarjacobson.com/use-cases-%E2%80%93-why-successful-and-popular/.
[2] https://www.pmi.org/pmbok-guide-standards/foundational/pmbok.

Object-Oriented Analysis and Design for Information Systems. DOI: https://doi.org/10.1016/B978-0-443-13739-6.00003-4

each use case in the beginning of the sprint and decide which ones will be single tasks (for being of the size acceptable by the team) and which ones should be divided into fragments to be more manageable during the sprint.

Notice that use cases do not have to be divided into technical tasks such as analysis, design, implementation, and test. What the team must do is to find different scenarios inside the main story. The most common scenarios are the *variants* and *exception handlers*, which are explained in this chapter. To find those fragments, the team needs to expand the use case and find its main flow of transactions, as explained bellow.

To proceed with the expansion of a given high-level use case, it could be useful to have at hand the system use case diagram, including all annotations or not functional requirements, and the supplementary specifications document. It would also be useful, for the first iteration, to have a version of the preliminary conceptual model. The team may use the conceptual model to help expand use cases, and at the same time, the expanded use cases would provide information to refine the conceptual model that after the first sprint is not "preliminary" any more, but "under refinement."

As use case expansion corresponds to the refinement of the functional requirements, the team must conduct a very detailed exam on the process incorporated into the use case *from the point of view of the user*. It would be very useful if the user is present when the team is discussing the use case expansion because the user is the best people to describe a list of tasks, variants, and exceptions that happens in her working journey.

In a first approach, the use case should be essential because in the beginning of analysis, the team may have no idea of its future interface. For this activity, the presence of the user is essential! After the essential flows are discovered, the team may propose one or more possible designs for the system interface. In this case, the team would appreciate if at least one competent designer is a member.

After deciding on the best proposal for the interface, the team may annotate the text of the use case and identify each action in the use case with one or more components of the interface. In this case, the use case evolved from essential to real or concrete.

6.2 Main flow

The *main flow* is the most important section of an expanded use case. It is the description of the use case process when everything goes right, that is, when no alternate flow occurs.

In the SISMOB example, a first draft of the main flow of the use case "Produce proposal assessment" could be something like this:

Use case: Produce proposal assessment

1. Reviewer search for process.
2. System presents list of processes allocated to reviewer, newest first.
3. Reviewer selects process.
4. System presents process name, status, priority, and validity.

5. Reviewer registers assessment and conclusion.

6. System confirms operation.

This is what is expected if everything goes well during the use case flow. But problems may arise. For example, for each business rule, there must be an exception handler, and variations of the main flow may exist.

As it can be seen, there is a pattern that repeats like:

1. The user informs...

2. The system informs...

Each pair of this kind is considered as a *transaction* and corresponds to the user taking some action followed by a reply by the system. The first transaction in the use case "Produce proposal assessment" is composed of steps 1 and 2, where the user asks for a list of projects and the system presents the projects that this reviewer has access.

The second transaction is composed of steps 3 and 4, where the user selects a project to work from the list provided by the system, and the system responds by showing some information on the selected process.

The third and final transaction is when the user writes an assessment about the project and concludes the operation what is responded by the system simply by confirmation that the data were received.

Observe that this is an essential use case. Thus information about user interface should not exist. There are no mentions to buttons, windows, menus, etc. It is not mentioned also by what kind of interface the information is passed or received. Most developers could be assuming keyboard, mouse, and screen. However, other options could be proposed, tested, and selected when it is time to propose and choose a good user interface. Later!

A use case flow is, therefore, a sequence of transactions. It is not an algorithm with loops and decision points. It is a straight line of events. Alternate flows are defined outside the main flow.

6.3 Alternate flows

A use case specifies a process that can be performed in real life in several different ways. In the last example, two people producing assessments would maybe take different sequences of steps. If the sequences are sufficiently similar[3], then the same flow must be used to describe both.

But in some situations, alternate flows must be used to indicate sequences that could occur in quite different ways.

---

[3] For example, one customer writes two lines and another customer writes fifteen lines: both actions may be described simply as "reviewer writes assessment" because the number of lines is irrelevant for understanding the process.

There are basically two kinds of alternate flows: *variants*, which indicate different ways to reach the same goal, and *exception handlers*, which indicate how to deal with obstacles to the flowing of the process.

6.3.1 Scenarios

A use case can be understood as a description or general specification that supports a set of different *scenarios*. Each scenario is a particular realization or *instance* of the use case. Usually, a use case has a *main scenario* (execution of the main flow) and *alternate scenarios* (executions of the main flow that pass by one or more alternate flows). However, the notion of main flow variants sometimes creates doubt on what should really be a use case. In the "Produce proposal assessment" example, considering that the process for writing an assessment may be long (even taking some days sometimes), we can consider that the use case has at least two finalizations:

- A reviewer writes a partially completed assessment and save it to continue another time (use case ends and could start again latter).
- A reviewer may write or not new information in the saved assessment and sends it to the system as a final decision (use case ends for good).

Is it a single use case with two alternative ends? Or should it be split into two use cases, one that ends with saving only and one that ends with sending a saved assessment?

Both options are equally valid, although one of them is possibly more useful than the other. The choices are:

- *Create more use cases* (*one for each scenario*). Each use case has a simpler structure, but there would be a high number of similar use cases. For example, one use case to write an assessment and another use case to send it as a final decision.
- *Group similar scenarios in a single use case*. There are a smaller number of use cases, but each of them would be more complex. For example, there is only one use case for writing an assessment and it can be finished by saving or by sending.

At this point, it is more important to discover the information exchanged between the actors and the system than to decide if two scenarios consist of one or two use cases. The team should evaluate and decide on the simpler solution. Moreover, one of the main goals here is to discover which is the user usual journey, and which transactions she must perform during this journey. It does not matter so much if the transactions belong to a single use case or to a pair of use cases; what is important here is to discover that they exist.

However, the advantage of joining alternate scenarios into a single use case is that the description of some steps must not be repeated in different use cases.

6.3.2 Variants

It is admitted, in principle, that the main flow of a use case is a strict sequence of transactions: it is neither branched nor nested.

A use case with two different endings such as "Produce proposal assessment" may have one scenario that is more typical (not necessarily more common, but it should be the natural path that comes to mind when someone describes the use case). In this case, the typical path is to write and assessment and send it as final. Deciding on continuing it another time could be considered as a variant.

Variants are not represented in use case as branches. The main flow is kept as a linear set of steps and the variants are referenced after the main flow. In our example, the "Produce proposal assessment" we should perceive that step 5 may not include sending the assessment. Then a variant can be defined for this step.

Use case: Produce proposal assessment (main flow)

1. Reviewer searches for process.
2. System presents list of processes allocated to reviewer, newest first.
3. Reviewer selects process.
4. System presents process name, status, priority, and validity.
5. Reviewer registers assessment and conclusion. [V1]
6. System confirms operation.

Variant V1: User decides to save for continuing latter

V1.1 Reviewer registers assessment and saves it.
V1.2 System confirms that the assessment is saved.
V1.3 Use case ends.

Saving the text to resume it later is not an *exception* (such as an *obstacle*) but an *option* for the user. That is not a condition that prevents the use case from concluding, because the use case still produces something: the assessment is saved and can be resumed later. One way to number variants is by using the letter "V" and a sequence of numbers, such as V1, V2. If a variant such as "V1" occurs only in one or a few steps, then it can be noted in the main flow, by using a label such as "[V1]." If the variant may occur in any step of the use case, it does not need to be referenced in the main flow.

6.3.3 Exception handling

After describing the main flow of a use case and adding variants (if any), the team can concentrate on identifying the *exceptions* that could occur and create an alternate flow for each one. Each *business rule* annotated for a use case will usually generate an exception. For example, if the use case for producing assessments has a business rule that states that the assessment must be send not later than 30 days after the proposal is received, trying to do that will be an exception. At this point, the team may consult the user about what can be done (or *if* something can be done) to surpass this exception and finalize the use case. In this example, when the deadline is closed without an assessment being sent, this reviewer cannot change or send it anymore. The process would have been probably already assigned to another reviewer at this time. Therefore this is a kind of exception that prevents the use case to be concluded with success. It fails because the user cannot reach the business goal.

In other cases, things could be different. For example, the user may insert a wrong password. The exception handler in this case usually provides another trial (maximum three, usually) and the "forget my password" option, which is almost universal nowadays in systems that demand passwords. If you get your password right on the second or third times, the use case may continue; if you recover your password, the use case may continue too. It means that the exception was handled. But, if you fail at the third try, you would be blocked by the system and probably a more complex process would be needed to recover your password.

The example below corresponds to the final form of the use case "Produce proposal assessment" with all variants and exceptions found by the team in the real case of SISMOB.

Use case: Produce proposal assessment (main flow)

1. Reviewer searches for process.
2. System presents list of processes allocated to reviewer, newest first.
3. Reviewer selects process.
4. System presents process name, status, priority, and validity.
5. Reviewer registers assessment and conclusion. [V1]
6. System confirms operation.

Variant V1: User decides to save for continuing latter.

V1.1 Reviewer registers assessment and saves it.
V1.2 System confirms that the assessment is saved.
V1.3 Use case ends.

Exception E1: Deadline reached BR-FNS.01[4].

E1.1 System presents message MODAL.114[5].
E1.2 User acknowledges.
E1.3 Use case fails.

Exception E2: Proposal was not prioritized BR-FNS.06.

E2.1 System presents message MODAL.371.

---

[4] BR-FNS.01 is a reference to the Business Rule (BR) that may be observed here and that is catalogued with the other business rules of the system.

[5] MODAL.114 is a reference to the message shown by a modal window that is catalogued with the other messages of the system. A modal window blocks navigation until the user acknowledges having read it.

E2.2 User acknowledges.

E2.3 Use case fails.

Like variants, exceptions are numbered by using the letter "E," and a numerical sequence.

Steps in alternate flows may use the code of the alternate flow as part of the number, such as "E1.1," or they may be numbered simply by a sequence 1, 2, 3, etc.

Each alternate flow must indicate if the use case ends with success, or if it fails, as in the example. Beyond success and fail, other possibility is to return to some step in the main flow after concluding the alternate flow. One good example of this case is when you are buying something on the Internet, and you have changed your address since the last buy. Changing address in the system does not belong to the main flow. It is a variant that consists of informing a new address and then returning to the main flow of the use case to conclude payment and anything else.

6.4 Writing recommendations

The writing style of a use case should follow a pattern such as "actor informs…/system informs…." Styles such as "system asks…" should be avoided because what must be represented in the use case is the *flow* of information, not the occasional *demands* that gave rise to those flows; those demands do not exist in every scenario, and in most of them they are not even necessary.

The team must avoid placing tests in the use case main flow. Tests such as "*if* the user has a record, *then* the system presents…" should be avoided. That kind of test is unnecessary because exception handlers should already be associated to the steps of the main flow. Then, if an exception occurs, it would be handled in an alternate flow.

These tests must not be placed in the main flow to keep it from becoming a complex flowchart instead of a straight, simple sequence of transactions. Lots of "if/then" statements can make the flow obscure, and the stakeholder would not know what the *expected* flow (happy path) is.

Another common writing concern is that a use case must alternate inputs and outputs of information (transactions). In other words, normally a use case has the form "actor informs …, system informs …, actor informs …, system informs …."

Sequences such as "actor informs …, actor informs …, actor informs …" or "system informs …, system informs …, system informs …" must be avoided.

The idea behind the alternating pattern is to reduce any discrepancy on the number of steps that different analysts could assign to the same use case. Without that rule, one analyst could write:

The customer provides name, ID[6], and phone number.

---

[6] Here and in further examples in this book, the *ID* provided by a customer is not a system-generated internal code, but the number of a personal document that belongs to the customer. In the United States, the *social security number* could correspond to the *ID* number, while in other countries, other numbers could be used.

On the other hand, another analyst could write:

1. The customer provides name.
2. The customer provides ID.
3. The customer provides phone number.

The most useful and correct version under this point of view is the first, because, among other things, the second would demand that the information be provided in the order of the steps: after providing the *ID*, the user cannot go back and correct her name. Thus the first version is more compatible with most information systems, which present interfaces where information in many fields may be entered and edited before it is finally sent to the system.

6.4.1 Essential versus real use case

A frequent doubt about use cases is *which* system must be described? The current one? Or the one that will be built? If the current operations are performed manually, and in the future, they will be performed with a computer, what must be the description provided by the use case? The answer is *none*, but *both*! The use case written for analysis purposes must describe the *essence* of the operations, not their concrete realization. Thus the analyst should always try to avoid mentioning the technology used to perform the process and concentrate only on the exchanged information. Instead of writing "the clerk writes the customer's name and address on a paper sheet," corresponding to a manual technology used normally in nonautomated systems, or "the customer fills in the name and address on fields F1 and F2 on the main screen," which corresponds to an automated technology, the analyst must register the operation simply as "the customer provides name and address." The last form is technology-free and interface-independent and represents, therefore, an essential description for the operation.

All use cases used for requirements purposes should be, in principle, *essential*. Essential in this context means that the use case is described in a language where only the essence of the operations is presented, not its concrete counterpart. In other words, the analyst must describe "what" happens between the user and the system without informing "how" that interaction happens. The analyst should not, therefore, while doing analysis, try to describe the interface technology between the user and system. This will be described during design time in which *real* use cases could be written after the real interface has been designed. Real use cases stay attached to a specific interface technology, while essential use cases are technology-free.

Why essential use cases? According to Ambler (2004), real use cases (those that mention technology) contain too many built-in assumptions, often hidden or implicit about the underlying technology of interface implementation strategies. That may be a good feature during design, but not during requirements analysis. An essential use case, on the other hand, states the user needs or intentions, and not the concrete technology that could support those needs.

As the description of the use case at that moment is made without reference to the interface technology, it is not necessary to decide what the interfaces look like, but only what *information* is exchanged between actors and system. References to menus, windows, buttons, and other graphical devices should be avoided in the text of the essential use cases.

So how do we describe use cases that seem to be particularly concrete such as drawing money from an automatic teller machine? How do we do that without describing technology? It is possible. Instead of saying "the user inserts a magnetic card," one could say that "the user provides identification." Instead of saying that the machine "prints the account details," one could say that the machine "presents the account details." Thus by eliminating the reference to the physical technology, only the essence remains. This opens the way for the design of innovative technologies later, that is, interfaces different than those that can be seen at a first glance. For example, the user could be identified by fingerprints, the receipt could be sent by SMS (Short Message Service), and even the money could be delivered in cash or in credits to a preloaded card.

It is the responsibility of the team to study the current processes of the company and produce an essential version of them in the form of essential use cases. Later, the team will give a new form to those processes by using technology to produce a new concrete version of the system. At this step, different proposals may be at stake, and some of them would be prototyped and tested before one is chosen.

6.4.2 Explicit information

For the sake of understanding use cases as functional requirements, it is recommended that the analyst makes explicit the individual data pieces exchanged between actors and the system. Thus instead of a laconic "customer provides data," the use case should say "customer provides name, ID, email, phone, and address."

Eventually, a term such as "customer" could be externally defined as meaning "name, ID, email, phone and address." An expression such as *customer = <name, id, email, phone, address>* could be written in documentation. If that definition is adequately registered, for example, in the conceptual model, or in a data dictionary, then it can be used in the use case text to avoid repeating the individual elements every time they have to be mentioned.

6.4.3 Identification and selection

A recurrent problem associated to use cases is how to identify people and things. For example, a reviewer must be identified and validated in order to perform the "Produce proposal assessment" use case. How does she do it? Username and password? Social security number? Fingerprints? Selecting the name from a predefined list or menu? To keep the use case essential, that particular action must be left generic, and references to possible ways for identifying a reviewer must be left to design. Furthermore, the computer security community already has established common methods to securely validate an identity, and these proven methods should be used instead of reinventing the wheel. For now, the use case could simply state that the user *provides identification*, without mentioning by which means that identification is obtained and validated.

Another example is the selection of a project for analyzing. Does the reviewer submit the number of the project? Select it from a list? Use a natural language speech interface? During use case expansion, these issues do not need to be decided (unless they are indeed nonfunctional or supplementary requirements). At the essential level of the use case, the user simply *selects a project*. Later, the design will present some options to provide the means for the user to make that selection in the most comfortable way.

6.4.4 Mandatory, complementary, and unsuitable steps

What steps are mandatory in an expanded use case? Are there some that are optional? In fact, two people that describe the same use case, unless they have a nicely established convention, may produce different flows with different steps.

In any scenario of a use case, the *mandatory* steps are those that cannot be suppressed without leaving the flow impossible to perform in terms of information changing between user and system. An assessment cannot be completed if a project is not selected, for example.

However, other steps that could be included may not be so important. If an analyst writes, "for example, that the system *asks* for an information," that step could be removed from the sequence and the flow could still make sense, given that in any case the user provides that information, with or without being asked to.

Analysts must be encouraged to build correct versions of the use cases, but they should not stop there: they may produce the smallest use case possible, by including only mandatory steps and avoiding optional ones.

Mandatory steps include information that is passed from the actors to the system and from the system to the actors. Without one of those steps, the flow may not make sense.

Other steps such as "ask for information" or "send confirmation message" are optional or *complementary*. They may help contextualize the use case, especially the real ones. But they are not fundamental because they do not transmit any information through the system boundary.

In a use case description, the information can not appear from nowhere. It is transmitted from the actors to the system and vice versa. The absence of any mandatory step may make the use case seem incomplete because information that is needed by the system is not sent by the user or vice versa.

Later, the information contained in the mandatory steps of a use cases could be used to refine the conceptual model.

Depending on the direction the information goes, mandatory steps may be identified as:

- *System events*: Steps that indicate that some information is transmitted from the actors to the system.
- *System returns*: Steps that indicate that some information is transmitted from the system to the actors.

Special care must be taken when considering system returns. For those steps to be mandatory, they must pass some information that the system stores or can access externally in other systems. That information must be something that in principle the actors do not have access to, except by querying the system.

Complementary steps are not fundamental in essential use cases because they do not correspond to system events or system returns, as they do not transmit information through the system boundary.

Some of them can be even mapped to navigation operations during interface design. For example, a real use case (design) could have a step like such as "the user opens window W32." That line does not correspond to a system event because at that time, the customer does not pass any information to the system (such as name, phone, address, and book title, etc.). That action corresponds simply to a change of state that will be implemented as interface navigation (a new screen is opened after the option is selected, for example).

The team must also keep in mind that, as the use case is a description of the interaction between actors and system, they must avoid including internal system processes, such as "the system stores the information into the database.." Those steps are considered *unsuitable* for the essential use case description. Considering the real version of the use case, those steps could be included if the internal process is not obvious. For example, every time a record is inserted or updated, there is a change in the database, and it must not be written in any version of the use case. However, if some exceptional internal operation happens, such as activating a thread for searching some information, it could be represented associated with a mandatory step.

The use case is a tool for describing the interaction between users and a system, not a tool to describe internal processing. The internal processes of the system will be better described during design with more adequate tools.

6.5 Included use cases and fragments

It is possible for two or more use cases to have coincident parts. For example, many use cases may include an *identification* fragment. In other cases, a use case may include not only a fragment, but a complete use case, such as for example, a *payment*. The "include" relationship should be used only when the duplicated fragment or use case is significant, that is, it should not be used when just one step is duplicated. An included use case or fragment may be called in a flow by using the "*include <fragment or use case name>*" expression.

Some care must be taken here. First of all, *use cases are not procedures like the ones used in programming languages*; they are linear descriptions of real-world processes. Teams are not encouraged to structure use cases as they do with code. Included use cases or fragments may be used *only* when the situation really justifies it.

However, the analyst must keep in mind that the goal of the expanded use case in analysis is to help in understanding the nature of the interactions between the system and its actors, and not to structure a computer program to simulate that interaction. Thus, the included use case or fragment calls must be used carefully.

6.6 Other sections of an expanded use case

Since the concept of a use case was created (Jacobson et al., 1992), different formats have been proposed. Each proposal includes different elements. The "main flow" and "alternate flows" sections are fundamental for any fully dressed use case description. However, other sections can be included if the team needs them. Some of the most popular are presented in the next subsections.

6.6.1 Stakeholders

There are often scenarios where groups other than actors are relevant to a use case. Other sectors of the organization could have some interest in the use case. For example, in the use case "Register proposal," the only actor is the Municipal Manager. But the results of that use case may interest other stakeholders, such as, for example, the law department of the municipality and the financial department, which may be interested in knowing if the proposal is adequate to the laws and finances of the municipality. Thus, even if those departments are not participants in the use case, they can be listed as *stakeholders*. And they may also be a source of requirements.

The utility of the stakeholders list for a use case is that the use case must *satisfy all stakeholders*. Thus, the documentation will be useful to remind the team to seek information that needs to be stored, processed, or transmitted, so that those interests can be satisfied.

6.6.2 Preconditions

Preconditions are facts assumed true before a use case starts. Preconditions must not be confused with exceptions: exceptions may be detected only after the use case has started. Exceptions are detected during a use case because most of the time it is not possible to verify if the conditions were true or not before the use case begins. For example, it is not possible to assure that the project has enough funds to be executed before starting the use case that sends the project to the National Health Fund; therefore, this is an *exception*. However, it is possible to admit that the user that sent the proposal is registered in the system. Thus assuming that the user is registered may be considered as a precondition.

As preconditions are accepted as true facts before the use case starts, they would not need to be checked during the use case flows, except if concurrent operation may turn the precondition invalid.

6.6.3 Success postconditions

Success postconditions establish the results of a use case, that is, what will be true after the use case is executed. For example, the "Send proposal" use case may have as a postcondition the following result: "the proposal was received by the federal manager."

6.6.4 Open issues

Sometimes, without the presence of the client or user, the team cannot decide about some issue that may depend on company policies. For example, may a project be sent with annexes? Is there a time limit between creating a new proposal and sending it?

If the client is not immediately available, these doubts must be recorded in the use case section "open issues" to be solved as soon as possible.

Other tool that can be used for this purpose is the CSD (Certainties, Suppositions, and Doubts) matrix. It can be a single matrix for the entire product, and it has three columns: the first states what the team knows for certain (former doubts or suppositions that were resolved by the client or user, and must not be asked again), the second is for suppositions, that is, issues that the team assume to be true, but that must be confirmed, and the third for doubts, that is, issues that the team has no idea how to deal with. The matrix is used to register doubts and suppositions and as soon as they are resolved, they must be moved to the first column where they stay to remind the team that they were once a doubt or supposition but was already confirmed.

At the end of the analysis activities of one sprint, it is expected that *all* open issues have been resolved and incorporated into the use case description.

6.7 Expansion of stereotyped use cases

Stereotyped or *pattern use cases* usually present low risk to the software development process because the structure of their flows and many business rules are already known. The most common pattern is identified by the $<<$ CRUDL $>>$ stereotype. If it is adequately documented, it may pass to the team a clear idea of what must be implemented for each of its instances.

Chart 6−1 is the documentation of the final version of every CRUDL use case in the SISMOB project. It was adapted from the SISMOB final documentation.

In the case of CRUDLs what can be said is that not every entity of the conceptual model is suitable to be managed by the CRUDL pattern. CRUDLs are expected to be the simplest entities. If they get more complex, a set of non-CRUDL use cases will be necessary for describing how the user works with them.

For instance, a *user* and an *assessment* are very simple entities and could be nicely managed by a CRUDL use case. On the opposite side, a *proposal* is one of the most complex entities of the SISMOB system. Proposals may be issued, canceled, completed, sent, resent, received back, etc. That does not characterize it as a CRUDL.

In the gray zone, there are concepts that the team must look at to decide if they may be adequately managed as a CRUDL or not. For example, is "Managing funds allocation" a CRUDL or not? Some time may be spent on analysis before the team can decide on that.

1. UC-CRU.01 – CRUDL – Real version

Represents the basic operations of CRUDL - Create, Retrieve, Update, Delete, and List.

Preconditions: The user is identified and authenticated. Access to the modules and their operations must be validated by access control as described in RN-AUT.02 - Access Control and must be consistent with the standardization of the system.

1.1. Main Flows

The CRUDL stereotype has four main flows, one for each of the CRUD operations. Listing is considered not to be a flow, but the default starting page of this group of use cases.

Create - Basic Path

1. The actor selects the option to create a register.
2. The system presents the registration screen with the save and cancel options.
3. The actor fills in the required information and selects the save option [V1].
4. The system validates the information, saves the record, displays the default success message, and returns to the screen before the registration [E1].

Update - Basic Path

1. The actor selects the option to update.
2. The system presents the registration screen with the options save, cancel, and delete.
3. The actor fills in the required information and saves [V1].
4. The system validates the information, saves the record, displays the default success message, and returns to the screen before editing the registration [E1].

Deletion - Basic Path

1. The actor selects the delete option.
2. The system displays the confirmation message MODAL.003.
3. The actor confirms the deletion.
4. The system deletes the record, displays the default success message, and returns to the screen before the record was deleted.

Retrieve - Basic Path

1. The actor selects the option to retrieve data.
2. The system presents the preview screen with the edit and delete options.
3. The use case is finalized.

1.2 Variant flows

V1: Cancel Create/Update – Variant

1. The actor selects the cancel option.
2. The system displays the default cancel confirmation message.
3. The actor confirms the cancellation.
4. The system discards the registered information and returns to the screen before the registration.

CHART 6–1 SISMOB CRUDL use case pattern.

1.3 Exception Flows

E1: Invalid information and/or mandatory fields – Exception

1. The system does not validate the information and displays the validation message.
2. The actor closes the validation message.
3. The system returns to step 3 of the main flow.

E2: Functionality or registry not available – Exception

1. The actor selects some system option, and the registry is no longer available, or the functionality can no longer be performed.
2. The system displays the error message MSG.359.

E3: No permission to access the registry - Exception

1. The actor selects some system option, and the user is not allowed access to the registry or functionality.
2. The system displays the error message MSG.179.

E4: Unexpected error – Exception

1. The actor selects some system option, and an unexpected error (ERROR_MSG) occurs.
2. The system displays the error message MSG.405.

E5: Database connection error – Exception

1. The actor selects some system option, and the connection to the database has been lost (CONNECTION_ERROR_MSG) or is invalid (ILEGAL_ERROR_MSG).
2. The system displays the error message MSG.406.

E6: Syntax or database structure error – Exception

1. The actor selects some system option, and an error occurs due to syntax failure, or the database structure is incompatible (SQLSYNTAX_ERROR_MSG).
2. The system displays the error message MSG.407

E7: Null mandatory information error – Exception

1. The actor selects some system option, and the query or operation does not return a required information to continue (NULLPOINTER_ERROR_MSG).
2. The system displays the error message MSG.407

E8: Server out of memory – Exception

1. The actor selects some system option, and an error occurs due to lack of memory on the application server (OUTOFMEMORY_ERROR_MSG).
2. The system displays the error message MSG.407

CHART 6–1 Continued.

1.4 NF-CRU.01 – Non-Functional Requirements for Create and Update

1. The operations of "Create""and "Update must be validated by access control according to BR-AUT.02 Access Control and must follow the standardizations defined in System Standardization.

2. The business rules and requirements are described in each module.

3. When selecting the "Create" option, the system should show the "Create" screen.

4. When selecting the "Update" option, the system should show the Create screen with the information of the selected record.

5. When selecting the "Save" option after editing a record, the system should display the message MODAL.094.

6. When trying to cancel or exit a new registration, if it has any information registered, it should show the message MODAL.001.

7. When trying to cancel or exit the updating or creation of a record where it is possible to save without finishing, if it has any information changed, it should show the message MODAL.002.

8. If any data from the registration is filled out/selected in a previous screen (pre-selection), this data should be considered as registered information.

9. The above messages must be in accordance with the module option (save, send, or confirm) and, if the option is to send, the finish message must be used.

10. Required fields must be validated and, if necessary, show the MSG.011 in error-type notification mode and an error-type hint for each field with the MSG.010 message.

11. The values of the fields must be validated and, if an invalid value field exists, show the MSG.007 in error-type notification mode and an error-type hint for each field with the MSG.006 message.

12. For mandatory fields and fields with invalid values in the same validation, it should show the MSG.012 message in error-type notification mode while retaining the aforementioned hints for each field. For free typing text fields, the validation of the maximum number of characters must be performed. If the user exceeds the maximum limit set in the data dictionary, the system must prevent the insertion of more characters.

13. When a record is successfully saved, the system should display the MSG.001 in success notification mode.

14. If the page refreshes and unsaved data is lost, it should display the message MSG.264.

15. A record cannot be changed by more than one user simultaneously. Thus, when attempting to edit a record and it is being edited by another user, the system should display the MSG.048 message in alert-type notification mode.

Breadcrumbs:

The description to be used in breadcrumb should be:

> *Insert/edit [name of entity]*

Example: "Insert/edit proposal", "Insert/edit User"

CHART 6–1 Continued.

1.5 NF-CRU.02 – Non-functional requirements for Deletion

1. The "Delete" operation must be validated by access control as described in RN-AUT.02 - Access Control.

2. Business rules and requirements are defined in each module.

3. When attempting to delete a record, the system should display the MODAL.003 confirmation message.

4. If the registry deletion is successful, it should display the MSG.031 message in success notification mode.

5. Deleting records should be logical, changing the record status to "Inactive".

6. A record cannot be deleted when it is being edited by another user.

7. When attempting to delete a record and it is being edited by another user, the system should display the MSG.048 message in alert-type notification mode.

1.6 NF-CRU.03 – Non-functional Requirements for Retrieve

1. Access to the modules and their visualization must be validated by access control as described in RN-AUT.02 Access Control.

2. When selecting the "Preview" option, the system should show the preview screen with the data from the selected record and, where allowed the "Update" and "Delete" options.

3. No changes to the registration are allowed through this option.

Breadcrumbs:

The description to be used in breadcrumb should be:
> *Information about [name of entity]*

Examples: "Information about user", "Information about proposal"

CHART 6–1 Continued.

1.7 NF-CRU.04 – Non-functional Requirements for Listing

1. Access to listings must be validated by access control as described in RN-AUT.02 - Access Control.

2. Business rules and requirements are defined in each module.

Filters:

3. The screen must display the "Clear Filters" option.

4. When selecting the "Clear Filters" option the system should clear all filter fields and update the listing.

5. The listing should be automatically updated with each filter fill or selection.

Column sorting:

6. If the list has columns with the option to sort, the selected column will be sorted in an ascending or decreasing manner according to the actor's need.

Select all items:

7. If the listing has the selection option, the system must present an "All" option at the top of the list so that all items are selected.

8. By clicking the option:
    *   If the items in the list are not selected, the system must check all items.
    *   If the items are already checked, the system must deselect all items.

Empty list:

9. If there is no data to be displayed in the listing, the system must display the message MSG.049.

10. For more details see RI-COM.03 - Listings.

Options:

11. The options available in the listings are described in each module and should be consistent with the RN-AUT.02 Access Control

Breadcrumbs:

The description to be used in breadcrumb should be:
> List of [name of entity in the plural]

Examples: "List of users", "List of Proposals"

CHART 6–1 Continued.

Questions

1. Variants and exception handlers are alternate flows for a use case. In which situations should one or the other be used?
2. What is the difference between an essential use case and a real use case? Why is the essential use case more interesting for requirements purposes?
3. Explain the differences between mandatory, complementary, and unsuitable use case steps.
4. What are preconditions for a use case?
5. Think or search for other examples of use case patterns, that is, general forms of use case, such as CRUDL, that can be defined generally and instantiated many times in different projects.

7

System operations

Key topics in this chapter

- System events
- System returns
- System commands
- System queries
- Sequence diagrams
- Stateless and stateful

7.1 Introduction to system operations

Among other uses, the text of the detailed use cases may be used as:

- A source of information to discover the concepts and attributes for refining the conceptual model.
- A source of information to discover *system operations*, which are the operations that encapsulate the domain tier of the system from its interface.

There are two kinds of system operations:

- *System commands*, which change data and must not return data.
- *System queries*, which return data and must not change data.

That follows the *Command-Query Separation* or *CQS* principle of software engineering (Meyer, 1988), which aims for better code reusability and maintainability. A query that changes data would be less cohesive than a query without collateral effect and a command without return.

System commands are methods that may be activated by a *system event*, that is, as a reaction to a user action. System commands, by definition, implement a flow of information from the outside to the inside of the system (input). Therefore system commands update the information that is managed by the system, usually in databases.

System queries are methods that correspond to the simple verification of information already stored. That information may be presented exactly as it is stored or modified by logical and mathematical operations. By definition, a system query may not be responsible for the insertion of new information into the system (that would be a *side effect*, a kind of anti-pattern). It should also not be responsible for updating or removing information from the system: it can only read information.

Object-Oriented Analysis and Design for Information Systems. DOI: https://doi.org/10.1016/B978-0-443-13739-6.00016-2

The set of system operations corresponds to the whole functionality of a system, that is, the set of all functions that can be performed by a user with the system.

Use cases are excellent sources for discovering system operations. System commands are basically associated to steps in which the user sends some information to the system (inputs). System queries are associated to use case steps in which the system sends information to actors (output).

7.2 Elements of a sequence diagram

One of the UML diagrams that can be particularly useful for representing the sequence of system events and returns in a use case is the *sequence diagram*. When a sequence diagram is used to represent a use case, it may be called a *system sequence diagram* (Larman, 2004). The system sequence diagram has elements that are instances of actors and other system components (expressions preceded by ":," as e.g.,:*User,:Interface*). In the first version of the system sequence diagram, only the actors and the system interface (or application tier) are represented (Fig. 7–1).

The activities related to use case analysis still do not deal with objects that are internal to the system. Thus the system must be represented as a single object: a black box. In this case, it can be represented by the interface symbol, as proposed by Jacobson et al. (1992) and seen in Fig. 7–1 (right side). One actor can only communicate with a system through its interface. Messages from the actor cannot reach directly any internal object, as shown in Fig. 7–2.

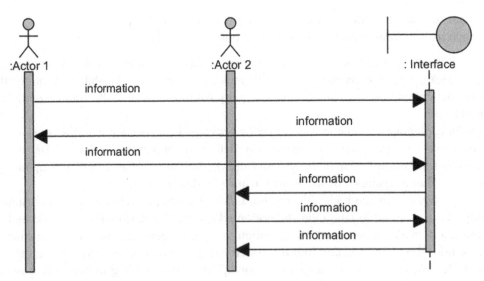

FIGURE 7–1 Information flows from/to users and interface.

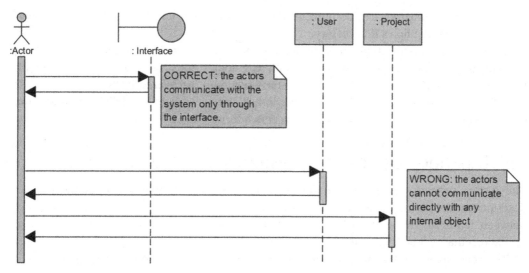

FIGURE 7–2 Example of antipattern where interface communicate with object surpassing the interface.

Actors, interfaces, and other elements of the sequence diagram have a lifeline, represented by a vertical line, where events may happen. When the line is dashed, the element is inactive. When the line is solid, the element is active (processing or waiting for the result of an operation being performed by another element). Human actors are always considered active.

The horizontal arrows represent the information flow. There are three kinds of information flows in this diagram:

- *Between actors*: Actors' communication among themselves without using the system, corresponding maybe to complementary steps of the expanded use case.
- *From the actors to the system*: Corresponding to *system events*, that is, steps that correspond to the inputs of the expanded use cases.
- *From the system to the actors*: Corresponding to *system returns*, that is, steps that correspond to the outputs of the expanded use cases.

The information exchange between actors does not belong to the scope of the system, but it may be useful to illustrate how information is exchanged from actor to actor until reaching the system, if necessary.

One thing to keep in mind when these diagrams are being built is that information usually does not appear from nothing; it must be transferred from actors to system and vice versa. The actor usually has some information that must be passed to the system to perform a process. A reviewer that wants to save and assessment should inform the system who she is, which project is being assessed, and what is the text of the assessment. In the beginning of this use case, the reviewer is the only one who holds all that information; the system has the registry of all projects and reviewers, but it cannot know who is going assess that specific project until someone provides that information.

The sequence diagram can be built for the main flow of a use case and completed with some or all alternate flows if necessary.

The most important thing at the moment is to discover *what* information is being exchanged between the actors and the system. The analyst must build a catalog with all system operations (which are explained in the next sections) discovered in the main and alternate flows of the use case. This information will be used later to define contracts that indicate how the system retrieves and transforms information.

7.3 Expanded use cases as system sequence diagrams

The system sequence diagram is a tool for achieving more formal and detailed use case descriptions. Additionally, developing the system sequence diagram makes the connection between requirements analysis (the expanded use case) and software design (the system operations that will be implemented).

The construction of the system sequence diagram may be done in two stages:

1. Representing the steps of the use case as *information* exchange between *actors* and the system *interface*.
2. Representing system operations as *operations calling* between the *interface* and the *façade controller*,[1] which encapsulates the domain tier of the system.

The first step is simple: for each use case input, there is an equivalent system event in which one actor sends information to the interface, and for each use case output, there is an equivalent system return in which an actor receives information from the system (Fig. 7–3).

Note that between actors and interface, the flows consist of sending and receiving uniquely information. Information may be sent by an actor, for example, by typing it in a form. Information can be received by an actor when it is printed on the screen. At this level, flows are not calling operations because actors usually are not computers.

The words or expressions used to represent information are sometimes a source of confusion and misunderstanding. To avoid such confusion, a writing pattern is suggested:

- Simple information (alphanumeric data) is represented by one or more words. For example, *name*, *assessment*, and *project number*.
- Complex information may be represented between " < " and " > " in the diagram if it is composed by a few elements (two or three). For example, <*name, date of birth, address*>.
- Complex information composed of numerous elements (more than three) may be represented in a separate note or data dictionary. Only the name of the complex concept is used in the diagram. For example, the data dictionary could contain this definition: *dto_project* = < *number, name, initial date, description, author, municipality, value* >. In this case, when all this information must be passed in a sequence diagram, the word "*dto_project*" should be used instead.

---

[1] A façade-controller provides "a unified interface to a set of interfaces in a subsystem. Façade defines a higher-level interface that makes the subsystem easier to use" (Gamma et al., 1995).

- A simple command that does not include alphanumeric information being passed may be represented between parentheses. For example, (*search for project*) or (*confirm*).
- A collection of values can be indicated by the suffix "*." For example, *dto_project** is a set of projects.
- When one object is selected from a collection presented by the system, the selection is indicated by the word "selected," as in Fig. 7−4, where "*selected project*" stands for a project that was selected from the set *dto_project** presented by the system.
- The information contained in a *dto_project* is probably a subset of the attributes of the *Project* class of the conceptual model; it does not necessarily correspond to the complete set of attributes of the *Project* class, but only the ones the user needs for choosing a project.

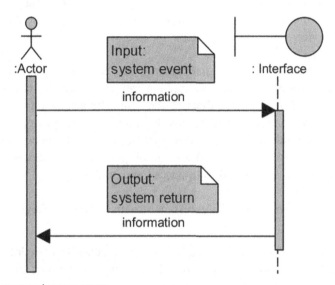

FIGURE 7–3 System event and system return.

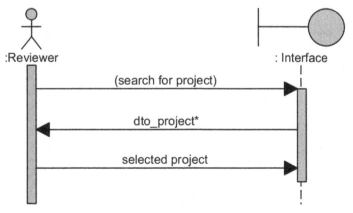

FIGURE 7–4 Commands and information flowing between user and interface.

- In the last step, when the user selects a project and informs the system which one it is, she does not have to send all the information contained in the respective *dto_project*. It only sends the project *identification* that usually should not even be known by the user. It is an information hidden to the user, that comes out as part of each *dto_project*, and is sent back to the system without explicit knowledge of the user. The user only knows that she has picked an option from a list.

7.4 Connecting the interface to the façade controller

System events are actions that a user performs over the system interface. When a web interface is used, for example, these actions consist of filling forms, pressing buttons, etc. These are not operations in the sense of programming languages, that is, these flows from an actor to the system and vice versa should not be labeled with operations or methods calling (messages).

However, *system commands* and *system queries* are computational operations that are necessary to implement system events and system returns, respectively. System commands and queries are activated by messages that are sent from the interface to the façade controller. Now, we have a system component that invokes another system component. In this case, it is the interface that sends a message, asking the façade controller to perform a method that consists of a command or a query. The set of all possible messages is equivalent to the whole functionality of the system: all data access and updating are done by system commands and queries.

Thus four kinds of arrows are of interest in system sequence diagrams, and they are shown in Fig. 7−5:

- *System event*: this is an action performed by an actor that sends some information to the interface. It can be a single command, single information, a complex information (DTO), or a list of information and DTOs, recursively.

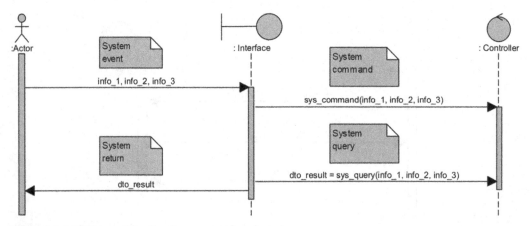

FIGURE 7–5 Adding second level: system commands and queries.

- *System return*: this is a flow of information from the interface to one or more actors. It usually consists of the same structures that are used with system events.
- *System command*: this is a message that is sent from the interface to the controller, usually in response to a system event. The system command must, by definition, change some information stored or managed by the system. In the diagram, this is represented by an arrow from the interface to the controller labeled with a message. The use of parentheses is always recommended to distinguish it from information flows, such as system events and returns. Thus even a message with no arguments should be represented here as *message()*.
- *System query*: this is a message that is sent from the interface to the controller to obtain some information from the system. Queries must not change data; they just return data. In the diagram, queries are represented by arrows from the interface to the controller labeled with a message with an explicit return value. In the example, the return value is represented by *dto_result*.

The domain tier of an application (the part of the system that contains all classes that perform the logical operations on data) is encapsulated by its façade controller, which is an instance of a class that implements all system commands and queries that must be accessed by a given interface or set of interfaces.

There are at least three subpatterns for the façade controller. The first one, for smaller systems, consists of implementing a single controller for the whole system. However, this would result in many operations implemented in a single class.

A solution to this is to divide it into *use case controllers*, that is, a different controller class for each use case. However, this is not a good solution when different use cases call the same methods, which should be implemented in different classes.

The most adequate solution for most medium or large systems is to implement *component* or *subsystem controllers*, that is, controllers that encapsulate the functionality of subsystems or components as defined by the system architecture.

The design of messages between the interface and the controller is made after an examination of the system events and returns using the following rules:

- A system event that sends data that must be stored, updated, or deleted, that is, data that cause a change in the internal state of the system, require at least one system command to be defined. More than one command may result from a single system event too.
- A system return that sends data obtained from the controller requires at least one system query between the interface and the controller, so that the data can be obtained from the controller in order to be presented by the interface.
- A sequence of system event and return, where the event just provides arguments for producing the return, requires a system query (not a command) where the information received from the system event is composed only by its arguments (Fig. 7−6).

The cause/consequence relation between events and commands and between returns and queries is not always so straight. Sometimes, a query can use arguments that were passed to the interface many steps earlier, or information passed by the actor to the interface can be used many times by different system commands and queries.

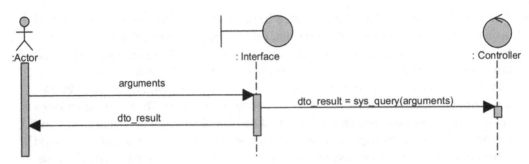

FIGURE 7–6 A query with arguments.

7.5 Stateful and stateless

When the system sequence diagram is being developed, each piece of information is passed from the actor to the interface just once. However, in the next level, between interface and controller, many different commands and queries may need the same arguments. For example, the customer *ID* may be necessary to perform many subsequent operations.

There is an antipattern named *stateful* that allows the controller to remember data sent by the interface even if these data are not registered in a permanent way. With the stateful pattern, the interface could send the ID just once, when the first operation is called, and maintain it in temporary memory so that the subsequent operations do not have to send the ID again.

This seems to be a good idea, because it avoids data being sent more than once between interface and controller. However, it has disadvantages. The main maybe is that it creates temporal dependence among operations. For example, the second operation needs the ID, but it is not sent by the interface because it was already sent for the first operation. In this case, the second operation has the ID as an implicit argument, which is stored someway in the controller memory. That problem is called *temporal dependency*. This is bad when we need to reuse operations in different contexts and thus must be avoided.

Instead, we should use the *stateless* strategy that assumes that the control does not have any temporary memory (does not have an internal state besides the database), and thus, each operation should receive every argument explicitly.

Fig. 7–7 shows how the system sequence diagram would look for the main flow of the use case "Update assessment" with a stateless strategy. The information is passed from the actor to the interface just once, but each time a system command or query needs that information, the interface should send it again as an argument to the controller. Observe that *selected_project* and *user_ID* are sent twice by different system operations.

Observe also that *user_ID* is known by the interface, it is not stored in the controller. That is why it is sent every time user identification is needed. Also, *user_ID* may be a complex information, not just a number. It may also be a hash number that codifies the user identification and password and can be extracted by the controller.

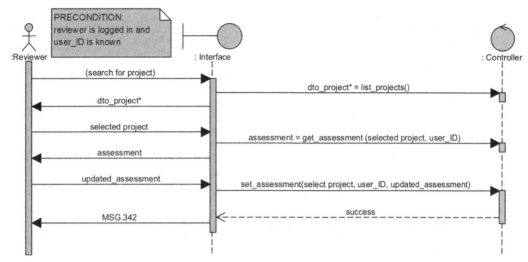

FIGURE 7–7 A stateless system sequence diagram for the main flow of the use case "Update assessment."

7.6 Alternate flows in system sequence diagrams

As seen before, use case steps, especially system events, may have exceptions, which are handled by an alternate flow (variant or exception handler).

The insertion of those alternate flows in a system sequence diagram may be done in stages. Initially, the exceptions may be indicated in the diagram where they occur by using *alt* fragments.

Suppose that *dto_project** is an empty list when the diagram in Fig. 7−7 is running. According to the requirements seen in Chart 6.1, it must show MSG.049. The user cannot proceed further. Her options are inserting a new project or quitting.

This is shown in Fig. 7−8 where a fragment *alt* is used. It works much like the *if-then-else* instruction in programming languages. If the condition [*dto_project** is empty] is true, then the first lane is executed (the one above the dashed line). Otherwise, the second lane is performed (the one below the dashed line).

In the first lane, there is also a fragment *ref* to indicate that another sequence diagram is executed at this point, in the case, *SQ.39 insert assessment*. The *ref* fragment works like a procedure call or a macro in programming languages. In the current example, there is no return and the use case simply ends after *SQ.39* is executed.

As quitting is an option that is usually allowed at any point in the flow, it should not be represented in the diagram.

The same happens to other exceptions that can occur at any time. The UML sequence diagram has no explicit way to represent *try-handle* structures. But we could represent the exceptions, if needed, after the main flow as *opt* fragments stereotyped with " << *exception* >>." The *opt* fragment should have only one lane and one condition, and it corresponds to an *if-then* structure, without the else.

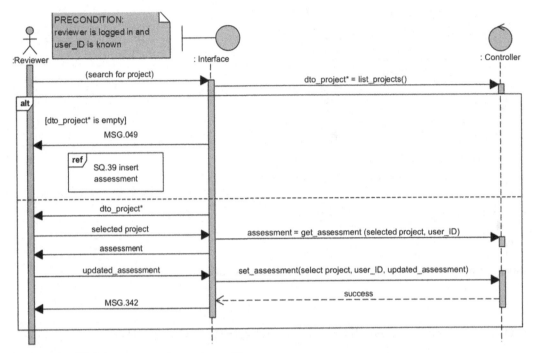

FIGURE 7–8 Adding fragments to represent exceptions.

Finally, when a variant makes the flow entering a loop, for example, a variant in step 5 sending control back to step 3, a *loop* fragment can be used. The loop works like a *"while"* structure in programming languages. It has a condition, and the flows inside it are repeated until this condition is false.

7.7 Discussion

Perhaps, the main practical result of the system sequence diagram modeling is the discovery and design of the system commands and queries that must be implemented to allow the functionality of the system to be available for the users. As seen in Fig. 7–8, the following system queries must be implemented:

- *list_projects():List of DTO*
- *get_assessment(a_project, a_user):Text*

  Besides, the following system command must also be implemented:

- *set_assessment(a_project, a_user, a_text)*

  Some of those operations could be in the usual pattern operations such as: *getter/setter*, *list*, and *get/add/remove/replace*. In this case, they must not be further inspected. However, other operations outside known patters can be expanded further, as seen in next chapters.

Questions

1. How are variants and exceptions modeled in a system sequence diagram?

2. Why is the *stateless* pattern preferable to *stateful*?

3. Which programming language structures are represented by the fragments: *alt, opt, loop,* and *ref*?

4. Can a simple system event send data to both a query and a command? Give an example.

5. Does every step in a real use case correspond to a system query or command?

8

Conceptual modeling: fundamentals

Key topics in this chapter

- Attributes
- Concepts
- Associations

8.1 Introduction to conceptual modeling

Domain analysis consists of discovering and modeling information that must be managed by the system. This means that the team should discover how the information must be structured and transformed. It starts early with the *preliminary conceptual model* and continues during the sprints, when that model is refined and completed with information obtained in the use cases and/or system sequence diagrams.

The team may analyze two aspects of information: *static* (also called *structural*), which is being introduced in this chapter, and *functional*, which will be introduced in Chapter 12. The static aspect of the information is therefore represented in the conceptual model and the functional aspect in the *system operation contracts*.

At this point, when the team is completing and refining the conceptual model, they are still looking the system as a black box. Information may enter and leave the system frontier, but the team is not worried about how it is processed internally. The *dynamic model*, consisting of the collaborations among objects, will be introduced in Chapter 13.

The conceptual model describes information that the system is going to manage. It is an artifact from the *problem* domain, not the *solution* domain. Therefore, the conceptual model should not be confused with the *Design Class Diagram*, which belongs to the software internal architecture.

The conceptual model should not also be confused with the *data model*, because the data model emphasizes stored data representation and organization, while the conceptual model aims at representing the comprehension of information by users and not its physical representation. Thus, a relational data model is just one of the possible physical representations of a more essential conceptual model.

An interesting way to comprehend the conceptual model is to imagine that the elements described by it correspond to information that initially exists only in the mind of the user, as represented in Fig. 8−1, and not in a physical store system.

A user sends information to the system and receives information back from the system through system events and returns, respectively. At this point, the system does not even

Object-Oriented Analysis and Design for Information Systems. DOI: https://doi.org/10.1016/B978-0-443-13739-6.00010-1

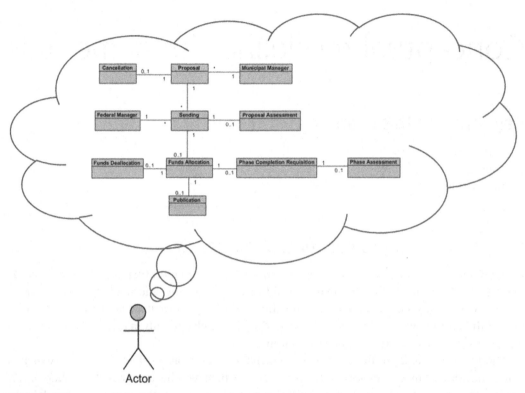

FIGURE 8–1 The conceptual model as a representation of the user knowledge.

need to be considered a *computational* system, because the information exists independently of computer support for storing and managing it. The goal of the analysis is to study the problem, not the solution yet.

The system solution could even be designed without computer technology. It is possible to analyze a whole situation and then propose a manual solution to implement it, in which, for example, data are stored in paper sheets, and operations performed by clerks using pencil, eraser, and staplers.

Just like essential use cases, the conceptual model is technology-independent. It should contain only elements that belong to the domain of the problem, leaving to the design the elements of the solution, that is, all elements related to technology, such as interfaces, storage, and communication.

The conceptual model represents only the static aspect of the information. Therefore, in the conceptual model, references to operations or dynamic aspects of the system cannot exist. Although the conceptual model is represented by the UML class diagram, the team *should not yet include any methods*. They will be included by using a specific technique introduced later in the book.

When the UML class diagram is used for conceptual modeling, there are precisely three kinds of elements to use for representing information:

- *Attributes*: Simple alphanumeric or primitive information, such as numbers, texts, and dates. Examples of attributes in the SISMOB project are reviewer's name, payment date, project title, and total cost of a work. An attribute is always connected to a more complex element: the concept.
- *Concepts*: The representation of the complex information that has coherent meaning in the domain. Concepts usually aggregate attributes and cannot be described merely as alphanumeric. Concepts also may be related to each other by associations. Examples of concepts in the SISMOB project are Proposal, Publication, Phase Assessment, and Municipal Manager (not to be confused with the *actor* "Municipal manager").
- *Associations*: A kind of information that links different concepts. However, associations are more than mere links: they *are* information. In the SISMOB example, associations should exist between proposals and municipal managers, and between funds allocation and publication, for example.

These three elements are detailed in the next sections. It is practically impossible to explain one without mentioning the others, because the three are strongly intertwined.

8.2 Attributes

Attributes are, in the conceptual model, the alphanumeric and primitive elements such as date, money, number, string, and interval.

Although most programming languages allow attributes to be defined as data structures such as lists, arrays, sets, and trees, it is not recommended that such structures could be used as attributes of a class. That would be an antipattern and would violate one of the most fundamental principles of object-oriented modeling, which is called *high cohesion*. Later, when discussing modeling patterns, this issue is revisited.

Complex concepts (classes) names should also not be used as attributes of other concepts (although, again, programming languages allow that). For example, a reviewer should not be an attribute of an assessment. If a relationship between reviewers and assessment should exist, then an *association* should be used instead, because reviewers and assessment are considered as complex concepts in the context of the SISMOB project.

8.2.1 Attribute types

Attributes may have a type, although this is not mandatory for the conceptual model. Fig. 8−2 show two versions of a class without and with attribute types.

Types in conceptual models have the same meaning they have in programming languages. In Fig. 8−2 (right), we have the classical types: *Integer* and *String*, and a primitive user-defined type: *Date*[1].

---

[1] Although for some programming languages, *date* may be also a primitive type.

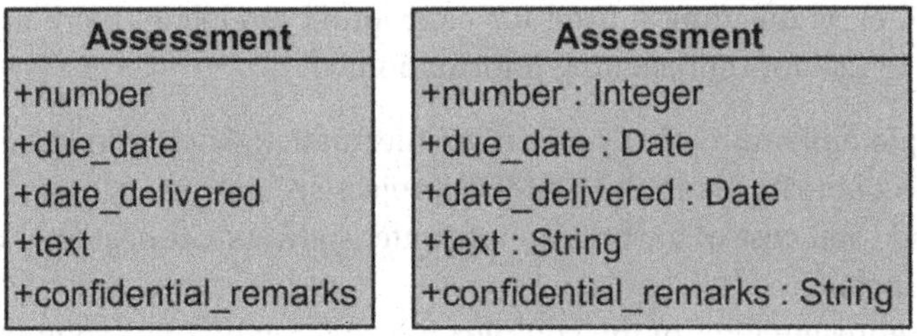

Assessment	Assessment
+number	+number : Integer
+due_date	+due_date : Date
+date_delivered	+date_delivered : Date
+text	+text : String
+confidential_remarks	+confidential_remarks : String

FIGURE 8–2 A class with untyped attributes (left) and typed attributes (right).

When an attribute is defined by formation rules, such as *date* and *phone*, it may be represented as a *primitive* class, which are highly reusable and used in the diagram as a type, not a class. Primitive types are introduced below in the text.

An *address* is something special. Is it an attribute or a complex concept? Is it simply a string or a complex concept composed of number, street, ZIP code, city, etc.? This case, as many others, is decided by analyzing the information needs of the users. If addresses are used just to print envelopes and send snail mail, then they behave merely as strings, and may be represented as attributes with type *String*. However, if addresses are used to calculate distances and routes, or if they are used to group customers that live in the neighborhood, then they behave as complex concepts and should be modeled initially as a primitive type. Furthermore, if they have a structure of associations between them or other classes, then they could be modeled as complex concepts.

8.2.2 Initial values

An attribute may be declared with an initial value. That means that every time a new instance of the concept is created, that attribute will automatically receive a defined initial value, which can be changed later if necessary. Unless stated differently, all attributes of a class are null when the class is instantiated. There are two ways to avoid an instance to exist without filling those mandatory attributes: the first, is to declare the attribute with an initial value, and the second is to pass the initialization value as an argument for the method that creates instances of that specific class.

In the SISMOB system, an *Assessment* instance may be created, for example, with a due date corresponding to the number of days, which is a known constant or variable, plus the current date. Considering that both values could be obtained from a service class such as "*Sismob*," the *Assessment* class could be represented like in Fig. 8–3. In that figure, it is also represented the number of the assessment being obtained as a system variable plus one and the text attributes initialized with the empty string (""), which is different from *null*. In the case of this class, the only attribute that would be null when the class is instantiated is *date_delivered*.

The definition of an initial value for an attribute may also be created with the use of the *Object Constraint Language (OCL)* (Object Management Group, 2010).

Assessment
+number : Integer = Sismob.last_assessment_number()+1
+due_date : Date = Sismob.today()+Sismob.assessment_term()
+date_delivered : Date
+text : String = ""
+confidential_remarks : String = ""

FIGURE 8-3 Attributes with initial value.

Every OCL expression should be declared in a *context* that corresponds to a class. Most OCL declarations also have a *subcontext*, consisting of a class property, that is, an attribute, association role, or even a method. When declaring the initial value for the attribute *due_date* in class *Assessment*, the context is *Assessment* and the subcontext is *due_date*. Thus, the OCL expression starts as:

```
Context Assessment::due_date
```

Optionally, the type of the attribute may be added:

```
Context Assessment::due_date:Date
```

In order to indicate that the OCL expression is defining an initial value for an attribute, the expression "*init*": is used, followed by the expression that produces the initial value for the attribute. As in the example, the initial value is a sum of two system variables, the complete expression may be defined as:

```
Context Assessment::due_date:Date
    init: Sysmob.today()+Sismob.assessment_term()
```

The expression may also be simplified a bit by omitting the type of the attribute:

```
Context Assessment::due_date
    init: Sysmob.today()+Sismob.assessment_term()
```

An attribute may have its initial value defined by more complex expressions too. However, the team must be aware that some values may not exist at the time that a class is instantiated and therefore, must be avoided as initial values.

8.2.3 Derived attributes

Derived attributes are understood as derived alphanumeric values only. If a "derived attribute" refers to objects or data structures containing objects, then they correspond to *derived associations* (Section 8.4.3). Derived attributes differ from normal attributes because they cannot be changed directly. In other words, they are *read- only*.

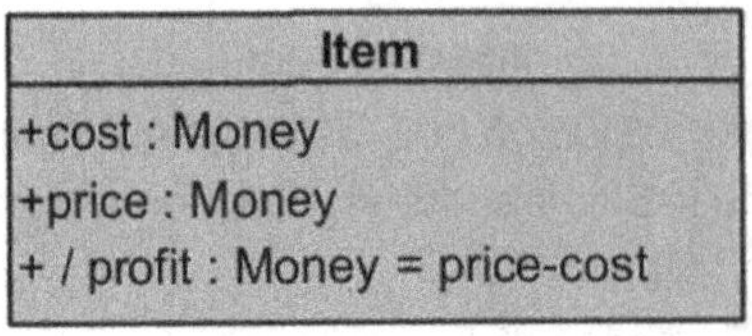

Item
+cost : Money
+price : Money
+ / profit : Money = price-cost

FIGURE 8–4 A class with a derived attribute.

A derived attribute is calculated and must be defined by an expression. In the class diagram, a derived attribute may be represented by a slash (/) preceding the attribute name (and type), followed by " = " and the (OCL) expression that defines the value of the attribute. Fig. 8–4 shows an example in which *profit* is defined as the difference between *price* and *cost*.

Derived attributes may also be defined by natural language or formal language. In this book, the formal language OCL will be used every time an expression must be used. The expression in this example has a class as context (*Item*) and an attribute as sub context (*profit*). It is followed by the word "*derive*": that indicates that the expression that follows it defines how the value of the derived attribute is calculated when it is read. The expression of the example of Fig. 8–4 defines *profit* by using the values of other two attributes of the same class: *profit* = *price* − *cost*. Thus, the OCL expression for defining this attribute is:

```
Context Item::profit:Money
        derive:
                price-cost
```

The OCL expressions *init*: and *derive*: need to be followed by a reference to an object. When this object is the instance which that corresponds to the context of the expression, it can be referred by the word "*self*," which works much like the expression "*this*" in Java and "*self*" in other object-oriented languages.

The notation *self.property* allows to access the value of a property (attribute, association role, or method) belonging to the object. For example, in the context of the class *Item*, the expression *self.cost* denotes the value of the attribute *cost* of a given instance of *Item*.

Thus, the OCL complete expression that defines the derived value for the attribute *profit* of class *Item* is:

```
Context Item::profit:Money
        derive:
                self.price-self.cost
```

In OCL, it is possible to omit the expression *self* when the context is not ambiguous. In the example above, the expression could be simplified to:

```
Context Item::profit:Money
        derive:
                price-cost
```

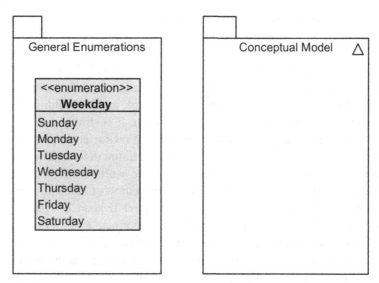

FIGURE 8–5 Enumeration.

In the *Item* context, *price* and *cost* may be nothing else but attributes of *Item*. Then, the word *self* may be omitted from the expression.

Derived attributes may not be directly updated. In the *Item* class of Fig. 8–4, only the attributes *cost* and *price* may be directly updated. The derived attribute *profit* is read- only: it is calculated as the result of its defining expression.[2]

8.2.4 Enumerations

Enumerations are a midterm between concepts and attributes. They are basically *strings* and behave like that. But there is a predefined set of *valid* strings that constitutes the enumeration domain. For example, a weekday type enumeration, such as, *Weekday*, can only assume a value in a set of seven possibilities: Sunday, Monday, Tuesday, Wednesday, Thursday, Friday, and Saturday. Thus, an attribute defined with that type, such as, *dayOff:Weekday* would only assume one out of those seven values, although it behaves just like an *string*.

Enumerations may appear in UML diagrams as stereotyped classes. It is suggested that enumerations that are domain-independent are not placed in the same diagram that contains the conceptual model, but in a special package intended to contain the enumerations, as shown in Fig. 8–5, because domain-independent enumerations (such as *Weekday*) are

---

[2] At this point, some readers that are also programmers could be worried about performance issues with the code that will be used to implement derived attributes. As they are by definition "calculated," it seems a waste of processing time to repeat those calculations if the original values of *cost* and *price* have not changed. However, the readers can stay calm because code optimization mechanisms are available for derived attributes. For example, the value calculated for a derived attribute may be kept in the *cache* and recalculated only when one of its components is changed. For example, *profit* must be recalculated only after the instance of *Item* changes the values of *price* or *cost*.

very reusable from application to application. Only domain-specific enumerations should be kept together with the other classes of the conceptual model so that people can see their meaning more easily.

In UML, enumerations are defined as stereotyped classes. While they *may* have associations and attributes of their own, the team is not encouraged to use those features because they would turn the enumeration into a complex concept, and it would probably lose reusability. For example, consider the *Weekday* enumeration. It is simply a list of seven names. Suppose now that the team adds some attributes to the *Weekday* enumeration, such as working hours. Then, Monday to Friday would have working hours defined from 9 a.m. to 5 p.m., Saturday from 9 a.m. to noon, and Sunday may have no working hours at all. In this case, what is the difference between this enumeration and a complex concept as it also has attributes and possibly associations and even methods later? Instead of creating attributes or associations for an enumeration, it would be advisable to create a new complex concept that accommodates the enumeration as is and the other attributes that need to be added. In the example seen in Fig. 8−6, a new concept *WorkingDay* could be created with two attributes: *day:Weekday* (still a pure enumeration), and *working_hours:TimeInterval* (a normal attribute as explained above). Thus enumerations that are thought to incorporate extra functionalities should be maintained as they are and included in normal classes.

To remain reusable, an enumeration should not be able to access any other class through an association. The fact that *WorkingDay* in Fig. 8−6 has an attribute labeled with *Weekday* allows the normal class *WorkingDay* to access the enumeration *Weekday* but not vice versa. This keeps the enumeration uncoupled from the classes that use it, and therefore, it maintains the enumeration largely reusable.

Enumeration values in OCL may be represented by the enumeration name followed by "::" and the value name, for example, *Weekday::Tuesday*.

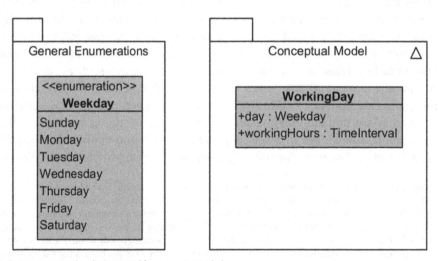

FIGURE 8–6 An enumeration being used by a conceptual class.

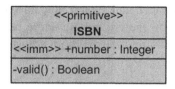

FIGURE 8–7 A primitive type.

8.2.5 Primitive types

The team can and should define *primitive types* when they deal with attributes that have formation rules, as in the case of International Standard Book Number (ISBN). Primitive types may be defined as classes stereotyped with ≪*primitive*≫, as shown in Fig. 8−7.

The *ISBN* class, stereotyped in such a manner, behaves like a *type* that can be used to define attributes. It is not a complex concept like *User*, *Proposal*, etc. It has a value with public access (marked with " + "), and a validation predicate that is private (marked with " − "), meaning that it can be accessed only by methods inside the class itself. That predicate will be called to verify if the ISBN value is valid or not, while it is created from an Integer, considering its formation rule.[3] That predicate is, therefore, used in the *constructor* (the method that creates instances of the class) to guarantee that only valid ISBNs are created. Remember that conceptual classes do not have methods, but primitive types are not conceptual classes. They are user-defined, reusable low-level components.

Although the value of the primitive type has public access, it is normally accepted that it is *immutable*. That means that the value of the primitive type can be defined only at creation time and not updated later. This is to make it consistent with the idea of primitive data elements as *constants*, and not as *objects*. Objects may change their internal state, and constants usually do not.[4] The immutable stereotype that may be used in attributes is ≪*imm*≫, for short.

Some primitive types, such as *Date* and *Money*, are already available in some programming languages and database management systems. Other not-so-common types may be created by the team and reused extensively.

The primitive type formation rule must be defined syntactically, that is, by evaluating expressions that do not need to consult data stored by the system. If a formation rule depends on consulting attribute or association values, then it is not, probably, the case for a primitive type, but for a normal class. For example, the *prime number* formation rule may be checked without consulting objects and associations, but a *registered city name* may not be a primitive type, because to check if a string is a registered city name, it is necessary to query existing names of current cities stored in the system.

A primitive type usually is *application-independent*, that is, its meaning usually is independent from the system or project being developed, just as general enumerations. An ISBN has the same meaning and formation rule in any application domain that uses it.

[3] The ISBN formation rule is explained in http://www.isbn.org/standards/home/isbn/us/isbnqa.asp.

[4] Some languages such as Smalltalk allow constants to change their value in runtime, but this is not usually the case and is not recommended for most applications.

However, concepts such as *User*, *Item*, and *Project* may have different definitions in different applications and cannot usually be reused without some refactoring effort. Primitive types, on the other hand, are usually 100% reusable, without adjustments or modifications.

8.3 Concepts

Concepts are more than alphanumeric values. They are also more than a bunch of attributes, because they carry meaning and may be associated to each other. Conceptual modeling may begin with concepts and associations only, as shown before, that is, attributes are not needed in the preliminary conceptual model. However, when concepts are examined in detail, they usually contain a coherent group of attributes.

8.3.1 Unique attributes

It is assumed that different instances of a concept are distinguishable from each other just by the fact that they were created independently. This is not the case with primitive types. Two dates, such as March 05, 2013 and March 05, 2013, are the same. But two customers named "John Doe" are not necessarily the same person. Some programming languages indeed use two comparison predicates, one to check if two objects are *equal* (they have the same values for their attributes) and another to check if they are *identical* (they share the same space in memory).

Different instances are therefore always distinguishable from each other, but additionally they may have attributes that are *unique* to them. Once an attribute has been stereotyped as ≪ *unique* ≫, two or more instances of the concept cannot have the same value for that attribute. One example of a unique attribute is the number of an assessment, which is unique for each assessment, while the other attributes may have identical values in different assessments (Fig. 8−8). Unique attributes usually are also immutable. It may be accepted as part of the definition of "unique," or else, the attribute should use the two stereotypes.

Unique attributes must not be confused with database primary keys. Primary keys are used especially for database design to provide a unique identification for an instance. But ≪ *unique* ≫ and primary keys are not identical, because a concept may have only one primary key, but more than one unique attribute. Primary keys must also be hidden from the user, while unique attributes are known and used by the user. Unique attributes are closer to the idea of *candidate keys* in relational databases (Date, 1982).

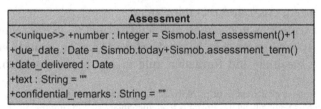

FIGURE 8–8 A class with a unique attribute.

FIGURE 8–9 A controller class.

8.3.2 System control class

Usually, the conceptual model is expected to be a connected graph, that is, every concept has a path (a sequence of associations) connecting it to every other concept. When that is not the case, it is supposed that something is missing, that is, important associations or concepts have not been discovered yet.

Although some authors oppose it, a concept that represents the system as a whole (in our example *Sismob*) may be useful in the conceptual model if some precautions are taken. First of all, that concept should be declared as a *Singleton*;[5] and second, it should not have attributes, being just a *control* class. This class corresponds to the *system controller* or *façade controller* already mentioned before. It does not represent any data; it serves only as a point of reference to add associations to other classes, as seen in the following sections.

All concepts are associated directly or indirectly to the controller class in order to be accessible by the application.

The system controller class may be stereotyped with ≪ *control* ≫ or drawn using Jacobson's (1994) icon, as shown in Fig. 8−9.

Later, the advantages of using the controller class are explained in detail. There are some situations that are nicely modeled as associations from the control class.

8.4 Associations

When complex concepts are related, it is said that there is an *association* among them. Associations usually happen only between two concepts, but they can also be defined among three or more concepts. There may also be reflexive associations between instances of the same class. For example, the association that links parents to children is defined as a reflexive association from *Person* to *Person*.

When classes are associated, then their instances may be *linked*. For example, an instance of *Assessment* is linked to an instance of *Reviewer* and an instance of *Proposal*.

Associations may be tricky to identify in use case texts, especially because sometimes deciding if something is a concept or association may be fuzzy. For example, is an *approval* an association between a manager and a proposal? Or is it a concept? If it is considered a concept, which are its own associations and attributes?

---

[5] A design pattern that states that a class with a single instance may be accessible globally.

Moreover, use case texts often mention *operations* that are not exactly static associations. Operations such as buying goods, or making a reservation, are dynamic transformations on data. They could produce instances of concepts to represent their existence. It is necessary to consider the difference between the (static) associations and (dynamic) operations:

- An *association* is a static relation that may exist between complex concepts, complementing the information about them in each moment (a snapshot of their state), or referring to new associative information (e.g., neighborhood or parent/children).
- An *operation* is the act of accessing and transforming existing information.

As a description of a dynamic process, a use case text is usually full of explicit references to operations; but associations usually must be inferred from the text, because they are implicit.

At a used car dealer, there are people who buy cars from other people. When someone buys a car, she is performing an operation. That operation changes the links between objects: one ownership link ceases to exist, while another is created in its place. But, as the transaction of buying has its own attributes, such as date, values, it would not be appropriate to represent an operation as an association, as shown in Fig. 8–10.

Why is that interpretation not adequate? The information about date of buying and value paid cannot be represented neither in the class *Person* nor in the class *Car*. A car may be sold many times and a person can buy many cars. Each time a car is sold to a person, a new piece of information is created, a *transaction*. In this specific case, a *Sale* (Fig. 8–11).

However, there are different ways people and cars may be associated besides ownership. A person may be *passenger* of a car, or its *driver*, or the association may represent merely that someone *likes* a given car. To eliminate such ambiguities, it is convenient in many cases to use a *role name* on one or both association ends to indicate which role a class plays.

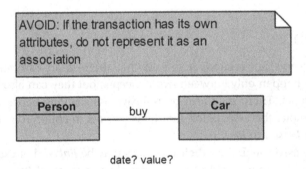

FIGURE 8–10 A operation unduly labeling an association.

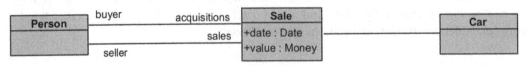

FIGURE 8–11 A transaction being represented by a class.

In Fig. 8−11, a sale has a buyer and a seller that are two (different) people. On the other way, a person has a set of acquisitions (of cars) and a set of sales. In the case of the two associations from *Sale* to *Person*, both ends (roles) are explicitly named.

In UML if a role is not explicitly named, then it may be referred by the name of the class at that end in lowercase. For example, still in Fig. 8−11, a sale has a "car" because the association does not explicitly label this end of the association. On the other hand, a car has a set of sales for the same motive.

If there are two or more (n) associations between the same classes, then at least $n − 1$ of the roles in both ends must be explicitly labeled. Otherwise, the diagram is ambiguous and not in compliance to the UML definition.

Although UML allows an association to have a name, this feature is not recommended. Instead of giving a name to an association as in Fig. 8−12 (left), consider naming its two roles (right).

It may be easier and more useful to work with role names instead of association names. In practice, the team can ignore the fact that associations may have a name. Conceptual models can be perfectly clear with role names replacing association names. Role names are easier to give because they define navigation possibilities between concepts and are useful also for naming derived programming code elements such as the variables that would represent the association when the code is generated.

If by any means an association name is still needed, it is always possible to create it by composing the role names; the reverse is not true. For example, an association between a car and a person could be called *fleet2owner*, *fleet_owner*, or *fleetXowner* if it indeed needs to have a name (e.g., for reference purposes). In this case, use the names of the roles if they are explicit. Otherwise, use the name of the class in lower case. Also, the order in that the roles appear in the name does not matter: *fleet2owner* is the same as *owner2fleet*.

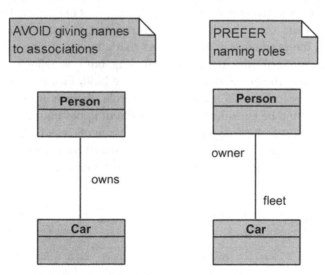

FIGURE 8−12 Naming an association versus naming roles.

8.4.1 Role multiplicity

In a conceptual model, it is fundamental to know how many elements a role accepts. For example, in the association between *Person* and *Car* with role name *driver* in Fig. 8–13, how many cars can someone drive? How many drivers can a car have?

The answer depends on a study of the nature of the problem and on the real meaning of the association, especially if it represents the present time or the past. For example, if the associations of Fig. 8–13 represent the present, then a car may have just one driver (one at a time). But if this association represents the past, then it is possible that a car had many drivers during different periods of time.

Thus, it is fundamental that the team decides clearly what the association means before deciding on its role multiplicity. They should remember that associations are static constraints; they represent links that may exist between the instances of the associated classes since the instant of their creation. Therefore, depending on the meaning of the association, it may have different role multiplicities.

There are, basically, two decisions to be made about the multiplicity of an association role:

1. Is the role mandatory or not? For example, should a person have at least one car? Should a car have at least one driver or owner?
2. Does the number of instances that may be linked through the role have a defined conceptual bound? For example, is there a maximum number or minimum number of cars that a person may drive or own?

The answers to these questions may be tricky. Regarding the first decision, for example, returning to the SISMOB project, it is expected that each proposal must have at least one assessment. But that does not qualify the *assessment* role for a proposal as mandatory, because a proposal can exist without an assessment for a period. Eventually, any proposal will hopefully be assessed, but not necessarily soon. Thus this role is *not* mandatory for the proposal.

The other tricky issue concerns the maximum number of elements that a role allows. Physically speaking, the maximum number of cars that a person may own is the number of cars that exist on planet Earth (the number is increasing, but it is defined at a given moment of time, even if it is hard to count). But as new cars are built, they may be purchased. Thus although there is a physical limit for the ownership role, there is no conceptual or logical limit. Thus the role should be considered virtually without upper bound.

Similarly, a proposal may have any number of assessments, even if a customary number is 3. If the maximum number of assessments is a *permanent requirement*, then the role may be labeled with 0..3 (meaning zero up to three assessments per proposal), and it will be

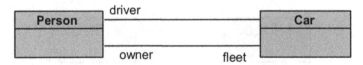

FIGURE 8–13 Associations without explicit multiplicity.

implemented by and array, probably. However, if this requirement is transient, then more flexibility is needed, and the role should be labeled with * (meaning zero or more assessments per proposal), and being implemented by a linked list, probably.

Role multiplicity in UML is represented by an expression where:

- The asterisk "*" means "any quantity," and indicates that there is no upper bound.
- The comma "," means "or."
- Two dots ".." means "up to."

The following are examples of the usual multiplicity limits for conceptual models:
1—exactly one
0..1—zero or one
*—zero or more
1..*—one or more
2..5—two up to five
2,5—two or five
2,5..8—two or from five up to eight

The multiplicity limits that include zero represent roles that are optional for a concept. All the other limits are mandatory.

Fig. 8–14 shows an example where one person may have a fleet with an undetermined number of cars (optional), and a person may be a driver of one car at most (also optional). On the other hand, it shows that a car must have a single owner (mandatory) and that it may have a driver or not (optional).

According to many countries' laws, a car may have more than one owner, or it may be owned by a corporation; in some situations, a car may also have no owner at all. The conceptual model (such as the one in Fig. 8–14) represents not necessarily a general truth, but the information needed for a given application. For some information systems, it could be mandatory that a car, in order to be registered, have a single owner and that this owner must be a person. In this case, the conceptual model should represent the specific and pragmatic information needs for that system.

8.4.2 Association direction

An association in a conceptual model should be *nondirectional* in principle, that is, the navigability of the association should not yet be determined (Booch et al., 2007). This is because for analysis purposes, it is only necessary to know whether two concepts are associated or not; *dynamic* design will decide on navigability later.

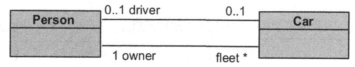

FIGURE 8–14 Associations with explicit multiplicity.

However, some exceptions may exist. For example, a derived association is necessarily unidirectional, and the same happens to associations coming from the façade controller, as seen below.

8.4.3 Derived association

Just as useful as derived attributes are *derived associations*, that is, associations that instead of being represented physically are calculated from available information. For example, suppose it is often necessary to know which proposals a given municipality has already sent in the SISMOB system. Considering that proposals are linked to municipal managers and the municipality is associated to this manager, then municipalities and proposals would not have a direct association, as seen in Fig. 8−15.

If proposals are not linked directly to the municipality in the conceptual model, referring to that information could be a bit more complicated than expected.

Fig. 8−16 shows a tentative for resolving this issue, but there is a need to guarantee that every time a manager adds a link to a proposal, the same happens to the municipality. If this is not done, the model would represent inconsistent information. Thus it would require some checking mechanism (e.g., allowing only assessments that were issued to be associated also to the municipality).

Fig. 8−17 shows an example of how a conceptual model for SISMOB could relate proposals to municipalities using a derived association "*/proposals.*" In this case, the association is unidirectional and only navigable from Municipality to Proposal. That means that a municipality may consult its own proposals directly (without using "Municipal Manager") but that a proposal not necessarily have direct access to its Municipality. If this is necessary, then a second derived association from *Proposal* to *Municipality* should be included.

The multiplicity of the destiny role of the derived association in Fig. 8−17 is multiple (*) because by navigating on the normal associations, it can be seen that a municipality may

FIGURE 8–15 *Proposal* and *Municipality* only have indirect association.

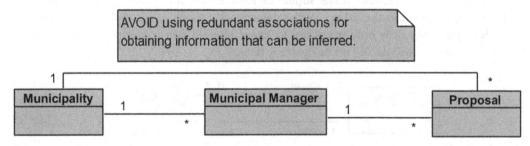

FIGURE 8–16 Redundant associations.

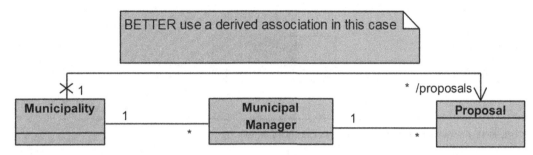

FIGURE 8–17 A derived association.

have submitted zero or more proposals. On the other direction, despite the derived association being not navigable from *Proposal* to *Municipality*, a constrained role may be indicated because one *Proposal* has just one *Manager* and one *Manager* has just one *Municipality*. Thus the origin of the derived association in this case has multiplicity "1."

Usually, the multiplicity of a derived association is defined by the product of the multiplicities of the roles that must be navigated to reach the target concept. The following rules may be used to determine that multiplicity:

- The lower bound of the derived multiplicity is the product of the lower bounds of the roles in the navigation path.
- The upper bound of the derived multiplicity is the product of the upper bounds of the roles in the navigation path.

For example, if the multiplicities found in the path are 1.0.5, 2..*, and 1, then the derived multiplicity is 2..*, because the lower bounds are 1, 2, and 1, and $1 \times 2 \times 1 = 2$. As the upper bounds are 5, *undetermined* (*), and 1, we have $5 \times undetermined \times 1 = undetermined$.

However, if filters are applied to the definition of the derived association, the resulting multiplicity may be different. For example, if the derived association is defined so that it links a municipality to the *last* proposal it has send, then the derived multiplicity should be 1, and not *.

As opposed to normal associations that allow links between individual objects to be added and removed, a derived association may only be consulted (just like derived attributes, which are read-only).

A derived association may be defined by an OCL expression as well. The example of Fig. 8−17 may be defined as:

```
Context Municipality::proposals
      derive:
              self.municipal_manager.proposal
```

The following observations can be made about this OCL expression:

- The context is the class at the origin of the derived association (*Municipality*). The subcontext is the role name of the derived association (*proposals*).
- The expression "*derive*": is used just like with derived attributes.

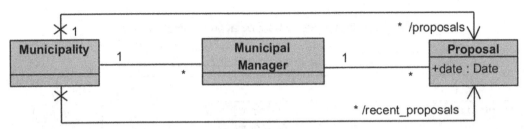

FIGURE 8–18 Another derived association that works like a filter.

- What determines if the expression is defining a derived attribute or association is the context and the type of information that is returned by the expression. Derived attributes are defined by expressions that return an alphanumeric, enumeration, or primitive type, while derived associations are defined by expressions that return an object or a collection of objects, recursively.

In object-oriented programming languages, usually the "." notation can be used only over a single object. OCL, however, allows it to be used over collections of objects.[6] If x is a collection, then the meaning of $x.y$ is the collection of y that can be obtained as properties of x. For example, if the context is *Municipality*, then *self.municipal_manager* denotes the set of municipal managers associated with that municipality. Moreover, *self.municipal_manager. proposal* is the set of all proposals linked to the managers of a given municipality.

8.4.4 Derived association with filter

A derived association may also be used to define a subset of objects from a set of linked objects by the application of a filter. For example, imagine that we want to have the information on the proposals sent by the municipality in the last 6 months only. This is a very dynamic derived association because its members may change as time passes or actions are done.

Let us complete our example by adding the attribute *date* to the class *Proposal* (Fig. 8–18). In this case, we could define another derived association that associates municipalities only with projects sent up to 6 months from now. Let us call this new association role *recent_proposals*.

It cannot be seen in the diagram, but the derived association in this case would have the following definition:

```
Context:Municipality::recent_proposals:Set<Proposal>
    derive:
        self.municipal_manager.proposal->select(:a_proposal|
            a_proposal.date+Sismob.Date(6,0,0)>=Sismob.today()
```

The OCL expression for this derived association has as the context the *Municipality* class, because it is at the origin of the association. The expression that defines the derived

---

[6] In fact, in OCL, even a single object is considered a collection with a single element. This is equivalent to the *natural* notion of a set, but not to the *mathematical* notion of set, because in set theory, a set with one element is not the element. In OCL a set with one element and the element are the same thing.

association must denote the set of proposals with date not older than 6 months. This can be obtained by the condition *a_proposal.date + Sismob.Date*(6,0,0) > = *Sismob.today*()

In this expression, the operation *Date* in class *Sismob* creates an object of the primitive class *Date* with 6 months, 0 days, and 0 years, following the order of the arguments.

The OCL expression to obtain a subset of elements that satisfy a given Boolean expression like this is *select*. The Boolean expression is placed inside parentheses after the *select* command. The Boolean expression usually starts with an iteration variable that in the case of the example is:*a_proposal|*.

The arrow notation "- >" is used before *select* instead of the dot (".") notation because the *select* function is applied over the structure of the set, not over its elements.[7]

OCL also allows the iteration variable to be omitted if the context of the expression is not ambiguous. Thus, we can simplify the expression by omitting the "*self*" expression as well as the explicit iteration variable:

```
Context:Municipality::recent_proposals:Set of Proposal
    derive:
        municipal_manager.proposal->select(
            date+Sismob.Date(6,0,0)>=Sismob.today()
        )
```

Observe that inside the parentheses after *select* the context is potentially ambiguous. There, the property *date* could refer both to a *Municipality* (broader context) and to a Proposal (narrower context). What allows us to eliminate the ambiguity is the fact that the property *date* does not exist in the class *Municipality*. If it existed in both classes, then the nonabbreviated notation should be used to eliminate the ambiguous expression.

8.4.5 Aggregation and composition

Some associations may be considered *stronger* than others in the sense that they define one kind of object that is composed of others. A house, for example, is composed of rooms, a book of chapters, an undergraduate career of courses, etc.

If the association is exclusive, in the sense that an object may not be part of another object at the same time, then it is considered a strong part-whole association, which is called a *composite aggregation*,[8] and it is drawn with a black diamond on the role that represents the whole (Fig. 8−19).

---

[7] In the case of a set of people *p*, if someone wants to get the set of all ages, she could write *p.age*. However, the size of the set is not a property of the people; it is a property of the *set structure*. Thus, to obtain the size of the set the expression *p- > size*() should be used. If it was written as *p.size*, then it would be representing the set of the sizes of each person (whether such information exists), not the size of the set.

[8] "An association may represent a composite aggregation (i.e., a whole/part relationship). Only binary associations can be aggregations. Composite aggregation is a strong form of aggregation that requires a part instance be included in at most one composite at a time. If a composite is deleted, all of its parts are normally deleted with it. Note that a part can (where allowed) be removed from a composite before the composite is deleted, and thus not be deleted as part of the composite. Compositions may be linked in a directed acyclic graph with transitive deletion characteristics; that is, deleting an element in one part of the graph will also result in the deletion of all elements of the sub graph below that element" (Object Management Group, 2011).

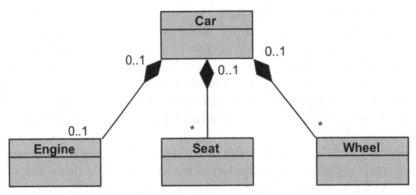

FIGURE 8–19 Example of composition.

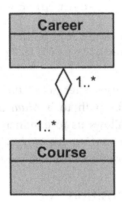

FIGURE 8–20 A shared aggregation.

The multiplicity of the role that represents the composite (the side where the diamond is), in the case of a composite aggregation, should be 1 or 0..1, and nothing else, because composites do not share parts, even with objects of the same class.

In the example, it is considered that a car is made of engine, wheels, and seats. However, as each of those components may be removed from a car and keep existence, both the role from the car and from the components is optional (0..1 or *).

Composite aggregation indicates exclusivity in the part-whole association. When this exclusivity is not mandatory (the part may be part of other aggregates), then a white diamond is used instead, and the association is called a *shared aggregation* (Fig. 8–20).

The white diamond indicates a shared aggregation where the part may belong to different wholes at the same time. In Fig. 8–20, a given *Course* may be part of one or more *Career*. This example shows a component that can be shared by many instances of the same class.

A different situation is when a component may be shared among instances of different classes. In Fig. 8–21, an *Item* must be part of an *Order*, but it could be part of a *Sale*.

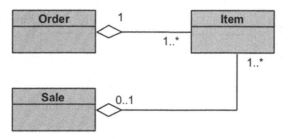

FIGURE 8–21 Shared aggregation of different classes.

Composite and shared aggregations are special associations and should be used with much parsimony, that is, they should be used only when the team is sure that it is the case that an object is really *part* of another and not just a normal association. Even the UML specification (Object Management Group, 2011) states that the precise semantics of a shared aggregation vary between application areas and modelers.

It is common to see aggregation and composition being abused in models when objects that are not part-whole related are linked by that kind of association. For example, a reviewer is not part of an assessment, if not for any other reason, but by the fact that a reviewer is a person and a text produced by a person does not become part of the person, neither the reverse.

Composite and shared aggregations should unite elements of the same nature: physical with physical, and abstract with abstract. If a *Car* is a physical thing, then its parts should be too. If a *Career* is an abstract thing, then its parts would also be abstract.

There are few real advantages in using aggregation in conceptual modeling. This is another reason to minimize or even abolish their use if the team still confuses the concepts. Among the advantages is that composite or shared aggregation parts usually have attributes and operations that are combined and derived in the whole. For example, the weight of a *Car* is derived as the weight of all its pieces, and if a *Car* is sold, all of its parts are sold too.

8.4.6 *n*-ary associations

Most associations are binary, that is, most associations have only two roles. However, there are situations where associations with three or more roles are needed. In UML, these associations can be represented by using a diamond that connects all the roles of the association, as in Fig. 8–22.

The example in Fig. 8–22 was taken from a budget control application. Each project may be associated to multiple budget items and multiple financial years. Each financial year may have a number of budget items per project. Each budget item is associated to a financial year and a project. A ternary association (i.e., an association with three roles) represents this situation better than binary associations.

A ternary association corresponds to a table with a triple index. Although it could be represented by binary associations with the introduction of an intermediate class, as in Fig. 8–23, the meaning is different. If a ternary is used, there can be only one combination

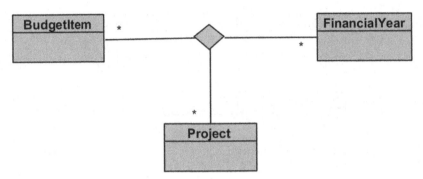

FIGURE 8–22 Example of tertiary association.

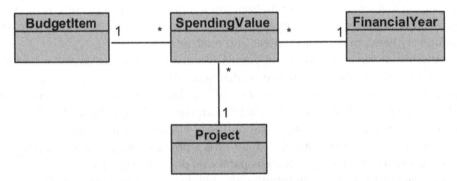

FIGURE 8–23 An option to a ternary association but with a different meaning.

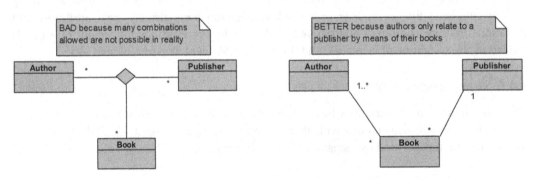

FIGURE 8–24 Correction of Fig. 8–23.

of *BudgetItem*, *FinancialYear*, and *Project*. In the example of Fig. 8–23, many occurrences of *SpendingValue* can exists with the same *BudgetItem*, *FinancialYear*, and *Project*.

These cases are not frequent, but they may appear in a project. Before deciding to use a ternary or *n*-ary association, the team should verify if they are not confusing it with a situation where a combination of binary associations should be used instead. For example, the case shown in Fig. 8–24 (left) is not correctly modeled as a ternary association, because the relation between the author and the publisher happens only when the author publishes a book with a publisher. Then, the configuration of Fig. 8–24 (right) is more adequate to the eventual requirements. Only in a scenario where the same author could publish the same book using a different publisher and the publisher could publish the same book with a different author would there be a case for a ternary association. But that is not the case.

Questions

1. Why should an attribute not be typed with a class name? Why should an attribute not be used to reference another class?
2. What is the difference between a normal association, an aggregation, and a composition? When to use each of them?
3. What is an Enumeration and how to use it in conceptual modeling?
4. List some examples of data types that could be defined as primitive and enumerations. The more the merrier.
5. What is the difference between initial valued and derived attributes?

9

Conceptual modeling: data structures and organization

Key topics in this chapter

- Collections: Set, Bag, Ordered Set, Sequence, Map, Partition, and Relation
- Organization of the Conceptual Model: Structural, Associative, and Temporal
- Invariants

9.1 Collections

Simple collections of objects that do not have any particular meaning or structure should not, in principle, be represented as concepts, but as association roles. Any association role *already* represents a collection of objects of the associated class. Thus considering the example of Fig. 9−1 (up), *fleet* associates a set of cars to a person. The model presented in Fig. 9−1 (up) is, therefore, unnecessary and redundant, because the model shown in Fig. 9−1 (down) is equivalent and simpler.

Thus unless the fleet has its own attributes, associations, or methods (e.g., a person having multiple fleets located in different places), the correct form to represent a simple collection of objects is through an association role, not through a class.

Thus the team must be aware that if the collection has particular attributes or associations, then it must be represented as a concept (methods will be introduced latter). For example, an *Order* is initially understood as a set of items, but an *Order* also has attributes such as issue date, total value, and discount and associations such as the one with the customer, who may have multiple orders. If that is the case, the collection is not a simple role but a concept, as shown in Fig. 9−2.

Association roles may be thought as representing *abstract data types* (Liskov, 1974) in conceptual models. In design models, they would also represent *concrete* data types. Abstract data types are defined only by behavior, not by structure. They appear, for example, in the following:

- The *set* structure, in which elements do not repeat and have no defined position.
- The *bag* structure, in which elements may repeat but still do not have a defined position.
- The *ordered set* structure, in which elements do not repeat but have a defined position.
- The *sequence* structure, in which elements may repeat and have a defined position.
- The *map* structure, in which keys are associated to values.
- The *partition* structure, in which keys are associated to sets of values.

Object-Oriented Analysis and Design for Information Systems. DOI: https://doi.org/10.1016/B978-0-443-13739-6.00008-3

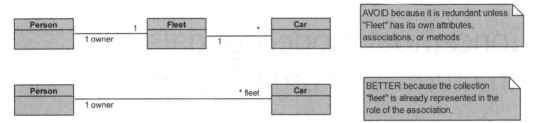

FIGURE 9–1 How to represent a collection with no particular features.

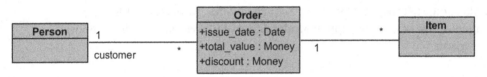

FIGURE 9–2 A collection with particular features being represented as a concept.

- The *relation* structure, in which sets of keys are associated to sets of values.

The *concrete* data types, on the other hand, are physical implementations for the abstract versions. For example, a list may be implemented in many forms, such as an array, binary tree, and linked list. In the case of concrete data types, besides behavior, there is a physical structure that defines them.

9.1.1 Set

In UML, an association role, by default, is a *set*, that is, a structure where elements do not repeat and where there is no defined position for them. In Fig. 9–3, the *fleet* is an example of a set. On the other side of the association, the role *owner* also represents a set, but in this case, it should be always a set with no more and no less than one element, due to the multiplicity of the role (1).

If someone tries to link the same car to the same person a second time, nothing happens, because it already belongs to the set, and the set cannot repeat elements. However, if someone is replacing the owner by another person, it is possible, unless the role is immutable.

9.1.2 Ordered set

Suppose a product that is not yet in stock has a list of people interested in buying it as soon as it is available. If it cannot be assured that the quantity of products received will fill all the orders, then the fairer way to attend to these customers is by establishing a line from the oldest reservation to the newest. This requires that the customers have a position in the line.

If the same customer cannot reserve the same product more than once, then it is still a structure with no elements repeated, but now with defined positions.

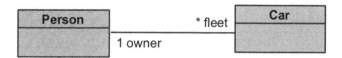

FIGURE 9–3 A set.

FIGURE 9–4 An example of ordered set.

This leads to the *ordered set* structure. In the diagram, the role may be marked with the constraint {*ordered*} to indicate that it is a collection where elements do not repeat but have defined positions, as seen in Fig. 9–4.

The constraint {*ordered*} over an association role means that the elements linked on that role have position (first, second, third, . . ., last), but still cannot be repeated. Also, it does not mean that this collection is necessarily sorted.

9.1.3 Bag

There are situations in which the position of the elements does not matter, but each element may appear more than once in the collection. That structure is called a *bag*.

For example, one may need to know how many people viewed the details of a product, and it may be important also to know how many times each one viewed it. It is not necessary to know who viewed it first, but the information on the number of views is necessary. That is a typical case for using a bag. Each time a person views the details of a product, a new link is added on the association role defined as a bag. The model is shown in Fig. 9–5.

9.1.4 Sequence

The *sequence* allows elements to be repeated and also assigns a position to them. For example, imagine that people who buy a given value worth of product qualify for receiving a gift, but a limited quantity of gifts is available. Thus a list of people that qualify to receive the gift may be built, and the gifts will be distributed to the first members of the list as soon as gifts become available. If someone again buys more than the limit established to receive a gift, she can enter the list again. Thus in that structure, the position of an element is relevant, and each element may appear more than once: this corresponds to a sequence structure, as seen in Fig. 9–6. This is a typical situation in which using a controller in the conceptual model can help building better models. Otherwise, a class for controlling reservations would need to be created especially to contain this association.

FIGURE 9–5 An example of bag.

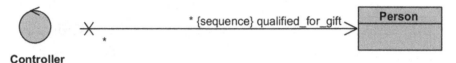

Controller

FIGURE 9–6 An example of sequence.

The multiplicity * on the *Controller* side means that not all customers are qualified for a gift and that they may qualify more than once.

The sequence has two important special cases. When the first element to be removed is always the oldest in the sequence, as in the case of Fig. 9–6, then the structure is also a *queue*. UML does not define a constraint for queues, but a stereotype on the sequence constraint would do the job: * *{sequence}* «*queue*».

When the first element to be removed is the newest in the sequence, then it behaves like a *stack* and may be stereotyped as such: * *{sequence}* «*stack*». Queues and stacks that do not repeat elements may be defined respectively as * *{ordered}* «*queue*» and * *{ordered}* «*stack*».

A general list may have elements removed and inserted at any position. Queues and stacks have elements inserted and removed only at predetermined positions, as explained above, although, in most cases, all their elements may be browsed.

A curiosity to be mentioned now is that in the real world, most collections are strict *sets* and not *sequences,* but even so, the most used programming structure is still the sequence or array, and not the set, which indicates a gap between reality and the data structures used in programming.

9.1.5 Map

When a concept has a unique attribute, a *map* may be created from that attribute to the concept, in such a way that it is easier to identify and find specific instances of the concept. For example, as the ISBN is unique for a book, associations to *Book* may be qualified by the ISBN, meaning that instead of having a set of books, the origin class has access to a map that allows immediate identification of any book if its ISBN is known. Fig. 9–7 shows an example of qualified association.

The small rectangle at the left side of the association in Fig. 9–7 represents a *qualifier* for the class at the opposite side of the association (*Book*). Notice that instead of "*," the role of the right side is now bounded by "0..1"; the association should now be read as follows: "for each possible ISBN there is no more than *one* book."

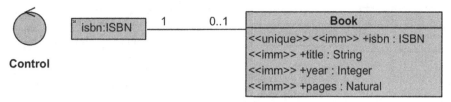

FIGURE 9–7 An example of qualified association.

Some valid ISBN values may not be associated to any book, because they were not registered in the system or because the ISBN, although valid, has simply not yet been assigned to any book; however, if one ISBN is taken by a book, no other book may share it. In practice, a qualified association is still an association "to many," but the objects belonging to the role may be accessed by one of their attributes, instead of being searched inside a collection.

The role at the left side (the qualifier side) is marked with "1," meaning that each book must have a single ISBN, neither less nor more. This must be necessarily true, because an ISBN is unique and not optional for the class *Book*, and therefore, it is mandatory and does not allow repetition. In this case, the ISBN is also immutable.

The qualifier is not only a method to access objects in an easier way. It is also a powerful modeling tool. For example, consider a situation where a person may own many phones, but only one of each kind. How do we represent this? The first naïve solution appears to be adding an attribute such as "*type*" in the class *Phone*. However, the type is not a property intrinsic to a phone; it is determined by how the person uses the phone. The phone can be a personal mobile, a professional mobile, a residence phone, etc. But it is not an attribute of the phone, it is a way a person relates to it. Then, a more elegant model for that situation is shown in Fig. 9–8.

In the case of Fig. 9–8, one person may have up to five phones, but just one of each kind. If more kinds are added to the enumeration later, then more phones may be associated to each person. If the role on the right side was 1 instead of 0..1, then one person should necessarily have five phones, each one of a different kind. That use of a qualified association with a mandatory role usually makes sense only when the qualifier is an enumeration or a finite set.

In the example of Fig. 9–7, the qualifier (ISBN) is an attribute of the qualified class, and in that case, it is called an *internal qualifier*. On the other hand, in Fig. 9–8, the qualifier (kind) is not an attribute of the qualified class, and it is called an *external qualifier*.

In Figs. 9–7 and 9–8, the multiplicity 1 or 0.1 on the right side of the figure means that the association is a *mapping*, that is, for each value of the key, there is at most one instance of the qualified class.

9.1.6 Partition

What if instead of "1" or "0.1," the multiplicity on the right side of the association was marked with "*"? In this case, the association would read as follows: "for each key there is a *set* of instances of the qualified class, not just one."

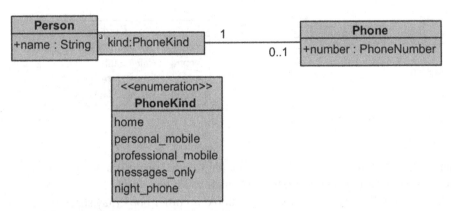

FIGURE 9–8 Modeling a situation with a qualified association.

For example, books may be classified by genre. As many books may belong to the same genre, then the *genre* attribute may not be unique. But it is possible to define a *partition* on the set of books based on their genre, as shown in Fig. 9–9.

Fig. 9–9 states that for each particular value of genre, there is a set of books associated (with zero or more elements). The role multiplicity "1" on the left side indicates that every book has one genre.

9.1.7 Relation

Now, imagine that a book may have more than one genre, for example, *The Hitchhiker's Guide to the Galaxy* (Adams, 1979), which can be classified both as science fiction and humor. For representing the possibility of a book having more than one genre, it would be sufficient to change the multiplicity on the left side of the association to * (if a genre is optional) or 1..* (if at least one genre is mandatory). Additionally, the genre should be removed from the attributes of *Book*, because it is not a single value anymore, and the qualifier becomes external, because the *genre* key now associates to multiple books. Fig. 9–10 shows the resulting relation.

The relation of Fig. 9–10 states that a book may have one or more genres and a genre has a set of books associated with it. As a book may have more than one genre, then the qualifier should be necessarily external.

9.2 Organization of the conceptual model

The elaboration of the conceptual model involves more than just putting concepts, attributes, and associations together. For the conceptual model to be a reliable and organized representation of real-world information, it is necessary to use some modeling techniques.

The main organizational techniques for concepts may be distinguished into three groups:

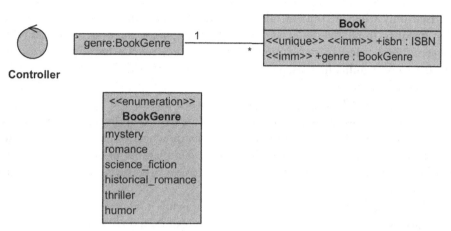

FIGURE 9–9 Example of partition.

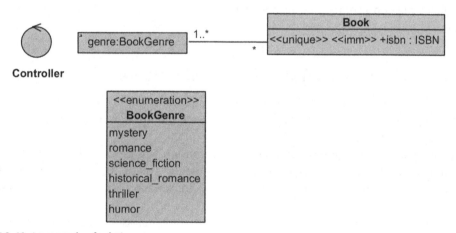

FIGURE 9–10 An example of relation.

- *Structural*: Representing generalizations among concepts, for example, *BankAccount* generalizing *SavingsAccount* and *CheckAccount*.
- *Associative*: Representing associative roles that some concepts may play related to others, for example, *Student* and *Professor* being roles a *Person* may play related to a school.
- *Temporal*: Representing relations among different states of a concept, for example, an *Order* being in states *AttendingPayment* and *Paid*.

Novice analysts and sometimes even experienced ones tend to think that the only way to factorize information is by using inheritance or generalization. However, it is necessary to apply some judgment before deciding on using this or another technique. Inheritance may be used only when a concept effectively has two or more subtypes. Although UML allows an instance to change its class, only a few languages, such as Smalltalk (Goldberg and Robson, 1989), tried to implement such a feature, maybe because there are some unresolved inherent difficulties associated to the fact that one instance could change its internal structure on the fly.

Most object-oriented languages ignore this feature due to the problems it raises, and since it is usually unnecessary, because most behaviors that could be modeled by this feature also have alternate simpler representations. Thus for practical terms, it is usually the case that an instance may not change its class: it is born as a member of one class, and it will die a member of the same class.[1] As students may become professors, they do not qualify as subtypes of people.

Another counterexample is *Worker* and *Customer* being modeled as subclasses of *Person*. This is bad first because no one is born a worker or customer; a person *becomes* a worker or customer when *associated* to a company. More than that, the same person may be a customer or worker in *more than one* company. Using inheritance in this case would create conceptual problems that can produce duplicity in records and data inconsistency.

The following subsections present details on the three approaches to the organization of concepts.

9.2.1 Generalization, specialization, and inheritance

For years, inheritance was considered the most important feature of object-oriented languages. Languages such as Smalltalk, for example, were built over a single hierarchy of classes based on inheritance.

As time went by, this emphasis lost strength, because it was perceived that inheritance is not always the best idea for solving modeling problems. Today, inheritance is considered just one of the techniques that help to factorize information that otherwise would be repeated in classes.

Inheritance, in object-oriented systems, occurs when two classes relate through a special association called a *generalization* (or a *specialization*, depending on the direction you look). A class that generalizes another class is its *superclass*, and the specialized one is the *subclass*.

Generalization should be used every time there is a set of classes $X_1, \ldots, X_n$ that have specific differences and common similarities, so that the similarities can be grouped in a superclass X (generalization of $X_1, \ldots, X_n$) and the differences maintained in $X_1, \ldots, X_n$.

Generalization/specialization has a semantic much different from the other associations of the conceptual model. It exists only between classes, not between instances as normal associations do. For example, if a class *Reviewer* is associated to the class *Assessment* by a normal association, then instances of *Reviewer* may be linked to instances of *Assessment*: the normal association allows those links to exist.

---

[1] More specifically, an object is also an instance of all of its superclasses. The idea is that the set of superclasses should not change after the instance is created.

On the other hand, if a class *BankAccount* is a generalization of *CheckAccount*, then every instance of *CheckAccount* is *also* an instance of *BankAccount* (Fig. 9–11). There are not two instances to be linked, just one instance with the properties defined in both classes.

In the example, every instance of *CheckAccount* has three attributes: *number, overdraft_limit*, and *overdraft_fee*. However, not every instance of *BankAccount* is an instance of *CheckAccount*: the generalization is antisymmetric. An instance of *BankAccount* has only one attribute: *number*.

Thus one of the reasons to use inheritance is when there are some similar properties (attributes, associations, or methods) in different classes, which may be factorized in an abstract construct such as a superclass.

If the superclass may have its own instances, then it is a normal class. However, most of the time superclasses are defined not to allow direct instances: only their subclasses may have instances. In this case, the superclasses are considered *abstract* classes. Abstract superclasses are represented in UML by a class with its name written in italic, or, more visibly, with the constraint {*abstract*} (Fig. 9–12).

In Fig. 9–12, the *BankAccount* class is abstract and therefore cannot have direct instances; only its subclasses may have instances. Instances of *CheckAccount* have *number, overdraft_limit*, and *overdraft_fee* as attributes; instances of *SavingsAccount* have *number* and *interest_rate* as attributes. Both subclasses also inherit the association to the class *Person*

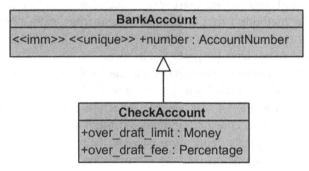

FIGURE 9–11 An example of generalization/specialization.

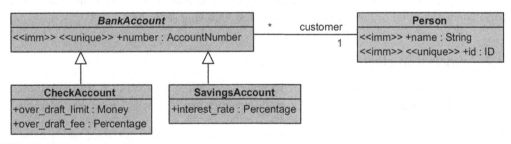

FIGURE 9–12 An example of abstract class.

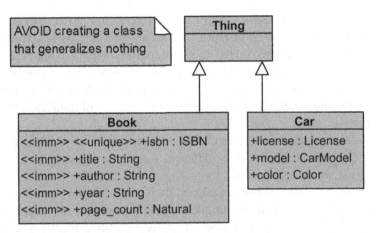

FIGURE 9-13 A case where a superclass is not necessary.

labeled as *customer*, and all instances of both classes must, therefore, be linked to an instance of *Person*.

Generalization in not advisable when the superclass has no properties, that is, no attributes, associations, or methods of its own (Fig. 9−13). In this example, *CarModel* and *Color* are enumerations.

Generalization should also not be used when subclasses do not have properties (attributes, associations, or methods[2]) that differentiate them from each other as in Fig. 9−14. One exception to this rule occurs when the superclass is abstract; in this case one, and just one, of its subclasses may not have properties of its own.

When subclasses do not have any properties, the ideal solution is to use a single attribute, possibly typed with an enumeration, to differentiate instance groups of objects (Fig. 9−15). In the example, we have considered that in some countries, name and gender may be changed legally. Thus we kept from considering those attributes immutable. Also, using an enumeration as gender, it is easier to add more genders if the requirements demand that; it should be only an update operation over an enumeration class. If subclasses were used, code should be written and compiled.

Besides these rules, before deciding on the use of inheritance, it is advisable to verify if the generalization really represents a structural classification of the elements and not an associative or temporal organization, as seen in the following sections.

9.2.2 Association classes

One issue frequently misunderstood in conceptual modeling is related to the definition of generalization among classes that are not really structural subtypes, but *roles*. For example, a

---

[2] Methods are only considered when design classes are being modeled. Remember that conceptual classes do not have methods.

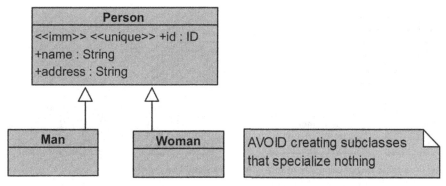

FIGURE 9–14 A case where subclasses are not necessary.

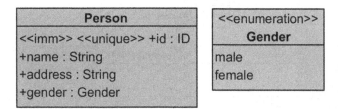

FIGURE 9–15 A better option for the situation of Fig. 9–14.

store may have two "types" of people: customers and workers. After discovering that both have a name, address, phone, etc., an analyst could assume that they are two concepts that should be generalized as *Person*. But that apparently simple solution (Fig. 9–16) generates a complicated problem because they are not different types of people, but different roles that people could play when relating to a company.

Why is this a problem? Imagine that a store worker decides to buy products at her workplace. In this case, the worker will be behaving like a customer. An unsuitable although very frequent solution to this is to create a second record for the worker as a customer, as if she was a different person. Consequently, the same person would have two records in the system: one as a worker and another as a customer. This produces data redundancy, and it is a source of data inconsistency, because, for example, if the worker record changes her address, the related customer record may keep the old address. Therefore as they are the same person, this information is inconsistent.

A more suitable solution is to consider that there exists a *Person* that may relate to a *Company* in at least two ways: as a customer and as a worker. The specific properties of a customer (credit limit, for instance), and of a worker (salary, for instance), would be properties of the associations and not of the person. To represent these association properties, an *association class* can be defined for each one, as shown in Fig. 9–17.

Therefore when the same object may play different roles related to other objects, these roles should not be represented as subclasses, but as *association classes*.

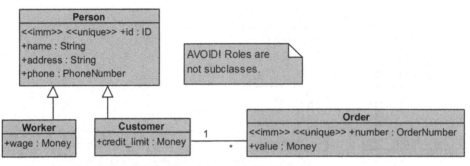

FIGURE 9–16 Unsuitable way of using inheritance when roles should be the case.

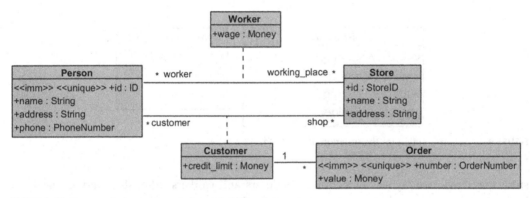

FIGURE 9–17 Concepts being represented as association classes.

To decide which situation demands inheritance and which situation demands association classes, it may be verified if the "subtypes" depend on the existence of a third class to make sense. If the "subtype" depends on a third class, then the solution consists of using an association class. For example, nobody may be simply an employee; if someone is an employee, then she must be associated to a company or at least to a boss.

Thus it is unsuitable to create classes that represent kinds of people that are not subclasses, but roles. Workers, teachers, students, principals, customers, etc., should not be subclasses of *Person*. Concepts like these only make sense if related to other concepts such as *Company*, *School*, and *Department*. A person may be worker *at* a company, student *at* a school, etc.

The difference between using an association class and an intermediary concept is subtle. Fig. 9–18 shows an example of a reservation being modeled as an intermediary concept (up) and as an association class (down).

In the case of Fig. 9–18 (up), a reservation associates a person to a flight. In the case of Fig. 9–18 (down), the person and the flight are directly associated, and the reservation is an association class.

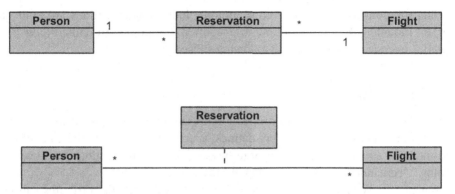

FIGURE 9–18 A reservation being modeled as an intermediary class and as an association class.

However, those representations are not equivalent. If an association class is used, then one person may have only one and just one reservation for a given flight. In the other case, the customer can have many reservations to the same flight.

9.3 Modal classes

Modal classes are used to model concepts with instances that can change from one state to another during their existence, changing, possibly, their properties' structure, including attributes, associations, and behavior. Although a few programming languages allow instances to change their structure by changing their class, this is not assumed as a modeling principle because such changes may create unpredictable structural problems and are usually unsafe.

Even if an instance could change its class, redefining its attributes and associations remains a problem. However, there are modeling techniques that allow to represent situations that would need objects that change class without using this feature. The idea is not to change the object class, but its *state*. For example, when a sale is paid, it does not become a new type of sale: it just changes its *state*.

Three increasingly complex situations related to state modeling may be identified:

- *Stable transition*: The different states of an object do not affect its structure, but only its property values (attributes and links). For example, a state may be represented by a single attribute.
- *Monotonic increasing transition*: As the object changes state, it may only keep its properties or acquire new ones. Associations and attributes can be gained, but not lost.

Nonmonotonic transition:[3] As the object changes state, it may keep, acquire, or lose properties. Associations and attributes may be gained and lost.

---

[3] The monotonic decreasing case can be considered here too (a transition that can only remove properties from an instance).

Modeling solutions for the stable and monotonic increasing transitions are quite simple. However, for modeling the nonmonotonic transition, a design pattern named *State* (Gamma et al., 1995) is necessary, as seen in the following subsections.

9.3.1 Stable transition

Frequently, different states of an object may be represented by a simple attribute. In fact, the set of all attributes and links of an object defines its state. For example, the state of an order could be modeled simply as a *state* attribute typed with an enumeration whose values may be "ongoing," "concluded," and "paid." (Fig. 9−19).

The transition is considered stable because just the value of the attributes can change. The inner structure of the object is kept the same. This does not happen with the two cases presented in the next subsections.

If all attributes are immutable, then the object cannot change state and behaves like a more complex constant.

9.3.2 Monotonic increasing transition

The situation is a bit more complex when the concept may acquire new attributes or associations as it changes state. For example, invoices that are waiting for payment have only *due_-date* and *due_value* as attributes. But an invoice that is paid additionally has *payment_date* and *paid_value* (Fig. 9−20).

It is said that the transition in Fig. 9−20 is *monotonic increasing* because new attributes and associations may be created for it, but not eliminated. This implies that a paid invoice cannot go back to be a new invoice again.

One solution that could be used in this case is to consider that the attributes that would be added after the object is created are optional, meaning that they can remain undefined until the invoice is paid. Fig. 9−21 shows optional attributes marked with the stereotype «*opt*». Although it may be a popular solution, it brings problems. First, it is necessary to assure that when *payment_date* is defined, *paid_value* would be too, and vice versa. An invariant could do the trick, if the team knows how to use them.

But this model is still not good because it generates a class with *low cohesion*, which has, in consequence, consistency rules that should be checked frequently. This kind of class is highly susceptible to programming errors.

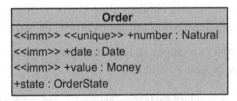
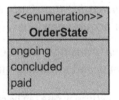

FIGURE 9–19 An example of a class with stable state transition.

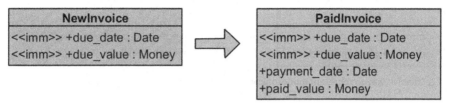

FIGURE 9–20 A class with monotonic increasing transition.

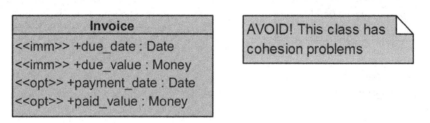

FIGURE 9–21 A class with optional attributes and cohesion problems.

It would be better to model the invoice concept so that the consistency of the objects could be constrained by the structure of the model itself and not by external rules. As it is a monotonic increasing transition, then it is possible to model this situation just by splitting the original concept in two: one that represents the invoice and another that represents its payment with the properties that were added when the payment occurred. These two concepts are, then, linked by a 1 to 0.1 association, as seen in Fig. 9–22.

Notice that in Fig. 9–22, the attributes that were optional before are now mandatory and immutable.

With the model presented in Fig. 9–22, it is impossible for an invoice to have a defined payment date and undefined paid value or vice versa. This is assured without performing any further verification on its attributes or associations.

We can still define the state of an invoice based on the existence or not of a payment. The state of an invoice can be, therefore, a derived attribute, which is calculated as follows: if there is no payment linked to the invoice, then the invoice is *new*; otherwise, it is *paid*. In OCL, that condition may be expressed as:

```
Context Invoice::InvoiceState
    derive:
        if self.payment->isEmpty() then
            InvoiceState::new
        else
            InvoiceState::paid
        Endif
```

This expression would be associated to the diagram shown in Fig. 9–23.

FIGURE 9–22 Effective way to represent monotonic increasing transition.

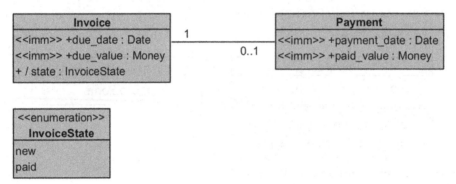

FIGURE 9–23 An invoice with a state as a derived attribute.

The expression above introduces two new OCL features:

- *if-then-else-endif*, which is one of the OCL selection functions and works like a *ternary* on programming languages. If the condition after the *if* is true, then the function results in the evaluation of the expression after the *then*; otherwise, it results in the evaluation of the expression after the *else*.
- *isEmpty()*, which is a function applied to a collection structure and returns *true* if the collection is empty and false otherwise. It is an easy way to check if there is some object linked to another object or not.

9.3.3 Nonmonotonic transition

With *nonmonotonic transition,* an object may both gain and lose properties as it changes its state.

Fortunately, it is not frequent that an information system requires any information to be *lost*. However, sometimes, that can be exactly what should be done.

For example, there are many ways to conceive and model a reservation system for a hotel. One of them consists of regarding the hosting as an entity that evolves from a reservation in three steps:

1. Initially, a potential guest makes a reservation indicating the days she intends to arrive and depart, the kind of accommodation, and the number of people. The hotel provides the fee.
2. When the guest checks in, the arrival date is registered (it may be the same date of the reservation or a different date). The hotel assigns a room that may be different from the one initially reserved if agreed and, if this is the case, it informs the guest of the new fee. The expected date of departure continues to exist, although it can be updated during the stay.

3. When the guest checks out, the expected departure date ceases to exist and the effective departure date is registered, and the bill must be paid.

This set of states may be modeled during business analysis with a state machine diagram like the one in Fig. 9–24.

If a hosting just acquires new attributes and associations as it evolves through the states of Fig. 9–24, then it could be represented by a chain of concepts such as *Reservation/CheckIn/ChechOut* shown in Fig. 9–25.

However, although usually we do not want to delete information there can be situations in which this is required by law (e.g., if there are data protection laws), or simply it may appear to be the right thing to do.

Thus we will consider that in our example, when a guest checks in, the estimated arrival is not necessary anymore and that it should be removed from the information system. The same happens to the estimated leave, after check-out. One solution would be simply erasing the value of the attributes *estimated_arrival* and *estimated_leave* in class *Reservation*. But in this case, the attributes are kept existing. Only their value would be nullified, and as they cannot be immutable the possibility of redefining those attributes after the lodging in finished would remain. Thus we need a way to remove those attributes from the system, not only their values.

Maybe the better possibility to represent this kind of situation is to use a design pattern known as *State* (Gamma et al., 1995). According to this pattern, a class should be separated

FIGURE 9–24 A state machine diagram modeling a simple hosting.

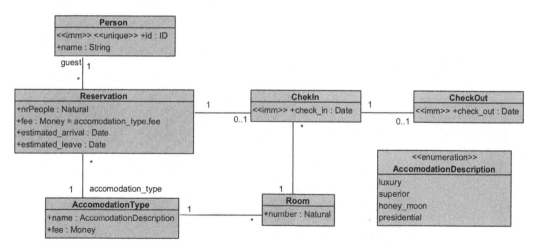

FIGURE 9–25 Possible model for reservations as monotonic increasing transitions.

from its states. Properties that are shared by all states are kept in the original class, and properties that belong only to one or a few states are moved to the respective states. These states are specializations of an abstract class, as shown in Fig. 9–26. Wait? Is it not the case that HostingState is not generalizing any property? No, this class is generalizing the association with class *Hosting*.

In Fig. 9–26, the attributes *nrPeople* and *fee* exist in every possible state of a hosting, and this is why they are represented in the hosting *Hosting* class that separates a reservation from its state. The other properties are distributed among the three possible states:

- *Reservation*: A hosting, in addition to the number of people and fee, has estimated arrival and leaving dates and the accommodation type (not yet a room), from which the initial value for the hosting fee is obtained.
- *CurrentLodging*: A hosting, in addition to the number of people and fee, has an immutable check-in date, estimated leaving date, and a room assigned. The *estimated_arrival* attribute and the straight link to the accommodation type are not necessary anymore and do not exist in this state.
- *FinishedLodging*: A hosting, in addition to the number of people and fee, has immutable check-in and check-out dates, and a room assigned. The estimated leaving date is not necessary anymore and does not exist in this state.

From the point of view of a *Room*, it can now be linked to at most one *CurrentLodging* (0..1), but it can be associated to many *FinishedLodging* (*). This way, the temporal property of that association is already modeled too, because the association of a room to lodging may be at most one in the present, but many in the past.

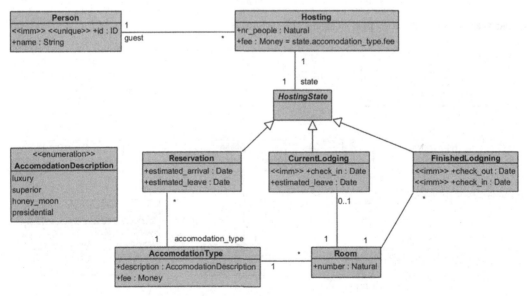

FIGURE 9–26 Nonmonotonic state transitions modeled with the *State* design pattern.

9.4 Invariants

There are situations where the expressivity of the diagrams is not enough to represent rules that should be recorded in the conceptual model. In some of these cases, the team should use *invariants*.

Invariants are general constraints over all instances of a given class. Some constraints are represented in the association roles when a multiplicity different from "*" is used.

However, not every possible constraint may be represented in the association roles. Consider the model shown in Fig. 9–27 that represents a situation in that a student may be registered in different courses, but the maximum limit is not the number of courses, but the number of weekly hours.

The maximum number of hours of a career may be represented as an attribute of the career, because it may be different for different instances of this class. Any course in this career has its number of hours, and the number of hours spent by a student is the sum of the number of hours of the courses he is registered in. The invariant is represented close to the name of class *Student*. It is the abbreviated form of the following OCL expression:

```
Context Student
       inv:
              self.courses->sum(:a_course|
                  a_course.hours
              ) <= self.career.max_hours
```

The expression "*sum*" in OCL is an operation that can be applied to collections. For each element in the collection, it evaluates the expression between parenthesis, which must denotate a numeric value, and produces the summatory of those values. If there is no expression between parenthesis, then it considers that it is being sent to a collection of numbers and proceeds to their summation. Thus the expression *courses->sum(hours)* could be, in principle, also written as *courses.hours->sum()*. However, as the default collection in OCL is the set, the result, in this case would not be correct, because a set does not allow a value to be

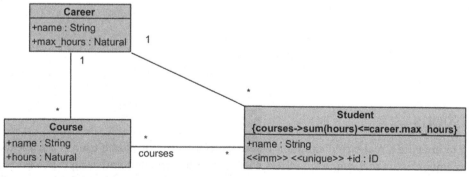

FIGURE 9–27 An example of a class with an invariant.

repeated. Thus if there are two or more courses with the same number of hours, only one occurrence would be added to the sum.

Another solution to this problem is to convert the set into a bag before taking the hours. OCL has messages to convert data structures, and in order to convert any other collection into a bag, the message "*asBag()*" may be used. Thus the expression can also be represented correctly as: *courses - > asBag().hours- > sum()*.

Observe that the invariant declaration in OCL does not have a subcontext; it must be true for every instance of the class, not for a particular attribute or association role.

Many software developers, when faced with the need to use constrains such as invariants, choose to incorporate these rules in methods that update the attributes and links of the objects. However, this approach may be riskier and more laborious.

The model presented in Fig. 9–27, however, may still have a problem. As it is, it allows a student to register in any course, no matter which career it belongs. If the business rule states that a student must only register in courses belonging to her career, another invariant should be used. A first approach to it could be something like:

```
Context Student
    inv:
        self.courses.career=self.career
```

The expression uses a feature of sets (not allowing elements to be repeated) to verify that all courses taken by the student belong to the student's career. The expression *self.career* results in the student's career (a set with a single element because of the multiplicity of the role from student to career). On the other hand, the expression *self.courses.career* results in the set of all careers associated to all courses taken by the student. If there are courses from different careers, then that set could not be equal to *self.career* (which has a single element). Otherwise, if all careers are the same, then the set *self.course.career* will contain a single element (because sets do not repeat elements). If that element is the same as *self.career*, then the invariant will be true and valid.

However, this expression is still incomplete, because if the student is not registered in any course, the expression *self.courses* will result in the empty set and therefore, *self.courses.career* will also be an empty set and so, different from *self.career*. To resolve this, a ternary can be used:

```
Context Student
    if self.courses->isEmpty() then
        True
    else
        self.courses.career=self.career
```

Questions

1. Try to imagine a real-world situation where the right structure to be used is a *sequence*. Remember that a real sequence allows elements to be repeated and assigns position to elements. Try not to get fooled by natural language use of the word "list." A "grocery list," for example, is not a sequence, because elements do not repeat and their position is irrelevant. Also, a student roll call may be organized in alphabetical order, but again, repetition is not allowed, and the order is again irrelevant although convenient for searching. Thus those are not real sequences.

2. Elaborate a list of concepts and subconcepts (subtypes of the original concept, e.g., *dog* and *beagle*) from common sense. Then, try to identify the type of each relation: structural, associative, or temporal. Try to have at least one example of each type in your list.
3. Try to elaborate three real-world examples of map, partition, and relation.
4. What is the difference between using an association class and an intermediate class?
5. Try to develop a real-world model that needs an invariant to be correct.

10 ▦

From use cases to conceptual model

Key topics in this chapter

- Finding Classes and Attributes
- Discovering Associations
- Independent and Dependent Concepts
- Iterative Construction of the Conceptual Model

10.1 Iterative construction of the conceptual model

This section shows how the conceptual model can be refined with information from the expanded use cases. Initially, we discuss how to find concepts and attributes from the use case texts. Next, we discuss how to identify new associations for the model. Finally, we present a complete example with some use cases from the first iterations of the SISMOB project and their contribution to the conceptual model.

10.2 How to find concepts and attributes

The process of discovering the elements of the conceptual model may vary. However, one of the most useful techniques is to look at the text of the expanded use cases or system sequence diagrams. From those artifacts, one can discover all textual elements that eventually refer to information to be managed.

Usually, these textual elements are composed of *nouns* such as "person," "order," "payment" or by expressions that denote nouns (known in linguistics as *noun phrases*), such as "payment authorization." Moreover, sometimes even verbs may represent concepts, when verbs express an act that corresponds to a noun, for example, the verb "to pay," which corresponds to the noun "payment."

The team should mind the project goals and scope when looking for the elements of the conceptual model. It is not advisable to represent information that is irrelevant to the system in the conceptual model. Thus not every noun, adjective, or verb should be considered as a model element. The team is responsible for understanding which expressions represent useful information for the system.

The process of identification of concepts and attributes consists of the following:

1. Identify in the expanded use case text or in the arguments of the operations in the system sequence diagram the words or phrases that correspond to concepts that are relevant to the system and therefore, must be maintained.

Object-Oriented Analysis and Design for Information Systems. DOI: https://doi.org/10.1016/B978-0-443-13739-6.00005-8

2. Group words or phrases that refer to the same entity, for example, "buy" and "acquisition," "customer" and "client," etc.

3. Decide which of the identified elements are complex concepts and which are mere attributes. Usually, attributes are the elements that may be considered alphanumeric (names, numbers, codes, monetary values, Boolean values, etc.), enumerations, or primitive (dates, ISBNs, etc.).

Even if there is no preliminary conceptual model, then, the first use case analyzed will be used to identify the first concepts. However, it is better if a structure like a preliminary conceptual model is available, because a better vision of the whole system is at hand in this case. If the preliminary conceptual model already exists, then the use cases will help to refine the model, indicating new concepts, new attributes, new associations, or structure changes.

If the team prioritizes the more complex use cases to be analyzed first, then significant new information may be added to the model quickly.

10.3 Dependent and independent concepts

A concept is *dependent* from others if it needs to be associated to them to make sense, that is, to represent information that is minimally meaningful.[1] For example, an assessment, as a single instance of class *Assessment*, alone does not have a complete meaning; the author of the assessment could remain unknown, but the object assessed must be known so that the assessment is meaningful.

A concept is *independent* if it has a meaning even without being associated to others.[2] For example, the *Person* concept may be understood just from its attributes, without being associated to other concepts. The existing associations for a person are optional. Thus the *Person* concept, in that sense, is independent.

But what purpose does this distinction serve? It was discussed before that only the simplest concepts may be managed by CRUDL use cases. This definition in most cases will include independent concepts, that is, usually, independent concepts are manageable by CRUDL.

However, dependent concepts should not be considered so simple in principle, because they have to be associated to others from the beginning, and this introduces complexity.

Concepts that are managed by CRUDL use cases are usually those that can be accessed directly when information is being retrieved from a system. If the team uses the controller-façade class in the conceptual model, in principle, the independent concepts must have mandatory links to the controller class. Being linked to the controller class means that the instances of the class may be accessed directly by it. For example, an instance of *Person* may be accessed directly by the controller by using its *id*. However, an instance of *Assessment* is not necessarily accessible directly by the controller.

---

[1] There is a parallel between dependent concepts and transitive verbs. The sentence "He opened" does not make sense, because the verb needs a complement, as for example, "He opened the can."

[2] A parallel exists between independent concepts and intransitive verbs. The sentence "He slept" makes sense because the verb does not require a complement. However, even intransitive verbs may have supplemental information (e.g., "He slept for 3 hours"), and independent concepts also may have such complements.

Therefore dependent classes in principle are not linked to the controller. But they may require a direct link in some cases. Although this is somewhat redundant, it may be the case. Fortunately, there are mechanisms to prevent this redundancy to become a problem.

10.4 How to find associations

If the information related to concepts and attributes is easily found in the use case texts, this is not the case for associations. As mentioned before, use cases contain references to operations that transform information, but when it is the case for associations, they are not so easily found.

So, how do we find associations between complex concepts? There are at least two rules that can be used:

- *Dependent concepts* (such as *Project*, *Assessment*, and *Cancellation*) should be necessarily associated to the concepts that complement them (which may be dependent or independent). The role opposite to the dependent concept is usually mandatory in this case, meaning that dependent objects are created with that role already filled.
- *Associative information*, that is, associations that are not mandatory but that add new information to the model should be represented by associations. For example, *Person* and *Car* may be considered independent concepts; however, they can be associated by a variety of modes, such as "owner," "driver," and "passenger."

Sometimes, associative information appears in the use case texts as concepts. For example, an order could be thought as an association between a customer and products, but it is sufficiently complex to be represented as a concept, because it has at least some attributes that must be owned by the association itself. In this case, an *intermediary concept* between *Order* and *Product* is necessary. If this intermediary concept is *Item*, then it should be associated to both *Order* and *Product* to make sense, because it is a dependent concept.

Let us talk a little about a mistake that sometimes happen. Complex concepts must be linked only by associations, meaning that one complex concept must not have an attribute typed with the name of another complex concept. If the team detects attributes with that characteristics, they should replace them by associations as soon as possible.

It is also not recommended to use alphanumeric attributes as *foreign keys* (Date, 1982). For example, if a *Car* has an attribute like *owner_id:ID*, we do not have the case of an attribute being typed by a complex concept name. However, the intention here is clear: the attribute *owner_id* is a reference to an instance of class *Person*. This must be avoided too, and this attribute is replaced by an association between the two concepts.

10.5 Example of iterative construction of the conceptual model

Let us proceed with a demonstration on how to evolve and refine a conceptual model by using expanded use cases. First, let us recall the preliminary conceptual model for the SISMOB project shown in Figure 4−5 and now presented also in Fig. 10−1.

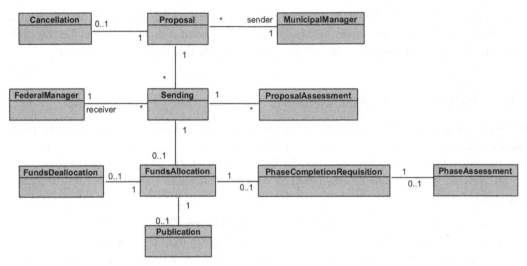

FIGURE 10–1 Preliminary conceptual model serving as example.

Notice that associations and their multiplicity are already present in the diagram as they were induced before by analyzing concepts and their dependencies. In this figure, we have already identified the roles of sender and receiver of a proposal, but they will be changed soon.

Initially, we should analyze the most complex use cases (save the CRUDL and reports for later). It is a temptation to start analyzing use cases by chronological order, starting, for example, with the use case that allows a municipal manager to introduce a proposal in the system. But we do not have to necessarily follow this order. Starting by the most complex use cases helps the team to cope with complexity in the beginning of the development process, and thus it may mitigate a lot of project risks as well as avoiding the need to refactor the model to accommodate complex use cases that were left to be analyzed later in the process.

So, we can begin by analyzing the use case already expanded in Chapter 6, "Produce proposal assessment." First thing to do is to mark nouns, noun phrases, adjectives, and even verbs that are candidate concepts. This is done below by using underline or double brackets.

Use Case: Produce proposal assessment (main flow)

1. «Reviewer» search for «process».
2. System presents list of «processes» allocated to reviewer, newest first.
3. Reviewer selects process.
4. System presents «process name», «status», «priority», and «validity».
5. Reviewer registers assessment and «conclusion». [V1]
6. System confirms operation.

   Variant V1: User decides to save for continuing latter.

   V1.1 Reviewer registers assessment and saves it.
   V1.2 System confirms that the assessment is saved.
   V1.3 Use case ends.

Exception E1: Deadline reached BR-FNS.01.

E1.1 System presents message MODAL.114.
E1.2 User acknowledges.
E1.3 Use case fails.

Exception E2: Proposal was not prioritized BR-FNS.06.

E2.1 System presents message MODAL.371.
E2.2 User acknowledges.
E2.3 Use case fails.

In this use case, specifically, only the main flow produced interesting candidates. We put brackets in "processes" in line 2 because there is a clue here that there are many assessments allocated to a reviewer (an association!) and that this queue is sorted or at least ordered.

Thinking about synonyms, maybe at this time the team would perceive that the term "project" is being used. Is this the same thing as "proposal"? The conceptual model uses that name to identify a concept that seems to coincide with the idea of project in the use case. As this is exactly the case, the team may rewrite the use case by replacing the term "project" by the more adequate term "proposal." Who decides on the more appropriate name is the user/client.

In this example, one new concept is revealed: *Reviewer* (or may it be a role?). *Proposal* and *Assessment* already belong to the model. The terms "reviewer" and "project" are repeated in the text and do not need to be marked more than once. Moreover, new attributes of *Proposal* are discovered now: *name*, *status*, *priority*, and *validity*. They must be introduced in the conceptual model.

It was created also an enumeration, *ProposalStatus*, the values of which are not yet known. This lack of information could be written at this time at the CSD matrix as a doubt to be answered by users or client later if they are not available immediately.

Also, it is observed in line 5 that the assessment has a conclusion, and it is a strong candidate for an attribute: a flag that indicates the state of the assessment.

Notice also that the attributes *concluded* and *text* of class *Assessment* should be added.

Finally, and more subtle, as the user may search proposals directly and choosing one to work with it may indicate that proposals must have an unique identification, and therefore, a potentially hidden attribute, but let us leave it public for now.

A deeper exam of the use case may show that when information about a proposal is shown an incomplete assessment could also be shown so that the user may finish it. This demands a modification on the use case for better conformance.

Thus, before going to the conceptual model, let us see how the use case seems after those discoveries. Only the main flow was modified and is shown below.

Use Case: Produce proposal assessment (main flow)

1. ≪ Reviewer ≫ searches for ≪ proposal ≫.

2. System presents list of «proposals» allocated to reviewer, newest first.
3. Reviewer selects proposal.
4. System presents «proposal name», «status», «priority», and «validity». It also shows the current saved version of the assessment if any, or empty string.
5. Reviewer updates assessment and «conclusion». [V1]
6. System confirms operation.

This revision of the requirements written in the use cases is normal and usually expected. And now, the refined conceptual mode can be seen in Fig. 10−2.

Now we are going to proceed with a change of perspective because as reviewers and federal and municipal managers are *roles* for people, it would be better to represent them as roles for the class *Person*. If those roles need any special attributes or associations later, they can be complemented by an association class each.

It can be seen in the model that *Sending* and *ProposalAssessment* should have a date each and that those dates must be not later than the date of the *validity* of the proposal. This can be represented by invariants in class *Sending* and *ProposalAssessment*. All those modifications are represented in Fig. 10−3.

Before analyzing another use case, let us observe that the role name "reviews" is applied to the class "*ProposalAssessment*." Are "review" and "assessment" synonyms? If they are, we should choose just one term to continue. This issue should be discussed with the user or client. For now, let us consider that they are in fact synonyms and that we chose to use the term "assessments" but to keep the class name "Reviewer." Thus the role name "reviews" must be changed to "assessments."

Next, we are going to analyze another use case for the same system. As suggested before, we would leave CRUDL and reports for later and try to explore first use cases that can help

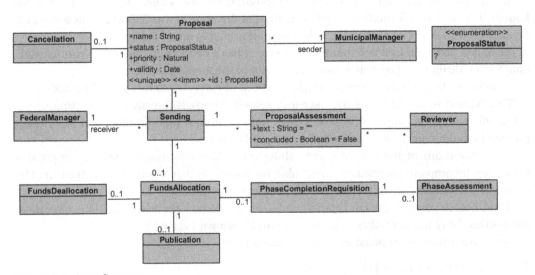

FIGURE 10–2 First refinement.

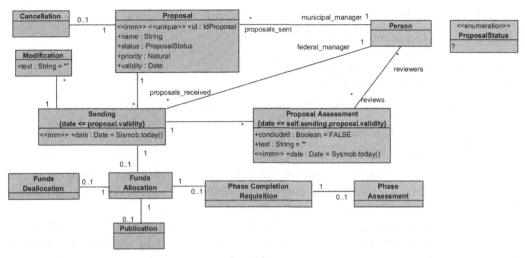

FIGURE 10–3 First refinement revised.

discovering new concepts, attributes, and associations. The use case "*Decide on proposal*" is associated to the federal manager, and a business rule states that a decision can only be taken after at least three assessments are available and necessarily before the deadline of the proposal. Considering the decision, the happy path is to continue with the project, but variants such as *cancellation* or *asking for modifications* are also possible.

Use Case: Decide on proposal (main flow)

1. Federal manager searches for «proposals qualified» to receive a «decision» (at least three assessments and before deadline).
2. System presents list of proposals, showing first the ones with «shorter deadline».
3. Federal manager selects proposal.
4. System presents proposal name, status, priority, validity, and the «list of assessments» attached.
5. Federal manager writes the «motivation» for her decision.
6. System confirms that all «conditions to decide» are ok. [E1]
7. Federal manager approves the «continuation» of the proposal. [V1] [V2]
8. System sends «email» to municipal manager.

Variant V1: Proposal is canceled

V1.1 Federal manager «cancels» the proposal.
V1.2 System sends email to municipal manager.
V1.3 Use case ends.

Variant V2: Proposal needs modifications

V2.1 Federal manager writes a «list of modifications» needed. [E2]
V2.2 System sends email to municipal manager.

V2.3 Use case ends.

Exception E1: Text of motivation is too «short»

E1.1 System presents message MODAL.482.
E1.2 Use case returns to main flow step 5.

Exception E2: Proposal needs modifications and the list of modifications is empty

E2.1 System presents message MODAL.483.
E2.2 Use case returns to step V2.1.

Just as before, first thing is to examine the text of the use case and marking words or expressions that are new candidates to concepts or attributes. To avoid repeating all the text of the use case, it was already done on its first presentation above.

Now, the use case is analyzed and compared with the conceptual model of Fig. 10–3.

In the first line of the main flow, we see that proposals must be qualified by having at least three assessments and being before deadline. Deadline is already an attribute of proposal (*validity*), but the limit number of three may be represented as a system variable accessible by a method such as *Sismob.minimum_assessments*(). Thus "qualified for decision" may be a derived attribute of class *Proposal*. However, when writing the OCL expression, the team may recall that a proposal may have multiple sendings and that the assessments are associated to the sendings and not to the proposal in order to allow many versions of the proposal to be analyzed. If the role from *Proposal* to *Sending* is marked with {*ordered*} «*stack*», then the most recent proposal can be retrieved by popping the top of the stack, which is the last element added.

The following OCL expression may represent it:

```
Context Proposal::qualified_for_decision:Boolean
    derive:
        self.sending->last().date <= self.validity
        AND self.sending->last().assessments->size()
            >= Sismob.minimum_assessments()
```

To avoid repeating the expression *self.sending->last*(), we can define a single identifier to this expression by using the "*def*": declaration of OCL:

```
Context Proposal::qualified_for_decision:Boolean
    def: last_sending = self.sending->last()
    derive:
        last_sending.date <= self.validity
        AND last_sending.assessments->size()
            >= Sismob.minimum_assessments()
```

Still in line 1, the federal manager should produce a decision that comes with a text and possibly an enumeration with *approved, canceled,* and *waiting_changes*. Those attributes may be represented in class *Sending*. As a decision is not necessarily made when the federal manager is attached to the sending, then both attributes may be optional ($\ll opt \gg$).

Continuing the analysis of the use case, in line 2, it is observed that the proposals are presented sorted by deadline proximity. Actions such as sorting lists may be done by the interface itself, but in this case, just to demonstrate the use of the controller class and a derived association, let us define a role from controller to proposal that consists of a sorted collection.

Thus the controller class may be included in the conceptual model and attached to the independent concepts that in this case are: *Person*, and? Just *Person*. All other concepts are dependent on another one. Then, a directed association from *Controller* to *Person* is added to the model.

In order to obtain a list of proposals sorted by deadline, we can create a derived association from *Controller* to *Proposal*. This association is *proposals_by_deadline*. We could, at this point, annotate in the CSD matrix a supposition: past deadline proposals are not shown in this list. Thus it must be confirmed later with the client, but now the team may assume it as true. Thus the OCL expression to define that derived association could be:

```
Context Controller::proposals_by_deadline: OrderedSet(Proposal)
    derive:
        self.person.proposals_sent->select(:proposal|
            proposal.validity < Sismob.today()
        )
        ->sortedBy(:proposal|
            proposal.validity
        )->asOrderedSet()
```

The first part of the expression is the filter "select" that returns only proposals for which deadlines are still valid. The function "*sortedBy*" places the objects in the set into an order that is given by the expression between parenthesis: *proposal.validity*. As *sortedBy* returns by default a sequence, we have changed it to be an ordered set by using *asOrderedSet()*.

In line 4, the "list of assessments" of a proposal may contain the assessments related to the last sending. This information can already be obtained in class *Proposal* by the OCL expression *self.sending->last()*.

In line 5, motivation is defined as an optional attribute of *Sending* that goes by the name *decision_motivation*.

In line 6, conditions to decide are a derived attribute of class *Proposal* named *qualified_for_decision*.

In Line 7, the continuation of a sending is represented by the optional attribute *final_status* in class *Sending*, which can receive one of the values of the new enumeration *DecisionType*.

Finally, the email mentioned in line 8 may be one of three kinds of preformatted texts including the decision motivation and final status. It reminds us that a Person, in this system, should have and email to receive communication. The attribute *email* added to class *Person* has a primitive type *Email* that checks its format.

In variant V1, the cancelation event is represented by one of the values of attribute *final_-status* of *Sending*.

The list of modifications mentioned in variant V2 could be a new optional attribute of *Sending*, or it can be considered as part of the text already in *decision_motivation*. It can be marked in the CSD matrix as a supposition that a new attribute is not necessary in this case. The team should opt for the simpler solution, but as this is not a certainty, it should be checked later with the user or client.

Exception E1 mentions the possibility of the motivation text to be too short. The minimum size can be stated in terms of characters and defined as a constant if it is a permanent requirement or as a system variable if it is a transient requirement. As the team does not know the value at this time, it should be marked as a doubt in the CSD matrix and resolved later. As in the case of a sorted list, this verification is purely syntactic, and it could be made by the interface itself. However, if the team prefers to represent it in the conceptual model, they should create a primitive type such as *MotivationText* that defines the acceptable sizes of this kind of text. Another option, more complicated, would be to create an invariant in class *Sending* stating that if the *decision_motivation* has a value, it should be a text with at least a certain number of characters.

Exception E2 mentions that the list of modifications may be empty. Well, this should make the team to revise a supposition from before and establishing the list of modifications as information to be associated to a sending. As it is a multivalued information, it cannot be an attribute of *Sending*, because we already mentioned that having attributes typed as collections is an antipattern that hinders the cohesion of the class. Thus *Modification* is added as a new class in the model, and it has a role "*" from *Sending* indicating that the "list" of modifications is in fact a set. If it was mentioned that the modifications have some type of priority, maybe that role could be changed to an OrderedSet, but there is no evidence for now that this is necessary. Fig. 10−4 shows the result after all those discoveries.

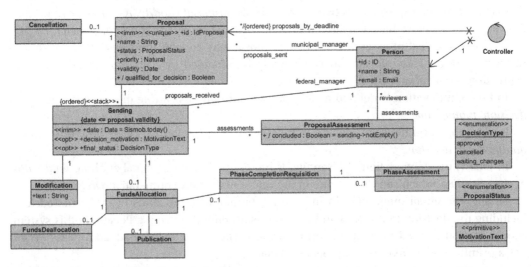

FIGURE 10−4 Conceptual model after analyzing a second use case.

Well, this finishes our presentation of this chapter. The team could continue to analyze other use cases and should continue to refine and complete the conceptual model from this point. As the more complex use cases are really examined before the others, it is expected that in the end of the process very few modifications would be necessary to the model because it would already have all important information. At this point, the team will be reaching a stable architecture, which is one of the conditions to start producing code.

Questions

1. What kinds of words are concepts and attribute candidates in the text of a use case?
2. How to differentiate concepts from attributes in the text of a use case?
3. How to find associations in the text of a use case?
4. What are dependent and independent concepts? Give three examples of each.
5. How to chose which use cases are going to be analyzed first?

11

Conceptual modeling: patterns

Key topics in this chapter

- High cohesion
- Specification classes
- Quantity
- Measure
- Strategy
- Composite
- Organizational hierarchy
- Account/transaction
- Interval
- Temporal patterns

11.1 Introduction to conceptual model patterns

Class diagrams that represent conceptual models almost always become more complex and harder to maintain than the team members would like. Naïve models may be unnecessarily complex. Fortunately, there exist techniques that reduce the complexity of such diagrams and, at the same time, improve their expressiveness.

These techniques are called *analysis patterns* and may be understood as a special case of *design patters* (Gamma et al., 1995) that are applied specifically to the conceptual model. Most patterns presented in this chapter were first described by Fowler (2003) and are here adapted to the UML notation and, sometimes, evolved.

Analysis or design patterns are not rules that must be obeyed, but recommendations based on previous experience. It is the responsibility of the analyst to decide when to apply a given pattern in the models.

11.2 High cohesion[1]

High cohesion is so important for object-oriented modeling that it is considered more a principle or guideline axiom than a pattern itself. A concept with high cohesion is more stable and reusable than a concept with low cohesion, which can become rapidly confusing and hard to maintain. Most systems could have all their information represented in a single table, but that would be an extreme worst case of low cohesion, and it would not be practical.

---

[1] Usually, high cohesion is mentioned in conjunction with *low coupling*. However, as coupling problems appear to emerge when object collaborations are designed, discussion on low coupling is left for a further chapter.

Object-Oriented Analysis and Design for Information Systems. DOI: https://doi.org/10.1016/B978-0-443-13739-6.00001-0

Almost every metric for class cohesion needs to compare attributes and methods (Miquirice and Wazlawick, 2018), and therefore, they may not be used during conceptual modeling, because methods are still missing from the model. In this chapter, however, we present not a metric, but a set of clues that may indicate that a class, even without its methods, is already suffering from cohesion problems.

Earlier, we mentioned that concepts should not have attributes that belong to other concepts (e.g., a car should not have the owner's ID as one of its attributes). Attributes also must not have class names or data structures (set, list, array, etc.) as data types because all those situations lead to low cohesion. A class with that kind of attribute is probably representing more than one single concept. For example, an instance of *Order* should not have an *items_list* attribute because items have their own attributes and associations; they should appear related to *Order* by a 1 to * association.

If a *Person* can have more than one address, instead of the naïve solution of creating attributes such as *address1*, *address2*, or even *address:Array < String>*, we should create a new concept (*Address*), which is associated to *Person*. Imagine how hard it would be to deal with the transformation of the single string address to a complex concept with attributes number, street, city, state, etc., if the addresses were modeled as multiple attributes or as an array of strings such as in Fig. 11−1.

The same Fig. 11−1 shows how to represent this concept by separating *Person's* attributes and *Addresses*.

Concepts and attributes should have a simple structure with high cohesion elements. Evidence of low cohesion includes scenarios where some attributes of a class may be null depending on the value of other attributes. If complex constraints (invariants) are necessary to keep a concept consistent, this is equivalent to using duct tape to keep the pieces of a broken pot together.

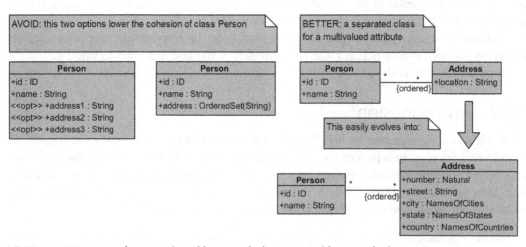

FIGURE 11–1 Naïve ways of representing addresses and a better way with more cohesion.

In Fig. 11–2, the attributes *paid_value* and *payment_date* are mutually dependent: either both are null, or both are not null. An invariant was added to the class to avoid the situation where one of them is null while the other is not, in order to avoid inconsistent instances. Invariants are good to represent business rules that must always be valid. But when an invariant just relates two attributes of a class like in this example, it is a strong clue of lack of cohesion.

A better way to model this situation is shown in Fig. 11–3, where the concepts *Order* and *Payment* appear separated but with high cohesion each one. In this case, there are no optional attributes depending on each other and *no need for constraints*.

Another potential problem related to low cohesion is the existence of groups of strongly correlated attributes, as seen in Fig. 11–4 where it can be observed that groups of attributes have stronger relations among them then outside the group. It happens to attributes such as *street, number, city*, and *state*, which together compose an address, or *ddd* (distance direct dialing) and *phone*, which are part of a complete phone number, or *passport_number* and *issuing_country*, which are part of passport information. In this figure, we have even used lines to divide the groups of strongly related attributes, but remember that this is not an UML notation, it is just a way to help in observing groups that are implicit in the set of attributes of the *Order* class.

The relation that exists inside each group appears implicitly in the position they are placed in the class description. This is bad, because if the attributes are moved from their original position, by being alphabetically sorted, for example, the weak structure of the groups would be messed up. The alphabetic order would be *city, ddd, issuing_country, name, number, passport_number, phone, state*, and *street* (see Fig. 11–5). Now it is harder to

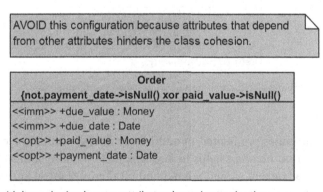

FIGURE 11–2 A class with low cohesion because attributes depend on each other.

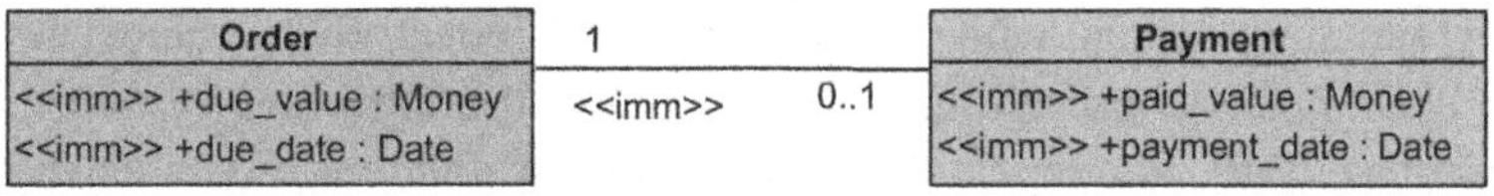

FIGURE 11–3 Modeling solution with high-cohesion classes.

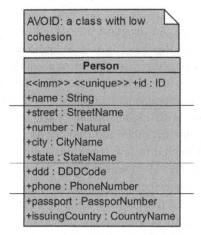

FIGURE 11–4 A class with low cohesion because of subgroups of strongly related attributes.

Person
+city : CityName
+ddd : DDDCode
<<imm>> <<unique>> +id : ID
+issuingCountry : CountryName
+name : String
+number : Natural
+passport : PassporNumber
+phone : PhoneNumber
+state : StateName
+street : StreetName

FIGURE 11–5 A class with attributes alphabetically sorted, which hinders comprehension.

comprehend which attributes are related to address, or phone number or passport, because they are mixed up, and no notation helps in knowing their weak relations. The understanding of the attributes of a concept should not depend on the ways those attributes are sorted.

A better solution to improve high cohesion in that model is shown in Fig. 11–6. This solution also eases the way to other modeling possibilities such as allowing a person to have more than one address or more than one phone or passport. In those cases, it is simply necessary to change the association role multiplicity.

Yet another situation occurs when some attributes repeat their values for a group of instances. Fig. 11–7 presents an example. In this figure, the attributes *customer_name, costumer_id,* and *customer_birth_date* repeat the same values for different orders when the customer is the same and has not changed her name, which is an extraordinarily rare situation.

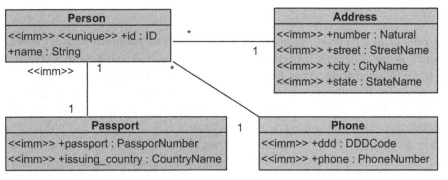

FIGURE 11–6 A model with classes with high cohesion.

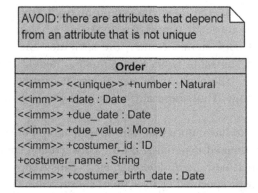

FIGURE 11–7 A class with low cohesion because it has attributes that repeat for a given set of instances.

FIGURE 11–8 A model with higher cohesion than the one in the last figure.

In database theory, we could say that in this case, the class has attributes that depend on another attribute that is not a *candidate key*. Namely, *costumer_name* and *costumer_birth_-date* both depend on *costumer_id*, and this last attribute is not unique for this class and therefore, not a candidate key.

This type of situation can be eliminated by splitting the concept into two associated concepts with better cohesion, as shown in Fig. 11−8. Notice that even attributes' names are shortened with this choice of model because they are not anymore misplaced attributes referring to another concept.

11.3 Specification classes

A special case of low cohesion happens when an object is confused with its specification. That situation is very frequent: sometimes, products or physical items share a common specification, while their exemplars may have some differences among them.

One example of specification is the difference between the concept of a book as a *published title* and a book as a *physical copy* of a published title. If both book concepts are not distinguished, lots of trouble will occur.

The class *Book* may refer to the published title, while *BookCopy* may stand for the physical copies. Thus an instance of *Book* is a *specification* for a set of instances of *BookCopy*, as seen in Fig. 11—9.

Depending on the information needs, it would be necessary to differentiate one copy from another. For example, if used books are to be sold, the conservation state should be kept for each copy. In this case, the *Book* class could be used as a specification for the class *BookCopy*, whose instances are single copies of a book.

The specification class *Book* should contain the attributes and associations that do not vary for different copies of the same book. For example, different copies of the same book have the same title, author, ISBN, base price, etc. However, conservation state and discount may be distinct for each copy. Thus these attributes (and associations, if any) are placed in the *BookCopy* class.

It is possible for a class to have more than one specification. For example, the discount of the book could be predetermined depending on the conservation state of the book (an enumeration with values such as new, *used, damaged*, etc.). Thus a copy, besides being specified by the published title, may be specified by its state of conservation. Thus *Conservation* would be a class with some instances that will associate the conservation state of any book with a predetermined discount. For example, all new books may have 0%, all used books, 10% and all damaged books 50%. This new situation is shown in Fig. 11—10.

The instances of class *Conservation* have two attributes. The first is the conservation state, which is a value obtained from the enumeration *ConservationState*. There are initially only three possible values: *new, used*, and *damaged*, which means that this class may only have three instances at maximum. The second attribute is the discount percentage that would be applied to

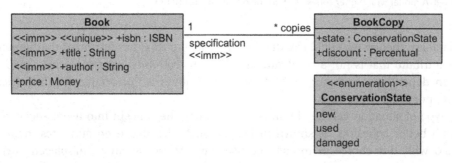

FIGURE 11–9 A class and its specification.

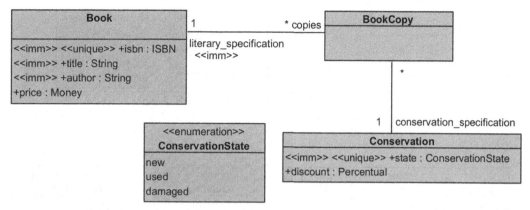

FIGURE 11–10 A class with two orthogonal specifications.

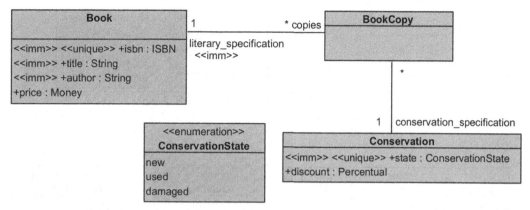

FIGURE 11–11 A class where a quantity is expressed by a predefined unity.

a copy depending on its conservation state. As it is expected that books with the same conservation state have the same discount, then the attribute *state* in class *Conservation* must be unique.

If that attribute was not unique, then the class *Conservation* could have any number of instances and different values of discount could be associated with the same conservation status.

11.4 Quantity

Frequently, the team faces the need to model quantities that are not merely numbers. For example, the weight of a book could be defined as 400. But 400 what? Grams? Pounds? Kilos? One solution is to define a specific type for the weight (*Pound*, for example), and then keep using it consistently. The attribute then could be declared as *weight:Pound* as seen in Fig. 11–11. But that demands that all books have their weight expressed in pounds.

In some cases, however, the system must be configurable to support different weight units. In some countries, grams and kilograms are used, while others use pounds, or even other units. If the attribute has a type that refers to a specific unit, then the system should suffer refactoring to accommodate new weight units.

However, the *Quantity* pattern allows different unit systems to coexist and to be easily exchangeable. The pattern consists of creating a new primitive type named *Quantity*, which has two attributes, *value* and *unit*, as shown in Fig. 11–12.

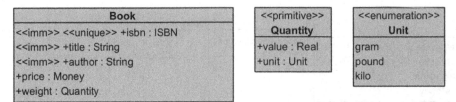

FIGURE 11–12 An example of use of pattern *Quantity*.

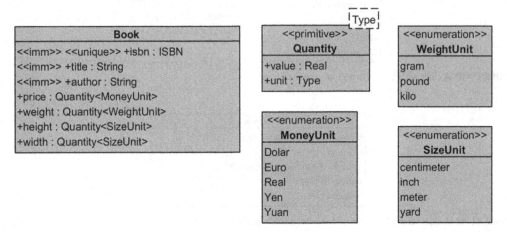

FIGURE 11–13 Different kinds of specialized units.

This way, the weight of each book is specified as a primitive quantity formed by a numeric *value* and a *unit*, whose type is an enumeration with possible values defined as *grams, pounds,* and *kilos.*

11.4.1 Different units

If different kinds of measures are necessary, then the units may be specialized, for example, time units, weight units, and size/distance units. One example is shown in Fig. 11–13.

In this figure, we introduce the concept of *genericity* or *generic class*, which is the case of class *Quantity* that can be instantiated necessarily with an existing type being bound to the parameter "*Type*." For example, *Quantity < SizeUnit >* is instantiated with attribute *unit* being typed with *SizeUnit*, which replaces *Type*. In this example, besides defining *WeigthUnit* and *SizeUnit* respectively to represent the weight of a book and its dimensions, we take the liberty to internationalize the *price* attribute of *Book*, by using *Quantity < MoneyUnit >* as type (let us assume that the user demanded that).

11.4.2 Unit conversion

If a unit conversion is needed, then an option is to use a new class *QuantitySpecification* that has a qualified association to the new class *Ratio*. This is an interesting kind of qualifier because the instance of *Ratio* is qualified by a derived attribute *destiny_unit*, which belongs to the class *QuantitySpecification*, but that is accessed by a different association (*destiny*). See Fig. 11−14 for more details.

From the point of view of the class *Ratio*, it has two associations with multiplicity 1 to the class *QuantitySpecification*. One is *origin* and the other is *destiny*. The class *Ratio* also has an attribute called *divider*. Its meaning is the following: the unit type in *origin* can be converted to the unit type in *destiny* if the value related to *origin* is divided by *divisor*. For example, if the *origin* is kilometer and the *destiny* is meter, then the *divider* must be 1000. More specifically, 5500 m divided by 1000 are equal to 5.5 km. Notice that there must exist an instance of *Ratio*, which is linked to *origin* kilometer and *destiny* meter and with divisor 1000.

Those ratios may be also used in OCL expression. Suppose that we want to return the value of the attribute *distance* from some class and necessarily converting it to kilometers (does not matter the original unit in which it is recorded), we could write an expression like this:

```
Context Anyclass::distance_as_kilometers(an_object):Float

    body:

        an_object.distance.value /

        an_object.distance.unit.destiny_unit[kilometers].divider
```

Here, *Anyclass::distance_as_kilometers* is the class and query we are defining. It returns a float number that we expect to be in kilometers. The argument *an_object* that is received should have an attribute named *distance* and its *unit* may be anyone, but hopefully a *DistanceUnit*. We can access the correct *Ratio* instance that converts any existing type of

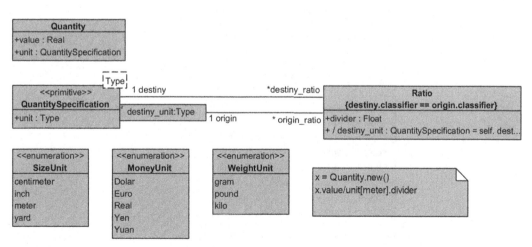

FIGURE 11–14 An extension of pattern Quantity with conversion ratios.

DistanceUnit into kilometers by writing *an_object.distance.unit.destiny_unit[kilometers]*. Notice that this is an association qualified by a derived attribute. Having the right *Ratio*, it is sufficient to divide the value of the original object by the *divisor*, which is an attribute of *Ratio*. The result value of this query is the quantity expressed in kilometers.

Notice that this approach works with many kinds of magnitude, except for temperature, as the different scales of temperature do not make the zero mark coincident to the others, which is a precondition to use *Ratio*. In those cases, special classes could do the mathematics in the place of *Ratio*.

11.5 Measure

An evolution of the *Quantity* pattern is the *Measure* pattern, which can be used when some different measures over an object must be taken possibly at different times. For example, a person in observation at a hospital may have many measures taken from time to time: body temperature, blood pressure, blood glucose level, etc. Thousands of different measures could be taken, but usually just a few are actually necessary for each patient. Therefore to avoid creating a concept with thousands of attributes with most of them likely being null, such as seen in Fig. 11−15, a better option is to use the *Measure* pattern as shown in Fig. 11−16.

Thus a patient may have a series of measures taken, each one assessing a different phenomenon and presenting a value that corresponds to a quantity (following the *Quantity* pattern).

It is still possible to make these patterns a little more sophisticated by adding attributes in the *Measure* class to indicate the instant of time at which the measure was taken and the validity of the measure. For example, the fact that a patient had a fever a couple of hours ago does not mean that she still has it. Instead of representing two attributes, one for time of

AVOID: A single class have a great number of readings which are not mandatory

Patient
+id : ID
+name : String
<<opt>> +age : Natural
<<opt>> +blood_pressure : Quantity
<<opt>> +temperature : Quantity
<<opt>> +height : Quantity
<<opt>> +weight : Quantity
<<opt>> +hart_frequency : Quantity
<<opt>> +glucose : Quantity
+an_so_on : ...

FIGURE 11–15 A class with too many optional attributes referring to readings about a patient.

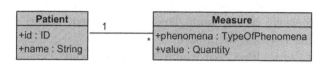
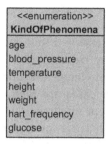

FIGURE 11–16 An example of application of pattern *Measure*.

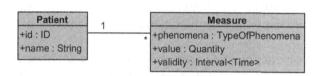
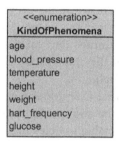

FIGURE 11–17 A sophistication of pattern *Measure* with an interval of validity.

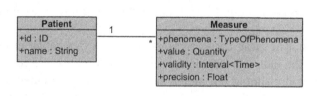

FIGURE 11–18 An evolution of *Measure* adding precision to its instances.

measure and another for time of validity, we used the pattern *Interval*, that is explained later in this chapter. It means that any measure has an interval of validity that in this case is composed of two instants of *Time*, as the genericity class is referred here as *Interval < Time>*. See Fig. 11−17.

Another evolution for this pattern is to add an attribute to define the *precision* or *accuracy* of the measure taken. For example, body temperature usually is measured with a precision of 0.1 degrees (Celsius or Fahrenheit). Weight of a person is usually measured with a precision of a pound or kilo, and so on. A precision of 0.001 means that some measure has a precision of three decimal places. See Fig. 11−18.

11.6 Strategy

It was mentioned that one of the great requirements challenges is to manage their change. Transitory requirements must especially be accommodated in the system design so that when they change, the impact to the system is minimized.

Some cases are relatively easy to address. For example, if it is already decided that the system must operate in different countries, the *quantity* pattern could be used to deal with currency and other measures that may vary from country to country as we already seen.

But there are much more complicated situations. For example, the tax calculation procedure may vary a lot from country to country and even from State to State in some countries. There are some taxes that are calculated in relation to the profit, others regarding the selling price, and so on. Methods for calculating taxes change from time to time, and in some countries new taxes are created every year. Systems must be prepared to cope with that, but the changes are completely unpredictable. Just configuring parameters usually is not enough.

Another example is a store's discount policy. Current policy could be applying 10% off on orders above 100 dollars, for example. However, after some time, creative and unpredictable policies may be defined by the sales department, such as:

- Give a free book with a value up to 50 dollars for orders above 300 dollars.
- Give 20% off for up to two books on the customer's birthday.
- Give 5% off on horror books on Friday the 13th.
- The customer spins a wheel, and it defines the discount she receives, from 1% to 10%.

Moreover, it would be possible to combine policies, if applicable, or choose the one that gives the higher discount.

The *Strategy* pattern suggests that in these cases, the procedure (e.g., calculate taxes or discount) must be separated from the data to which it applies. In other words, if a discount is applied to an order, then the discount should not merely be a method implemented in the *Order* class. The discount should be defined as something easier to change. The solution proposed by the *Strategy* pattern is to create an abstract class associated to the order. This abstract class may have concrete subclasses that represent concrete discount policies, as shown in Fig. 11−19.

Thus each instance of *Order* is associated to an instance of one of the subclasses of the *Discount* strategy. UML does not allow an attribute to be declared {*abstract*}; only classes and methods may be declared so. However, as derived attributes will be implemented by methods eventually, the idea of an *abstract derived attribute* stereotyped with «*abstract*» as shown in Fig. 11−19 is coherent to the UML spirit.

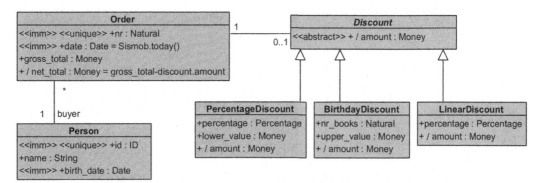

FIGURE 11-19 Strategy pattern.

Thus the abstract class *Discount* implements an abstract derived attribute *amount*, which is implemented in a concrete way in each of its subclasses. If some of the strategies need data from the customer or from the order to calculate the discount, that data can be accessed through the associations from the discount abstract class to the classes that own the information.

To complete the example of Fig. 11−19, the definition of the *amount* of each discount strategy is given below:

```
Context PercentageDiscount::amount:Money

    def: gross = self.order.gross_total

    derive:

        if gross >= self.lower_value then

            self.percentage * gross

        else

            0

        endIf
```

In this case above, if the gross total of the order is higher than the lower value of the discount, a percentage of discount is applied to the gross total, otherwise zero discount is applied. Other strategy is:

```
Context BirthdayDiscount::amount:Money

   def:

      birthday = self.order.buyer.birth_date

      today = System.today()

   derive:

      if birthday.day() = today.day()

      AND birthday.month() = today.month() then

         percentage * self.order.gross_total

      else

         0

      endIf
```

In this case above, if today is the birthday of the buyer, a linear discount defined by *percentage* is applied. Finally:

```
Context LinearDiscount::amount:Money

   derive:

      percentage * self.order.gross_total
```

In this last case, a linear discount is applied to the gross total without any conditions. Remember that *amount* is the quantity of money that is subtracted from the *gross_total* in the *Order* for obtaining the *net_total* that is a derived attribute in the same class.

This pattern minimizes two problems related to requirements change. First, it keeps the discount strategy applied when the order was issued, even if strategies change in future. Second, if new strategies are created later, the team just must implement one or more subclasses for *Discount*. This usually does not affect the old strategies or the old orders.

11.7 Composite[2]

Different class instances may be grouped and treated as a single object recursively. The easier place to observe this pattern is by looking at drawing applications that allow

---

[2] *Composite* is the classic name for this pattern. However, if basic elements may be shared by different composite elements, it is the *shared aggregation* association that is used instead of the *composite aggregation*. This happens, for example, when strategies are composed.

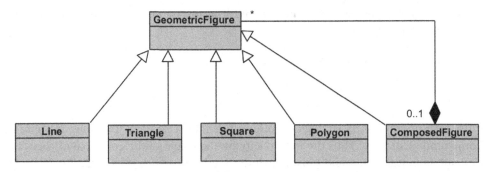

FIGURE 11–20 An example of recursively composed classes.

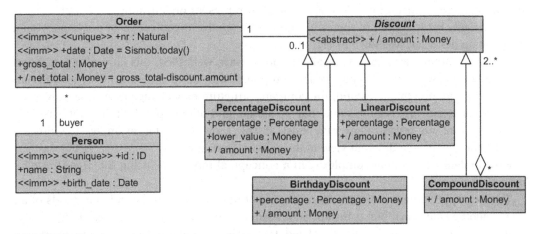

FIGURE 11–21 The composite pattern being applied to strategies.

independent geometric figures to be joined and treated as a new individual object. It can be seen in Fig. 11−20 where a geometric figure has five subclasses, line, triangle, square, polygon, and composed figure. On the other hand, a composed figure may be composed of any kind of geometric figure, lines, triangles, squares, polygons, and recursively composed figures.

The same idea can be applied to the strategies seen in the last subsection. The combination of different discount strategies can be obtained, for example, by the sum of the values obtained for the derived attribute *amount* for each individual strategy, or by choosing the highest or lowest values among them. The choice of one or another combination produces different aggregated strategies.

Fig. 11−21 shows the definition of the *SumDiscount* strategy that can be a combination of two or more strategies. The *amount* attribute in *SumDiscount* is simply the sum of the value of the component strategies whichever they are.

At the same time, the expression below could be the definition of the derived attribute *amount* in class *SumDiscount*.

```
Context SumDiscount::amount:Money
    derive:
        self.discount->sum(a_discount|a_discount.amount)
```

In the case of composing strategies, nothing prevents a strategy to belong to more than one compounded strategy. Thus the multiplicity on the origin of the composition association is "*," meaning that the diamond must be white to indicate a shared aggregation.

11.8 Organizational hierarchy

Another common situation consists of the need to represent organizational hierarchies. It is commonplace, for example, to represent the administrative organization of a company as a composition hierarchy as shown in Fig. 11–22.

However, hierarchies like this usually do not behave well. First, this kind of organization is not followed by every company: other companies may have different levels or different compositions among them. Second, the company structure may change over time. New divisions or offices may be created, some may be joined, and others split. Last, but not least, different views of an organization may exist at the same time; for example, the finance department may have a different view of the same organization.

How to deal with all that complexity in a conceptual model? By using the *organizational hierarchy* pattern.

The first approximation of a solution consists of not considering the different levels of an organization as concepts, but as instances of a single concept, as shown in Fig. 11–23.

In this way, flexibility is gained related to dealing simultaneously with organizational structures from different companies. Also, eventual changes in the organizational structure,

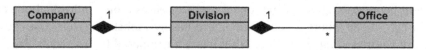

FIGURE 11–22 Straight representation of a company's organizational structure by using classes for the different levels of composition.

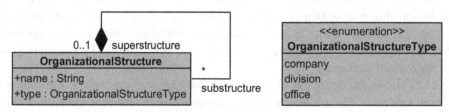

FIGURE 11–23 A simple application of the organizational hierarchy pattern.

such as adding more levels, or changing dependencies, may be easier to accomplish, because no code must be rewritten; only data accessible by the user must be changed.

This pattern has some variations that may be used if concurrent hierarchies, superseding structures, or equivalent structures should also be represented.

The case for concurrent hierarchies involving some of the same structures may be solved with the use of a class which instances are the different views of the hierarchy. Let us suppose, for example, that some offices informally view themselves in groups, which are not a structure of the formal hierarchy. There are, then, two visions, the formal and the informal one, in which groups appear. In the formal hierarchy, offices are linked to divisions, but in the informal hierarchy, offices are linked to groups and groups are linked to divisions. Fig. 11−24 shows how to represent those parallel hierarchies.

Now, the *View* class may have two instances, one with *name* "formal" and other with *name* "informal." The link between two organizational structures has an association class that associates the respective subordination to one of the views. Now, substructures may have different superstructures in different or in the same view. If it is the case that a substructure has only one superstructure in the same view, then an invariant could be applied:

```
Context OrganizationalStructure
    inv:
        self.superstructure->forAll(:a_superstructure|
            self.superstructure->select(:b_superstructure|
                b_superstructure.subordination.view =
                a_superstructure.subordination.view)
            ->size = 1
        )
```

This invariant states that for each superstructure of an instance, the size of the set of superstructures with the same view as the original superstructure (*a_superstructure*) must be 1.

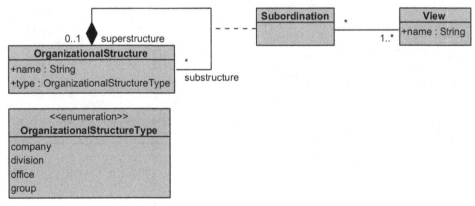

FIGURE 11–24 Parallel hierarchies.

Looking at the model again, the team may perceive that it is very lousy regarding subordination relationships. In fact, any type of organizational structure can be sub or superstructure to any type of organization structure. Well, it could be verified by code, but it can also be represented in the conceptual model with an additional class *Rule* and a new invariant. The new class is shown in Fig. 11–25.

The model shows that instances of *View* may have a set of rules that establish that inside that view a structure of type A can only be a superstructure of type B if there is an instance of *Rule* with attributes *sub* valued with B and *super* valued with A. For example, in the official view of the organization discussed before, the existence of a rule with *sub* equals to *office* and *super* equals to *division* allows an office to be a substructure of a division. This is not enforced by the model as it is, however. To make it mandatory, an invariant must be created:

```
Context Subordination
    inv:
        self.view->forAll(:a_view|
            a_view.rule(a_rule|
                self.substructure.type = a_rule.sub
                AND self.superstructure.type = a_rule.super
            )
        )
```

This invariant states that for each subordination and each view associated to it, there exists a rule associated to the view with attributes *sub* and *super* corresponding respectively to the types of the substructure and superstructure of the subordination.

In the two last invariants, we introduce two new operations of OCL: *forAll* and *exists*. They behave in a very similar form that their equivalents in logic and mathematics: ∀ and ∃.

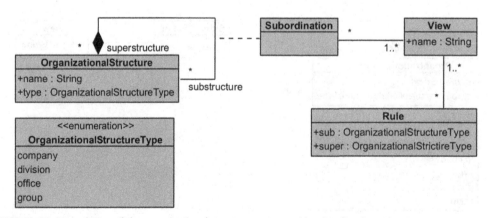

FIGURE 11–25 An evolution of the organizational structure pattern with subordination rules.

11.9 Object joining

One of the team's assumptions that usually fails is that users will do everything right. That is not always the case. User failure (and sometimes sabotage) is still frequent, despite the efforts to build failsafe interfaces. A user could, for example, register a new person in the system and later discover that it was already registered. Entering an incorrect code or the impossibility of having a unique identification for a real-world object may cause this situation. The result is that two objects are registered in the system, both representing the same person, and each of them may possibly have its own set of treatments associated, some repeated, some not. In Brazil, the public health system must attend any person (citizen or not) that needs health care. Suppose someone that is unconscious and without identification. This person would be probably registered as John Doe with a special identification number and receive health care. If later the identity of this person is discovered, then the registry for this John Doe must be added to the registry of the identified person.

The solution when this kind of situation happens is to join the objects, usually copying one over the other. Thus the system may be prepared to do so.

Besides, it is not always an *error* that causes the need for a join. In some situations, there are objects considered equivalent by one group of people and not by another, and both situations must be represented simultaneously. In other cases, as in multiple view organizational hierarchies, it may be necessary to indicate that two structure elements in different views are equivalent, or that one succeeds another in time.

The following subsections present the main strategies to deal with these kinds of situations.

11.9.1 Copy and replace

The first strategy that comes to mind when it is necessary to join two objects consists of copying the data of one object over the second (*copy and replace*). The copy/replace command could be defined by a contract (see Chapter 12), and the team should define, for each attribute and each association, what must happen during the copy/replace command. Rules should be defined to decide if an attribute is going to be copied over the other, or if their values are to be added, or if the newest or highest of them must prevail, etc. Regarding the associations, the team must decide what happens: if one replaces the other, or if their properties are added, and so on.

The registry of the date of the last inclusion or change of a concept may be useful for deciding which attribute must be kept in the case of a conflict. For example, if a registered customer makes a new record, and it is going to be resolved, then the most recent address must be kept, not the oldest one. On the other hand, all her orders must be added to the resulting instance.

After performing the copy/replace command, the instance that was copied must be destroyed, and any references to it must be redirected to the instance that received the data.

To avoid losing data by thinking that two registers are the same and after merging them discovering that that was not the case, it would be useful to use one of the temporal patterns in the class that may be merged. Temporal patterns are described in the end of this chapter, and they would allow to recover the original objects after merging.

11.9.2 Superseding

Superseding is a technique that can be used when the original object must be kept and not destroyed. Superseding is applicable, for example, in the case of organizational structures that are succeeded in time. Suppose that the departments of marketing and sales are joined into a single department of *customer contact*; the original departments must be marked as no longer active, and a new department must be added as their successor. The superseding strategy may be implemented by a reflexive association, being an evolution of the organizational hierarchy pattern in this case, as shown in Fig. 11−26.

The derived attribute *active* indicates if the structure is active or if it has been superseded. It is true if the set of superseders is empty and false otherwise.

To maintain the original organizational structure even if it is not active anymore may be important for registry purposes. Someday someone may need to know how much a given department that does not exist anymore spent on toothpicks.

It would be useful to add an association class to the *superseded/superseder* association; its attributes could indicate, for example, the date when the superseding event taken place, or the context or view in which it must be considered. This can be seen in Fig. 11−27.

In this case, when an organization is divided into two, for example, there will be two links between the superseded organization and the superseder organizations, and two superseding events may be linked to both links.

If there is a need to account for the multiple superseding links that belong to the same event, a specification class for *SuperSeding* can be added for grouping the links that were created by the same event, as seen in Fig. 11−28.

To deal with this kind of situation, the team should also consider applying one of the temporal patterns seen in the end of the chapter.

11.9.3 Essence/appearance

Another situation that can still often happen is the existence of objects that are considered equivalent but must be kept as separated objects. This is not a registry error, and it is not an object that supersedes another: this is *object equivalence*.

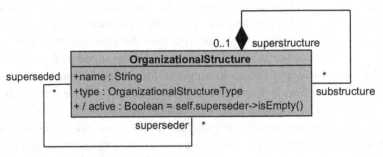

FIGURE 11-26 An example of superseding strategy.

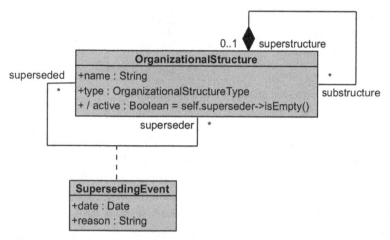

FIGURE 11–27 Evolution of the supersede pattern.

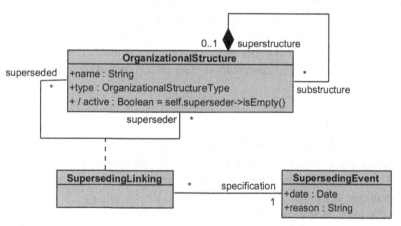

FIGURE 11–28 Superseding links grouped by a single superseding event specification.

Object equivalence may be modeled using an essence object that is associated to a set of equivalent objects. As opposed to *copy/replace*, the original objects are kept, and as opposed to *superseding*, there is no active or superseded object: all associated objects are equivalent. Fig. 11−29 shows an example of a class (*Book*) that accepts that its members share a common essence.

In the example, we consider that the same book in essence, especially a classic work, may be published by different publishers. Each publication is distinct, with a different ISBN and number of pages. Even the title and author's name may vary (proper names may be translated or abbreviated sometimes). But the essence of the text is the same. Some users may be interested in ordering Plato's *The Republic* from a specific publisher, and others may be interested in the book independently of the edition or publisher. Thus the users interested in a specific publication are looking for the appearance (a given instance

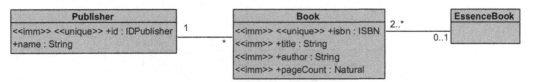

FIGURE 11–29 An example of application of pattern *Essence/Appearance*.

of *Book*), and the users interested in the text are looking for the book in essence—the publisher does not matter. The second group of users, when viewing any edition of *The Republic*, must also be allowed to view other instances of *Book* linked to the same *EssenceBook* if they exist. In other words, if you look for book *a_book* and if *a_book.essence_book->notEmpty()*, then you will see *a_book.essence_book.book*, which is a set of books with the same essence.

Not *every* Book must be linked to an *EssenceBook*, only those that participate in an equivalence class. Also, there must be at least two equivalent books to create an *EssenceBook*. This is why the association role from *EssenceBook* to *Book* is marked with 2.*.

Objects are considered equivalent if they are linked to the same essence object. The essence object exists only to establish that equivalence; usually it will not have any other properties. Otherwise, maybe the *specification class* pattern could be used instead.

11.9.4 Undoing a join

Just when the team thinks that the real world cannot be more complex, it becomes so. Therefore if there is a possibility of joining objects, it is also possible that joined objects must be separated again. Once again, these commands may be performed through well-planned operations available at the system's user interface.

To allow the joins of the *copy/replace* technique to be undone, a backup of the original objects must be kept, because the technique destroys one of the objects and disfigures the other. A log on the operations done over the object after the merge must also be kept and possibly redone in one of the original objects after splitting.

The *superseding* technique allows the join to be undone too. Despite there are other ways to do that, maybe the best one is to perform the merging or splitting operations in reverse order. For example, if the departments of marketing and sales are merged into a department of customer care, undoing this operation would be just to split the department of customer care into a new department of marketing and a new department of sales.

In the case of *essence/appearance*, it is necessary to remove the association (and the essence object if less than two links to it remain).

However, in every case it is important to decide how to deal with eventual changes within the object that occurred while it was joined with the others. Again, temporal patterns may help doing things in these cases.

11.10 Account/transaction

The *account/transaction* pattern is closely related to business, but it has wide applicability. Products in a store may be cataloged, ordered, received, delivered, discarded, etc. Such movements, as well as the financial transactions involved with them, give origin to concepts such as *Order, Delivery, Discard, Return, Payment,* and *Receiving,* each one with its own attributes and associations.

However, it is possible to identify a common core for all these concepts and many more, which is constituted by a single and powerful pattern.

An *Account* is a concept that bears quantities of *something* (such as products or money). An *Account* has a balance that usually consists of the sum of every deposit or withdrawal.

On the other hand, deposits and withdrawals are usually just transactions of goods or money from an account to another. Thus a *Transaction* consists of two movements: a deposit in one account and a withdrawal of the same value from another account. Fig. 11−30 illustrates those classes.

A consistent transaction with two entries such as the one in Fig. 11−30 needs two entries with the same absolute value but opposite signs. In other words, if a transaction takes 5 dollars from an account, it must necessarily deposit 5 dollars into another account; the withdrawal has a negative sign and the deposit a positive sign. Thus the *Transaction* class needs the following invariant:

```
Context Transaction
     inv:
           self.movement->sum(:a_movement|a_movement.value)=0
```

This means that for each instance of *Transaction,* the sum of the value of the two associated movements must be zero.

The derived attribute *balance* of class *Account* is defined as the sum of every movement linked to that specific *Account:*

```
Context Account::balance
        derive:
              movement->sum(value)
```

Many situations related to the store example could be modeled from a set of instances of class *Account,* such as:

- For each *supplier,* there is an instance of *Account* from which products are "withdrawn," that is, it is an *entry account,* and its balance becomes more negative as products are ordered from the supplier.

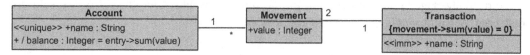

FIGURE 11–30 Classes for the *Account/Transaction* pattern.

- There is an account for *orders expected*, which contains the products that were ordered from the supplier but that had not yet arrived.
- There is an account for *stock* containing the available products.
- There is an account for *sold products* containing products sold but not yet delivered.
- There is an account for *delivered products* containing products delivered but not yet confirmed by the customer.
- There is an account for *confirmed delivery* containing products delivered and confirmed by the customer. Its balance represents the whole set of products that the customer has bought from the store.

In parallel to product transactions, there are concomitant money transactions. There are receivable accounts, payable accounts, received accounts, paid accounts, investment, debts, values saved for paying taxes, etc.

Thus many transactions of the bookstore example could be modeled as an instance of *Transaction*. For example:

- An *order* is a transaction that takes products from a *supplier* entry account and deposits them into an *expected orders* account.
- The *arrival* of the products is a transaction that takes from the *expected orders* account and adds to the *stock* account.
- A *sale* is a transaction that takes from the *stock* account and adds to the *sold products* account.
- A *delivery* is a transaction that takes from the *sold products* account and adds to the *delivered products* account.
- A *return* is a transaction that takes from the *delivered products* account and adds to the *stock* account (if the products are in good shape).
- A *confirmation of delivery* is a transaction that takes from the *delivery* account and adds to the *confirmed delivery* exit account.

As an example, imagine a company that just started, where five instances[3] of the *Account* class were created: *supplier, pending orders, stock, sold*, and *delivered*. Fig. 11−31 shows the initial state for those objects when all accounts have a zero balance.

Fig. 11−32 shows the resulting set of objects when a *purchase order* (instance of *Transaction*) is created. The order was issued for 50 products. Account *supplier* balance is now −50, and account *pending orders* is +50.

Fig. 11−33 shows the state of the accounts if only 40 of the 50 ordered books arrive. In this case, 10 products are still pending and 40 are in stock. Still −50 are in the balance of the supplier.

Fig. 11−34 shows the state of the accounts after 25 products are sold. In this case, *supplier* keeps −50, *pending orders* are 10, *stock* is updated to 15, and *sold* to 25.

And finally, Fig. 11−35 shows how the accounts look like after the 25 books sold are delivered. Account *sold* is updated to 0 and *delivered* to 25.

---

[3] The example deals with only five instances for simplification. Many others could be included.

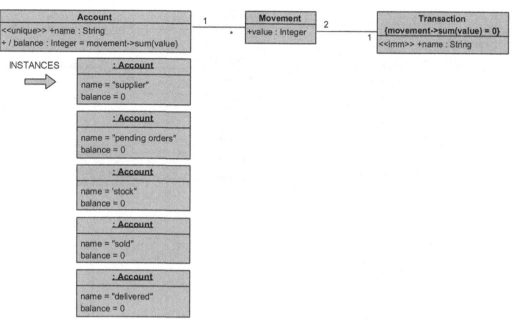

FIGURE 11–31 Initial state of an accounting system for products.

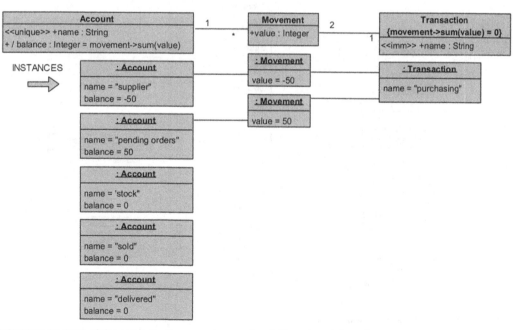

FIGURE 11–32 State of the accounts after a purchase order of 50 products is issued.

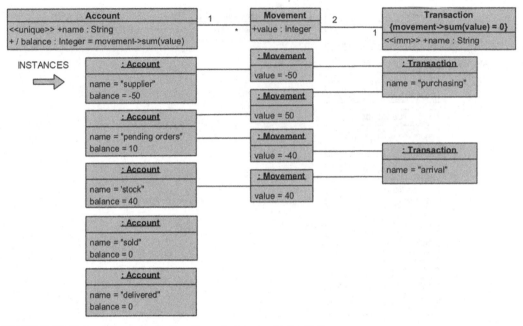

FIGURE 11–33 State of the accounts after 40 products arrive at the stock.

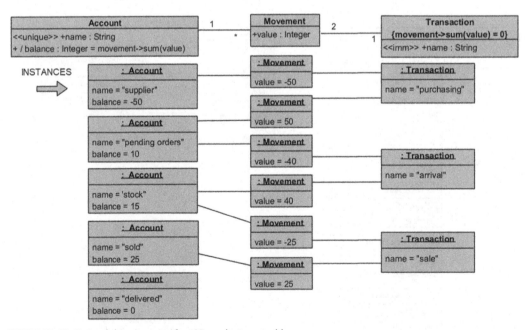

FIGURE 11–34 State of the accounts after 25 products are sold.

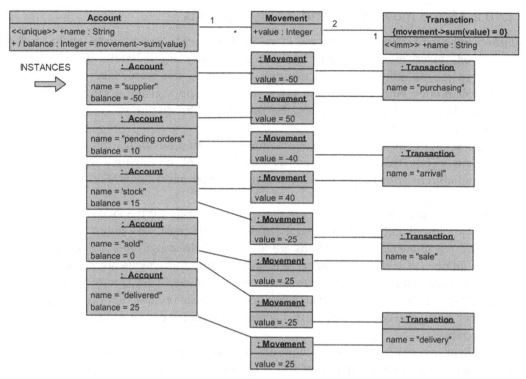

FIGURE 11–35 State of the accounts after the delivery of 25 products.

New transactions and accounts may be created dynamically (i.e., without having to recompile the system). For example, a new transaction may be created for returning products, which moves products from the *delivered* account back to the *stock* account. Also, a new transaction for discarding products could be created moving products from the *stock* or *sold* accounts to a new account for *discarded* products. Parallel financial transactions could be created as well by using *Account* and *Transaction*.

11.10.1 Multilegged transactions

This pattern is very interesting as an example of how a simple powerful idea can deal with so many different situations. It has many variations and sophistications. For example, *multilegged transactions* may be created, if necessary, for moving from more than one account to a single account, or from a single account to more than one account, or even from more than one account to more than one account at the same time. To accomplish this variation, the multiplicity role from *Transaction* to *Movement* should be changed from 2 to 2.*.

11.10.2 Memo movements and memo accounts

Another important variation is the use of *memo movements*. For example, when money is received, taxes must be paid, but not necessarily immediately. Thus when a transaction moves money from a customer account to the store balance account, a quantity of money equivalent to the taxes due could be registered into a tax memo account. When it is time to pay taxes, the balance of the memo account registers the amount to be paid.

Memo accounts and normal accounts share the same attributes but not the same associations. Thus they are defined as subclasses of an abstract class *Account*. The same happens with memo movements and normal movements. Fig. 11−36 shows the model.

Memo and normal movements are not distinguished except for the kind of *Account* subclass they are linked and to the fact that a *Transaction* still must have only 2 normal movements, or 2.* if multilegged transactions are allowed. At the same time, a *Transaction* can have any number of memo movements, and those memo movements are not used in the invariant in class *Transaction*. Only normal movements should sum zero in a *Transaction*. Fig. 11−37 shows the initial state of an example where a sale transaction can be registered with money being moved between normal accounts and a tax of 15% being registered in a memo account.

What happens next is a sale when 400 Mira is transferred from the client account to the target organization account and a tax of 15% is registered in the *tax due* memo account. The resulting situation is depicted in Fig. 11−38.

Notice that at this point, the taxes are not being paid. Money is transferred between the two normal account and sum zero, and the 15% of taxes due is simply registered in a memo account for future providences.

Finally, let us see what happens when the day to pay taxes arrives. Then the balance registered in the *taxes due* must be transferred from the organization's account to the government account, and the memo account should be reset to zero. This is shown in Fig. 11−39.

And this completes our example.

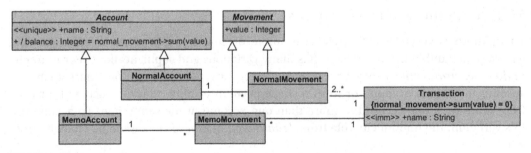

FIGURE 11-36 Memo and normal accounts and memo and normal movements.

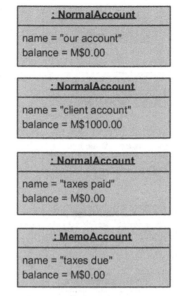

FIGURE 11–37 Initial state of a transaction with a memo account.

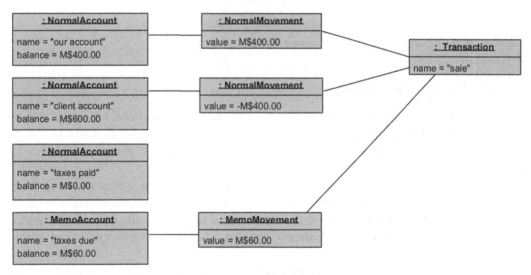

FIGURE 11–38 The status of the objects after a sale is registered.

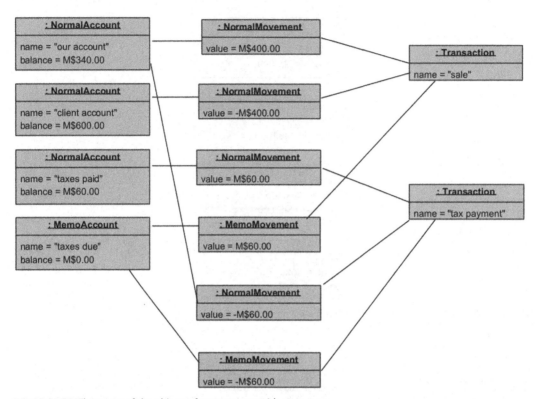

FIGURE 11–39 The status of the objects after taxes are paid.

11.11 Range or interval

When an object has a pair of attributes indicating the beginning and end of some phenomena, such as initial and final date, instead of representing it as two separated attributes, it is advisable to declare a single attribute type such as *Interval* (or *Range*), as shown in Fig. 11–40.

The primitive *Interval* is parameterized, meaning that when an instance is created, it must indicate the *Type* to be used to define its attributes. For example, an interval over *Date* could be referred to as *Interval < Date>*, and an interval over a quantity defined as *Distance* could be referred to as *Interval < Distance>*. See Fig. 11–41 for an example of use of this pattern.

There are at least two reasons for using an interval instead of two attributes:

- If the lower and upper bounds are separated attributes in a conceptual class, they would have a strong relation between them. This violates the high cohesion principle explained in Section 11.2.
- Operations that are specific to intervals (e.g., checking if a value is inside an interval) will be needed. If there is a specific *Interval* primitive type, these operations may be

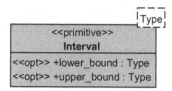

FIGURE 11–40 A primitive type *Interval* with genericity.

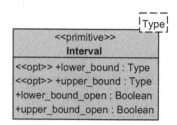

FIGURE 11–41 An example of use of pattern *Interval*.

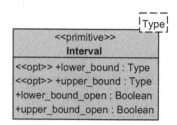

FIGURE 11–42 Interval with open and close options for bounds.

implemented once just in the primitive. If two attributes are used instead, each class where they are declared should implement its own version of the operations on intervals.

It is much more reasonable to implement operations just once in a high-cohesion class, than implementing them many times in low-cohesion classes.

As seen in Fig. 11−41, both attributes of the *Interval* class are optional, which means that intervals may be undefined in one or both ends. For example, an interval that starts at January 1, 2023 and has no upper bound could be defined with *lowerBound* = "01/01/2023" and *upperBound* = *null*.

Evolutions of this pattern could consider the mathematical properties of intervals. For example, there are *open* and *closed* intervals: [0.10] is a closed interval that includes 0 and 10, while (0.10) is an open interval that excludes 0 and 10. Furthermore, (0.10] excludes 0 and includes 10 and [0.10) includes 0 and excludes 10. This evolution could be implemented simply by adding two Boolean attributes to the class *Interval*: *lower_bound_open* and *upper_-bound_open* as seen in Fig. 11−42.

Finally, to enforce the definition that an interval must have a *lower_bound* smaller than its *upper_bound*, if they exist, an invariant can be added to the *Interval* class:

```
Context Interval
    inv:
        self.lower_bound->notNull AND selfupper_bound->notNull
        IMPLIES self.lower_bound <= self_upper_bound
```

Here we considered that an interval with the same lower and upper bounds is valid, such as [10..10]. Also, the invariant above uses the operator *IMPLIES* of OCL. This is a predicate equivalent to the implication operator in propositional logic, and *X IMPLIES Y* is false if and only if X is true and Y is false.

11.12 Temporal patterns

Frequently, the analyst faces the need to deal with time. For example, it may be necessary to represent the relations between people and their jobs. But, if the association between people and jobs represents only the present time, then the information of former jobs will be lost when someone quits the job. This section discusses some patterns that deal with that important notion.[4]

11.12.1 Effectivity

When an object is valid for some time. For example, when the temperature of a patient is measured, it is considered valid for a certain period. In an extreme example, a temperature measure taken today will not be considered valid after 7 days. Other measures may have longer periods of validity. For example, if an adult measure 6 feet, this measure may be considered valid for years.

The period between the act of taking a measure and the end of its validity is the *effectivity* of the measure, and in is the name of the first temporal pattern.

Effectivity may be represented as an interval attribute in a class that represents the object that has validity time, as seen in Fig. 11−43.

It can also be applied to products, such as medicine, renting contracts.

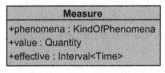

FIGURE 11−43 Temporal pattern *Effectivity*.

[4] Martin Fowler presents a nice summary on many temporal patterns at http://martinfowler.com/eaaDev/timeNarrative.html. Consulted in: May 31, 2023.

11.12.2 History

If historical information must be stored about the past states of an association, attribute, or even a whole object, then the *History* pattern may be used. In the example of Fig. 11−44, the stereotype «history» is used to indicate that a person may have only one job at an instant, but her former jobs are remembered by the association.

Notice that the stereotype is applied to the whole association and not only to a role. This means that if the association is navigable in two ways, both roles maintain history: the person remembers the organizations she worked before and the organization remember persons that worked for it, but that are not employed anymore.

The stereotype of the association of Fig. 11−44 means that a person must have just zero or one job currently, but she may have had other jobs in the past. These past jobs may be recovered as items in a list. In other words, it is possible to recover the last job, the job before the last, and so on.

When it comes to design, each class with an association with a navigable role implements a method for accessing the elements linked. In the example of Fig. 11−44, the design class for *Person* would have a getter query *get_job()* that returns the organization where this person is working or the empty set if this person is unemployed. If the association is stereotyped with «*history*», in addition to that standard method *get_job()*, there would exist another method with a parameter, *get_job(index:Natural)*, where *get_job(0)* returns the current job and is the same as *get_job()*. However, *get_job(1)* returns the last job before the current one. Also, *get_job(2)* returns the job before the job before the current one, and so on. If there is no job for the index given, then the query returns the empty set.

In practice, this pattern can be implemented by two associations, as shown in Fig. 11−45: one representing the current job, if any, and the other representing a sequence (yes, a sequence because one can work in the same organization more than once) of jobs. The stereotype is, then, a way to abbreviate a more complex structure, replacing it with a simpler one.

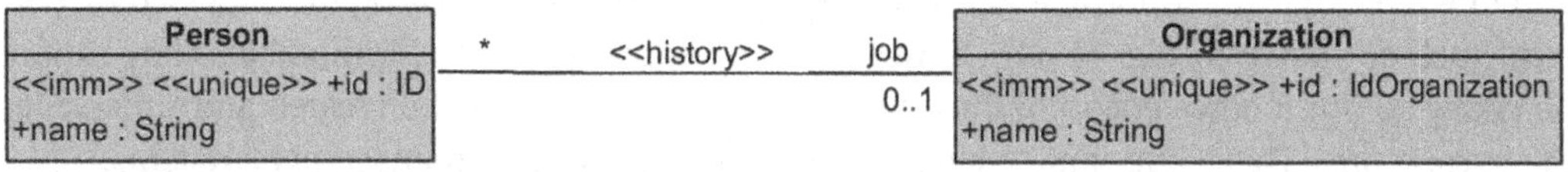

FIGURE 11–44 History patters applied to an association.

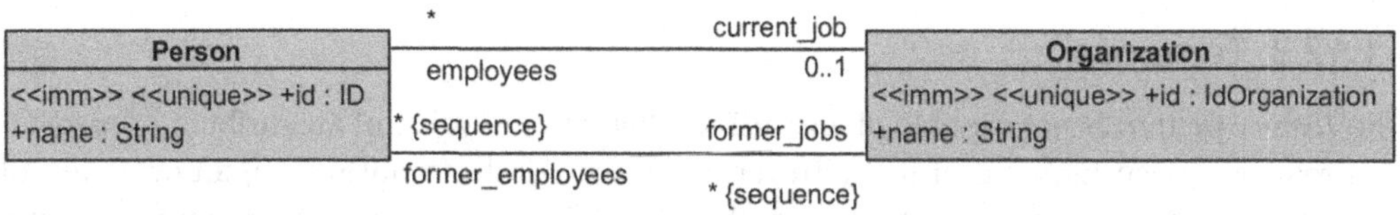

FIGURE 11–45 A possible implementation for the *History* pattern for an association.

Person

<<imm>> <<unique>> +id : ID
<<history>> +name : String
<<history>> +address : String

FIGURE 11–46 An example of attributes with *History* pattern.

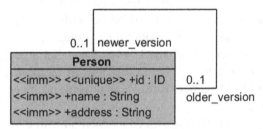

FIGURE 11–47 A possible implementation of attributes with history using superseding.

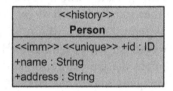

FIGURE 11–48 A whole class stereotyped with «*history*».

This pattern can also be applied to attributes. If a person changes name and address and we should maintain this information for any reason, then the pattern can be used, as in Fig. 11–46.

On interesting way to implement this pattern in attributes is by using the superseding pattern, such as shown in Fig. 11–47. Here name and address become immutable. They cannot be changed, but a new version of the object with other values may be created and supersedes the current one. This is the same technique used by configuration management systems.

This implementation already works for all attributes of the class that are not immutable and can be used as well when the whole class is stereotyped with this pattern as seen in Fig. 11–48.

11.12.3 Temporal

The *History* pattern is not capable of answering what was the value of an attribute or association role at a given moment of time. To represent that kind of information, an evolution of that pattern may be used: an association that in addition to sequential memory has time memory, as shown in Fig. 11–49.

FIGURE 11–49 Temporal pattern applied to an association.

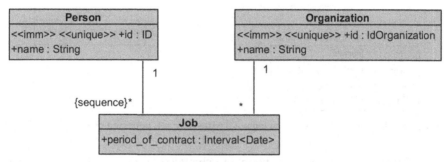

FIGURE 11–50 A possible implementation for the *Temporal* pattern.

A temporal association or attribute has at least three methods to consult its value. In the case of the example, where the job role association is temporal, the following methods would exist:

- *getJob*(): Returns the current job of a person or the empty set if the person is currently unemployed.
- *getJob*(*index:Natural*): Returns the current or former job of a person depending on the index argument, or the empty set if there is no job at that index. For example, *getJob* (0) returns the current job, if any, *getJob*(1) returns the job before the current one, if any, and so on.
- *getJob*(*date:Date*): Returns the job a person had at the end of a given date or the empty set if the person was unemployed at that date.

If it was required to know the job of a person at a given time of the day, then the primitive type *Date* can be replaced by *Time*, which refers to year, month, day, hour, minute, and second. For applications that demand more precision, milliseconds, microseconds, and so on could be used additionally.

Fig. 11−50 presents a possible implementation the ≪ *temporal* ≫ stereotype.

The *Job* class does not have a pair of attributes such as *initial_date* and *end_date*, but a single attribute *period_of_contract* with type *Interval* < *Date* >, representing an interval between hiring and firing.

In the case of attributes or classes that need to know their values in given dates in the past, as shown in Fig. 11−51, the implementation can also follow the superseding pattern as shown in Fig. 11−52. But, in this case, a stamp of time is added to the supersede association.

Person

<<imm>> <<unique>> +id : ID
<<temporal>> +name : String
<<imm>> +birth_date : Date

FIGURE 11–51 A class with temporal attributes.

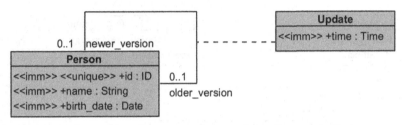

FIGURE 11–52 A possible implementation of the temporal pattern for attributes and objects.

For example, some countries allow people to change their names after marriage, divorce, or decision of a judge. In Fig. 11–51, the ID and birthdate of a person are not supposed to change. However, the different names of that person may be remembered by the system, and the time each change happened too.

11.12.4 Bitemporal

Not only in science fiction but also in many current information system applications, time may be considered two-dimensional. There is a dimension of time in which events occur and another dimension where we acknowledge that an event occurred.

This is a new pattern known as *Bitemporal*, because it has two dimensions for time: the time when an event happened and the time we were informed that the same event happened. Those times not always are coincident. For example, it is said that when Lincoln was murdered, the news took 15 days to reach Europe. Fig. 11–53 shows a situation where a bitemporal pattern is applied to an association.

Looking at this model, imagine that the association says that a *Person* named Mary is currently working for Organization X. However, today we discovered that in fact Mary is not working at that organization for the last three months. There are two dates to be recorded here: the date Mary changed jobs and the day our information system received that information.

This knowledge may justify eventual actions done during the time when our system was not updated. If only the date of change is recorded, than it would be impossible to know that this information was not available for a certain time.

Sometimes, especially for accountability or legal procedures, knowing when a record was changed is crucial. The bitemporal pattern is an elegant way to keep track not only of the line of events but also the line of our knowledge about events.

Now a new getter may be introduced for the role *job*: *getJob*(*change_date, knowledge_- date:Date*). The first argument is the instant of time we are interested in, and the second

FIGURE 11–53 Bitemporal pattern.

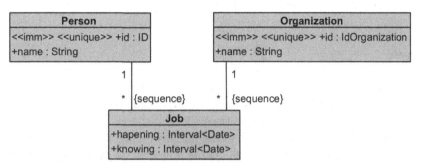

FIGURE 11–54 A possible implementation for pattern bitemporal.

argument is the instant of time of our knowledge about it. For example, if we want to answer the question "On June 15, 2023, where did we believe that Mary worked on June 1, 2023?" we could use the query *get_job*("06/01/2023," "06/15/2023").

If we want to know where Mary worked on June 1, 2023, based on our current knowledge, we could use the getter mentioned for the temporal pattern: *get_job*("06/01/2023"), which is short for *get_job*("06/01/2023," *today*).

Fig. 11−54 presents a possible implementation for that stereotype.

Now there are two date ranges in the class *Job*, one for registering the time the job was effective (*happening*) and the other to represent the range of time when this information was considered true (*knowing*).

Each time our knowledge about the job of a person is changed, a new instance of *Job* is created. The *happening* attribute establishes when the job was effective, and the *knowing* attribute establishes the point from when we believed that. The upper bound of the two intervals in *Job* would usually be kept undefined while it represents our current knowledge, that is, while that information was not overridden by newer (eventually contradictory) information.

The bitemporal pattern can also be applied to attributes or entire classes, just like the temporal pattern and again using the supersede pattern.

11.13 Discussion

A good conceptual model produces an organized structure that is suitable to generate an already normalized database. It incorporates structural rules that prevent information from being represented in an inconsistent way; it also simplifies the code that will be generated because it minimizes and organizes consistency checks, and several verifications that are guaranteed by the model itself do not need to be performed by the code.

The use of suitable design patterns in situations where they are necessary simplifies the conceptual model and gives it more flexibility and quality. It is, therefore, a powerful tool for agile modeling. Many other patterns exist, and teams may create their own new patterns. It just should be kept in mind that the creation of a pattern is justified only when its benefits pay for the effort expended in creating and remembering it.

Questions

1. In Fig. 11–30, there is no explicit invariant that states that a *Transaction* cannot be linked to movements that are linked to the same account, because the structure of the model already demands is. Why is it not necessary?
2. Apply the *Account/Transaction* pattern to the parallel financial transactions of the example shown in Figs. 11–31 to 11–35. As the bills may be paid forward, it may be necessary to use memo entries. Define the set of instances of *Account* and *Transaction* that are necessary and describe them.
3. Use Google or another search mechanism to find examples of conceptual models including classes with attributes. Analyze those classes and check if they present cohesion problems. Propose alternative solutions to them if necessary.
4. A system for registering genealogical trees allows different users to check if they have coincident people in their own trees. If this is the case, the shared person is marked in each tree as equivalent to the other. Thus two cousins, for example, who have the same grandfather, may have a coincident registry in their trees. Which of the three strategies of object joining is best for dealing with this case? Why? Elaborate a model for representing people in the genealogical trees using that pattern.
5. Look at Fig. 11–19 and create a new discount strategy that gives a percentage of discount for sales with more than a certain number of products.

12

Functional modeling with object constraint language contracts

Key topics in this chapter

- Preconditions
- Postconditions
- Query returns
- Exceptions
- System Operation Contracts

12.1 Introduction to functional modeling

Before functional modeling begins, the analysis process may have already produced two artifacts:

- The *refined conceptual model*, which represents statically the information managed by the system.
- The *expanded use cases* or *system sequence diagrams*, which show how potential users exchange information with the system, without mentioning how that information is processed internally by the system and in some cases even without mentioning the interface technology.

When system sequence diagrams are built, the system commands and queries that must be implemented are identified. Each system command and query imply a user intention or goal; for example, the reviewer may be providing information on which proposal she is going to asses, or she may be looking for the list of assessments she has done in the last 30 days. That intention is captured by *system command contracts* and *system query contracts*, generically referred to as *system operation contracts*, which corresponds to the functional model of the system.

A *system command contract* may have three sections:

- *Preconditions* (optional): Logic statements that are assumed to be true by the command and therefore should not be checked by it. For example, "all assessments in the list are completed."
- *Postconditions* (mandatory): Logic statements that explain how the command changes existing information if it is successfully executed. For example, "one assessment was created and associated to the proposal and reviewer."
- *Exceptions* (optional): Logic statements that contain conditions that could prevent the command from succeeding, and that will be checked by it. For example, "the deadline for the assessment is past."

Object-Oriented Analysis and Design for Information Systems. DOI: https://doi.org/10.1016/B978-0-443-13739-6.00004-6

On the other hand, a *system query contract* may have the following sections:

- *Preconditions* (optional): Logic statements that explain what is assumed to be true by the query and therefore should not be checked by it. For example, "The assessment list is not empty."
- *Results* (mandatory): A data structure that defines the information that the query returns. For example, "a list with all reviewers sorted by seniority."
- *Exceptions* (optional): Logical conditions that were added by the designer to prevent the system from performing the query in some situations. For example, "the user has no authorization to change this record."

Preconditions exist in both types of contracts. They define constraints that are complementary to the ones already existing in the conceptual model. Preconditions are assumed to be true by the operation. This means that preconditions are *not* tested by the operation that is defined by the contract; they must be tested and assured *before* the operation is performed.

Postconditions, on the other hand, exist only in system command contracts because they specify *how the information kept by the system was changed*. Special care must be taken to not confuse postconditions with query *results*. By the *Command-Query Separation* principle (Meyer, 1988), it is not appropriate for a command to return any result (except in special justified cases). Queries, on the other hand, must return some result, but cannot produce any change in the existing information. Therefore system queries must have *results* and system commands must have *postconditions* usually.

As opposed to preconditions that must be true before the operation is called, *exceptions* are situations that usually cannot or should not be tested before; exceptions are tested by the operation itself. Exceptions are events that, if they occur, prevent the operation from succeeding.

Exceptions in command contracts and exceptions in query contracts may have distinct purposes. In command contracts, exceptions are used when arguments or existing information does not satisfy a given business rule (e.g., trying to register a customer that is already registered).

However, in query contracts, exceptions have a different meaning. As a query does not change information, there is no invalid argument that could possibly prevent a well-defined query from being performed. If a user queries a system about a person that does not exist, the query is not prevented from being performed: it would answer that there is no person for the query; this is the right answer, not an exception.

Exceptions in queries would be used only if by any chance the team decides that for a given condition, the query *must not* be performed. Usually, those conditions are related to security issues, or other technological concerns such as multiwindow interface, concurrency, and communication. As these issues are usually not addressed by functional modeling, exceptions in queries contracts are not frequent at this point.

Normally, in an operation contract, be it a command or query, an exception can be transformed into a precondition and vice versa. The decision on designing an issue as a precondition or exception determines which part of the system is responsible for testing that issue: the *calling operation* or the *called operation*. Usually, in large multiuser systems, *concurrent*

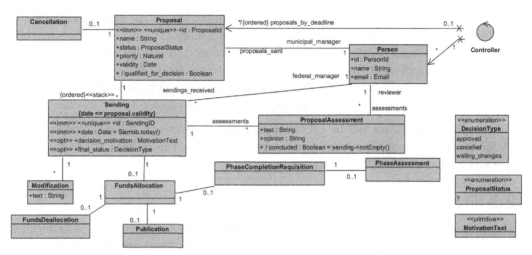

FIGURE 12–1 Conceptual model to be used in examples.

race conditions[1] may lead to choosing to avoid preconditions; however, if the system is not subject to complex concurrency or a concurrency control mechanism that prevents data from changing during transactions exists, then a design based on preconditions may be the better choice.

For the examples in this chapter, a partial refinement of the conceptual model presented in Fig. 10−4 will be used, now represented as Fig. 12−1.

Also, we will be using the sequence diagram of Fig. 7−7, now represented as Fig. 10−2 to identify the system operations that are necessary for this use case. A few modifications were done to reflect new knowledge about the project. For example, what are being searched in this use case are not projects, but their sendings. Also, when a reviewer looks for an assessment, she wants to know only her assessments, not everyone's. That is while the argument *user_id* was added to the *list_sendings* query.

As a precondition for this sequence diagram, we see that *user_id* is known because it is guaranteed that the user logged in before this use case started.

The system operations we are looking for are in the space between the interface and the controller. As we are using the stateless strategy, the operations would look like:

- *list_sendings*(*user_id*):*OrderedSet* < *DTO_Sending*>. In this case, remember that *DTO_Sending* is a list of alphanumeric values defined in the data dictionary of the project and the return of the query is defined as an *OrderedSet*, which could be sorted by different criteria on the interface. It is not a regular *Set* because it would need to be converted before sorting, and it is not also a *Sequence* because there is no need to repeat objects in this list. The attribute *user_id* was added as an argument to avoid the user to receive sendings to which she is not associated with.

---

[1] For example, after a user orders a product, while the user is closing the order and providing payment, the only available product could be sold to another user. This must be avoided with concurrency control mechanisms.

- *get_assessment(selected_sending, user_id):Text.* This query returns the existing text of an unfinished assessment or the empty string if none is available.
- *set_assessment(selected_sending, user_id, updated_assessment).* This is the only system command in this use case, which updates the text of the verified assessment by the reviewer. Although a sending may have multiple assessments, they must all be from different reviewers. An invariant should be written to guarantee that (consider it as an exercise).

In the next sections, we will be presenting the components of a system operation contract: preconditions, returns, postconditions, and exceptions. The chapter finished with the presentation of standard CRUDL contracts.

12.2 Preconditions

Preconditions establish what must be true when a system query or command is performed. For example, for every operation in Fig. 12−2, there is a preliminary precondition that states that the user is logged in and that her id is *user_id.*

Thus the three operations in that diagram could establish that this fact did not change until they are performed by declaring the same precondition in the definition of their functionality. Observe that all three operations are implemented in the class *Controller* and that they are being called by the interface. Thus *Controller* will always be the context for system operations. This is the precondition for *list_sendings*:

```
Context Controller::list_sendings(user_id:UserId):OrderedSet<DTO_sending>
    pre:
        self.person->exists(a_person|
            a_person.id = user_id
        )
```

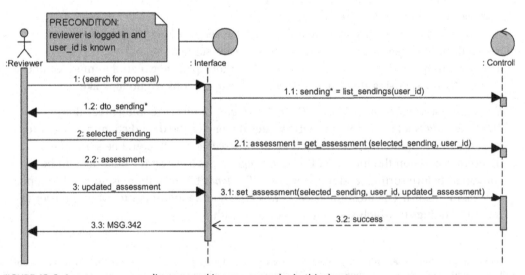

FIGURE 12–2 A system sequence diagram used in some examples in this chapter.

Abbreviated form:

```
Context Controller::list_sendings(user_id)
    pre:
        person->exists(
            id = user_id
        )
```

The precondition would be the same for the other two operations as they both receive *user_id* as argument.

Looking closely to the precondition, it becomes true if exists at least one person with a given *id*. It could be the case that many persons could exist with the same *id*. However, as the *id* attribute of *Person* is unique, that cannot be the case. Only one instance of *Person* can have the given *id*.

To be useful for software development, preconditions must be expressed in a careful way. They must reflect facts that can be identified in the previously developed conceptual model, or the model must be updated to reflect the new information just discovered. This justifies the use of formal languages such as object constraint language (OCL) for writing contracts (Warmer and Keppe, 1998) instead of natural language.

Preconditions may be classified into two groups:

- *Parameter guarantee*: Preconditions that assure that the arguments of a command or query correspond to valid objects (e.g., "there exists a person with the *id* passed as an argument").
- *Complementary constraint*: Preconditions that further constrain the conceptual model when performing a given command or query, to assure that the information is in a given state when the operation is being executed. For example, in a context where an instance of *Sending* can be associated with zero or more assessments, a precondition such as "the sending has received no assessment" is a complementary constraint that reduces the possibilities from zero or more to zero only.

12.2.1 Parameter guarantee

There is a systematic way to know if a given system operation must have a parameter guarantee precondition (or exception). This feature is also related to the operation's functional test, as seen later in this book. The team must look at each parameter of the operation and ask if there are any valid and/or invalid values considering the type of the parameter.

As an example, let us consider the third operation in our example sequence diagram: *set_assessment*(*selected_sending, user_id, updated_assessment*). The types are absent from the expression, but they are easy to infer:

- *selected_sending*: *SendingId*. The class *Sending* does not have a ≪ *unique* ≫ attribute, and although identifying its instances by looking at the reviewer and proposal is possible, it demands a lot of work. Thus the solution of creating an *id:SendingId* unique attribute for this class may solve the problem in an easier way. In fact, every class could have its unique attribute, but they are not always necessary. That is why they are created as the demand arises. In case of need, they can be used by the interface to uniquely identify an instance. However, the user must never have access to this value.

- *user_id: PersonID*. Remember that this is a unique code for identifying users and that it is not recommended to use codes that are known in the real world, such as social security number. This is so because the government may change the format of this number or even extinguish it without notice and also because people outside the United States usually do not have this identification number. Thus it does not serve for identification purpose in our system.

- *updated_assessment: String*. This is simple, except if we are considering that the updated text must have a minimum size. However, as the assessment is not necessarily sent just after being updated, we can accept at this point any size of text and leave the verification of its size to the operation that concludes the assessment.

The first and second variables of this operation have a very similar case: both receive a value that must conform to validity rules and that must correspond to valid objects stored by the system. For both cases, there is one class of valid objects (id's that correspond to a valid object of the respective kind in the system) and one class of invalid objects (id's that do not correspond to any valid object of the respective kind in the system).

In the case of the third parameter, at this time, any string can be accepted. Thus there is one class of valid objects including every string and no invalid class.

Now, there is a rule:

For each invalid class comprehended in the parameters, the contract of this operation MUST have one precondition or exception to deal with it.

We will explain the issue with exceptions later. They are interchangeable. But let us concentrate on the preconditions for now.

The first parameter has one invalid class; thus, the precondition must certificate that this is not the case. The same happens to the second parameter. The third parameter does not demand the creation of any precondition for now. Thus the declaration of this operation with its preconditions could be like:

```
Context Controller::set_assessment(selected_sending, user_id,
                                   updated_assessment)
    pre:
        self.person.assessments.sending->exists(a_sending|
            a_sending.id = selected_sending
        ) AND
        self.person->exists(a_person|
            a_person.id = user_id
        )
```

Abbreviated form:

```
Context Controller::set_assessment(selected_sending, user_id,
                                   updated_assessment)
    pre:
        person.assessments.sending->exists(
            id = selected_sending
        ) AND
        person->exists(
            id = user_id
        )
```

12.2.2 Semantic and syntactic preconditions

Regarding parameter guarantee preconditions, special care must be taken not to confuse *semantic* preconditions with simple *syntactic* verifications. Semantic preconditions require that the database is consulted: for example, verifying if there is a person with a given *id*. However, syntactic verification may be done preferably by mechanisms other than preconditions.

If a parameter has a type *Natural*, it is not necessary to query a database to verify if a given argument belongs to the type or not, because it is sufficient to ask if it is an integer greater than zero to reach that conclusion. Then, when a parameter is declared as *x:Natural*, it is not necessary to write any preconditions to assure that *x* is a positive number: the type already states that.

Another example is the ISBN, which has a formation rule, and can be checked syntactically. Instead of writing preconditions to verify if a parameter is a well-formed ISBN, the team should simply create a primitive type *ISBN* with a verification method and use it forever.

What about *PrimeNumber*? Could it be a type? The answer is *yes*, because to know if a given number is a prime number, a syntactic verification is sufficient. Simply verify if any prime minor or equals to its half divided by it produces an integer number. If it has an integer divider, then it is not a prime number. No databases must be consulted.

Types must be defined in the system operation signature. If the desired type does not exist, a primitive type can be defined by the team. For example, Fig. 12−1 uses primitive types such as *IdProposal*, *MotivationText*, and *DecisionType*[2] that may incorporate not only identification and checksum mechanisms but also security mechanisms, because those identifiers could be encrypted to avoid unauthorized access. In both cases, primitive types could be defined to deal with the complexity of the verification mechanism.

12.2.3 Complementary constraints

A complementary constraint consists of assuring that certain constraints stronger than those of the conceptual model are valid while a given command is performed. Thus if the

---

[2] Their description, however, do not appear in the diagram.

conceptual model states that a given role has multiplicity 0.1, for example, a complementary constraint could just say that when performing a given command that role is filled (1) or not (0). For example, in general, a *Sending* may have zero or more *ProposalAssessment* associated with it. But the command that finalizes a *Sending* could have a precondition that states that at least a minimum number of *ProposalAsssessment* is linked to it. This number can be a constant (e.g., 4) or a system variable, such as *Sismob.minimum_assessments*.

A precondition can never contradict the conceptual model. If the conceptual model states 0.1, then no precondition could state a multiplicity of 2 or more for the same role. But if the conceptual model states 0.2, then the precondition can further restrict it, stating, for example, 0.1 or 1.2, or even, just 0, 1, or 2.

12.2.4 Precondition assurance

As the preconditions are not tested by the command that declares them, an external mechanism should exist to assure that they will be guaranteed before the operation is called.

This guarantee can be made by explicitly calling a query that verifies if the condition is true before calling the operation or by interface mechanisms that prevent the operation from being called with invalid data.

For example, instead of allowing the user to type any string in an ISBN field, the user could be led to select from a list of valid ISBNs, also with other information about books, such as, title, author, and price. That way, the parameter ISBN would be validated before performing the command that places one copy of that book in the shopping cart.

Usually, the flow of messages expressed in the system sequence diagram is a way to verify if preconditions are valid. For example, in Fig. 12–2, observe that the *user_id* is valid because the use case has a precondition that states it. Unless one of the operations in the sequence diagram deletes that user, it may be assumed that it continues to be valid until the end of the sequence. In some cases, concurrent processes by other users may be considered. It should be the case that a concurrent process deletes the instance. In this case, protections such as atomic transactions can be used or simply the observation that a given instance can never be deleted because of structural constraints.

12.3 Exceptions

Exceptions in contracts are fail conditions that the designer cannot or does not wish to avoid before starting performing the command itself.

Sometimes, conditions identified as exceptions may be converted into preconditions. If it is possible to transform an exception into a precondition, it is generally advisable to do so, because it is preferable to avoid problems as soon as possible. It is preferable to keep the user from performing a mistaken action rather than allowing her to do it and then reporting the error later.

OCL does not present a specific expression to manage exceptions, but they can be simulated in contracts by conditional postconditions (Section 12.6) such as:

```
post:
    if <condition> then
        <raise exception>
    else
        <all other post conditions, including other exceptions>
    endIf
```

As it would not be easy to represent many exceptions using this nested approach, we propose a new stereotyped expression, *exception:*, which is a shorter version of the expression above:

```
exception:
    <condition> IMPLIES <raise exception>
```

Now, for a contract to indicate an exception, it is sufficient to identify the condition that produces the exception and name the exception. Those names are usually represented by a code in a dictionary, and this code appears in the contract instead of the description.

A contract just indicates that exceptions may occur, but their handling must be defined only during the design of the interface or application tier, because if an exception is raised by the façade controller, it should be handled by the tier immediately above: the application or interface tier.

Imagine then in the contract for *set_assessment* it was not possible to guarantee that the *Sending* being passed as argument was not deleted by any other thread. In this case, instead of considering its existence as a precondition, the contract should indicate that it will try to use it, and if it by any chance does not exist, an exception will be raised. The partly defined contract with this exception would be something like:

```
Context Controller::set_assessment(a_sending, a_user, updated_assessment)
    pre:
        self.person->exists(a_person|
            a_person.id = a_user
        )
        ...
        NOT self.person.assessments.sending->exists()
            IMPLIES Exception.throw(E235)
        )
```

Here, a basic *throw* message is used to signal the exception to a class named *Exception*, which is not a basic OCL class, but that can be created to manage exceptions. Notice that when a precondition is transformed into an exception, the condition itself is always negated.

It is assumed that when an exception is raised, the system operation cannot be executed and none of its postconditions or results are obtained, because the data must be kept in a consistent state even when an exception occurs.

Some exceptions may be converted into preconditions if the designer devises a way to assure the condition *before* calling the command. In this case, the condition is negated again. But remember that *NOT NOT condition* is the same as *condition*.

Only conceptual elements (concepts, attributes, and associations) may appear in the OCL expressions of the contracts. These elements are necessarily related to the business rules of the system being analyzed. The exceptions mentioned here must be exceptions related to the business rules and not exceptions related to hardware or communication problems. Exceptions that may occur in physical storage, communication, or external devices must be addressed by specific mechanisms in the tiers where those elements belong. Usually, users are not even aware of them.

12.4 Preconditions and exceptions versus invariants

Invariants are used in the conceptual model to represent rules that should be always valid, independently on any system operation. *Preconditions* and *exceptions* are used for rules that are valid only during the execution of a given system operation.

When an invariant already exists in a given class, it is equivalent to the existence of an exception rule for each of its methods. For example, if there is an invariant that states that a student may enroll only in courses related to her career, then this invariant works as an exception in any method implemented in this class. Thus commands for enrolling a student may consider that the exception already exists in the form of the invariant, and if the student tries to enroll in a course that does not belong to her career, an exception would be raised.

Thus an invariant is equivalent to a set of exceptions, but not equivalent to preconditions. The existence of an invariant does not assure that the design or the user does not try to violate it. When an invariant violation happens, an exception is raised, just as in the case of exceptions. However, an operation may add a precondition that states that the invariant is assured before this operation is executed. This is a complementary mechanism that states that in the case of that specific operation, the invariant will not be violated because it has already being guaranteed by the design of the code.

Test mechanisms can be defined to verify if the invariants, preconditions, and postconditions are not being violated during the system execution. If those conditions are violated at any moment, they would raise exceptions. In those cases, the designer of the code must revise the structure of the program to correct the defect or handle the exception so that it will not happen again. When the system is delivered to the final user, it must be assured at the best of the team's capacity, that no invariant, precondition, or postcondition is violated at any time.

Exceptions, however, may occur because of concurrency issues or as the result of failures, not bugs. For example, the code may be bug-free, but even so the network may be down. This is an exception that must be raised and treated, and it is not due to a failure in programming. This has to do with fault tolerance.

12.5 Query return

As mentioned before, system commands change data while system queries just return data to the user. The contracts for system queries must define what is returned, and this can be done in OCL by using the *body* expression.

Expressions that represent preconditions are all Boolean, but expressions that represent the return of a query may have other types. They can return strings, numbers, lists, tuples, or even more complex structures. The following examples are based on the models of Figs. 12−1 and 12−2. Initially, we present the query that returns the list of sendings associated to a person as a reviewer.

```
Context Controller::list_sendings(user_id:ID):OrderedSet<DTO_sending>
    pre:
        self.person->exists(a_person|
            a_person.id = user_id
        )
    body:
        self.person->select(:a_person|
            a_person.id = user_id
        ).assessments.sending.proposal->collect(:a_proposal|
            Tuple {
                name = a_proposal.name
                status = a_proposal.status
                priority = a_proposal.priority
                validity = a_proposal.validity
            }
        )->asOrderedSet
```

Abbreviated form:

```
Context Controller::list_sendings(user_id:ID)
    pre:
        person->exists(
            id = user_id
        )
    body:
        person->select(
            id = user_id
        ).assessments.sending.proposal->collect(
            Tuple {
                name = name
                status = status
                priority = priority
                validity = validity
            }
        )->asOrderedSet
```

This query introduces two new functions of OCL, *collect* and *Tuple*. Collect is a function over collections that takes each element of the original collection and puts in the target collection the result of the expression evaluated inside parentheses. For example: $\{1, 2, 3, 4, 5\}-> collect(x|2 \times x)$

produces {2, 4, 6, 8, 10}. Applying it to collections of objects the idea is the same, an expression such as *self.person-> collect(a_person|a_person.email)* will return the set of emails of each person in the set *self.person*.

In fact, collect and the dot notation produce the same result. But the dot notation can be used only when the operation after the dot is postfixed (the operator goes after the expression.)

For example, we can write: *self.person.email* or *self.person-> collect(a_person|a_person. email)*. Both expressions produce the same result.

However, an operation that is not postfixed, such as " $\times$," which is infixed (the operator goes between operands) cannot be written with the dot notation. For example, writing {1, 2, 3} $\times$ 2 is not syntactically correct in OCL. It must be written as {1, 2, 3}-> *collect(x|x $\times$ 2)*.

The expression "Tuple" is not postfixed too; it is prefixed because the operator comes before the parameters. Tuple defines a kind of a key/value set, where the key is any identificatory chosen by the team, and the value must be a valid OCL expression that returns an object, data structure, or attribute value.

In the query before, a tuple is created with four keys: name, status, priority, and validity, and the respective values are all taken from the *Person*'s neighboring class *Proposal*.

It is recommended that system queries never return objects to the interface to keep both tiers logically separated. For example, instead of returning an instance of *Person*, the system query should return a simplified version of the information, such as a tuple with the values of the attributes of an instance of *Person*. There are some techniques that can be used to transform any OCL expression into simple data structures with alphanumeric values, such as JSON, XML, and proxies DTOs[3].

12.6 Postconditions

Postconditions establish what changes in the information managed by the system after some command is performed. Postconditions also must be carefully specified in terms that can be immediately recognized on the conceptual model structures. Thus although contracts can be written in natural language, they should be carefully written so they can be immediately translated into OCL expressions.

In order to classify the types of postconditions that can be used in a contract, we must take into account that the conceptual model has three basic elements, which are concepts, attributes, and associations. Thus considering that instances of classes can be created and destroyed, association links can be added, removed, and replaced, and attribute values can be changed, only six types of postconditions are necessary to express any change in data:

- Change an attribute value.
- Create a class instance.

---

[3] *Data Transfer Objects* are a design pattern that indicates that objects passed by the façade controller to the interface and vice versa cannot be instances of conceptual classes (those in the conceptual model). They must be pure data, with no behavior attached. This may be implemented with objects that only have attributes and their respective getters and setters (if any), nothing else. The JSON structures and the OCL *Tuple* are examples of *DTOs*.

- Destroy a class instance.
- Add an association link.
- Remove an association link.
- Replace and association link.

These postconditions are the most fundamental or basic commands that may be defined for an object-oriented system. They may not be decomposed any further, and all other commands are defined as combinations of them.

Thus a *basic command* is a command that performs one of the six postconditions listed above. The meaning and behavior of a basic command are predefined.

The basic commands, as defined in the following subsections, are effectively basic in the sense that they do the task without performing certain consistency verifications. For example, a command that adds a link between two objects would not verify if the upper bounds for both roles of the association were surpassed. That kind of consistency verification is preferably made by preconditions or exceptions in the contract, and the design of the contract should not violate them.

12.6.1 Changing an attribute value

One of the basic postcondition types consists of indicating that the value of an attribute was changed. That is usually written in OCL as

```
object.attribute = value
```

But, as OCL is a declarative language, this expression must not be understood as an assignment. It has, in fact, three possible ways to become true:

- *object.attribute* may be changed to become equal to *value*. This is usually the default interpretation.
- *value* may be changed to become equal to *object.attribute*.
- Both *value* and *object.attribute* may be changed to a third value and become equal.

Therefore in terms of code generation, this kind of expression may produce ambiguous interpretations. Cabot (2007) proposes a default semantic for interpreting such expressions so that ambiguity is reduced. However, another approach is possible, which does not require changing the original semantics of OCL. The idea is to use the "^" (caret) predicate instead of the " = " (equals sign) predicate, as explained below.

We can indicate without ambiguity that an attribute was changed just by declaring that a basic message concerning the change was sent to the object. The basic message is predefined, and its name should start with the prefix "*set*" followed by the name of the attribute. The new value is passed as an argument.

The message *set_attribute* may be sent to an instance of a class that contains the attribute. For example, if we are interested in changing the *priority* of a given *Proposal*, the following OCL expression could be used:

```
Context Controller::change_priority(a_proposal_id:ProposalId,
                                    a_priority:Natural)
    post:
        self.person.proposals_sent->select(b_proposal|
            a_proposal_id = b_proposal.id
        ).priority = a_priority
```

But we have already seen that it can be interpreted in ambiguous ways. The expression below expresses the same intention but without any ambiguity:

```
Context Controller::change_priority(a_proposal_id:ProposalId,
                                    a_priority:Natural)
    post:
        self.person.proposals_sent->select(b_proposal|
            a_proposal_id = b_proposal.id
        )^setPriority(a_priority)
```

Abbreviated form:

```
Context Controller::change_priority(a_proposal_id, a_priority)
    post:
        person.proposals_sent->select(
            a_proposal_id = id
        )^setPriority(a_priority)
```

The caret notation means that the message at the right *was sent* to the object or collection of objects at the left. Thus it is a Boolean predicate, and the result of the expression above is Boolean.

All these postconditions could be simplified if there was a qualified association between the Controller and the class Proposal, as seen in Fig. 12–3.

In this case, the postcondition could be written as:

```
Context Controller::changePriority(a_proposal, a_priority)
    post:
        all_proposals[id].priority = a_priority
```

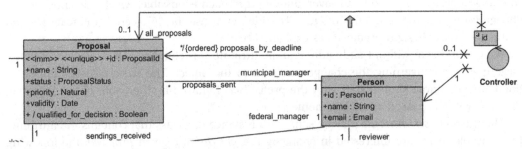

FIGURE 12–3 A qualified association between the controller and the *Proposal* class.

Or:

```
Context Controller::changePriority(a_proposal, a_priority)
    post:
        all_proposals[id]^setPriority(a_priority)
```

The expression *all_proposals[id].priority = a_priority* means that two values are equal no matter how that result was accomplished. But *all_proposals[id]^setPriority(a_priority)* states unambiguously that the attribute *priority* of object *all_proposals[id]* was changed to *a_priority*.

This form of writing is still considered a declarative specification, not imperative. The expression *with* "^" just states that an object has received a message; it does not say who sent that message. The decision about which object is going to send that message is left for dynamic modeling (Chapter 13).

12.6.2 Creating an instance

The command that creates an instance must just do that: create a class instance. Although OCL is not an imperative language, it has a constructor to indicate that a new instance of a class was created. This is expressed as a property of an object and is referenced as follows:

```
object.oclIsNew()
```

Its meaning, when used in a postcondition, is that the *object* was created during the command being specified by the postcondition. This property may be used in conjunction with another that declares the class of the object:

```
object.isTypeOf(Class)
```

However, as it would be a bit tedious to keep declaring the creation of an instance using two expressions, the definition of a single predicate that states that an object was created as an instance of a given class is suggested. The expression *object.new_instance_of(class)* is therefore defined as being equivalent to:

```
object.oclIsNew() AND object.oclIsTypeOf(class)
```

Thus a postcondition that declares that a new instance of *Person*, referred to as *new_person*, was created can be defined as *new_person.new_instance_of(Person)*.

In this case, the caret notation is not used because it is not a message sent to an instance of *Person*. It is a declaration that an instance *new_person* of class *Person* was created.

The message *new_instance_of* does not say anything about the instance's attributes and links, even the mandatory ones. As before, it can be assumed that other expressions will initialize mandatory attributes and links, and that the new instance's consistency will be checked for the contract as a whole and not for each individual basic command.

Attributes with initial values are considered automatically initialized when the instance is created. Thus it would be redundant to specify postconditions to update the attributes with initial values, unless values different from the default are desired.

Derived attributes, on the other hand, are calculated and cannot be directly modified. Thus they are not initialized too.

Attributes stereotyped with «optional» may be kept undefined at creation time; defining a value for them is not mandatory and usually is avoided.

But what happens with other (normal and mandatory) attributes when an instance is created? The basic command represented by the predicate *new_instance_of* simply produces the instance. It does not initialize attributes and links except for those that are defined with default initial values. If mandatory attributes and links are not initialized, the instance may be inconsistent; thus the contract should specify further postconditions that assure that all mandatory attributes and links are initialized when an object is created.

We have seen so far postconditions to create instances and change attributes. This allows us to combine them to create a contract for a CRUDL command that creates a new instance of *Person*. The system command *create_person* may have the following as a contract:

```
Context Controller::create_person(person_id:PersonID, a_name:String,
                                  an_email:Email)
    post:
        new_person.new_instance_of(Person) AND
        new_person^set_id(person_id) AND
        new_person^set_name(a_name) AND
        new_person^set_email(an_email) AND
        self^add_person(new_person)
```

Thus this contract establishes that when the message *create_person* is sent to the controller, some modifications happen in the information structure. A new instance of *Person* was created, and its mandatory three attributes are initialized. An association from the controller for this class is mandatory from the site of the controller, and despite it being not able to navigate in that direction, it must be created anyway. Thus the message *add_person* sent to the controller establishes a link between it and the new person.

This class has other associations besides that with the controller, but they are all optional from the side of *Person* and do not need to be added at creation time.

12.6.3 Destroying an instance

Although destroying objects is rare in object-oriented systems, it may sometimes occur. Usually, past deadline proposals and rejected proposals are not deleted physically: they are simply marked as inactive. In the Sismob project, this is even a supplementary requirement: no object is destroyed. Only data protection laws recently have introduced with more emphasis the need to really destroy information in a system.

Considering that an instance of an object is to be destroyed physically, there are two approaches to do it:

- *Explicit*: It is declared that the object was destroyed by sending an explicit destruction message to it.
- *Implicit*: All associations to the object are removed so that it becomes inaccessible. In programming languages, it is possible to implement *garbage collection* to remove from memory objects that are not accessible anymore.

In this book, the explicit approach is chosen because it makes the modeler's actual intention clearer. An object that has to be destroyed, then, must receive a basic message such as the following:

```
object^destroy()
```

The meaning of this expression is that the referred object was destroyed during the execution of the command.

It is assumed that all links to the destroyed object are removed as well. If any object formerly linked to it becomes inconsistent, then the contract must specify what happens to that object (if it is removed as well, or if the role is replaced by a link to another object). If there are objects that depend on the destroyed object, there are three options, which will be detailed later in this chapter:

- *Precondition*: the destruction of the object is prevented if it has dependent objects.
- *Exception*: the operation may try to destruct the object, but if it detects dependent objects, it fails.
- *Postcondition*: the operation removes the object and any other object that depends directly or indirectly of it. This option is not applicable in all circumstances, though.

12.6.4 Adding a link

As mentioned earlier in the chapter, another kind of basic command is one that states that a link was added between two objects. Although link additions are bounded by the multiplicity of the roles, this is only checked for the contract as a whole and not for each individual basic command. Thus a basic command can surpass the upper limit of a role only if another command in the same contract removes one element from that role, maintaining the number of objects in the role within the limit.

Usually, an OCL postcondition to indicate that a link was created would look like the following:

```
object.role->includes(another_object)
```

But, again, this expression may be ambiguously interpreted at the code generation stage, because there are at least four ways for it to become true:

- Include *another_object* in *object.role*.
- Assign to *another_object* an object that is already in *object.role*.
- Assign a third object to *another_object* and include it in *object.role*.
- Assign the empty set to *another_object*, because independently of the contents of *object.role*, it includes the empty set.

Usually, the first option is the intended meaning. But again, we suggest a notation that does not cause ambiguous interpretations and at the same time is more familiar to software developers. Once again, the "^" notation and a basic command are used to indicate that a link was created.

There are many dialects for naming commands that modify association roles. Here, we use the prefix *add* followed by the name of the role. Another common option would be to use the *set* prefix, as in the case of attributes. However, attributes have their values changed, while links are added; thus, perhaps, different goals should have different names.

Considering the association between classes *Person* and *Proposal*, and considering two instances, *a_person* and *a_proposal*, respectively, a link between the instances may be created in two different ways. First, from the point of view of a *Person*:

```
a_person^add_proposals_sent(a_proposal)
```

The use of the role "proposals_sent" assures that the person is a municipal manager. Second, from the point of view of a *Proposal*:

```
a_proposal^add_municipal_manager(a_person)
```

Both expressions are symmetric and produce exactly the same result: a link based on the association is created between the instances, and it is not directional.

Associations with mandatory roles, such as the one from *ProposalAssessment* to *Person*, usually require that their links are created in the same contract that creates the object that must have the role filled. Thus a link from *ProposalAssessment* to *Person* will be added always when an instance of *ProposalAssessment* is created, as shown below:

```
Context Controller::create_assessment(a_person_id:PersonID,
                                       a_sending_id:SendingID,
                                       a_text:String, an_opinion:String)
    post:
        new_proposal_assessment.is_instance_of(ProposalAssessment) AND
        new_proposal^set_text(a_text) AND
        new_proposal^set_opinion(an_opinion) AND
        self.person->select(a_person|a_person.id = a_person_id)
            ^add_assessments(new_proposal_assessment) AND
        self.all_proposals.sending->select(a_sending|
            a_sending.id = a_sending_id
        )^add_assessments(new_proposal_assessment)
```

Abbreviated form:

```
Context Controller::create_assessment(a_person_id, a_sending_id,
                                      a_text, an_opinion)
    post:
        new_proposal_assessment.is_instance_of(ProposalAssessment) AND
        new_proposal^set_text(a_text) AND
        new_proposal^set_opinion(an_opinion) AND
        person->select(id = a_person_id)
            ^add_assessments(new_proposal_assessment) AND
            all_proposals.sending->select(
                id = a_sending_id
            )^add_assessments(new_proposal_assessment)
```

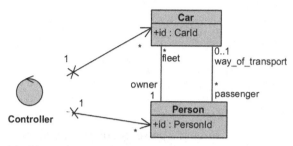

FIGURE 12–4 A simple model with mandatory and optional associations.

As can be seen, the postcondition states that a new instance of *ProposalAssessment* is created. There are two mandatory attributes (*text* and *opinion*) that are initialized with the values received as arguments. There are also two mandatory associations to *Sending* and *Person* that must be filled with a link. The link between the *Person* and *ProposalAssessment* is easier to create because a *Person* can be directly identified by its *id*, and the link between *ProposalAssessment* and *Sending* is a bit more indirect, because, first, the controller should access all proposals and then localize a specific assessment attached to one of them.

12.6.5 Removing a link

A single operation of removing a link can only be executed when an optional association exists between two objects. If the association is mandatory in one side at least, the link cannot be removed, but replaced to keep the consistency of the conceptual model.

All associations in the current example of Sismob have at least one mandatory role. Thus they do not serve as example to this basic operation. Let us then consider a situation where a *Car* has an *owner* (mandatory) and a number of *passengers* (optional). Se Fig. 12–4 for it.

As the figure shows, the association *fleet/owner* is mandatory, and it cannot be removed by a contract or an instance of *Car* would be inconsistent without an owner. This association can only be replaced, that is, we can substitute an owner by another. However, the association *way_of_transport/passenger* can be removed (if any exist) because it is not mandatory.

The removal of a link between two objects is made by a basic command prefixed by the word *remove*,[4] followed by the role name and receiving as a parameter the object member of the role that must be removed.

Then, a contract to remove a certain person from a certain car could be written like this:

```
Context Controller::remove_passenger(a_person_id:PersonId, a_car_id:CarId)
    def:
        a_car = self.car->select(:b_car|b_car.car_id = a_car_id)
        a_person = self.person->
            select(:b_person|b_person.person_id = a_person_id)
    post:
        a_car^remove_passenger(a_person)
```

---

[4] Some dialects might use *unset*.

Abbreviated form:

```
Context Controller::remove_passenger(a_person_id, a_car_id)
    def:
        a_car = car->select(id = a_car_id)
        a_person = person->select(id = a_person_id)
    post:
        a_car^remove_passenger(a_person)
```

In this case, if this person is not currently a passenger of that car, an exception would be raised.

When the multiplicity of the destination role of the link to be removed is 1 or 0.1, it is optional to inform the parameter, because there is only one possible link to be removed. If instead of removing the link from the point of view of the *Car*, it was done from the point of view of the *Person*, the result would be the same, but the basic command would not need a parameter:

```
Context Controller::remove_passenger(a_person_id:PersonId)
    def: a_person =
        self.person->select(b_person|b_person.person_id = a_person_id)
    post:
        a_person^remove_way_of_transport()
```

Abbreviated form:

```
Context Controller::remove_passenger(a_person_id)
    def: a_person = person->select(id = a_person_id)
    post:
        a_person^remove_way_of_transport()
```

12.6.6 Replacing a link

It is clear that replacing a link can be obtained by removing and adding a link, but this is an operation so important that it deservers to be included in the group of the basic commands.

Replacing a link can be used even when one of the roles is mandatory. It is considered an atomic operation, and thus, the mandatory role does not become inconsistent. One thing, however, that must be observed is if the role is immutable or not. It depends on the semantics of the model. Fig. 12−5 shows two situations, one where replacing a role is possible and other where it is not.

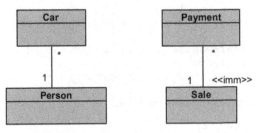

FIGURE 12−5 A mutable and immutable role.

This decision is totally dependent on the interpretation of the association. In the left side we have a car that must have an owner. We cannot add a second owner and neither remove the only owner for a period of time because during that period, the objects would be inconsistent. This is the case where the replace basic command can be used. Suppose that *a_car* is an instance of *Car* and *a_person* is an instance of *Person*. We could write an OCL expression such as *a_car^replace_owner(a_person)*, which would change the former owner of this car by another one. This can be made because cars can change owners.

However, in the case on the right of the figure, an installment necessarily belongs to a sale, but contrary to the situation with cars and persons, an installment once attached to a sale cannot have its sale replaced by another one. Once an installment is added to a sale, there it remains.

12.6.7 Well-formed postconditions

If we assume that the basic commands do not check if the objects and links are left in a consistent state, then the team must assure this verification when they are specifying the system command contracts.

The verifications that must be done are, at least, the following:

- A command that creates an instance must also have postconditions stating that all the instance attributes were initialized, except for (1) derived attributes (which are calculated), (2) attributes with an initial value (which are predefined by an *init* expression, unless a different value is desired), and (3) optional attributes, which can be null (in that case, initialization is optional too).
- All mandatory links for a newly created instance must be added.
- If after that the newly created object does not have a direct or indirect path to the controller, one must be created by one or more links.
- All created links must stay within the lower and upper bounds defined by their association roles multiplicity.
- All invariants affected by changes in attributes, links, or instances must not be violated, if possible.

The invariant-checking mechanism does not assure that the designer is writing a contract that keeps all invariants true. It is the responsibility of the designer to be aware of the invariants and avoid raising unnecessary exceptions. If an invariant happens to raise an exception that is not handled by the system, then there is certainly a design problem. Thus when it is impossible to prevent an exception, at least it must be handled by the upper tier (the interface).

Another issue involves attributes declared with initial values. If the definition of the initial value of an attribute uses information that may be obtained only by navigating its links, how can it be calculated before the links are created? The team must consider that the initialization of attributes with initial values will be one of the last tasks in the programming code that implements a contract, that is, attributes with initial values may be defined only after all links are added and the instance is (almost) consistent. In Fig. 12−6, it can be seen that the *Item.value* attribute may only have its initial value assigned after a link between the instance of *Item* and *Product* is added. Otherwise, the value of the attribute would be undefined.

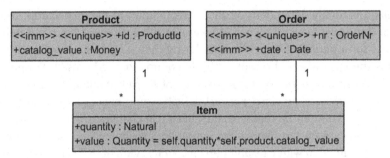

FIGURE 12–6 An example of an initial value that depends on another object.

12.6.8 Combination of expressions

Usually, OCL expressions used in preconditions, postconditions, exceptions, and body may be joined by the *AND* operator. This means that all expressions in the chain of *ANDs* must be true.

But it is also possible to use the *OR* operator, which establishes that just one of the expressions must be true in order to the combined expression to be true. For example:

```
Context Person::chose_wardrobe():String
      body:
          if System.rains() then
              "umbrella" OR "raincloath"
          else
              "normal clothes"
```

The problem with using this kind of expression is that it is inherently ambiguous. If it is raining, we cannot know for sure if the person is using an umbrella, a raincoat, or both. This kind of ambiguity is often avoided in usual information systems.

Another operator that can be used to connect OCL expressions is the *IMPLIES* operator, which has the same meaning of the implication operator of Boolean logic. *IMPLIES* is used when a postcondition is to be obtained only if a certain condition is true. For example, the following contract allows a user to change the text of a *ProposalAssessment* only if it is not concluded:

```
Context Controller::change_assessment(a_person_id:Person_Id,
                    a_proposal_Assessment_Id:Proposal_assessment_Id,
                    a_text:String)
    def:
        person = self.person->select(a_person|a_person.id = a_person_id)
        assessment = person.assessments->select(an_assessment|
              an_assessment.id = a_proposal_assessment_id)
    post:
        NOT assessment.concluded IMPLIES
            assessment^setText(a_text)
```

Abbreviated form:

```
Context Controller::change_assessment(a_person_id, a_proposal_Assessment_Id,
                                      a_text)
    def:
        person = person->select(id = a_person_id)
        assessment = person.assessments->select(
            id = a_proposal_assessment_id
        )
    post:
        NOT assessment.concluded IMPLIES
            assessment^setText(a_text)
```

Remember that the NOT operator has precedence over implication. Then, the postcondition may be read as "if the assessment is not concluded, then its text is changed."

The advantage of *implies* is that it is shorter than *if-then-endif*, but they have the same meaning. The advantage of *if-then-endif* or *if-then-else-endif* is that it is more familiar to programmers and includes a way to specify what must be obtained for both cases of a Boolean expression that is shorter than using two *implies* structures.

12.6.9 Former values

Sometimes a postcondition is built upon values that attributes and roles had before the command is performed. Those former values are referred to by the function *@pre* to indicate that they do not correspond to the value of the attribute *after* the command is performed (which could be different). For example, a postcondition that establishes that a quantity in stock for a given product has increased may be expressed as:

```
Context Controller::add_to_stock(product_id:ProductId, a_stock:Natural)
    def:
        product = self.products->select(a_product|a_product.id = product_id)
    post:
        product^set_quantity(product.stock@pre + a_stock)
```

Abbreviated form:

```
        Context Controller::add_to_stock(product_id, a_stock)
            def:
                product = products->select(id = product_id)
            post:
                product^set_quantity(product.stock@pre + a_stock)
```

Thus why was *@pre* used above? Because after the command is performed, the quantity in stock would already be incremented, and the argument for the basic command must be defined as the *previous* quantity plus the new quantity. That is why we have to write *product. stock@pre* (the former value) instead of *product.stock* (the newer value).

Remember that OCL is declarative, just as arithmetic is. Ada Lovelace already noticed in the 1830s that $x = x + 1$ is not a true statement in mathematical notation, because it cannot be true for any value of x. But when you write $x = x + 1$ in a *programming language*, it means the same as $x = x@pre + 1$.

12.6.10 Postconditions covering collections of objects

It is possible with a single OCL expression to state that a whole set of objects was changed. For example, an expression that states that the price of every product was raised by $x\%$ may be written using the *forAll* expression:

```
Context Controller::raise_product_price(x:Percent)
    post:
            self.product->forAll(:a_product|
                a_product^set_price(a_product.price@pre*(1+x))
    )
```

If the price is going to be raised by a value that does not depend on its former values, such as M$0,50 for each product, then there is no need to use the *@pre* notation. For example, if the price of all products has to be raised by x mira, then the following expression could be used:

```
Context Controll::add_to_product_price(x:Money)
    post:
            self.product->forAll(:a_product|
                a_product^setPrice(a_product.price + x)
    )
```

Remember that in our examples, *product* is a role of an association from the controller to the class *Product*.

12.6.11 Postconditions and real-world events

The process of creating contracts is intimately related to the expansion of the use case and the conceptual model. The conceptual model should be used as a reference at every moment because it is the source of information with which assertions can be made about the information.

Contracts should be always written with expressions that can be interpreted in terms of elements of the conceptual model. Thus assertions like "the products were shipped" or "the product was lost" would hardly be postconditions because they do not represent information contained in the conceptual model; they describe *real-world* events. If the team wishes to express this in a contract, they should create a conceptual structure (attribute, role, or concept) to represent it. For example, the fact that the products were shipped could be represented by creating an instance of the *Delivery* class and linking it to the current instance of *Order*.

12.7 Pattern contracts for CRUDL

The following subsections present models for contracts for typical CRUDL commands. There are three system command contracts and two system query contracts. The commands and queries examples are performed within the *Person* class, defined in accordance with the model of Fig. 12−7.

As in the case of CRUDL use cases, seen before, CRUDL system contracts can also be considered as patterns. It is our intention to show with this special model all contractual possibilities of these operations.

From now on, we abandoned the more verbose version of OCL to deal only with the most abbreviated version for each contract.

12.7.1 Contract for *create*

The contract for a *create* command usually should include the instantiation of a new object, initialization of its mandatory attributes, and addition of its mandatory links. The list below summarizes what we have to do with each attribute and association in the example:

- Attribute *id*: must be filled with a parameter of the *create* function, or with a new number created by a system service class.
- Attribute *name*: must be filled with a parameter of the *create* function.
- Attribute *date_of_birth*: must be filled with a parameter of the *create* function.
- Attribute *municipality_of_residence*: nothing is done because it is a derived attribute.
- Attribute *date_of_registry*: it does not need to be filled now because it has an initial value that is calculated by the system. As it is also immutable, it would not be changed in the future.

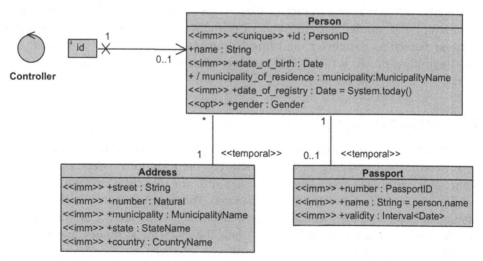

FIGURE 12–7 Basic conceptual model for examples in this section.

- Attribute *gender*: as it is an optional attribute and not immutable, it does not need to be created now. It can be filled latter.
- Role *address*: as it is a mandatory role, when a *Person* is created, her *Address* must be defined at the same time. In some cases, especially when the association is mandatory in both ends, the attributes of the address should be passed together with the attributes of the person in a single operation that creates both objects simultaneously. But as the role to the side of *Person* is optional, we can create an *Address* independently, and then pass it as argument to the operation that creates a *Person*. Notice also that the same address may belong to more than one person.
- Role *passport*: as it is an optional role, it does not need to be filled now. It can be added later or never.

Now, let us see the contract for *create* an instance of *Person* accordingly to this model:

```
Context Controller::create_person(an_id, a_name, a_date_of_birth, an_address)
1     pre:
2           person[an_id]->isEmpty()
3     post:
4           new_person.new_instance_of(Person) AND
5           new_person^set_id(an_id) AND
6           new_person^set_name(a_name) AND
7           new_person^set_date_of_birth(a_date_of_birth) AND
8           new_person^add_address(an_address) AND
9           new_person^set_date_of_registry(System.today) AND
10          self^add_person(new_person)
```

Lines were numbered to easy explanation. The precondition in line 3 establishes that there is no *Person* in this system with the same *id* as the one received as parameter. This is for avoiding violating the *unique* constraint in this attribute.

Line 4 established that an instance of *Person* was created. Lines 5, 6, 7, and 9 initialize the mandatory and nonderived attributes of this class. Finally, line 8 creates a link with the address passed as parameter, and line 10 creates a link with the controller. As this last one is unidirectional, it must be a message received only by the controller and not vice versa.

12.7.2 Contract for *update*

The CRUDL *update* command usually involves changing the value of some attributes. Before defining a contract for updating an object, however, the team must check which attributes are immutable. Attributes and association roles with the «*imm*» stereotype cannot be changed by any command after the object is created. Those properties are read-only.

The update command then will change normal attributes that are not immutable, neither derived. In the case of a *Person* in Fig. 12−7, only the following attributes may be updated: *name* and *gender*. Regarding roles, they usually are changed by specific operations. For example, one operation could replace the address of the *Person* and another could add a new *Passport*. Usually this is not done by the CRUDL update. The update contract in this case might look like the following:

```
Context Controller::update_person(an_id, a_name, a_gender,
                                  an_address, a_passport)
1    def:
2        a_person = person[an_id]
3    pre:
4        a_person->notEmpty()
5    post:
6        a_person^set_name(a_name) AND
7        a_person^set_gender(a_gender)
```

In this case, we defined a precondition in line 4 to establish that there is a person in the system with the *id* provided. Notice that this is the opposite of the precondition for the creation operation.

In lines 6 and 7, we update the value of the only two attributes that can be updated. Notice that in this case, it is not necessary to create a link between the controller and the instance of person, because it already exists.

The class *Controller* would have also operations to replace the *Address* and add a *Passport* to an instance of *Person* (passports usually cannot be replaced neither removed).

12.7.3 Contract for *delete*

The command that *deletes* an object must consider structural rules of the conceptual model before deciding if an object can or cannot be destroyed.

In the case of Fig. 12−7, for example, an instance of *Person* cannot be deleted if one or more passports are linked to it, because, from the point of view of the passport, the link is mandatory. This does not happen to addresses, because an *Address* can exist without being linked to a *Person*. In this case, it is the *Person* that cannot exist without an *Address*.

Thus before planning to delete an object from the system, it is convenient to verify if there are associations that prevent this operation to be performed.

In order to perform deletion without violating any structural rules, one must choose one of these three approaches below:

- Assure by *precondition* that the object being deleted would not leave other objects inconsistent regarding the lower bound of their associations. With this approach, only persons with no mandatory associations to them may be deleted. In the example, a *Person* with no *Passport* *may be deleted* but a *Person with a Passport* should not be deleted so easily. It can be highlighted in the system interface: the objects that cannot be deleted may be gray or without the delete icon, while others have normal color and/or the presence of the icon.
- Use an *exception* to abort the delete command if it is attempted for an object that will leave other objects inconsistent. If a user tries to delete *Person* that has passports linked

to it, an exception would be raised. In this case, the interface shows every person and provides the delete option for anyone. But if the operation is tried on an object that cannot be deleted, an error message produced by an exception will appear and avoid the operation to be concluded.

- Assure by *postcondition* that all objects that would be left inconsistent after deletion are deleted as well in cascade. In this case, all passports linked to a *Person* to be deleted would be deleted as well.

The third approach is used when we want to propagate the delete command to every object that has mandatory associations to the object being deleted. This propagation is recursive: deletion will continue until no more objects with mandatory links to objects that were deleted are found.[5] This approach may *not* always be used; there are situations in which propagating deletion is against business rules. In the case of *Persons*, for example, deleting an *Address* linked to a person will leave that person inconsistent. However, it probably is not the case to propagate the deletion to the *Person* as well. In this case, what happens is that deleting an *Address* linked to a *Person* is prohibited. However, deleting a *Person* with all her *Passports* is acceptable, because if a *Person* is deleted, those *Passports* have no reason to continue to exist.

Let us see the three possible contracts to delete a *Person*. First one, prevented by precondition:

```
Context Controller::delete_person(an_id)
1    def:
2         a_person = person[an_id]
3    pre:
4         a_person->notEmpty() AND
5         a_person.passport->isEmpty()
6    post:
7         a_person^destroy()
```

In line 4, the precondition states that the person exists, and line 5 states that it is not linked to any passport. Thus it can be deleted, as done in line 7.

Now let us see the contract where exception is used to prevent an invalid deletion to happen:

```
Context Controller::delete_person(an_id)
1    def:
2         a_person = person[an_id]
3    pre:
4         a_person->notEmpty()
5    post:
6         a_person^destroy()
7    exception:
8         a_person.passport->notEmpty() IMPLIES Exception.throw(278)
```

---

[5] In fact, in the general case, the lower bound of the role is the information that must be considered. For example, if a role has multiplicity 3.*, than removing a link when only 3 are left already makes the object inconsistent.

In this case, the precondition only checks if the person exists. Postconditions are tried to be achieved but cannot because an exception raises if a *Passport* is attached to the *Person*.

Finally, let us see how the deletion would happen if it were cascaded by preconditions. Remember that this option is not always valid, it depends on the semantics of the objects and their links. The contract is this:

```
Context Controller::delete_person(an_id)
1    def:
2         a_person = person[an_id]
3    pre:
4         a_person->notEmpty()
5    post:
6         a_person^destroy() AND
7         a_person.passport^destroy()
```

As there are no other classes dependent to *Person* or *Passport*, so this is sufficient. Otherwise, a list of other objects to be deleted would be added to the *post* section of the contract.

A programmer used to imperative languages could find strange to destroy an object and then destroy the objects linked to the original one. In most imperative languages, it would be an error and the order of those expressions should be inverted. However, OCL is declarative, and the "AND" expression means really "and" and not "then" as in imperative languages. Thus the idea is not a sequential flow of commands, but a single logic expression glued by some "ANDs" that must be true after the operation is executed.

Observe also that the caret notation can be used with collections of objects, as in *a_person.passport^destroy()*. In this case, it is a set of objects (passports) that are declared as destroyed.

However, usually, information systems do not allow information to be deleted. A person that is removed from the system, for example, is not really deleted, but marked as *inactive*. For implementing this approach, one simple solution is to define a new Boolean *active* attribute for the class whose members may be inactivated instead of deleted. The default value for this attribute is *true* because the object usually is active when it is created.

12.7.4 Contract for *retrieve*

The simple CRUD *retrieve* query returns information about the attributes of a class as they are; that is, without doing any calculation, filtering, etc. In this case, normal attributes, immutable, derived, and attributes with initial value, all of them can be returned. The exception would be private attributes, but they are not used yet in conceptual model.

These queries do not return data that are not explicitly in the class definition. Queries that return data calculated from one or more objects are *reports*, not *retrieve* queries.

A simple retrieve query for the class *Person* of Fig. 12–7 could be defined as follows:

```
Context Controller::retrieve_person(an_id:):Tuple
    def:
        person = person[an_id]
    body:
        Tuple {
            id=person.id,
            name=person.name,
            date_of_birth=person.date_of_birth,
            municipality_of_residence=person.municipality_of.residence
            date_of_registry=person.date_of_registry
            gender=person.gender
        }
```

As discussed before, the retrieve query returns a tuple or record with the data from the attributes of the object selected by the query parameter.

12.7.5 Contract for *listing*

Finally, the second query of CRUDL is a query that lists all objects belonging to a class or those that correspond to a Boolean filter. Usually, not every attribute will be shown in a listing. Thus the team may consult to user/client (or use the CSD matrix) to decide which attributes are relevant for a listing. Usually, only attributes that help the user to recognize the record she is looking for are used. In this example, we chose as attributes to locate a *Person*, the following items: *name*, *date_of_birth*, *municipality_of_residence*, and *gender*.

If no filter is applied, then every object will be listed. The contract in this case could be:

```
Context Controller::list_person():Set<Tuple>
    body:
        person->collect (
            Tuple {
                name=person.name,
                date_of_birth=person.date_of_birth,
                municipality_of_residence=person.municipality_of.residence
                gender=person.gender
            }
        )
```

We discuss some patterns for the application of filters to listing later in the book.

12.8 Discussion

An expanded use case is a chain of commands and queries that will be performed in a given sequence. Usually, each operation will supply information or assure preconditions for other operations. The best approach to write contracts for this sequence of operations is to follow the use case flow that is depicted in the system sequence diagram. In this sequence, the team must ask:

- What is the goal of each operation?
- What do they produce in terms of information?
- How do they change attributes and object links?
- Do they create or destroy or deactivate objects?
- What do they expect their predecessors have produced?
- Which exceptions could happen during execution?
- Can their exceptions be reconfigured as preconditions?
- Do their parameters include groups of values that are invalid? If positive, this demands preconditions or exceptions.
- Do the operations follow a known pattern?

When answering these questions, the designer will be building contracts that allow the commands and queries to be performed in a consistent way in the context of the use case transaction. If it is necessary to add new queries or commands to the sequence diagram to assure certain preconditions, then this is the right moment to do that.

Questions

1. Explain and present an example on how an exception may be transformed into a precondition and vice versa.
2. What is the difference between exceptions in command contracts and in query contracts?
3. What are the six possible postconditions, and what basic commands define each of them?
4. In Fig. 12–2, although a *Sending* may have multiple assessments, they must all be from different reviewers. The current model does not guarantee it. Write an invariant that deals with this issue.
5. Give an example of a mandatory link that can be replaced and another that cannot be.

13

Domain tier design

Key topics in this chapter

- Responsibility
- Visibility
- Low Coupling
- Delegation
- Dynamic Modeling
- Design Class Diagram

13.1 Introduction to domain tier design

Software design in general aims to produce a solution to a problem that has already been sufficiently clarified by analysis. The static aspects of the *problem* are represented in the conceptual model, and the functional or transformational aspects are represented in the expanded use cases, system sequence diagrams, and system operation contracts. Now it is time to design a *solution* to implement the logical and technological aspects of the system. In this sense, *design is a solution for a problem modeled by analysis.*

During iterations, after expanding use cases, refining the conceptual model, and writing contracts, the team may conduct design activities, which can be divided into two groups:

- *Logical design* (this chapter), which includes the aspects of the problem that are related to the business logic. Usually, the logical design is represented in the *design class diagram* (*DCD*), which evolves from the conceptual model, and by *interaction diagrams*, which show how objects exchange messages to perform system operations and achieve the postconditions of the contracts.
- *Technological design*, which includes all aspects of the problem that are inherent to the technology used: interface, data storage, security, communication, fault tolerance, etc. Some activities related to technological design are addressed in this book:
  - *Interface tier design* (Chapter 16), which consists of designing the user interface and preferably keeping it decoupled from the domain tier.
  - *Persistence tier design* (Chapter 17), which consists of the definition of a persistency mechanism to allow data load and save, which can be performed automatically, preventing the designer from being overconcerned about those aspects.

Logical design is also known as *domain tier design*. The domain tier corresponds to the set of classes that perform all data transformation and queries. Other tiers implement technological aspects of the system: persistency, interface, communication, security, etc. They

Object-Oriented Analysis and Design for Information Systems. DOI: https://doi.org/10.1016/B978-0-443-13739-6.00011-3

are usually derived from and dependent on the domain tier, and their utility is to connect the pure logic of the domain to the physical computer aspects (communication networks, human interfaces, storage devices, etc.).

The design of the domain tier consists basically of two activities that can be performed iteratively:

- *Dynamic modeling*, which consists of building execution models for the system operation contracts. In object-oriented systems, such models are usually represented by interaction diagrams such as communication or sequence diagrams or even as pure text algorithms.
- *DCD building*, which consists basically of adding to the conceptual model, some information that was not possible or desirable to obtain earlier, such as the association's navigation direction, and the methods to be implemented in each class. Those aspects can be effectively included in the software design if dynamic modeling is done. Additionally, the structure of design classes may be a little different from the conceptual model as new classes or a different class organization may be necessary to perform some concrete functions that will be required at this point.

The logical design can be performed systematically if the team is in possession of two artifacts:

- The evolving conceptual model that will be converted into the DCD.
- The functional model represented by system operation contracts.

The logical design activities consist of building interaction diagrams for system operations found in the system sequence diagrams, considering the DCD and the respective system operation contract.

Dynamic modeling, as mentioned before, can make use of communication or sequence diagrams, or even algorithms. Each of those forms has advantages and disadvantages:

- *Algorithms*, for programmers, are easier to write, but it may be difficult to clearly realize the connections among objects in simple text. Thus the choice for algorithms to use object-oriented dynamic modeling may raise the risk of high coupling among classes, generating bad design. One of the worst results of the common use of this tool is that programmers tend to write methods as if they are using 1970s structured programming and not object-oriented programming.
- *Communication diagrams* are better than algorithms for visualization and responsibility distribution purposes, and they are better than sequence diagrams for providing an explicit view of the visibility lines between objects. However, these diagrams may be difficult to organize and in the case of complex collaborations, they may become harder to read than sequence diagrams. Maybe because of that, the OMG is not evolving the chapter dedicated to communication diagrams in the UML handbook.
- *Sequence diagrams* are usually easier to read than communication diagrams, but they do not show explicitly the visibility lines between objects. If the designer is not vigilant, invalid or impossible communications may be included in the diagram. However, as it is

the most used interaction diagram of UML and the fact that we already used them to systematize use cases, this will be our choice in this chapter given that they are always used with one eye in the conceptual model or DCD.

Thus this chapter uses sequence diagrams for dynamic modeling in order to ease the visualization of the communication between objects.

The class diagram examples in this chapter assume that it is design time. Thus associations may be directed, and classes may have methods and private attributes.

The chapter initially discusses object responsibility, which is a key concept in understanding how to distribute methods among objects. Knowing which object should implement which responsibility allows design classes to be highly cohesive.

Another key concept that is presented in detail is *visibility*, which establishes that communication among objects can occur only when visibility lines exist. If the quantity of those lines is minimized, *low coupling* (Meyer, 1988) is achieved in the design.

Finally, the chapter explains how to transform contracts into dynamic models by using responsibility distribution and visibility, as well as other design patterns, to produce the best design possible.

13.2 Object responsibility distribution

Responsibility distribution among objects has to do with the following question: *What methods must be implemented in which classes?*

Many designers find it difficult to build an elegant solution to that problem when they simply try to add methods to a class diagram. The use of interaction diagrams and design patterns may, however, provide a more efficient and effective way to *discover* the most suitable place to implement each method.

The DCD is built from the conceptual model, which provides the basic set of classes, attributes, and associations that are needed. Then, it is necessary to develop interaction diagrams for each system operation contract; not necessarily everyone the just one sprint, because this can be done iteratively and cumulatively. Those diagrams show objects exchanging messages to achieve the postconditions of the respective contracts. There are techniques that help in building those diagrams in an elegant way. The use of diagrams is better than algorithms, especially for novice designers, because with algorithms, the designer may fall for the temptation of concentrating all responsibilities in a single class, while the diagrams allow better visualization of the distribution of responsibilities among the objects. An example of that situation is presented later in this chapter.

When a team builds object-oriented code without an adequate method for dynamic modeling (that is, simply making a class diagram and adding ad hoc methods to it) there is a risk that the responsibilities may be poorly distributed among the classes, and the result may be as unstructured as the old *spaghetti code*. Usually, object-oriented systems are well organized at the class level, but unhappily the code written inside methods is often poorly designed.

Thus for a system to be elegant, responsibilities must be well distributed. If a systematic method is not used, responsibilities can become concentrated in the controller class, or in classes that represent business actors, such as *Person* or *Company*. In the end, classes such as *Project, Assessment,* and *Payment* would have no relevant method besides their own attribute's getters and setters.

When one or two classes do all the work, and others are passive, there is no object-oriented code worthy of that name, but a concentrating structure.

On the other hand, designers, sometimes, make the mistake of believing that an object-oriented system is a simulation of the real world. But that is not usually true. An object-oriented model represents *the information* about the real world and not the *things* themselves. The difference is subtle: methods do not correspond to real-world action, but to the internal information processing of the system. That is why concepts such as *Project* that are passive in the real world may perform commands in object-oriented systems.

Thus designing object-oriented software must be understood as a precise method, guided by learned patterns, and not simply as the act of creating classes and associating ad hoc methods to them.

Before explaining how to distribute responsibilities among objects, a taxonomy of those responsibilities will be defined. Basically, there are two high-level groups of responsibilities:

- The responsibility of *knowing*, which corresponds to the getters or queries on objects.
- The responsibility of *updating*, which corresponds to the commands performed by objects, set in the case of attributes, add, remove, and replace in the cases of roles, and nonpattern others.

Both high-level groups are divided into three subgroups:

- Things that the object knows or updates within *itself* (getting and setting its attributes).
- Things that the object knows or updates in its *neighborhood* (adding, removing, and replacing its links).
- Other things that the object knows or updates that are not classified in the previous two groups. Normally these things correspond to *derived knowledge* (derived attributes and associations, and other queries in general) and *coordinated activities* (delegate methods).

In the case of the responsibilities of *knowing*, the three subgroups could be characterized as follows:

- *Things that the object knows about itself.* This is equivalent to being able to access the attributes of an object. Such responsibilities are incorporated to the classes by basic query methods named with the prefix *get* followed by the name of the attribute.[1] For example, if the class *Person* has an attribute *birth_date*, then the method *get_birth_date* has the responsibility of knowing the value of that attribute.

---

[1] That is valid for normal attributes belonging to classes of the conceptual model, though. During the construction of the DCD, new design attributes that represent the internal state and influence the behavior of an object may become necessary and those attributes do not necessarily have to be accessed by other objects: in that case, they should not have getters (they are private or protected).

- *Things that the object knows about its neighborhood*: This is equivalent to being able to access directly linked objects. This responsibility is incorporated in the methods that obtain the set of objects linked through a given role. Such methods are usually prefixed with *get* and followed by the role name (or the name of the class in the absence of the role name). For example, if *Car* is associated to *Person* and the role name for *Person* is *driver*, then the method *get_driver* returns the set of people that are drivers of a given car it may be zero person, one person, or more.

- *Derived things that the object knows*: This is equivalent to information that is composed or calculated from other information. This responsibility may be associated to derived attributes and derived associations, in which case the methods are also prefixed by *get* followed by the name of the derived attribute or association. For example, if *total_value* is the name of a derived attribute of class *Order*, then *get_total_value* is a method that returns that derived attribute. Derived knowledge also includes other queries about an object that cannot be represented as derived attributes or associations, such as queries with parameters; in that case, names may vary.

In the case of responsibilities related to *updating* information, the three subgroups could be characterized as:

- *Things that the object does over itself*: This corresponds to the basic command that updates a single attribute, which is prefixed with *set*,[2] followed by the attribute name. For example, if the class *Person* has an attribute *weight*, then *set_weight* is a method that incorporates the responsibility of changing that attribute.

- *Things that the object does over its neighborhood*: This corresponds to the basic commands that add, remove, and replace links between objects. These commands are identified respectively by the prefixes *add, remove*, and *replace* followed by the name of the association role. For example, if the class *Customer* has an association with *Reservation*, the methods *add_reservation, remove_reservation*, and *replace_reservation* incorporate that responsibility.

- *Things that the object coordinates*: This corresponds to commands that perform multiple tasks, possibly in different objects. These commands are known as *delegated methods*, and they are crucial for class design because the methods of the other groups are just basic commands with previously known behavior; but delegate methods must be designed for created nonbasic behaviors. For example, if all the products in a given order must be marked as delivered, the coordination of the marking activities must be made by the instance of *Order* itself, because it is the object with the most immediate access to the objects that participate at the operation.

Table 13−1 summarizes the six kinds of responsibilities and the methods typically associated to each kind.

---

[2] Remember that not every attribute may have a setter. Immutable attributes should not have a setter. Derived attributes never have setters, and private attributes also should not have public setters.

Table 13–1 Object responsibilities.

	Know	Update
About itself	Query on attributes: – *get_attribute()*	Update attributes: – *set_attribute()*
About its neighborhood	Query on association roles: – *get_role()*	Update links: – *add_role()* – *remove_role()* – *replace_role()*
Others	Queries on derived attributes and roles, and other general queries: – *get_attribue()* – *get_role()* – names vary in the case of other general queries	Delegated methods: – names vary

There is no standard name for delegated methods and general queries, which are named depending on the operation they perform. Usually, these names must not include the name of the class where they are implemented. For example, if *Decision* implements a command to finish it, do not name it as *a_decision.finish_decision()*; it is better not to mention the name of the class in the method. Then, *a_decision.finish()* would do it better.

13.3 Visibility

For two objects to be able to exchange messages to perform their responsibilities, it is necessary that some kind of *visibility* exists between them. There are four basic forms of visibility between objects:

- *By association*: If there is a link between two objects defined by an association between their classes.
- *By parameter*: If an object, when performing a method, receives another object as parameter.
- *Locally declared*: If an object that is performing a method receives another object as a query return.
- *Global*: If an object is visible by any other object.

None of the visibility forms are necessarily symmetric. That is, if *x* has visibility to *y* that does not mean that *y* necessarily has visibility to *x*. Visibility by association may be symmetric if the association is bidirectional, but this is not always the case.

13.3.1 Visibility by association

There is visibility by association between two objects only when there is an association between their respective classes. The kind of visibility allowed depends on the role multiplicity and other features, such as the association being qualified, ordered, and so on.

FIGURE 13–1 Unidirectional association between classes with multiplicity 1.

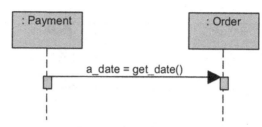

FIGURE 13–2 Object visibility to a single object.

An association role may be considered a collection of instances, especially if its upper bound is greater than 1. But, in the case of multiplicity 1 or 0.1, it is possible to interpret the role as a set or as an individual object. OCL, in these cases, considers the role both as an object and a collection. Regarding multiplicity, then, the following kinds of visibility may be identified:

- If the multiplicity is 1, then there is straight visibility to one instance and to the set that contains that instance.
- Any other multiplicity allows only visibility to a set of instances[3].

The DCD is not the only specification that determines the multiplicity of a role. It is complemented by the preconditions of the contracts, which can constrain multiplicity bounds even more, as seen in the following sections.

13.3.1.1 Visibility to a single object

Fig. 13–1 shows a *Payment* class that has a unidirectional association to *Order* with multiplicity 1. In this case, any instance of *Payment* has straight visibility to an instance of *Order*.[4]

In this way, when an instance of *Payment* is represented in an interaction diagram, as shown in the sequence diagram in Fig. 13–2, it can send messages directly to the instance of *Order* that is linked to it.

---

[3] It could be considered that a 0..1 role is filled with a single object or a null value. However, that is not coherent with the interpretation of other multiplicities such as, for example, 0..2 or *, where 0 stands for the empty set and not for the null value. To avoid such inconsistency it is preferable to consider that multiplicity 0..1 refers to a set that can be empty or contain a single element.

[4] And additionally, to a set that contains that order.

FIGURE 13–3 Unidirectional association between classes with multiplicity *.

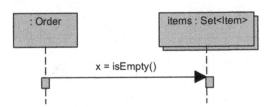

FIGURE 13–4 An object with visibility to a set of objects sending a message to the set structure.

13.3.1.2 Visibility to multiple objects

Multiplicity values different from 1, such as *, 1.*, 0.1, or 5, provide visibility to a collection[5] of objects, not just to a single instance. From now on, all those cases will be generally addressed as * multiplicity, or association *to many*.

Fig. 13–3 shows class *Order* with a unidirectional association with multiplicity * to class *Item*.

In this case, an instance of *Order* can send a message to a set of instances of *Item*. It is possible to send messages to the set structure itself,[6] as shown in Fig. 13–4. In the example, the message verifies if the set is empty.

But it is possible to send a message iteratively to each element of the set, as shown in Fig. 13–5. In the example, the message requests the subtotal value of each item.

Thus messages, in sequence diagrams, may be addressed to the collection structure or to the collection elements individually. When a message is sent to the structure, the type of the object that receives the message should be a collection, such as *Set < Item>* in Fig. 13–4. The fact that the message is iterative and sent to all elements in the set is represented by the *loop* fragment that involves the message. The condition [*for all*] indicates that all elements of the set receive the message.

A filter could be used here if the message was intended just for some selected elements. For example, if the message *get_subtotal* is intended only for items with *quantity* greater than 1, then the condition into the loop fragment could be written as *item|item.quantity > 1*, instead of *for all*. Thus it is identical to the OCL expressions used inside parentheses of the *select* operation.

---

[5] A *set* by default.

[6] In this text it is assumed that the operations available for sets and other collections are the ones defined by OCL (Object Management Group, 2010). However, if different languages or packages are used, a different set of operations would be available.

13.3.1.3 Visibility by association with ordered roles

If the association role is ordered with the use of the {*ordered*} or {*sequence*} constraints, the visibility to the collection as a structure is kept, but additionally straight visibility to individual elements indexed by their position is allowed.

Fig. 13−6 presents a class diagram with a unidirectional association with an ordered role. In Fig. 13−7, different types of visibility allowed by that association are shown.

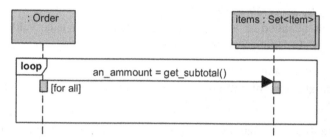

FIGURE 13–5 An object with visibility to a set of objects sending a message to each element of the set.

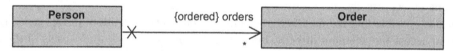

FIGURE 13–6 Unidirectional association between classes with ordered multiplicity.

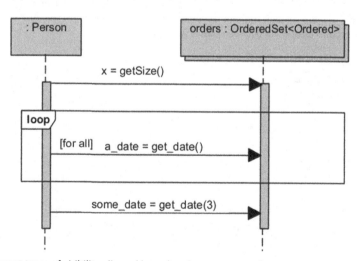

FIGURE 13–7 Different types of visibility allowed by ordered or sequence roles.

In Fig. 13−7, the first message is sent to the OrderedSet structure as a whole and asks how many elements there is in the OrderedSet. The second message is enclosed in a loop fragment and corresponds to asking each *Order* in the OrderedSet its date. The third message is a new type when compared to the other situations seen above, it accesses a given element in the OrderedSet by its index. In this case, it returns the date of the element in position "3." If there is no element in this position, then it returns the empty set.

13.3.1.4 Visibility by association with qualifiers

If the association is qualified as a map (only one element for each value of the qualifier), there are at least two forms of elements visibility:

- Visibility to the set of elements (as if it were a regular set).
- Visibility to a single element if the object has a key to access the element in the association role.

Fig. 13−8 presents a class diagram with a qualified association from *Person* to *CreditCard*.

Fig. 13−9 shows that the structure as a whole can be addressed. It shows also that all elements of the role can be accessed just as if the qualified association has a set in the opposite role. It also shown that if the origin class has one of the keys for the mapping, then it can access one object directly.

It is also possible that the qualified association represents a partition. In this case, there is no way to access one element directly, but only the complete set or the subsets of the partition. Fig. 13−10 shows a link that defines a partition. Card numbers are immutable and

FIGURE 13–8 Unidirectional association between classes with qualifier.

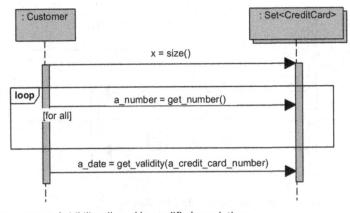

FIGURE 13–9 Different types of visibility allowed by qualified associations.

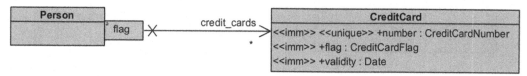

FIGURE 13–10 Unidirectional association between classes with qualifier defining a partition.

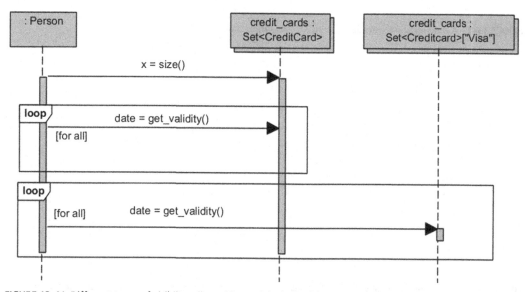

FIGURE 13–11 Different types of visibility allowed by qualified associations that define partitions.

unique, but card flags are just immutable. A person can have more than one card with the same flag. Thus this example defines a partition.

In this case, the whole set may be accessed. But the use of the qualifier allows also accessing cards belonging to a given subset. Fig. 13–11 shows the modes available.

In this figure, the first message accesses the structure as if it was a simple set. The second message is sent to each element of the whole set. The third message is sent only to a subset in which *flag* is equal to "Visa."

13.3.1.5 Visibility by association with association class

As explained before, when a link with an association class is added, an instance of the association class is created and attached to the link. When the same link is removed, then the respective instance of the association class is destroyed. Thus if *Person* has a unidirectional association to *Organization* and that association has an association class *Job*, as shown in Fig. 13–12, when a link between instances of *Person* and *Organization* is added, an instance of *Job* is created; and every time a link from *Person* to *Organization* is removed,

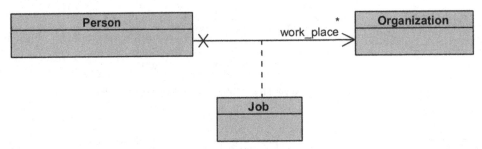

FIGURE 13–12 A unidirectional association with an association class.

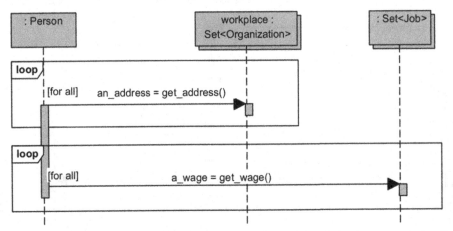

FIGURE 13–13 Two types of visibility that a class has when a unidirectional association has an association class.

the respective instance of *Job* is destroyed. Therefore an instance of *Person* has visibility to two sets[7] with the same size: one with instances of *Organization*, and another with instances of *Job*. As it is a unidirectional association, an instance of *Job* has visibility only to a single instance of *Organization*.

If the association in Fig. 13–12 were bidirectional, then an instance of *Organization* would also have visibility to a set of *Person* and a set of *Job*. Additionally, any instance of *Job* would have visibility to one instance of *Person* and one instance of *Organization*.

It is important to highlight that if the association is bidirectional, there is only one instance of *Job* attached to the link, not two.

Fig. 13–13 shows two kinds of visibility from the point of view of *Person*. The first represents the visibility that an instance of *Person* has to the set of instances of *Organization* as work places. That corresponds to the default visibility obtained for a role with multiplicity *.

---

[7] The association probably would be physically implemented not as two sets, though, but by a dictionary. Here the visibility means that two sets of objects may be obtained by an instance; this does not mean that they are implemented like that.

The second one represents the visibility that an instance of *Person* has to a set of instances of *Job*, the association class.

The association class also works as a mapping in a way that is very similar to the qualified association. The qualified association maps an alphanumeric into an object, but an association with association class maps an instance into another instance. The model in Fig. 13−12 is equivalent to mapping a job for each organization a person works for. Thus if an instance of *Person* has visibility to a specific instance of *Organization* (key), it may find the correspondent instance of *Job* (value) as illustrated in Fig. 13−14.

Also, in Fig. 13−14, we can see that *an_organization* must be an instance of *Organization* and that the instance of *Person* must have some kind of visibility to it in order to use it to access the respective instance of *Job*. In the example, we used an instance of *SomeClass* to return *an_organization* to *Person* such that the necessary visibility is achieved.

Finally, Fig. 13−15 shows the visibility that instances of the association class have to the instances of the link participating classes: a visibility that is strictly one.

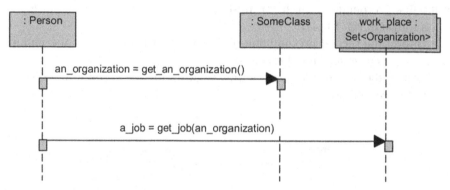

FIGURE 13–14 An instance of a class in the origin of a unidirectional association that has visibility to an instance on the other side also has visibility to the corresponding instance of the association class.

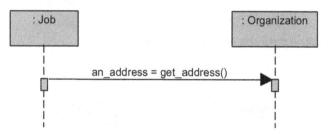

FIGURE 13–15 Instances of association classes have visibility to a single instance at the destiny (if unidirectional) or both ends of the respective link (if bidirectional).

13.3.1.6 The influence of preconditions on visibility by association

When a precondition in a contract states a multiplicity that is more restrictive than the one allowed in the class diagram, it is the visibility established by the precondition that must be considered in the context of that operation.

For example, consider the class diagram of Fig. 13–16, which defines that an order may or may not have a payment linked to it.

Consider now that a given operation contract has a precondition that states:

```
pre:
    anOrder.payment->notEmpty()
```

Or:

```
pre:
    anOrder.payment->isEmpty()
```

Then, both contexts are restricting the explicit multiplicity of the class diagram. In the case of the first precondition, the team must consider that the multiplicity in the *Payment* role is 1, as shown in Fig. 13–17.

In the case of the second precondition, the team must consider that the multiplicity in the *Payment* role is 0, as shown in Fig. 13–18.

In both cases, the new restrictions are only valid during the scope of the operation that has the specific precondition.

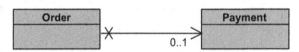

FIGURE 13–16 A class diagram used in examples.

FIGURE 13–17 A precondition that makes an optional role mandatory.

FIGURE 13–18 A precondition that makes an optional role absent.

13.3.2 Visibility by parameter

Visibility by parameter is obtained when an operation running in object *A* receives an object *B* as a parameter. In that case, the object *A* can communicate to *B* even if their classes are not associated.

Consider the example of Fig. 13–19, where the *Product* class has no association to the *Delivery* class. Therefore no instance of *Product* can send a message directly to an instance of *Delivery* or vice versa.

Consider now an instance of *Order* that is linked to one instance of *Product* and to one instance of *Delivery* as shown in Fig. 13–20. Now, consider that the instance of *Order* sends a message like *register_weight* to the instance of *Delivery*, passing a reference to the instance of *Product* (*a_product*) as an argument. Then, the instance of *Delivery* acquires visibility *by parameter* to that instance of *Product*.

Good design practice demands care with visibility by parameter. This is not the same kind of coupling that is obtained with visibility by association. With visibility by association, the participating classes are already coupled by a semantic association, that is, they are linked anyway because the meaning of one is attached to the meaning of the other (e.g., an

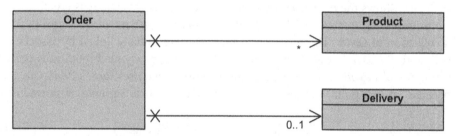

FIGURE 13–19 A model where a *Product* and a *Delivery* cannot communicate directly.

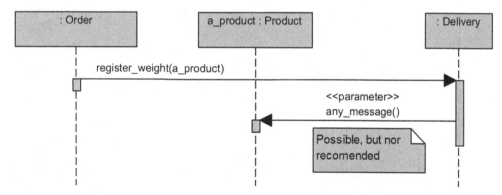

FIGURE 13–20 An object that should not be sending a message to a parameter.

order and its items). But in the case of visibility by parameter, any object may be passed as a parameter to another object, even if they have absolutely no relation between them.

Each time a class declares methods with parameters belonging to other classes that are not yet associated, a new (and possibly unnecessary) coupling would be created. High coupling means poor design. Thus it is convenient to avoid that whenever possible.

The best use for visibility by parameter is to receive and resend objects until they reach the terminal (basic) operations. In practice, what happens is that certain objects will be passed to other objects in a chain until they reach some object that has association visibility to it and can therefore perform the required operation, as seen in Fig. 13−21.

In summary, objects received as parameter that have not association visibility to the object running the operation must not receive any messages; they can only be passed along as arguments. That would contribute to the low coupling principle that states that objects must keep the minimum possible links.

13.3.3 Locally declared visibility

Another form of visibility happens when an object sends a query to another and receives as return a third object. Fig. 13−22 shows the class diagram that serves as basis for this example and Fig. 13−23. Shows the objects communicating so that local visibility is created.

In the example, an instance of *Person* sends a message *get_payment* at position 1 to an ordered collection of *Order*. The person and the order are initially linked by association, but the person and the payment are *not*. However, after the *get_payment* method is performed, and an instance of *Payment* is returned to the person, it acquires *local visibility* to the payment, because, at that point, the payment is assigned to a local variable (*a_payment*) of the

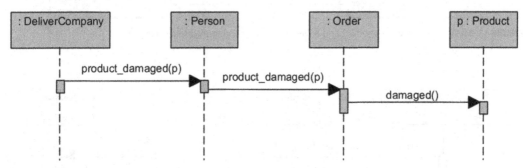

FIGURE 13–21 A chain of delegation.

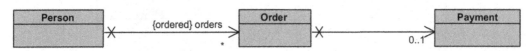

FIGURE 13–22 Class diagram used in example.

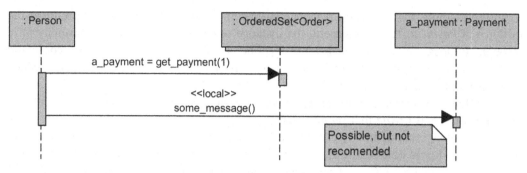

FIGURE 13–23 Local visibility.

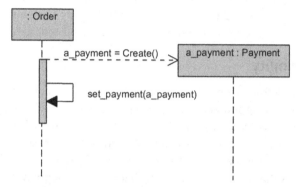

FIGURE 13–24 An object that creates another and receives its reference by local visibility that is transformed into association visibility.

method the instance of *Person* is executing. From this moment on, the instance of *Person* acquires local visibility to the payment and may communicate directly with it.

However, a design pattern known as *Don't talk to strangers* (Larman, 2004)[8] does not recommend that an object send messages to objects that are only locally visible. According to that pattern, the person should not send messages to *a_payment*. As seen before, there is always a design option that avoids this kind of communication. The problem here again is high coupling: if the person acquires local visibility to an instance of *Payment*, it acquires a link that is not semantically supported by the conceptual model. On the other hand, the price to pay for low coupling in this case is sometimes having to implement more delegate methods, as seen later.

An acceptable use for local visibility occurs when a basic command that creates an object is invoked. When an object is created, the new instance is usually referenced by a local variable. That local visibility may be immediately transformed into visibility by association, as shown in Fig. 13–24.

---

[8] A summarization of the *Law of Demeter* (Lieberherr and Holland, 1989).

In the example, the message *Create* is a basic command, a constructor that produces the instance of *Payment*. At that moment, the instance of *Order* gets a new local visibility to it, through the local variable *a_payment* that contains the returning value of the command *Create*. The message *set_payment* links that new instance of *Payment* to the *Order*, which acquires visibility by association to it.

Here there are two important exceptions related to already mentioned design patterns: first, the command *Create* that modifies data can also return an object, but only if it is the object it created; second, an object is allowed to send messages to an object with local visibility because it was obtained from a method that specifically created it. Thus those exceptions refer to the patterns *Query-Command-Separation* and *Do not speak to strangers*.

Both local and parameter visibilities are valid only in the scope of the method that originated them; just like parameters and local variables in programming languages, they are only valid inside the methods where they have been declared. But visibility by association is more permanent, persisting until it is explicitly removed by a basic command that removes a link.

13.3.4 Global visibility

There is *global visibility* for an object when it is accessible by any object at any time. The *Singleton* design pattern (Gamma et al., 1995) suggests that an instance may be globally visible if it is the *only instance of a class*. This makes sense, because if that class has only one instance, it is not necessary to create associations from other objects to it. Also, if that class has a single instance, it is not necessary to pass it as an argument to a function because the idea with parameters is that they may vary, and that does not happen if the class has a single instance. Global visibility is the choice in this case.

Examples of singletons are classes that represent services, such as *CurrencyConverter*, *TimeCounter*, and *OrderNumberGenerator*. There must be a single instance of service classes that can be accessed by any object at any time. An example is shown in Fig. 13−25.

If the singleton pattern is overused, it may turn into an *antipattern*. Designers must not use singletons for entities of the conceptual model; for example, if the system is single user and a single order may exist at a time, it should not be declared a singleton because it is a conceptual entity, not a service class. A conceptual entity that is unique now may admit multiple instances in the future and declaring it a singleton would hinder the evolution of that class.

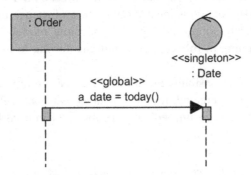

FIGURE 13−25 An object with global visibility.

Also, a singleton, in principle, should not have direct references to entities, because that reduces its reusability potential and creates high coupling problems. Service classes, such as *Date*, must not be associated to entity classes; they are globally visible and grant access to every instance.

13.4 Dynamic modeling based on postconditions

We saw that system command contracts present a set of postconditions that correspond to certain basic commands for creating and deleting instances, adding, removing, and replacing links, and modifying attribute values. These contracts only indicate *what* is supposed to happen, but they do not show *how* messages are exchanged between objects to achieve those goals. UML interaction diagrams may be used to exactly design how these collaborations may happen. The following principles are recommended:

- The kind of visibility among objects depends fundamentally on the role features, such as multiplicity, ordering, and qualification, that are defined in the class diagram and sometimes further constrained by preconditions.
- Each postcondition in the contract must be achieved in the interaction diagram by a message that calls a basic command in the object that holds the responsibility.
- The control flow in a dynamic model begins at the instance of the façade controller that receives a message from the interface.
- When an object that is executing has no visibility to the object that must perform an operation, it should *delegate* the responsibility and the execution to another object that is closer to the one that holds the responsibility.

Santos (2007) presents a systematization of those principles by defining an automatic search-based production system capable of generating well-designed communication diagrams from a broad selection of contracts.

In addition to these principles, design patterns should be applied whenever possible to help the designer build methods that are effectively reusable and maintainable.

13.4.1 Creating instances

When a contract establishes that some instance was created, some other object must actually create it by sending a basic *Create* message in the respective sequence diagram. The *Creator* design pattern (Larman, 2004) states that the choice should be preferably:

- An instance of a class that has a composite or shared aggregation to the class of the object to be created.
- An instance of a class that has a *one-to-many* association to the class of the object to be created.
- An object that has the initialization data for the object to be created, and that is preferably associated to it.

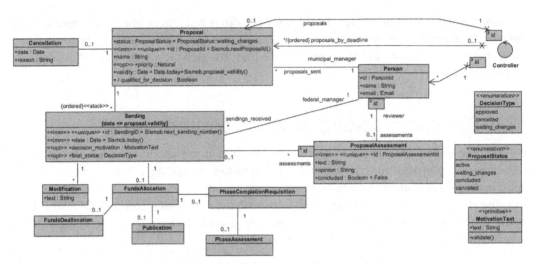

FIGURE 13-26 Conceptual model updated to be used as example in this chapter.

Each rule applies only if the previous one does not apply.

To serve as a reference for the following examples, let's go back to our example of Sismob. Fig. 13—26 presents an updated version of the model where some qualifications were added and where we discovered that *ProposalAssessment.concluded* must not be derived but can have an initial value.

As a first example, let us work on the contract and dynamic model of an operation where a municipal manager creates an instance of *Proposal* that will not being sent yet.

The postconditions then would establish that an instance of *Proposal* is created, its *status* will be "waiting changes," because it was not yet submitted. The *id* of the *Proposal* now is created by a service class called "Sismob." The priority was discovered to be optional because it is the federal manager and not the municipal manager that defines it. The *Proposal validity* now is calculated automatically also using a function from a service class. The *name* of the proposal is received as argument by the system command.

After creating this instance, the link between the *Controller* and *Proposal* with role *"proposals"* must be created. Nothing to do with the link *proposals_by_deadline* because it is derived.

A link must be created between the person identified as the municipal manager and this proposal. And that is it. The OCL contract would be like:

```
Context Controler::create_proposal(a_person_id, a_name)
    post:
        new_proposal.new_instance_of(Proposal) AND
        a_person[a_person_id]^add_proposals_sent(new_proposal) AND
        new_proposal^set_name(a_name) AND
        self^add_proposals(new_proposal)
```

Now let us see this same contract represented as a sequence of messages sent from one to another object. This is depicted in Fig. 13–27.

The sequence diagram used for dynamic modeling here has different kinds of messages:

- A message that invokes a *system operation*, which is sent by the interface and received by the controller: *create_proposal*, in the example.
- A basic query message that locates a specific person in the *proposals* role from the *Controller* to *Person* (*get_person*).
- A delegate message from *Controller* to the instance of *Person* (*a_person*) delegating the responsibility of creating and initializing a new *Proposal*.
- A basic command message from *a_person* that really creates the instance *new_proposal* (horizontal dashed arrow).
- Two more basic messages from *a_person* to *new_proposal* adding *a_person* as municipal manager and setting the name of the proposal to *a_name*.
- Finally, the controller sends to itself a basic command to add the new proposal to the role *proposals*.

Let us now see another example to emphasize the importance of using delegation to obtain low coupling in a project. We are going to specify the operation in which the municipal manager finishes its proposal and produces a *Sending*. In this case, a new instance of *Sending* should not be created by the *Controler* because there are no straight links from *Controller* to *Sending*. *Proposal* and *Person* are equally candidates to create a *Sending*. Having this equivalence, we simply chose *Proposal* to be the creator. It would be the case to consider a *Proposal* as a composite of *Sending*, although we decided not to officialize it. Considering a *Sending* as part of a *Person* would be nonintuitive.

Thus the context is: there is already a proposal linked to a municipal manager and we need to create a *Sending*, fill in its attributes, linking it to the proposal and linking it to a

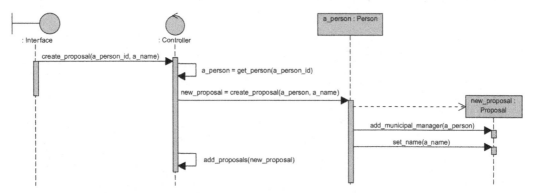

FIGURE 13–27 A sequence diagram that corresponds to the dynamic flow of the contract above.

Person as a *federal manager* because it is a mandatory link from the *Sending*. First let us see the contract:

```
Context Controller::send_proposal(a_proposal_id:ProposalId,
                                  a_federal_manager_id:PersonId)
    def:
        a_proposal = proposals[a_proposal_id]
        a_federal_manager = person[a_federal_manager_id]
    pre:
        a_proposal->notEmpty() AND
        a_federal_manager->notEmpty()
    post:
        new_sending.new_instance_of(Sending) AND
        a_proposal^add_sending(new_sending) AND
        new_sending^add_federal_manager(a_federal_manager)
```

In this contract, only a new instance and its two links are created. The *Sending* attributes are all with initial values or optional and thus do not need to be initialized during creation.

Now, for the dynamic model of this contract, we must remember that as the controller does not have association to *Sending*, it must delegate this creation, and it will be done by *Proposal*. In Fig. 13–28 first, the controller identifies the proposal and the federal manager by their ids. Then, a delegate message is sent to the proposal, with the federal manager as argument. The proposal then creates a new_sending, adds it to its role *sending*, and adds the federal manager to the new sending.

Now let us consider what happened if we do not follow the *Do not speak to strangers* design pattern. In Fig. 13–29, we allowed the controller to create the sending.

What happens here are two problems: first, a new visibility line that did not exist before was created between *Controller* and *Sending*. This increases the coupling of the system, which should be maintained low for a better organization of the code. Second problem is that the *Controller* is doing everything; the other objects are only arguments passed from one side to

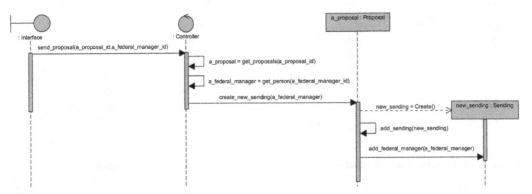

FIGURE 13–28 A sequence diagram with a delegate message.

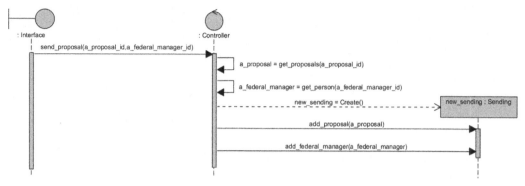

FIGURE 13–29 Violating the *Do not speak to strangers* pattern.

the other, but none of them has any proper behavior. This concentrates the processing and is as bad for object-oriented programming than spaghetti code is for structured programming.

13.4.2 Destroying instances

The destruction of an instance is dynamically modeled by sending a *destroy* basic message to an object. The same principles of the creator design pattern apply here: the object that destroys an instance must have a shared or composite aggregation relationship with the object that is supposed to be destroyed, or an association from one to many, or, at least, be associated to the object.

Care must be taken to avoid leaving objects with mandatory links inconsistent after an object is destroyed. If the contract is well formed no orphan objects will be left, and the sequence diagrams only need to represent the postconditions that are mentioned in the contract.

As an example, let us present a situation where a reviewer can remove/destroy a proposal assessment of her authorship. The condition to the removal is that the proposal assessment is not concluded yet, accordingly to the attribute *concluded*.

```
Context Controller::remove_proposal_assessment(a_reviewer_id,
                    a_proposal_assessment_id)
    def:
        a_reviewer = person[a_reviewer_id]
        a_proposal_assessment = a_reviewer.assessments[a_proposal_assessment_id]
    pre:
        a_reviewer->notEmpty() AND
        a_proposal_assessment->notEmpty() AND
        a_proposal_assessment.concluded = False
    post:
        a_proposal_assessment^destroy()
```

This contract assumes that the person who is the reviewer exists, and that the proposal identified exists also and is not concluded. Fig. 13–30 shows the sequence diagram that

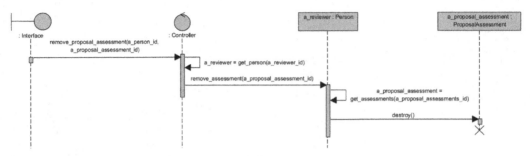

FIGURE 13-30 A sequence diagram for destroying and object.

implements this contract. In this diagram, the one responsible to destroy the proposal assessment is the reviewer that created it.

Observe that the message *remove_assessment* between the *Controller* and *a_reviewer* is a delegate message. There is also a mark that ends the line of life of the proposal assessment just after it receives the message *destroy()*.

13.4.3 Adding, removing, and replacing links

Our Sismob example, up to this point, does not have any operation that just creates a link between two existing objects. Every link is created just after a new object is created too.

Examples of links being created can be seen in Fig. 13–28 in the case of the operations *add_sending* and *add_federal_manager*, which are both basic commands to create links.

Methods to add links may be implemented usually in any of the participant classes. If the association is unidirectional, they should be implemented in the origin.

The same happens in the case of removing or replacing a link: *add_role*, *remove_role*, or *replace_role*.

The object that sends the message to create a link may be one of the participants of the link as in the case of *add_sending* sent by *a_proposal* to itself in Fig. 13–28. But it can also happen that the message that adds a link is sent by an object that does not participate in the link, such as in the case of the message *add_federal_manager*. In this case, the message should be sent to one of the participants of the link, and it should send the other participant as a parameter.

13.4.4 Modifying attributes

Another kind of postcondition that must be considered in dynamic modeling is the *attribute value modification*, which may be achieved by the basic *setter* message that can be sent by the object that owns the attribute or by one of its neighbors.

In the Sismob example, we could work with a command that changes the *concluded* attribute from a *ProposalAssessment* to *True*. The contract would be like this:

```
Context Controller::conclude_assessment(a_person_id, a_proposal_assessment_id)
    def:
        a_person = person[a_person_id]
        a_proposal_assessment = a_person.assessments[a_proposal_assessment_id]
    pre:
        a_person->notEmpty() AND
        a_proposal_assessment->notEmpty() AND
        a_proposal_assessment.concluded = False
    post:
        a_proposal_assessment^set_concluded(True)
```

The sequence diagram for implementing this contract is shown in Fig. 13–31.

13.4.5 Conditional postconditions

As explained before, sometimes a postcondition must be obtained only if some given conditions are valid. In these cases, it is possible to use conditional messages in interaction diagrams that are similar to the guard conditions used in machine state and activity diagrams.

As an example, let us consider that a *ProposalAssessment* can only change the attributes *text*, *opinion*, and *concluded* if the attribute *concluded* is *False*. The contract for this operation is similar to the contract of a CRUDL update command, but the difference is in the fact that the postconditions can only be achieved if anther condition is *True*. The contract can be like this:

```
Context Controller::update_proposal_assessment(a_person_id,
                    a_proposal_assessment_id,
                    a_text, an_opinion, is_concluded)
    def:
        a_person = person[a_person_id]
        a_proposal_assessment = a_person.assessments[a_proposal_assessent_id]
    pre:
        a_person->notEmpty() AND
        a_proposal_assessment->notEmpty()
    post:
        if a_proposal_assessment.concluded then
            Exception.raise(123)
        else
            a_proposal_assessment^set_text(a_text) AND
            a_proposal_assessment^set_opinion(a_opinion) AND
            a_proposal_assessment^set_concluded(is_concluded)
        endIf
```

FIGURE 13–31 A sequence diagram where a value of an attribute is changed.

Following our previous definitions, the postconditions in this case are conditioned. There are two cases do be dealt with: "assessment concluded" that produces to an exception and "assessment not concluded" that leads to its update with the parameters received.

The diagram of Fig. 13–32 in this case would need to use an *alt* fragment to deal with the two exclusive options.

Notice that the message sent from the controller to the person is a delegate one. It has the same name of the system command sent from the interface, because it has the same purpose. Then, the instance of person that has visibility to proposal assessments will coordinate the basic commands and queries necessary to do the job.

13.4.6 Exceptions

Sometimes preconditions cannot be converted to exceptions. Then they must be tested by the operation itself. UML unfortunately does not have a notation specific for dealing with exceptions in sequence diagrams. After seeing some proposals in literature and evaluating their complexity, we propose one that seems to be the most simple to draw. First, let us define a contract with exceptions, a contract to delete a *Person* that can only be completed if this person is not associated to proposal *assessments*, *sendings_received*, or *proposals_sent*:

```
Context Controller delete_person(a_person_id)
    def:
        a_person = person[a_person_id]
    post:
        a_person^destroy()
    exception:
        a_person.assessment->notEmpty() IMPLIES Exception.throw(491)
        a_person.sendings_received->notEmpty IMPLIES Exception.throw(492)
        a_person.proposals_sent->notEmpty IMPLIES Exception.throw(493)
```

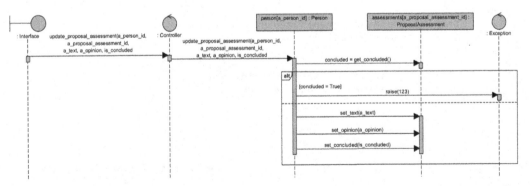

FIGURE 13–32 A sequence diagram with an *alt* fragment.

Our proposal to deal with that is to put the postconditions into the first shape of the fragment *alt* defining as condition "[*try*]." Then, the other shapes of the *alt* fragment could be used to indicate the exceptions that can occur. Fig. 13−33 shows the appearance of this sequence diagram.

In this diagram, we replace the *opt* fragment in the case of the exception by guard conditions, that is, conditions that go between "[" and "]." This makes the diagram easier to read.

13.4.7 Postconditions over collections

When system commands have contracts with postconditions that specify updates over collections of objects, the iteration structure may be used in the communication diagram to indicate that a message is iteratively sent to every element in the collection. For example, the following system command increases the *validity* of every proposal within a deadline given by a number of days:

```
Context Controller::extend_validity(a_number_of_days)
    post:
        proposals_by_deadline->forAll(
            ^set_validity(validity@pre+a_number_of_days)
        )
```

In this case, a message *set_validity* will be sent to a set of objects iteratively. The respective sequence diagram could be like the one in Fig. 13−34.

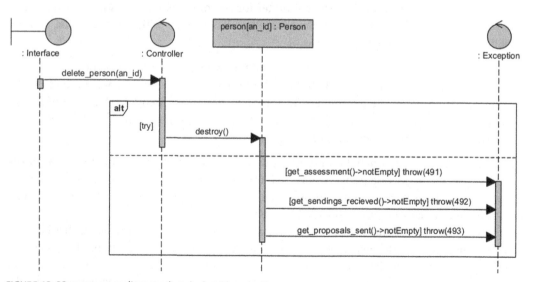

FIGURE 13–33 a sequence diagram that deals with exceptions.

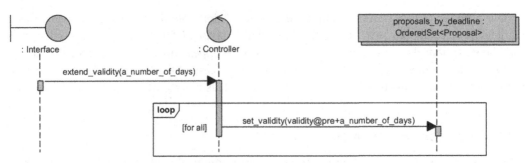

FIGURE 13–34 A sequence diagram that updates a collection of objects.

13.5 Delegation and low coupling

Up to this point, we have seen some techniques for building sequence diagrams. But in most situations, there is more than one design option and more than one way to send a message.

As discussed earlier, sometimes the object that has control does not have visibility to the object that can perform the responsibility. In this case, two opposite design approaches can be identified:

- The object that has control tries to obtain a reference to the object that can perform the responsibility and communicate directly with it.
- The object delegates the message to another object that is closer to the object that can perform the responsibility.

To understand the difference between these two approaches, imagine that Mary is the boss of Peter. The boss wants to order a buffet for the office party, but she does not know any catering companies. The boss knows that Peter has contact with some catering companies, and then, two approaches are possible:

- The boss asks Peter for the phone numbers of the companies and makes the arrangements herself. The only thing that Peter does is to pass his contacts to the boss.
- The boss sends Peter the parameters for the party: how many people, what kind of food, how much to spend, etc., and asks Peter to do the arrangements. The party happens, and the boss delegated the most part of the work to Peter.

Although in real life, it may be interesting to contact many people and companies, this is not the case in object-oriented systems. When objects are highly coupled, the system is more complex than it really needs to be. Thus it is necessary to avoid creating connections between objects that were not connected in the first place.

The first approach discussed just above is called *concentration*. With it the object that has execution control manages to obtain references to all objects needed and performs the operation itself. The second approach is called *delegation*, and it consists of making the objects delegate responsibilities when they cannot perform those themselves. The second approach is usually preferable, because it provides more potential for reusing classes and methods, because the intermediary queries or delegated methods that this approach creates usually are reusable.

Let us repay attention to a contract shown before, in which a user, a municipal manager, sends a proposal to the system after having registered it.

```
Context Controller::send_proposal(a_proposal_id:ProposalId,
                                  a_federal_manager_id:PersonId)
    def:
        a_proposal = all_proposals[a_proposal_id]
        a_federal_manager = person[a_federal_manager_id]
    pre:
        a_proposal->notEmpty() AND
        a_federal_manager->notEmpty()
    post:
        new_sending.new_instance_of(Sending) AND
        a_proposal^add_sending(new_sending) AND
        new_sending^add_federal_manager(a_federal_manager)
```

We can recall that the diagram in Fig. 13−28 shows a possible implementation for this contract that does not increase the number of links between objects because it uses only the association links already present.

With the concentration approach, the whole process would be implemented in the *Controller* class. As seen in Fig. 13−29, this class would obtain all necessary data to perform the system command. In the concentration sequence diagram, all the messages are sent by the *Controller*. No delegation happens, as no object sends messages and the *Controller* instance acquires visibility to all objects that it interacts with.

Both approaches solve the problem. But by using the delegation approach, the query can be implemented with more cohesion and less coupling.

Fig. 13−35 shows the flow of messages between objects and therefore the dependencies that must exist between classes.

In the concentration diagram, a new link between the controller and an instance of *Sending* is created although a path from *Controller* to *Sending* already exists through *Proposal* and also through *Person*.

The price for using delegation is usually having more methods declared in the intermediary classes. However, reusable methods are usually produced to counteract this issue. The price for using the concentration approach is having a design where responsibilities are concentrated in the façade controller instead of being distributed among the objects; this produces a model that is hard to evolve and maintain in the long term.

13.6 Design class diagram

One of the goals of the logical design is to build and refine the DCD, which is created from the conceptual model and from information obtained during dynamic modeling (when the interaction diagrams for the contracts are being built).

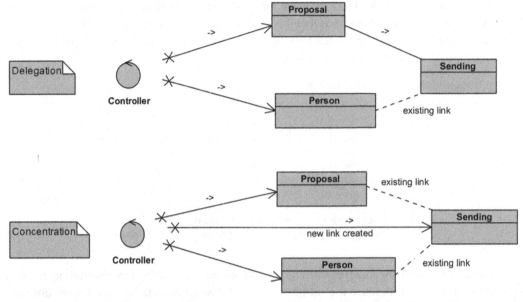

FIGURE 13–35 Dynamics of message sending between instances of classes with the delegation and the concentration approaches.

The first version of the DCD is an exact copy of the conceptual model, which will be modified later. The basic modifications that are made in the DCD during domain tier design are the following:

- *Methods are added.* During analysis, only system commands and queries were discovered and added to the façade controller class. During design, delegate and basic methods belonging to other classes are added.
- *Associations are directed.* During analysis, associations were nondirectional. During design, their direction is determined by the direction of the messages flowing between objects in the interaction diagrams.
- *Attributes and associations may be detailed.* It is not mandatory to present details about attributes and associations during analysis. These details may be added during design. Additionally, in analysis, only abstract data types are used to specify association roles, and they may be replaced by concrete data types during design (e.g., replacing *sequence* by *array list* or *linked list*).
- *The structure of classes and associations may change.* It may be necessary to create new classes to implement certain design structures, such as strategies and services, for example. Thus it is possible that the class structure of the DCD does not correspond exactly to the structure of the conceptual model, in some cases.
- *Possible creation of protected and private attributes.* In the conceptual model, all attributes are public because they represent static information and not behavior. However, when

the dynamic aspects of objects are represented, it may be necessary to work with private attributes to encapsulate internal states that determine the behavior of some objects. These attributes sometimes may not be directly accessible through a getter or setter, but their influence on some methods is felt.

During the construction of a communication diagram, each time an object receives a delegated message, its class must implement the corresponding method.

The DCD may also include information about the direction of the associations if the designer chooses not to implement every association as bidirectional. This is usually the case because unidirectional associations tend to be simpler to implement and more efficient when compared to bidirectional associations.

Deciding whether an association is unidirectional or bidirectional depends on the flow of messages on the interaction diagrams. No association should be, in principle, navigable in the direction of the controller: the controller sees the classes, but they do not see it. Other associations may be unidirectional if the messages only flow in one direction, and bidirectional if messages flow in different directions, even if that happens in different sequence diagrams.

Associations that links were not used by messages are left undefined (nondirectional) until another diagram eventually decides on their direction.

If other sequence diagrams developed for different system operations require messages navigating in the opposite direction as those that were already discovered, then the respective associations should be bidirectional.

The logical design activity finishes when the DCD has enough information to implement the domain tier classes. That usually happens when all system operation contracts have been examined and their dynamic models incorporated into the design.

Questions

1. What are the six kinds of responsibilities that objects may have? What kind of method is used to perform each responsibility?
2. What are the four kinds of visibility that may exist between objects? Are they symmetrical? How does each of them influence high coupling among classes?
3. Explain the influence of contract preconditions and exceptions in dynamic models. How do they affect the complexity of the dynamic model?

14 ⣿

Code generation

Key topics in this chapter

- Code generation for classes, attributes, and associations
- Code generation for delegated methods and system operations
- Patterns for bidirectional associations

14.1 Introduction to code generation

In order to have running systems, it is necessary to generate code for the classes from the domain tier and for the other technological tiers of the system. This chapter concentrates on code generation for the domain tier.

Once the sequence diagrams and the DCD are produced, code generation is an activity that may be systematized to a point that it can be practically done automatically. Automatic code generation is feasible for domain classes, which perform all the logical processing specified by the system operation contracts.

This chapter presents rules for code generation for the DCD and sequence diagrams. Examples are presented in Python, which is nowadays a dominant language in learning and business. It also has structures that are much closer to those of the algorithms than other languages.

DCD classes are usually directly converted into programming language classes. Class attributes are converted into *private instance variables* in the respective class. In many languages, those variables must be *declared*. But this is not necessary in Python. As soon as a new identifier is used in the context of a class, it is assumed to be a new instance variable.

Although Python does not demand variables to be labeled, any variable has a type that is the type of the object that is stored in the variable. As explained before, variables that represent attributes must store alphanumeric values, such as *Integer*, *Real*, *String*, and *Boolean*, primitive ones, such as *Date*, *Money*, and *ISBN*, or enumerations such as *CalendarDay*, *Gender*, and *PhoneType*.

If other objects can access the attribute, then it is *public* and should be implemented with a *getter* method. If the attribute can be updated, then it must be implemented with a *setter*, which can be a simple *set_attribute* method or another variation such as *increment_attribute*, if the attribute is numeric. Fig. 14−1 presents an example of design classes that are used to show how programming code can be generated.

Object-Oriented Analysis and Design for Information Systems. DOI: https://doi.org/10.1016/B978-0-443-13739-6.00017-4

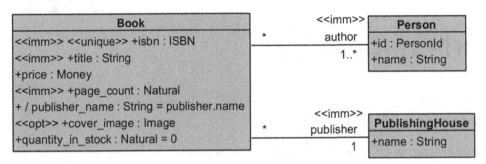

FIGURE 14–1 A reference class model for code generation.

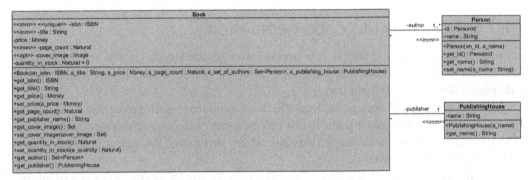

FIGURE 14–2 A design version for the conceptual model in Fig. 14–1.

First let us open a BIG parenthesis here to show the difference between a conceptual and a design class. What we see in Fig. 14–1 is a conceptual version of classes *Book, Person,* and *PublishingHouse*. Now compare it to Fig. 14–2 to see what a design or dominion definition for these classes could be:

Let us examine the differences and how the former diagram was transformed into this one. First, all attributes are transformed from public to private. And, if there is any derived attribute or association, it must be transformed into a public method.

In each of the classes, only the mandatory basic commands should be implemented. First, the Creator command, which in the case of *Book* has a lot of initialization parameters, including a set of *Person* and an instance of *PublishingHouse*.

All attributes that were public before now have a getter to access their values. All nonderived and nonimmutable ones will also have a setter that allows to change their values. In the case of roles from *Book*, in this diagram, both are immutable. Thus they implement only the getter methods and not the add, remove, and replace methods.

The derived attribute *publisher_name* from the conceptual model was found to be redundant here because the name of the publisher can be easily obtainable through the method *get_publisher*; thus, this derived attribute is wiped out of the model.

The two associations from *Book* are considered (for now) to be unidirectional, because during development, it was always the book that sends messages to the person or to the publishing house. Vice versa never happens. In this case, the associations are considered unidirectional until a case is found where a message must navigate to the opposite side. In this case, the association becomes bidirectional and must be implemented as that. At least a *get_book* method should be implemented in any class that may have access to the book.

Given all this features, we believe that for educational purposes, we should continue to work with the conceptual version of the classes, not the design one. Remember that the transformation from conceptual to design may be done at any moment between modeling and code implementation. Therefore in the following examples, we will take the conceptual classes as basis and generate code directly to python without making explicit the design version of each class.

Now, let us close those BIG parentheses and continue our analysis on the conceptual model.

Initially, we are going to program the class *Book*. First, declare the name of the class with the expression "*class Book:*." In Python, upper and lower cases are considered different symbols. Thus if you write *Class Book:*, you will get an error because the expression *Class* is unknown to Python, but *class* is.

First thing usually is to define the initialization of the class. The constructor is a predefined command we do not need to worry by now. What we need to know is that the constructor, when activated to create a new instance of any class, will call a special method *__init__* (two underlines before and after the word *init*. No spaces!). The parameters of *__init__* should be, first, a special variable called "*self*" followed by a list of parameters necessary to initialize the mandatory attributes and associations.

This list comprises attributes that are not *optional* neither *derived*. *Unique* attributes must be checked. But for now, we assume that this is going to be done later and proceed with them as if this stereotype is not present.

The first object that must appear as parameter of *__init__* is self. Then, we can include the parameters the multiplicity of which does not accept 0, that is, the list would contain usually roles for which multiplicity is 1 or 1..*, or any other variation excluding 0.

In our example, the initial lines for creating the class *Book* in Python would be something like:

```
class Book:
    def __init__(self, an_isbn, a_title, a_price,
                 a_page_count, a_publishing_house, a_set_of_authors):
```

Next, we must assign to each attribute or association, which will be the instance variables, the values received by *__init__*. Later, we will discuss a more adequate approach to deal with associations, but for now we will just treat them as mere attributes. We just separate attributes and associations in two blocks marked by comments as seen below:

```
class Book:
    def __init__(self, an_isbn, a_title, a_price,
                 a_page_count, a_publishing_house, a_set_of_authors):
    #ATTRIBUTES
        self.isbn = an_isbn
        self.title = a_title
        self.price = a_price
        self.page_count = a_page_count
        self.quantity_in_stock = 0
    #ASSOCIATIONS
        self.publishing_house = a_publishing_house
        self.authors = a_set_of_author
```

Now we will define the methods that are necessary for dealing with the attributes. Remember that:

- A normal attribute has methods *set* and *get* even if it is *optional* or have an *initial value.*
- *Immutable* attributes have only the *get* method, not the *set.*
- *Derived* attributes have only the *get* method that usually must be implemented as a more complex query than in the other cases.

In the case of associations:

- Normal associations have *get, add,* and *removal* methods unless other rules apply.
- Derived associations only have *get.*
- If the association is *immutable,* then it implements only the *get* method.
- Associations to 1 may have a *get* method. They also have a *replace* method if the business rules allow the object in that role to be replaced. They do not implement *add* and *remove.*
- Associations with a qualified role in the origin may implement *get, add,* and *remove,* normally, but they can also implement the method that finds an instance depending on its key: *get_at(key).* They can also have a second *remove* method: *remove_at(key).* The original one, applied on collections in general, receives the object to be removed as parameter (*remove_role(object)*). If it is a qualified association, though, it can also have a *remove* method based in the key (*remove_role_at(key)*). Also, if the qualifier is external, then the *add* method must explicitly indicate the key, such as *add_role(key, value).* In this case, the add method implemented to other collections with only the object to be added does not exist.
- In the case of an ordered role, *get, add,* and *remove* based on the object's position may also be implemented additionally to their counterparts that use only the object as parameter. If this association has a *replace* method, then another *replace* method based on position may also be implemented.

The final code to implement the *Book* class with its basic methods would be like:

```
class Book:
    def __init__(self, an_isbn, a_title, a_price, a_page_count,
                 a_publishing_house, a_set_of_authors):
        #ATTRIBUTES
        self.isbn = an_isbn
        self.title = a_title
        self.price = a_price
        self.page_count = a_page_count
        self.quantity_in_stock = 0
        #ASSOCIATIONS
        self.publishing_house = a_publishing_house
        self.authors = a_set_of_authors

    #ATTRIBUTES
    def get_isbn(self):
        return self.isbn

    def get_title(self):
        return self.title

    def get_price(self):
        return self.price

    def set_price(self, new_price):
        self.price = new_price

    def get_page_count(self):
        return self.page_count

    def get_cover_image(self):
        return self.cover_image

    def set_cover_image(self, new_cover_image):
        self.cover_image = new_cover_image

    def get_quantity_in_stock(self):
        return self.quantity_in_stock

    def set_quantity_in_stock(self, new_quantity):
        self.quantity_in_stock = new_quantity

    #ASSOCIATIONS
    def get_publisher(self):
        return self.publishing_house

    def get_authors(self):
        return self.authors
```

Table 14–1 Minimum set of basic methods to implement according to the kind of attribute role.

	(default)	<<imm>>	<<opt>>
get	get_role():alphanumeric	get_role():alphanumeric	get_role():alphanumeric
set	set(alphanumeric)	-x-	set(alphanumeric)
Parameter in __init__	Yes	Yes	No

	Derived	Initial value
get	get_role():alphanumeric	get_role():alphanumeric
set	-x-	set(alphanumeric)
Parameter in __init__	No	No

Table 14−1 presents a summary of the basic methods that must be implemented for each kind of association role. Notice that some conditions can be combined. For example, a role may be to 0..1 and immutable at the same time. In this case, the strongest restriction applies. In the example, despite an association to 0..1 may implement add and remove methods, they will not be implemented because the stereotype « *imm* » does not allow it.

Observe that in Table 14−2, each kind of association has a different set of methods for accessing and changing links. The implementation of these methods follows definitions that are usually very similar from class to class. The following subsections show examples of some of those methods.

14.2 Unidirectional associations

Unidirectional associations with no multiplicity constraints at the origin may be implemented similarly to attributes as *instance variables*, and according to Table 14−2, they should have methods for updating and querying.

However, if there are multiplicity constraints at the origin role, these associations must be considered as *bidirectional*, even if they are not navigable in both directions. Fig. 14−3 shows an example of that situation, where although the association is only navigable from *Car* to *Person*, every car must be linked to a single person.

If the association is implemented as an instance variable in the *Person* class, it will be hard to assure that a car belongs to a single person, which is a constraint in the origin.

There are still some considerations we must discuss about the differences between an attribute and a unidirectional association. First, attributes are always implemented by variables whose types are alphanumeric, primitive, or enumerations. Associations, on the other hand, are implemented by variables whose types are domain classes (in the case of associations to one) or data structures (in the case of associations *to many*).

In addition, considering different role multiplicities and other features of associations, there are distinctions to be made regarding the methods to be implemented for each type of association.

14.2.1 Unidirectional association to 1 and 0..1

The unidirectional association with role multiplicity 1 may be stored in a single instance variable in the origin class, and its type should be the destination class. Fig. 14−4 shows a unidirectional association *to one* from *Car* to *Person* with role name *owner*.

Table 14–2   Minimum set of basic methods to implement according to the kind of attribute role.

	to 1 (set)	to 0..1 (set)	to * (set)	to 1..* (set)
get	get_role():Object	get_role():Set	get_role():Set	get_role():Set
add	-x-	add_role(object)	add_role(object)	add_role(object)
remove	-x-	remove_role()	remove_role(object)	remove_role(object)
replace	replace(object)[1]	-x-	-x-	-x-
Parameter in __init__	Yes	No	No	Yes

	<imm>	derived	with initial value
get	get_role():Set	get_role():Set	get_role():Set
add	-x-	-x-	add_role(object)
remove	-x-	-x-	remove_role(object)
replace	-x-	-x-	-x-
Parameter in __init__	Yes	No	No

	Bag	OrderedSet	Sequence
get	get_role():Bag	get_role():OrderedSet get_role(position):Object	get_role():Sequence get_role(position):Object
add	add_role(object)	add_role(position,object)	add_role(position,object)
remove	remove_role(object)	remove_role(object) remove_role(position,object)	remove_role(position,object)
replace	-x-	replace_role(position,object)	replace_role(position,object)

	Map (internal qualifier)	Map (external qualifier)
get	get_role():Set get_role(key):Object	get_role():Set get_role(key):Object
add	add_role(object)	add_role(key,object)
remove	remove_role(object) remove_role(key)	remove_role(object) remove_role(key)
replace	-x-	replace_role(key,object)

	Partition (internal qualifier)	Partition (external qualifier)
get	get_role():Set get_role(key):Set	get_role():Set get_role(key):Set
add	add_role(object)	add_role(key,object)
remove	remove_role(object)	-x-
replace	-x-	-x-

	Set with association class	Array
get	get_role():Set get_association_role():Set get_role(key_object):Object	get_role():Sequence get_role(position):Object
add	add_role(object,association_object)	-x-
remove	remove_role(object)	-x-
replace	-x-	replace_role(position,object)

FIGURE 14–3 A unidirectional association to many with a restriction at the origin.

FIGURE 14–4 Unidirectional association to 1 with no restrictions at the origin.

The implementation of the *Car* class requires an instance variable named *owner* implemented with type *Person*. Regarding the association methods, following Table 14−2, only *getOwner* and *replaceOwner* should be implemented. In the code below, we represent only the lines that are necessary to implement those specific associations. The *__init__* method also would have only the necessary arguments to clarify this example by leaving other possible arguments out of the code:

```python
class Car:
    def __init__(self, an_owner):
        self.owner = an_owner

    #ASSOCIATIONS
    def get_owner(self):
        return self.owner

    def replace_owner(self, new_owner):
        self.owner = new_owner
```

In the case of a role with multiplicity 0..1, we must be concerned that there are two possibilities when we get the value of the role: either an object is returned or something else that represents *no object* is returned. Some languages have *null* objects that usually are a problem because any message sent to them results in raising an exception.

Woolf (1998) proposed a design pattern named *Null object* which consists of creating a special object that is interpreted as null but that behaves differently, being capable, for example, to respond to some messages.

Python implements this idea with the object *None*. It represents "no object," but you can use it in expressions. Thus instead of returning a set with one element or a set with no element, we can implement returning an object or *None*. This decision is necessary because, differently to OCL that uses the natural notion of sets, Python uses the mathematical notion of sets, which means that a set that contains one element is different than the element.

If we assume that the role multiplicity in Fig. 14−5 is 0..1, we could then implement the basic methods as with *get, add* and *remove,* according to Table 14−2, and the payment must not be informed in the *__init__* method.

```python
class Order:
    def __init__(self):
        self.payment = None

    def get_payment(self):
        return self.payment

    def add_payment(self, a_payment):
        self.payment = a_payment

    def remove_payment(self):
        self.payment = None
```

In this example, when an object that already has a payment receives the message *add_payment*, it will replace the old payment by the new one. This behavior may be defined to be different in other projects, which would, for example, produce an exception or prevent the execution of the operation. Similarly, when an order does not have a payment and the *remove_payment* is executed, nothing results from that. In other approaches, an exception could be the case in some situations.

14.2.2 Unidirectional association to set

The unidirectional association *to many* may be implemented as a collection. If it is a simple association with multiplicity * in the destination role, then it may be implemented as a *set*. Below is a Python example for the association represented in Fig. 14−6.

```python
class Person:
    def __init__(self):
        self.assessments = set()

    def get_assessments(self):

    return self.assessments

def add_assessment(self, an_assessment):
    self.assessments.add(an_assessment)

def remove_assessment(self, an_assessment):
    self.assessments.remove(an_assessment)
```

As defined in Table 14−2, it must implement the operations *get*, *add*, and *remove*, and no initial value is passed to the *__init__* function that just initializes the set of assessments as an empty set.

Here we deal with a set collection that prevents operations such as "get last element" or "get element in position *x*." Thus we must deal with the structure with the ways that are proper to it. For example, suppose each assessment has a *concluded* attribute, as shown in Fig. 14−7.

FIGURE 14–5 Unidirectional association to 0..1.

FIGURE 14–6 A unidirectional association to many.

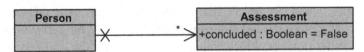

FIGURE 14–7 An evolution of Fig. 14–5.

In this case, the class *Assessment* must provide the methods *get* and *set* so that its attribute can be used. As we cannot usually address members of a set by their positions, we usually deal with the whole set at a time. For example, suppose that the class *Person* has a method to conclude all assessments linked to it. For accessing each element in the set of assessments, an iterator operator will be useful. In this case, we can write a Python expression such as *for an_assessment in self.get_assessments(): an_assessment.set_concluded(True)*. The complete code for both classes is shown below:

```python
class Assessment:
    def __init__(self):
        self.concluded = False

    def get_concluded(self):
        return self.concluded

    def set_concluded(self, a_boolean):
        self.concluded = a_boolean


class Person:
    def __init__(self):
        self.assessments = set()

    def get_assessments(self):
        return self.assessments

    def add_assessment(self, an_assessment):
        self.assessments.add(an_assessment)

    def remove_assessment(self, an_assessment):
        self.assessments.remove(an_assessment)

    def conclude_all_assessments(self): #new delegate method
        for an_assessment in self.get_assessments():
            an_assessment.set_concluded(True)
```

In the new delegate method, we could also write *for an_assessment in self.assessments:*. It would work the same way. However, even inside the same class, it is preferable to use the method *get* to access an instance variable than using the name of the instance variable itself. This is because in some cases the *get* method may execute hidden operations that are necessary.

FIGURE 14–8 A model with a bag.

14.2.3 Unidirectional to bag

Python does not implement any structure like a bag. However, it can be implemented by using a common list as a base and by implementing only *get*, *add*, and *remove*. As stated in Table 14−2 for bags. That is, we are not implementing methods to access an element by its position. Fig. 14−8 shows the base class diagram with a bag and its Python code could be like:

```python
class Product:
    def __init__(self):
        self.viewers = []

    def get_viewers(self):
        return self.viewers

    def add_viewer(self, a_person):
        self.viewers.append(a_person)

    def remove_viewer(self, a_person):
        self.viewers.remove(a_person)
```

14.2.4 Unidirectional to sequence

The sequence is the most used structure in Python programming although, as seen before, it is relatively rare in the real world. Fortunately, Python implements the sequence structure with the datatype *list*. Fig. 14−9 shows a situation (*list*) where a sequence is the right structure to use in the role.

The following code shows the implementation of this role in Python:

```python
class Controller:
    def __init__(self):
        self.qualified_for_gift = []

    def get_qualified_for_gift(self):
        return self.qualified_for_gift

    def get_qualified_for_gift_at(self, position):
        return self.qualified_for_gift[position]

    def add_qualified_for_gift(self, position, a_person):
        self.qualified_for_gift.insert(position, a_person)

    def remove_qualified_for_gift(self, position):
        self.qualified_for_gift.pop(position)

    def replace_qualified_for_gift(self, position, a_person):
        self.qualified_for_gift[position] = a_person
```

14.2.5 Unidirectional to ordered set

Python also does not implement a structure such as ordered set. There are different ways to implement or simulate this structure. Here we present one of the simplest ones using Python lists to simulate ordered sets. A new class *OrderedSet* is defined, so that the structure can be reused as if it was a primitive type in Python. Fig. 14−10 shows an structure with an ordered set.

Remind that ordered sets are lists that do not repeat elements but where elements have position. Thus we can create a new class *OrderedSet* by using a list as a base and controlling duplicates in the methods *add_role* and *replace_role*.

By project decision, we must decide how the abovementioned methods behave. For example, if you have an ordered set [5, 2, 8, 9, 4] and you *insert* the element "8" at different positions, you can have the following results:

- Position 0: [**8**, 5, 2, 9, 4]
- Position 1: [5, **8**, 2, 9, 4]
- Position 2: [5, 2, **8**, 9, 4]
- Position 3: [5, 2, 9, **8**]
- Position 4: [5, 2, 9, 4, **8**]

To obtain these results when an element is inserted into an ordered set, the idea is to check the list and, if the element already is in the list, to delete it from its old position and then insert it in the new position. If the element already appears at the indicated position, nothing needs to be done.

Regarding the *replace_role* method, the results are not very clear. What if the element already appears in the list; should it be removed before or after the replacement? Let us get again the list [5, 2, 8, 9, 4] and see in Table 14−3 what happens when the repeated element is removed before or after the *replacement*.

Here we can see that if the element already is in the ordered set, we have different results if the original element is at or after the new position where it will be placed.

We adopt the "before" strategy because it seems more adequate to say that the element in position *n* will be replaced by a new one. We only must have in mind that if the element already was in the list, then after the replacing operation, it may go to the position *n* − *1*, and not to *n*, if the identical element in the least was before the position where the new elements will be placed. This approach also prevents the error that would happen if the element were placed in

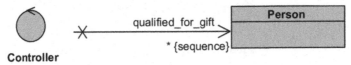

Controller

FIGURE 14–9 A model with a sequence.

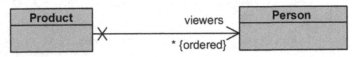

FIGURE 14–10 A model with an ordered set.

Table 14–3 Different results obtained by replacing a repeated element in an ordered set depending on the positions.

Position	Original list	Insert "8" before removing from the position	Insert "8" after removing from the position
0	[5, 2, 8, 9, 4]	[**8**, 2, 9, 4]	[**8**, 2, 9, 4]
1	[5, 2, 8, 9, 4]	[5, **8**, 9, 4]	[5, **8**, 9, 4]
2	[5, 2, 8, 9, 4]	[5, 2, **8**, 9, 4]	[5, 2, **8**, 9, 4]
3	[5, 2, 8, 9, 4]	[5, 2, **8**, 4]	[5, 2, 8, **8**]
4	[5, 2, 8, 9, 4]	[5, 2, 9, **8**]	<<index error>>

the last position of the ordered set. Thus if the element is already in the list, we first replace it and then remove the old one, except if the old one is also the replaced one.

Having this into consideration, this would be the Python code for defining the *OrderedSet* data structure:

```python
class OrderedSet:
    def __init__(self):
        self.representation = []

    def get(self):
        return self.representation

    def get_at(self, position):
        return self.representation[position]

    def add(self, position, object):
        for element in self.representation:
            if element == object:
                self.representation.remove(element)
                break
        self.representation.insert(position, object)

    def remove(self, object):
        self.representation.remove(object)

    def remove_at(self, position):
        self.representation.pop(position)

    def replace(self, position, object):
        self.representation[position] = object
        for index in range(0, len(self.representation)):
            if self.representation[index] == object and index != position:
                self.representation.pop(index)
                break
```

Now we can create a role with {*ordered*} in any class that would need it. Thus we can write Python code for the role in Fig. 14—10:

```python
import ordered

class Product():
    def __init__(self):
        self.viewers = ordered.OrderedSet()

    def get_viewers(self):
        ordered.get(self.viewers)

    def get_viewers_at(self, position):
        ordered.get_at(self, position)

    def add_viewers(self, position, a_person):
        ordered.add(position, a_person)

    def remove_viewers(self, a_person):
        ordered.remove(a_person)

    def remove_viewers_at(self, position):
        ordered.remove_at(position)

    def replace_viewers(self, position, a_person):
        ordered.replace(position, a_person)
```

14.2.6 Unidirectional to array

An array is a list with fixed size. Python does not have the array as a built-in data structure, but we can simulate an array by creating a list with a given size, filling it with None's or zeros, for example, and then not implementing methods that could change the size of the list. Therefore an array will just have the *get* and *replace* methods, and its size will always be the same.

An example of an array could be a tray of eggs, as seen in Fig. 14—11. There are always 12 positions to place eggs in a Tray, and some of them can contain an Egg while others contain None.

It is not necessary to use a constraint or stereotype to inform that a given role is an array because its multiplicity will denote that. In the example, the role *egg* has 12 positions, not more not less.

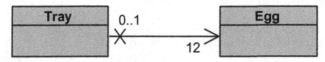

FIGURE 14–11 A model with an array.

When we define a role as an array, the number of positions must be informed when the object is instantiated. Therefore the method *__init__* would receive the size of the array as a parameter. The code blow represents the class Tray with the array *representation* with 12 spaces, numbered from 0 to 11, that can contain an Egg or None:

```python
class Tray():
    def __init__(self, size):
        self.representation = []
        for i in range(size):
            self.representation.append(None)

    def get_eggs(self):
        return self.representation

    def get_egg_at(self, position):
        return self.representation[position]

    def replace_egg_at(self, position, an_egg):
        self.representation[position] = an_egg
```

14.2.7 Unidirectional qualified association

The unidirectional qualified association is implemented like the association with multiplicity to many. However, instead of the data type *set*, we use a mapping, or dictionary structure (*dict*) that associates an alphanumeric, primitive, or enumeration type (key) to one object or a set of objects (values).

As for any other unidirectional associations, we must keep in mind that the unidirectional implementation is only possible when the association has no multiplicity bounds in its origin, that is, the origin role must have multiplicity *. If this is not the case, a bidirectional implementation must be considered.

Fig. 14−12 shows a model with a qualified association defining a map to 0..1 with an internal qualifier. When the qualifier is internal, it does not need to be passed as argument in the *add* method, because the value is already stored in the object. The Python code would be like this:

```python
class Person():
    def __init__(self):
        self.phones = dict()

    def get_phones(self):
        return self.phones

    def get_phone_at(self, key):
        return self.phones[key]

    def add_phone(self, a_phone):
        self.phones[a_phone.get_number()] = a_phone

    def remove_phone(self, a_phone):
        self.phones.pop(a_phone.get_number())

    def remove_phone_at(self, a_key):
        self.phones.pop(a_key)
```

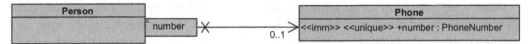

FIGURE 14–12 A model with a qualified association with internal qualifier.

The *replace* method is not implemented in this case because it would not make sense to replace an object with a unique attribute in a dictionary that uses that same attribute as qualifier.

It is important to stress that the design of the qualified association with an internal qualifier works better if the qualifier attribute is immutable. If this was not the case, the attribute could change, and that change would not necessarily propagate to the value that is the key for the association. This would create an inconsistency. That constraint, however, does not apply to maps with external qualifiers, because in that case the qualifier is not an attribute of the qualified class.

Fig. 14–13 presents a map with an external qualifier. The corresponding code is shown below:

```python
import phone

class Person():
    def __init__(self):
        self.phones = dict()

    def get_phones(self):
        return self.phones

    def get_phone_at(self, a_key):
        return self.phones[a_key]

    def add_phone(self, a_key, a_phone):
        self.phones[a_key] = a_phone

    def remove_phone(self, a_phone):
        for key in self.phones.keys():
            if self.phones[key] == a_phone:
                self.phones.pop(key)
                break

    def remove_phone_at(self, a_key):
        self.phones.pop(a_key)

    def replace_phone(self, a_key, a_phone):
        self.phones[a_key] = a_phone
```

In the case of Fig. 14–13, there is an issue to be considered: as the origin of the association has no multiplicity restriction, and the qualifier is not an attribute of the class, nothing

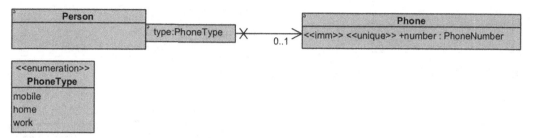

FIGURE 14–13 A model with an external qualifier.

assures that the same phone is not associated to two or more keys. For example, the following sequence of commands would produce a phone associated to two different types:

```
a_person.add_phone("residential", a_phone)
a_person.add_phone("comercial", a_phone)
```

If that is what is expected, nothing else must be said. But if that does not agree with
the business rules, then the role on the left side should be 1 and the association should be
implemented as a bidirectional association, so that control mechanisms could avoid a phone
from being associated to more than one type.

Now, let us see the case of unidirectional qualified association that is the "partition" (relations must be bidirectional) with internal qualifier. For the next example, we consider that a
person may have a set of phones for each type (Fig. 14–14). And the Python code for the
qualified role is:

```
class Person():
    def __init__(self):
        self.phones = dict()

    def get_phones(self):
        return self.phones

    def get_phones_at(self, a_key):
        return self.phones[a_key]

    def add_phone(self, a_phone):
        key = a_phone.get_idd()
        if not key in self.phones.keys():
            self.phones[key] = set()
        self.phones[key].add(a_phone)

    def remove_phone(self, a_phone):
        for key in self.phones.keys():
            if a_phone in self.phones[key]:
                self.phones[key].remove(a_phone)
                if len(self.phones[key]) == 0:
                    self.phones.pop(key)
                break
```

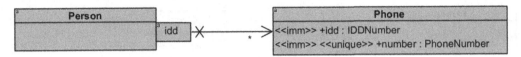

FIGURE 14–14 A model with a partition and an internal qualifier.

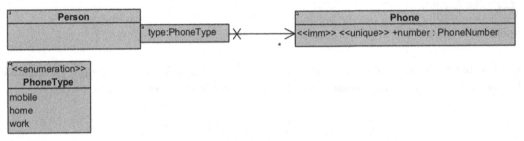

FIGURE 14–15 A model with a partition with external qualifier.

Finally, if the partition has an external qualifier as seen in Fig. 14–15, the code would be like:

```
class Person():
    def __init__(self):
        self.phones = dict()

    def get_phones(self):
        return self.phones

    def get_phones_at(self, a_key):
        return self.phones[a_key]

    def add_phone(self, a_key, a_phone):
        if not a_key in self.phones.keys():
            self.phones[a_key] = set()
        self.phones[a_key].add(a_phone)
```

14.2.8 Unidirectional association with association class

When the association has an association class, it is necessary to implement the creation and destruction of instances of that class each time a corresponding link is added or removed.

Association classes may exist in associations with any multiplicity. However, they are more common and useful in associations that are many to many.

One possible implementation for this kind of association is to create a *dict* associating instances of the opposite class to instances of the association class.

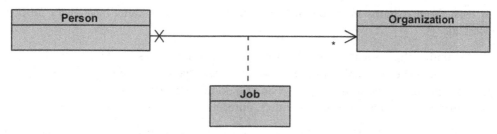

FIGURE 14–16 A model with an association class.

Fig. 14—16 shows an association class, and its implementation is shown below:

```
from job import Job

class Person():
    def __init__(self):
        self.organization_job = dict()

    def get_organizations(self):
        return set(self.organization_job.keys())

    def get_jobs(self):
        return set(self.organization_job.values())

    def get_job_at(self, an_organization):
        return self.organization_job[an_organization]

    def add_organization(self, an_organization):
        new_job = Job()
        self.organization_job[an_organization] = new_job

    def remove_organization(self, an_organization):
        self.organization_job.pop(an_organization)
```

In Fig. 14—16, we see that when a new link is created from *Person* to *Organization* with *add_organization*, a new instance of *Job* is automatically created.

As Python has garbage collector, it is not necessary to explicitly destroy the instance of *Job* in *remove_organization*, but some care must be taken to confirm whether there are no other classes with mandatory associations to the association class.

14.3 Bidirectional associations

As mentioned before, the unidirectional implementation of associations is only possible when they are navigable in one direction and there is no multiplicity constraint in the origin role. In other situations, the bidirectional implementation is necessary.

At least three patterns for implementing bidirectional associations have been proposed (Fowler, 2003):

- Implementing the association as two unidirectional associations (*mutual friends*).
- Implementing the association as a unidirectional association in just one of the classes, and making navigation to the opposite side be done over a derived association.
- Implementing an intermediary object that represents the association.

In all the cases above, if the association is navigable in both directions, the *get* method must be implemented in both participating classes, because navigation must be allowed in both directions. However, if we have the case of a unidirectional association with a multiplicity restriction at the origin, then the *get* method must be implemented only at the origin class.

The *add*, *remove*, and *replace* methods, if required, may be implemented only in one of the classes, because if they exist in both classes, they would be redundant as they would do the same thing.

14.3.1 Mutual friends

The option for implementing bidirectional associations in both directions is the best in terms of time efficiency, but it is less efficient in terms of space allocation because each association is implemented twice. It may also require more control overhead because the implementation of the association in both classes must be synchronized.

The implementation of the unidirectional components of the association follows the recommendations given before.

If both roles are optional and no other constraints are present, then links may be added and removed at will. Otherwise, care must be taken not to violate structural rules. As links must be added and removed from both sides of the association, auxiliary methods would be needed to add and remove the individual unidirectional links in one of the classes.

These auxiliary methods must not be called in any other place except the *add* and *remove* methods. That is why they must be declared as *private*, but the opposite class must have access to them; thus, they are exported exclusively to that class.

Fig. 14–17 presents a bidirectional many-to-many association, and the corresponding implementation code is shown below:

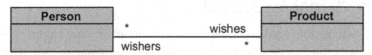

FIGURE 14–17 A model with a bidirectional association with no restrictions.

```
class Person():
    def __init__(self):
        self.wishes = set()

    def get_wishes(self):
        return self.wishes

    def add_wish(self, a_product):
        self.wishes.add(a_product)
        a_product._add_wisher(self)

    def remove_wish(self, a_product):
        self.wishes.remove(a_product)
        a_product._remove_wisher


class Product():
    def __init__(self):
        self.wishers = set()

    def get_wishers(self):
        return self.wishers

    def _add_wisher(self, a_person):
        self.wishers.add(a_person)

    def _remove_wisher(self, a_person):
        self.wishers.remove(a_person)
```

The methods *_add_wisher* and *_remove_wisher* implemented in class *Product* are considered as *protected* and must not be used by other methods besides the ones they were designed to. Python does not have real protected methods. Thus programmers usually prefix the name of the method with "_" to indicate that it is protected.

As mentioned before, the access methods (*get*) must be implemented in both classes if the association is navigable in both directions. But the *add* and *remove* methods may be implemented in just one class. In the example above, they are implemented only in class *Person*.

In any case, one class implements the *add* and *remove* methods and the other implements the auxiliary protected methods *_add* and *_remove*.

14.3.2 Unidirectional implementation

Even if the association is bidirectional, it may be the case that navigation occurs much more often or is more critical in just one direction. If that happens, an option is to implement the association physically in *only one direction* and implement the *get* method for the opposite side as a derived association. The advantage is that the code is simpler, faster in one direction, and space saving. The disadvantage is that the navigation from the opposite direction would be much slower.

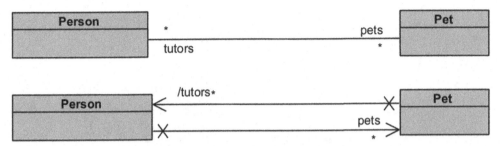

FIGURE 14–18 Representation and implementation of a bidirectional association with unidirectional implementation.

This form of implementation is also easier when the role on the origin of the implemented direction has no multiplicity restriction. If there is a restriction, then the unidirectional implementation is possible only if additional mechanisms to control multiplicity at the origin of the association are implemented, with more loss of performance. Fig. 14–18 shows an example of a bidirectional association (upper) and its implementation as a normal unidirectional association from *Person* to *Pet* and a derived association from *Pet* to *Person*.

Observe that the lower part of the figure represents the design implementation of the conceptual upper part of the figure. In the lower part, navigation from *Pet* to *Person* is only possible through the derived association/*tutors*; *pets* is not navigable. ON the other hand, navigation from *Person* to *Pet* is only possible through the unidirectional association with role *pets*, and which is not navigable to the other sense. The Python code would be the following:

```
Class Person():
    def __init__(self):
        self.pets = set()

    def get_pets(self):
        return self.pets

    def add_pet(self, a_pet):
        self.pets.add(a_pet)

    def remove_pet(self, a_pet):
        return self.pets.remove(a_pet)


from person import Person

class Pet:
    def __init__(self):
        pass

    def get_tutors(self):
        all_persons = Person.all_instances()
        tutors = set()
        for person in all_persons:
            if person in self.get_tutors():
                tutors.add(person)
        return tutors
```

Python does not implement the function *all_instances* and many consider it as an antipattern. Thus maybe this is not really the best choice for implementing bidirectional associations.

14.3.3 Association proxy

A bidirectional association may also be implemented by means of an intermediary object that represents the association. The intermediary object consists of a class that represents a table with pairs of linked instances. This table is highly reusable. First, there will be slightly different implementations for the table depending on the multiplicity and other restrictions in roles. Let us see one possible implementation for a * to * bidirectional association:

```python
table = dict()

def create(name):
    table[name] = []
    return table[name]

def link(a, name, b):
    table[name].append((a, b))

def unlink(a, name, b):

    table[name].remove((a, b))

def get_from_key(name, key):
    result = set()
    for pair in table[name]:
        if pair[0] == key:
            result.add(pair[1])
    return result

def get_from_value(name, value):
    result = set()
    for pair in table[name]:
        if pair[1] == value:
            result.add(pair[0])
    return result
```

After trying and studying diverse forms of implementation of the *association proxy*, the simpler form seems to be implementing it as a global variable that contains a dictionary that relates names of associations (*role1_role2*) to a list of pairs that represent the linked elements. The methods in this case are all static.

This solution could be used in cases like the one in Fig. 14−18 to represent the bidirectional association that is completely balanced in terms of execution time relative to its roles. The get methods must be implemented in both classes while add, remove, and replace only in one class. This is the code of the class *Person* that uses the Association Proxy to implement all methods for association *wishers_wishes* between classes Person and Product:

```
import association

WW = 'wisher_wish'

class Person():
    def __init__(self):
        if not WW in association.table.keys():
            association.create(WW)

    def get_wishes(self):
        return association.get_from_key(WW, self)

    def add_wish(self, a_product):
        association.link(self, WW, a_product)

    def remove_wish(self, a_product):
        return association.unlink(self, WW, a_product)

    def remove_wish(self, a_product):
        return association.unlink(self, WW, a_product)
```

The code for the other participating class is simpler:

```
import association

WW = 'wisher_wish'

class Product():
    def __init__(self):
        if not WW in association.table.keys():
            association.create(WW)

    def get_wishers(self):
        return association.get_from_value(WW, self)
```

Care must be taken to use the same name for the association in both classes. In order to avoid repeating the string "wisher_wish" many times, a constant *WW* was defined to be used in its place.

For a second association in the same class, a new association name must be created and the methods *get*, *add*, and *remove* implemented for this specific association in both participating classes.

That leads to the temptation of changing methods like *add_wisher(self, a_product)* by *add* (*self, "wisher," product*). In this case, a lot of methods would not be written, but only if they conform to the general form. Any different configuration of multiplicity or constrains in the roles would need a different table structure.

The association proxy approach tends to be much simpler and maintainable than the former ones. It also mimics the structure of a relational database because associations are indeed implemented as intermediary tables, which correspond to the intermediary object here.

The disadvantage of this method is that getters are slower in both directions when compared to the bidirectional approach and the global visibility of the intermediary object may cause design hazards if not used carefully.

14.4 Delegated methods and system operations

To this point, we have shown how to generate code for classes, attributes, associations, and their corresponding basic methods that may be considered part of their basic structure. Now it is the time to explain how to implement delegate methods and system operations. These should be implemented by following the dynamic models explained before.

In a system sequence diagram, system operations are implemented as a sequence of messages that are sent by the controller. Some of those messages could be basic operations so that their code is already known, as explained by the patterns in this chapter. However, some messages are not basic, but delegate, and they have to be discovered and implemented considering the sequence of messages that are sent by the same object that received the delegate method in continuation for this.

Let us look again at Figure 13−28, reproduced here as Fig. 14−19.

In this diagram, we observe five basic operations: *get_proposals* and *get_person*, that are basic queries on roles from: *Controller* to itself. On the other hand, *send_proposal* is a system operation that is usually delegated, and *create_new_sending* is a delegate message from: Controller to *a_proposal*.

Let us forget for now the basic operations and deal with the implementation of those two nonbasic messages. First, the *send_proposal* system operation should be implemented in class Controller as a sequence of messages that directly follow it in the sequence diagram

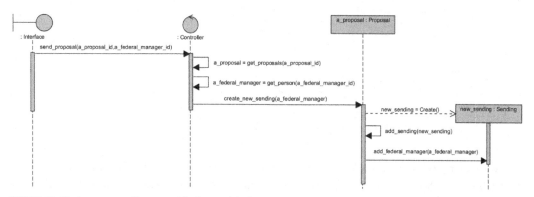

FIGURE 14–19 A sequence diagram with the model of a system operation.

considering just one level in deepness. This means that *send proposal* will *not* be implemented as:

1. get_proposals
2. get_person
3. create_new_sending
   3.1 new_sending
   3.2 add_sending
   3.3 add_federal_manager

The implementation of the messages at the second level (3.1, 3.2, and 3.3) is delayed. Instead of that, only the three messages at the first level after *send_proposal* are implemented:

1. get_proposal
2. get_person
3. create_new_sending

The other messages from *Proposal* to *Sending* and Proposal to *Proposal* are sent from *a_proposal* to *new_sending* and *a_proposal* in the implementation of the delegate method *create_new_sending*:

1. Create
2. add_sending
3. add_federal_manager

It would be a problem if messages from different levels were mixed in the same method implementation. For example, if the *Create()* message to sending was implemented inside method *send_proposal*, a problem of cohesion would arise, as seen before.

That said, the code for the system and delegate methods in the diagram (ignoring other basic methods for now) could be:

```
class Controller:
    #...
    def send_proposal(self, a_proposal_id, a_federal_manager_id): #SYSTEM OPERATION
        a_proposal = self.get_proposals(a_proposal_id)
        a_federal_manager = self.get_person(a_federal_manager_id)
        a_proposal.create_new_sending(a_federal_manager_id)


class Proposal:
    #...
    def create_new_sending(self, a_federal_manager):     #DELEGATE METHOD
        new_sending = Sending()
        self.add_sending(new_sending)
        new_sending.add_federal_manager(a_federal_manager)
```

As it can be seen, this implementation avoided increasing coupling because it does not return the new *Sending* to the controller. Instead of *concentration*, this code works with *delegation*.

Questions

1. Explain in detail how a delegate message that appears in a sequence diagram must be implemented.
2. What are the basic operations that must be implemented for most kinds of associations?
3. Considering Fig. 13-26, a *Proposal* has an association to *Sending* that is 1 to *{ordered} ≪ stack≫. Considering that this association is bidirectional, show the mutual-friends implementation of its representation and its methods.
4. Consider Fig. 13-28, try to present a *concentration* version of this diagram and present the corresponding (smelling) code.
5. Produce a design domain version of the classes in Fig. 12-7.

15

Testing

Key topics in this chapter

- Functional testing
- Stubs and drivers
- Test-driven development
- Unit testing
- System testing with use cases

15.1 Introduction to testing

No matter how sophisticated the modeling and specification techniques used to develop software are, no matter how disciplined and competent the team is, there is a factor that makes software testing always necessary: *human error*. It is a myth to think that good developers working with state-of-the-art tools are capable of developing error-free software (Beizer, 1990).

Murphy's Law (Bloch, 1980) in many of its corollaries seems to speak directly to the software industry. For example:

- Anything that can go wrong will go wrong (at the worst time ever).
- If everything seems all right, you have not checked appropriately.
- Nature always sides with the hidden flaw.

For many years, software-testing activities were considered a punishment to programmers. Testing was considered as a waste of time because software was supposed to be correct from the beginning.

However, things have changed. The test discipline now is considered extremely important. Today, it is an integral part of the software development process and one of the most fundamental disciplines in software engineering.

Furthermore, leading software development companies started to outsource software testing, by hiring *test factories*. That means that not only developers but also teams are especially trained to conduct testing.

This chapter presents test activities that are strongly adapted for use with the techniques shown in previous chapters. In special, this chapter will deal with two important levels of test: unit tests and system tests.

Unit tests are used basically to check the behavior of classes, including their basic and delegate methods. If automatic code generation is used, such tests may be suppressed, because it is assumed that automatic code generators do not make human errors.

Object-Oriented Analysis and Design for Information Systems. DOI: https://doi.org/10.1016/B978-0-443-13739-6.00007-1

On the other hand, *system tests* can be performed as systematic *use case tests*. Each use case is a script that establishes normal and alternate flows for accomplishing business goals. Use case tests also may be executed manually or automatically. If the client executes use case tests following the system tests proposed, then they are called *acceptance tests*.

There are two major categories of test techniques:

- *Structural tests*, which evaluate the internal structure of the code.
- *Functional tests*, which evaluate operations based only on their inputs and outputs.

In this book, only functional techniques applied specifically to the two levels of testing mentioned are introduced:

- Functional unit test applied to any kind of methods, but especially to system operations, which already have contracts that ease the process of identifying the test cases.
- System tests based on system use cases. This kind of test has variants. If conducted by final users, they are acceptance tests. As the development team gives the user more proactivity and less control during the tests, they can also be called α or β tests.

Meszaros (2007) and Beck (1989) are good references to understand automated tests and its patterns.

15.2 Functional testing

Functional testing consists of a sequence of tests that define entry values for an operation and observe if the result is what was expected. Functional tests may be run without any knowledge of the programming code that implements the operation; only its behavior is observed. The quantity of tests to be conducted to assure that an operation is correct may be virtually undefined. However, functional testing may use techniques to reduce the number of necessary tests without losing coverage. The most useful techniques for accomplishing that goal are *equivalence partitioning* and *limit value analysis*, which are explained in the following subsections.

15.2.1 Equivalence partitioning

One of the principles of functional testing is the identification of equivalent situations. For example, if an operation accepts a set of data (normality) and rejects another set (exception), then it may be said that there are two *equivalence classes*[1] of input data for that operation: *accepted* and *rejected values*. It is usually impossible to test every value included in those classes, because they may be virtually infinite. Thus the technique of *equivalence partitioning* indicates that at least one element in each equivalence class must be tested (Burnstein, 2003).

---

[1] As literature usually uses the term *equivalence classes*, which is a mathematical concept, to refer to the set of objects than can or cannot be accepted, the reader must avoid confusing them with *classes* from the conceptual or domain models.

Classically, the equivalence partitioning technique considers the division of the inputs through the following criteria (Myers et al., 2004):

- If the valid values are specified as an *interval* (e.g., from 10 to 20), then we define one valid class (10 to 20) and two nonvalid classes (less than10 and more than 20).
- If the valid values are specified as a *quantity of values* (e.g., a list with five elements), then we define a valid class (list with five elements) and two nonvalid classes (lists with less than five elements and lists with more than five elements).
- If the valid entries are specified as a *set of acceptable values* that may be processed in different forms (e.g., the strings of an enumeration such as "adult" and "minor"), then we define a valid class for each of the valid options and an invalid class for all other values.
- If the valid values are specified by a logical condition (e.g., a comparison between dates: "*today must be greater than birth date*"), then we must define a valid class (when the condition is true. E.g., today = 07/12/2023 and birthday = 09/29/1967) and an invalid class (when the condition is false; e.g., today = 07/12/2023 and birthday = 03/22/2233). Consider dates being represented as MM/DD/YYYY.

The classes of valid inputs may be defined not only in terms of restrictions on the input data but also in terms of the results that may be produced. If the operation that is being tested has different behavior depending on the value of the input, then different valid sets must be defined for each behavior. For example, consider a simple operation *half(x:Integer):Integer*. Business rules state that this operation accepts only positive numbers for x. Thus the operation is defined to fail if trying to accept zero or negative numbers. Finally, consider that the operation produces $(x - 1)/2$ for odd numbers and $x/2$ for even numbers (the results also belong to the domain of Integer). Thus we must consider that *half* has three equivalence classes for the parameter x:

- A valid class composed of odd positive integers: 1, 3, 5, . . .
- A valid class composed of even positive integers: 2, 4, 6, . . .
- An invalid class composed of nonpositive integers: 0, −1, −2, −3, . . .

The equivalence class values must be always restricted to the domain defined by the type of the parameter. For example, if the type of the parameter were something other than *Integer*, then different equivalence classes would be defined. If the operation was *half(x:Natural):Integer*, then the equivalence classes should be redefined so that they remain inside the *Natural* domain, which does not include zero and negative numbers:

- A valid class composed of odd Naturals: 1, 3, 5, . . .
- A valid class composed of even Naturals: 2, 4, 6, . . .
- No invalid classes.

On the other hand, assume the operation is defined with a broader parameter type such as *half(x:Float):Integer*; then the equivalence classes would be:

- A valid class composed of odd positive integers: 1, 3, 5, . . .
- A valid class composed of even positive integers: 2, 4, 6, . . .
- An invalid class composed of positive nonintegers: 0, 3.1, 4.5, 17.334, 0.003, . . .
- An invalid class composed of negative float or integer numbers: −3, −8, −4.1, −17.6, −100, . . .

We can see from the examples above that if the designer restricts the type of the parameter as much as possible (using *Natural* instead of *Integer* or *Float* in this example), then fewer or simpler invalid equivalence classes would be defined. That is why examples in previous chapters use the *Natural* type instead of *Integer* whenever zero or negative numbers could not be accepted. And that is why enumerations should be used rather than unrestricted strings whenever possible. Having less classes to test contributes to agility.

15.2.2 Limit value analysis

People who work in software testing used to say that (software) bugs hide in the slits. Due to this, the equivalence partitioning technique is often used in conjunction with another technique known as *limit value analysis*.

Limit value analysis consists of avoiding choosing random values from an equivalence class but choosing one or more limit values if they can be determined.

In those domains, such as numbers, this criterion may be applied. For example, if an operation requires an integer parameter that is valid only if included in the interval [10..20], then there are three equivalence classes:

- Invalid for any $x < 10$.
- Valid for $x \geq 10$ and $x \leq 20$.
- Invalid for any $x > 20$.

Limit value analysis suggests that eventual errors in the logic of a program do not happen at random places in the code, but they concentrate at the boundary points where two intervals of data meet. Thus if the domain of the parameter is *Integer*:

- For the first invalid class, the value 9 must be tested.
- For the valid class, 10 and 20 must be tested.
- For the second invalid class, the value 21 must be tested.

Thus if there is a logic error in the operation for some of these inputs, it is much more probable that it will be found in this way rather than if a random value is chosen inside each interval that defines an equivalence class.

15.3 Stubs

Frequently, parts of the software must be tested apart from the main body of code, but at the same time, they must communicate with those other parts.

Let us get one example from combinatorics. If you are familiarized with the concepts of *factorial* and *combination*, you will understand easily. When a method *combination* (that is going to be tested) needs to call operations such as *factorial* that has not yet being implemented, then the component *factorial* may be replaced by a simplified version of it that implements only the behavior that is necessary to perform the test of *combination* operation. This simplified component that is used in the place of a component that has not yet been implemented is called a *stub*.

For example, suppose that a method *combination* needs a *factorial* calculator that has not yet been implemented. A simplified version of *factorial* may be implemented just for allowing the method *combination* to be tested. Suppose that given the formula $C(n, p) = n!/(p!(n - p)!)$ with $p \leq n$, we decided to test *combination* with the following values:

- C(0, 0) == 1
- C(1, 0) == 1
- C(1, 1) == 1
- C(2, 0) == 1
- C(2, 1) == 2
- C(2, 2) == 1
- C(3, 0) == 1
- C(3, 1) == 3
- C(3, 2) == 3
- C(3, 3) == 1

In this case, we would be testing the limit value (0, 0) and some additional values. Notice that in order to test *combination* with those values, we do not need a factorial calculator; we just need to know the values of 0!, 1!, 2!, and 3!. Thus the stub *StubFactorial* defined below must be enough for this purpose. The name of the file that will contain the following code could be *stub_factorial.py*, but it implements the method *factorial* with the same name as in the definitive class to simplify refactoring when the stub is finally replaced by the definitive class.

```python
def factorial(a_natural):
    if a_natural == 0:
        return 1
    elif a_natural == 1:
        return 1
    elif a_natural == 2:
        return 2
    elif a_natural == 3:
        return 6
    else:
        return None
```

In this way, the operation *combination* may be tested without investigating and defining a possibly more complex operation to calculate factorials.

```python
from stub_factorial import factorial


def combination(n, p):
    return factorial(n) / (factorial(p) * (factorial(n-p)))
```

If we run the tests with the values above for $C(n,p)$, we will see that they are correct.

Although stubs may be considered as mock-ups and therefore disposable after the real component is implemented, it could be a good idea to maintain stubs in a components library. That could accelerate the testing of the class that uses the stub. Imagine that the stub usually will have a few lines of code and use little memory, while the real class that the stub represents may be linked to a series of other classes that may include many lines of code as well as a large testing database. In this case, stubs would be the fastest option to test the original class.

Stubs are useful especially if top-down development happens; but, as we have seen, in other situations too.

15.4 Drivers

If the relation of a class and a stub is represented as *class* → *stub* because the class calls for methods implemented in the stub, then another way to address this relation is by using *drivers*. The relation between a driver and a class that implements the methods that the driver will call may then be *driver* → *class*.

Thus, one use for drivers is to allow bottom-up development similarly as stubs do with top-down. However, drivers may be a much more powerful tool if we implement them systematically. The idea is to make a driver calling a given function for any valid or invalid equivalence class in its parameters. In this way, the driver will be an automatic tester for a given method or class.

In our first example, shown in Fig. 15−1, the element chosen to be tested is the method *get_age*() in class *Person*. We will proceed here with the simplest way of testing it so that the idea can be better understood without the introduction of more complex structures.

The class *Person* has only two attributes: *name*, and *date_of_birth*, and four methods, *Person*(), the constructor, *get_name*() and *set_name*(), the basic methods for the attribute *name*, and a derived method *get_age*(), which returns the age, in years calculated from the *date_of_birth* and today. The *date_of_birth* attribute is immutable and private, but, combined with the date of today, it can allow to derive the age of the person.

Of course, there are algorithms already implemented in Python for calculating age from date of birth, but the idea here is to show a sequence of commands programmed

Person
-name : String
-date_of_birth : Date
+Person(a_name : String)
+get_name() : String
+set_name(a_name : String)
+get_age() : String

FIGURE 15−1 A fragment of a model to be used as example in this section.

to do this calculation with one mistake placed on purpose, just to see if the test can detect it.

```
from datetime import *


class Person:
    def __init__(self, a_name, a_date_of_birth):
        self.name = a_name
        self.date_of_birth = a_date_of_birth

    def set_name(self, a_name):
        self.name = a_name

    def get_name(self):
        return self.name

    def get_age(self):
        today = datetime.date.today()
        t_day = today.day
        t_month = today.month
        t_year = today.year
        b_day = self.date_of_birth.day
        b_month = self.date_of_birth.month
        b_year = self.date_of_birth.year
        age = t_year - b_year - 1
        if t_month > b_month:
            age = age+1
        elif t_month == b_month and t_day > b_day:
            age = age+1
        return age
```

To systematically test the *get_age*() method, we will write a driver for it. The driver is a sequence of tests where we are supposed to at least apply the techniques of equivalence partitioning and limit value analysis seen before in this chapter.

Despite the *get_age*() method not having any explicit parameter, it has an implicit one, which is the date of *today* and a private attribute *date_of_birth* that is used to calculate the age of the person.

Considering the two techniques explained before, we could think of testing the following values:

- An aleatory date in the past (andrew).
- A person who is going to celebrate birthday tomorrow (beth).
- A person who is celebrating birthday today (charles).
- A person who is celebrating 1 year tomorrow (daisy).
- A person who is celebrating 1 year today (edward).
- A person born today (florence).
- A person who will be born tomorrow (gerald). An invalid class—all other classes are valid.

The following is the code that creates the *fixtures*, that is, objects that will be used exclusively in the driver to test the different equivalence classes. For now, we ignore *gerald* on purpose because it belongs to an invalid equivalence class and should be tested differently from the other values.

```
from person import *
from datetime import *

andrew = Person("Andrew", date(1967, 9, 29))   # YYYY/MM/DD
beth = Person("Beth", date(1980, 8, 10))
charles = Person("Charles", date(1980, 8, 9))
daisy = Person("Daisy", date(2022, 8, 10))
edward = Person("Edward", date(2022, 8, 9))
florence = Person("Florence", date(2023, 8, 9))
gerald = Person("Gerald", date(2023, 8, 10))
```

After creating the fixtures, the sequence of tests is defined. In this case, each *assert* is a command that compares the result of the method *get_age()* for the different objects in different equivalence classes with the expected result:

```
# today = 08/09/2023

assert(andrew.get_age() == 55)
assert(beth.get_age() == 42)
assert(charles.get_age() == 43)
assert(daisy.get_age() == 0)
assert(edward.get_age() == 1)
assert(florence.get_age() == 0)
```

After running the driver, we obtain the following output:

```
Traceback (most recent call last):
  File "D:/.../diver_person.py", line 17, in <module>
    assert(charles.get_age() == 43)
AssertionError


Process finished with exit code 1
```

Thus there is something wrong with the age of *charles*. If we examine the code, we will see that the function *get_age()* is returning 42 instead of 43 for *charles*, which is an error because he is celebrating birthday today and 43 would be the right sum. This error is caused by a line in the original file *person.py* that mistakenly used the "$>$" comparator instead of "$>=$." To be more specific, the error is in the line that starts with "elif" in *get_age()*.
Thus in order to fix the mistake, the line:

```
elif t_month == b_month and t_day > b_day:
```

must be replaced by:

```
elif t_month == b_month and t_day >= b_day:
```

After correcting this error, the function *get_age*() will pass in all tests. But we still have the problem with *gerald*. As future birthdays are not allowed in most systems, they belong to an invalid class of unborn people. In the case of an operation receiving or returning values from invalid classes, many different things could happen. Suppose that in this case we want the *get_age*() method to raise an exception. Then, the driver, when finding such a situation, should detect this exception, or else, the test is failure.

Thus we can use the following code to finish this driver where we try to execute *get_age*() over *gerald*:

```
try:
    assert(gerald.get_age())
    print("Error: exception not detected")
    raise Exception
except:
    print('pass')
```

If the function *get_age*() stops with an exception for *gerald*, then the driver will consider that the test succeeded. However, if the expression *gerald.get_age*() runs without an exception, then the driver will consider that the test failed, and we obtain the following result:

```
Error: exception not detected
Process finished with exit code 0
```

The problem of future dates being registered, however, does not start with the method *get_age*(). In fact, when the instance of *Person* is created, it should already detect that the date passed as argument is not valid. Thus instead of checking for this problem in method *get_age*(), it would be better to test it in the *__init__* method of *Person*. An assert that the argument *date_of_birth* is equal or past *today* will then be used in this method, and unborn people would not even be created:

```
class Person:
    def __init__(self, a_name, a_date_of_birth):
        assert a_date_of_birth <= datetime.date.today()
        self.name = a_name
        self.date_of_birth = a_date_of_birth
```

Thus stubs and drivers are simple implementations that simulate the behavior of other components. The stub is used in the place of a component that should be called but is not yet implemented. The driver is used in the place of a component that should call the component to be tested in a systematic and reproducible way.

Both stubs and drivers must be maintained as code assets, the first to avoid the developer to load many classes to test a simple operation and the other to allow the developers to systematically test their code in an automatic way.

15.5 Test-driven development

Test-driven development or *TDD* (Beck, 2003) is a technique and a programming philosophy that incorporates automatic testing to the process of producing code. It works like this:

1. First, the programmer that receives the specification of a new functionality that must be implemented should create or modify a set of automatic tests for the code that does not yet exist or that are now anymore correct, respectively.
2. This set of tests must be executed and observed to fail. This is done to show that the tests won't succeed unless a new feature is implemented in the code. If the test passes at this time, there are two explanations: either the test is badly written or the feature that is being tested is already present in the code.
3. After the tests fail, the code must be developed with the only objective being passing the tests. (If any other feature is identified by the team, then the tests must be updated before this new feature is introduced in the code. In that case, the process restarts from step 1.)
4. After the code passes all tests, it must be cleaned and improved if necessary, in order to meet internal quality standards. After passing the final tests, it is considered stable and may be integrated into the main body of code of the system.

The contracts that were developed with OCL and the dynamic models in system sequence diagrams are exceptional sources of information for developing complete and consistent test cases before producing any code.

The motivation for TDD is to incentivize the programmer to keep the code simple and to produce a test asset that allows any part of the system to be automatically tested.

15.6 Unit testing with TDD

Unit tests are the most elementary tests and consist of verifying if an individual component of the software was implemented correctly. Usually, a *test case* will verify all conditions for a given method in a class. Let us use a version of the class *Person* depicted in Fig. 15−2 where

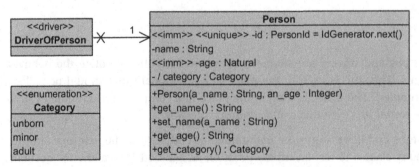

FIGURE 15–2 A new version of *Person* to be tested.

the *age* attribute was used instead of birthday. In this case, *age* is immutable. This is a situation that is common in some systems when you need to know the age of the person on the date of her registration and not the updated age of today.

This class to be tested has four variables and five methods. Let us explain initially the variables and relate them to the methods that will be included in the test cases.

The first attribute of class *Person* is *id*. This is a special variable used to differentiate one object from another. It is not known by the user and therefore does not have a getter or setter available to the user. The test of this kind of attributes is made by an internal mechanism that examines the control class *IdGenerator*, which is used systemwide. Thus we are not worrying with testing it now, at least, not in the context of testing the class *Person*.

15.6.1 Testing methods related to a public mandatory and immutable attribute

The third method in class *Person* is *age*. It is a public, nonderived method and therefore should have a getter and a setter. However, it is also immutable, and because of that it will not have a setter, just a getter. Also, as it is mandatory, it should appear as an attribute of the *Person*() method.

Thus we must test the method *Person*() to see if the result of *get_age*() obtained just after an instance of *Person* is created is really the one that was informed by the method *Person*().

As stated by TDD, the code that tests the class must be written first. However, if a file *person.py* does not exist yet, you must create it. Leave it blank except for the two lines below:

```
class Person:
    pass
```

Then, let us use the library *unittest*, already available in Python, to write the first version of the *driver_person.py* file. In this example, we must create an instance of *Person* with the method *Person*(*an_age*) and verify with the method *get_age*() if the value returned from this method is equal to *an_age* as sent to *Person*(). The code belong will be written in a different file, usually: the class *Person* is in file *person.py* and its driver is in file *driver_person.py*.

As we see, the file *driver_person.py* has a class *DriverPerson* that is a driver that corresponds to a subclass of *TestCase*, implemented in *unittest*. Inside this class, there is a method *test_age* that would verify if a person created with *ANI_AGE* would return the same value when the method *get_age*() is invoked. The code for the driver file is the following:

```
import unittest
from person import *


ANY_AGE = 50


class DriverPerson(unittest.TestCase):
    def test_age(self):
        a_person = Person(ANY_AGE)
        self.assertEqual(a_person.get_age(), ANY_AGE)
```

The idea now is to run this driver and see if it finishes with success or error. Obviously, an error will occur because the class *Person* that is being tested was implemented with just a *pass* command. Notice also that this set of tests is minimal in the sense that it tests only the feature regarding *age* that was discussed. There is no mention to the person's *name* neither *category*.

Next step is to implement in class *Person* the minimum features that just allow it to pass in the *DriverPerson* test. This is a possibility:

```
class Person:
    def __init__(self, an_age):
        self.age = an_age

    def get_age(self):
        return self.age
```

As you see, the code is clear and simple, it does not cover features that will be tested in future and present a clear test as described above. If you try to run *DriverPerson* again, it will inform that 1 test was performed and no errors found. This concludes the first loop on the test-driven approach in our example.

15.6.2 Testing methods related to a public, mandatory, and mutable attribute

For the second loop, let us examine the attribute *name* of class *Person*. It is a simple attribute that is public, mandatory, and mutable. It means that the attribute *name* must have getter and setter and appear in the list of parameters of *Person()*. For this set of methods, we should test two configurations:

1. If the value of *get_name()* just after *Person(an_age, a_name)* is executed is equal to *a_name*.
2. If the value of *get_name()* just after *set_name(another_name)* is executed is equal to *another_name*.

For that, lets first change the code of the driver by adding these two new tests:

```
import unittest
from person import *


ANY_AGE = 50
ANY_NAME = 'John'
ANOTHER_NAME = 'Mary'


class DriverPerson(unittest.TestCase):
    def test_age(self):
        a_person = Person(ANY_AGE, ANY_NAME)
        self.assertEqual(a_person.get_age(), ANY_AGE)

    def test_name_creator(self):
        a_person = Person(ANY_AGE, ANY_NAME)
        self.assertEqual(a_person.get_name(), ANY_NAME)

    def test_name_setter(self):
        a_person = Person(ANY_AGE, ANY_NAME)
        a_person.set_name(ANOTHER_NAME)
        self.assertEqual(a_person.get_name(), ANOTHER_NAME)
```

The result probably is that three tests were tried and three failed, even the test on *Person* and *get_age*() that already had success now failed because now the method *Person* has two parameters and not just 1. Now, we continue to develop the class *Person* so that it would pass all three tests. A change will be needed here at the method Person() that now has one more argument. The code for this new version of class *Person* could be:

```
import unittest
from person import *


ANY_AGE = 50
ANY_NAME = 'John'
ANOTHER_NAME = 'Mary'


class DriverPerson(unittest.TestCase):
    def test_age(self):
        a_person = Person(ANY_AGE, ANY_NAME)
        self.assertEqual(a_person.get_age(), ANY_AGE)

    def test_name_creator(self):
        a_person = Person(ANY_AGE, ANY_NAME)
        self.assertEqual(a_person.get_name(), ANY_NAME)

    def test_name_setter(self):
        a_person = Person(ANY_AGE, ANY_NAME)
        a_person.set_name(ANOTHER_NAME)
        self.assertEqual(a_person.get_name(), ANOTHER_NAME)
```

Now, all three tests run with success, as expected.

15.6.3 Testing methods related to a derived attribute with more than one valid class

Finally, we must deal with the derived attribute or method *get_category*(), which is a little more complex because it depends on values already stored in *age* and a series of equivalence classes that must be tested for their limits. Look at Table 15−1 to recall the definition of the attributes related to this method.

Instead of representing the output of this method as strings, we created an enumeration *Category* that is already depicted in Fig. 15−2. An enumeration can be defined in a Python file, which in this case contains a class *Category* that is a subclass of *Enum* that is imported from the Python library *enum*. The code of category.py, therefore, is:

```python
from enum import Enum


class Category(Enum):
    UNBORN = 1
    MINOR = 2
    ADULT = 3
```

Now we have an enumeration called *Category*. It has only three members: *Category. UNBORN*, *Category.MINOR*, and *Category.ADULT*. If you try to write *Category.X* for any other *x*, it will be refused by the system.

As new functionality is going to be tested, we have first to rewrite the driver with a test comprehensive enough to cover the upper and lower limits of all equivalence the instance of *Person* that is being tested. In the case of equivalence classes that do not have lower or upper limits (those marked with the infinite symbol), we can use any other value inside the equivalence class.

Now we are going to rewrite the driver to take account of the query *get_category*(). Values to be tested are given in Table 15−2.

Table 15-1   Categories of people.

Validity	Interval	Category
Valid	−∞..−1	unborn
Valid	0..17	minor
Valid	18..∞	adult

Table 15-2   Limit values to each equivalence class.

Validity	Interval	Category	Lower	Upper
Valid	−∞..−1	unborn	−234	−1
Valid	0..17	minor	0	17
Valid	18..∞	adult	18	7622

In order to conduct the tests, we will write the following code to the driver:

```python
import unittest
from person3 import *
from category import *


ANY_AGE = 50
ANY_NAME = 'John'
ANOTHER_NAME = 'Mary'
UNBORN_LOW = -234
UNBORN_HIGH = -1
MINOR_LOW = 0
MINOR_HIGH = 17
ADULT_LOW = 18
ADULT_HIGH = 7622


class DriverPerson(unittest.TestCase):
    def test_age(self):
        a_person = Person(ANY_AGE, ANY_NAME)
        self.assertEqual(a_person.get_age(), ANY_AGE)

    def test_name_creator(self):
        a_person = Person(ANY_AGE, ANY_NAME)
        self.assertEqual(a_person.get_name(), ANY_NAME)

    def test_name_setter(self):
        a_person = Person(ANY_AGE, ANY_NAME)
        a_person.set_name(ANOTHER_NAME)
        self.assertEqual(a_person.get_name(), ANOTHERNAME)

    def test_get_category(self):
        a_person = Person(UNBORN_LOW, ANY_NAME)
        self.assertEqual(a_person.get_category(), Category.UNBORN)

        a_person = Person(UNBORN_HIGH, ANY_NAME)
        self.assertEqual(a_person.get_category(), Category.UNBORN)

        a_person = Person(MINOR_LOW, ANY_NAME)
        self.assertEqual(a_person.get_category(), Category.MINOR)

        a_person = Person(MINOR_HIGH, ANY_NAME)
        self.assertEqual(a_person.get_category(), Category.MINOR)

        a_person = Person(ADULT_LOW, ANY_NAME)
        self.assertEqual(a_person.get_category(), Category.ADULT)

        a_person = Person(ADULT_HIGH, ANY_NAME)
        self.assertEqual(a_person.get_category(), Category.ADULT)
```

Notice that we use a lot of constants in the program. This is to avoid using *magical numbers* in the code, that is, using a constant UNBORN_LOW in the code may be more comprehensive than just using a number such as −234. If another programmer looks at this code, she would take a lot of time trying to figure out what that number represents and from where it was generated.

Now, run this driver, it will fail. Now it is time to implement the final version for the class *Person*:

```python
from category import *


class Person:
    def __init__(self, an_age, a_name):
        self.age = an_age
        self.name = a_name

    def get_age(self):
        return self.age

    def get_name(self):
        return self.name

    def set_name(self, a_name):
        self.name = a_name

    def get_category(self):
        if self.age < 0:
            return Category.UNBORN
        elif self.age < 18:
            return Category.MINOR
        else:
            return Category.ADULT
```

If you have not mistyped anything, this implementation of the class will pass all the tests. Class and driver may be considered DONE and committed to the build.

After some time, however, requirements may change, and now we will see why TDD is so important for the agile principle "Welcome changing requirements, even late in development. Agile processes harness change for the customer's competitive advantage."[2]

15.6.4 Testing after requirements change

No problem if the requirements for one or more methods change in agile development. The team will be prepared, and one of those preparations is to use systematic tests, especially TDD. Now, take the Table 15−2 and imagine that the categories of age were changed to the ones represented in Table 15−3.

---

[2] https://www.agilealliance.org/agile101/12-principles-behind-the-agile-manifesto/. (Accessed 08 February 2023).

Table 15–3   New limit values to be tested.

Validity	Interval	Category	Lower	Upper
Invalid	-∞..-1	Unborn	-234	-1
Valid	0..17	Minor	0	17
Valid	18..64	Adult	18	64
Valid	65..120	Aged	65	120
Invalid	121..∞	Too old	121	7622

Observe that now we have two invalid classes. One appears when the class UNBORN is changed from valid to invalid; they are no longer a category, but an invalid value that must be rejected by the operation *get_category*(). The former category ADULT is now divided into two valid classes, ADULT and AGED, and one invalid class TOO_OLD. According to TDD, first thing to do is to rewrite the driver to reflect the new requirements. Let us do this:

```python
import unittest
from person import *
from category import *


ANYAGE = 50
ANYNAME = 'John'
ANOTHERNAME = 'Mary'
MINOR_LOW = 0
MINOR_HIGH = 17
ADULT_LOW = 18
ADULT_HIGH = 64
AGED_LOW = 65
AGED_HIGH = 120
UNBORN_LOW = -234
UNBORN_HIGH = -1
TOO_OLD_LOW = 121
TOO_OLD_HIGH = 7622

class DriverPerson(unittest.TestCase):
    def test_age(self):
        a_person = Person(ANYAGE, ANYNAME)
        self.assertEqual(a_person.get_age(), ANYAGE)

    def test_name_creator(self):
        a_person = Person(ANYAGE, ANYNAME)
        self.assertEqual(a_person.get_name(), ANYNAME)

    def test_name_setter(self):
        a_person = Person(ANYAGE, ANYNAME)
        a_person.set_name(ANOTHERNAME)
        self.assertEqual(a_person.get_name(), ANOTHERNAME)
```

```
def test_get_category(self):
    a_person = Person(MINOR_LOW, ANYNAME)
    self.assertEqual(a_person.get_category(), Category.MINOR)

    a_person = Person(MINOR_HIGH, ANYNAME)
    self.assertEqual(a_person.get_category(), Category.MINOR)

    a_person = Person(ADULT_LOW, ANYNAME)
    self.assertEqual(a_person.get_category(), Category.ADULT)

    a_person = Person(ADULT_HIGH, ANYNAME)
    self.assertEqual(a_person.get_category(), Category.ADULT)

    with self.assertRaises(Exception):
        Person(UNBORN_LOW, ANYNAME)

    with self.assertRaises(Exception):
        Person(UNBORN_HIGH, ANYNAME)

    with self.assertRaises(Exception):
        Person(TOO_OLD_LOW, ANYNAME)

    with self.assertRaises(Exception):
        Person(TOO_OLD_HIGH, ANYNAME)
```

If run, some errors will be detected as expected, but, most important, look at the last lines of the driver, the ones starting with "*with.*" Those are the tests for invalid classes. Each expression expects that a call to *Person*() will produce one exception because the predicate *assertRaises* is used instead of *assertEqual*. If the expression including creating a person and calling *get_category*() does not produce an exception, the test fails.

Now it is time to refactor the *Person* class in order to accommodate those new requirements:

```
from category import *


class Person:
    def __init__(self, an_age, a_name):
        assert 0 <= an_age <= 120
        self.age = an_age
        self.name = a_name

    def get_age(self):
        return self.age

    def get_name(self):
        return self.name

    def set_name(self, a_name):
        self.name = a_name

    def get_category(self):
        if self.age < 0:
            return Category.UNBORN
        elif self.age < 18:
            return Category.MINOR
        else:
            return Category.ADULT
```

Notice that among other things, an assert was placed just after the *__init__* declaration. If the expression with $0 <= an\_age <= 120$ is False, then an exception will be raised at this point. This makes this class pass the test for invalid classes of the driver.

15.6.5 A top-down approach to minimize the need of unnecessary tests

All discussion that happens in Section 15−6 presumes that what are going to be tested are the different modules or classes of a system. If the team does not have a little automatization in the testing process, this can take a large quantity of time. However, there are other ways to think about how to organize the tests in a big project. Maybe all agree that testing getters and setters one by one in a big system is a big loss of time. But if a setter or getter is failing, they will eventually propagate their error to higher-level operations. Then a kind of top-down approach to testing may be used if the team starts with the highest-level operations and only test lower-level operations if some error is found in those tests.

As the higher-level operations in a well-structured object-oriented project are the system operations (commands and queries), then they are our natural candidates to be tested first. It also comes with another vantage: system operations have contracts since the analysis was conducted over them, and those contracts are exactly what a tester needs to organize a test suit that covers all the system because we already know that the system operations of the use cases already cover the entire functionality of the system.

A team that uses this approach will apply functional test to all system operations considering all scenarios established by the business rules represented in the preconditions and exceptions of each contract. Different success scenarios also may be analyzed by different test cases. If one scenario does not pass the test, then the team will look closely to the system operation, and if no mistake in code is found, they will establish contracts to the lower-level operations used. This continues recursively until an operation is found with an error or a basic operation is found. If that basic operation is ok, then another branch of the operations tree must be analyzed.

The system operations test, then, consists of verifying if the desired postconditions are really obtained in a contract, and if in abnormal conditions, exceptions are effectively raised. System operation tests are very similar to unit tests, except that now the operation has a contract, which eases the identification of the necessary test cases.

15.7 Use case testing

There are many levels of testing that can be applied to a system. Unit test is the most basic type, and it usually is produced by the programmer and not by a test team.

The same kind of test can be used to produce integration tests, which may consist of applying the same tests of the drivers in an integrated version of the system, not in an isolated part.

Above this level of testing, there are the so-called *system tests*. A system test is conducted not on the code, but on the interface of the system. The drivers that were produced to unit and integration tests are not used. A system test consists of a person or automatic system (test robot) using the interface of the system in order to see if all use case paths work from the point of view of the user.

In the case of system tests, the team may and should use the use cases as guides. Thus the purpose of the system tests is to see the system working when trying to execute the main flow and the alternate flows as well. Usually, use case tests do not fail because the use case must run from its beginning to an end; if it must pass by exception handlers, the exceptions will be handled, and if it passes on variants, the variants will be concluded, and the main flow resumed in order to terminate the use case with success. However, sometimes a use case cannot produce its desired result because the user does not have the information or other resources to proceed, for example, a user that has no authorization to register a new user. In those cases, we can say that the use case fails because it must be aborted.

If the test is run by the development team in the place of the real user, then it is called *system test*. If the test is run by the client or under her supervision, then it is an *acceptance test* or *homologation test*. If a whole set of system use cases related to a business use case is performed in a logical sequence such as the one defined by the business activity diagram, then it is a *business cycle test*.

The *use case test* aims to verify if the current version of the system correctly performs the use case processes from the point of view of a user that performs a sequence of system operations in an interface (not necessarily a graphic one) and is able to obtain the expected results.

The use case test may be understood as a systematic execution of the use cases flows. For example, if a use case has three variants and five exception handlers, then the following tests must be run:

- One test in which only the main flow is followed (the happy path).
- Three tests, each one passing on a different variant and concludes normally.
- Five tests, each one passing on a different exception handler at least one time. The exception must then be handled and the use case concludes normally.

It is possible to automate these tests so that they can be performed by a test robot that simulates the actions of the user on the interface.

In Bridge, we run the first system test by hand, because the human eye is important to detect imperfections that the robot cannot see. This test is documented as a use case and is shared with the team. After the test is completed without major errors, then it is passed to the test automation team that will create a robot that would repeat this same test automatically every time it is necessary.

Let us take, for example, the use case "Produce proposal assessment" from Chapter 6, reproduced below:

Use case: Produce proposal assessment (main flow)

1. Reviewer searches for process.
2. System presents list of processes allocated to reviewer, newest first.
3. Reviewer selects process.
4. System presents process name, status, priority, and validity.
5. Reviewer registers assessment and conclusion. (V1)

Table 15–4 Documentation for testing a use case.

Use case: Produce proposal assessment				
Code	Purpose	Status at end	How to obtain	Result
15.6.0	Main flow	Success	1, 2, 3, 4, 5, 6	A finished assessment and conclusion are registered. Assessment is ended.
15.6.1	Variant V1	Success	1, 2, 3, 4, 5, V1(1, 2, 3)	An unfinished assessment and conclusion are registered. Assessment is not ended.
15.6.2	Exception E1	Fail	1, 2, E1(1, 2, 3,)	Message MODAL.114 is shown.
15.6.3	Exception E2	Fail	1, 2, E2(1, 2, 3)	Message MODAL.371 is shown

6. System confirms operation.

Variant V1: User decides to save for continuing latter.

V1.1 Reviewer registers assessment and saves it.

V1.2 System confirms that the assessment is saved.

V1.3 Use case ends.

Exception E1: Deadline reached BR-FNS.01[3].

E1.1 System presents message MODAL.114[4].

E1.2 User acknowledges.

E1.3 Use case fails.

Exception E2: Proposal was not prioritized BR-FNS.06.

E2.1 System presents message MODAL.371.

E2.2 User acknowledges.

E2.3 Use case fails.

This use case has one variant and two exception handlers. It means that it needs at least four tests in order to cover any path possible.

The system test, then, may be structured in a table that relates some important information, such as the purpose of the test, the type of result, and how to execute it. See Table 15–4 that could be a documentation for system test for the use case "Produce proposal assessment."

Furthermore, a whole set of *nonfunctional tests* may be necessary depending on the supplementary specifications and nonfunctional requirements of the system. Examples of nonfunctional tests are compatibility, compliance, endurance, load, localization, performance, recovery, resilience, security, scalability, stress, and usability. Explaining all these kinds of tests is beyond the scope of this book. Nonfunctional testing demands heterogeneous techniques and are covered by many books such as: Molyneaux (2009) on performance testing, Nelson (2004) on stress testing, and Nielsen (1994) on usability testing.

---

[3] BR-FNS.01 is a reference to the Business Rule (BR) that may be observed here and that is cataloged with the other business rules of the system.

[4] MODAL.114 is a reference to the message shown by a modal window that is cataloged with the other messages of the system. A modal window blocks navigation until the user acknowledges having read it.

Questions

1. Look at Fig. 9-19 and produce an identification of tests that must be made for this class and implement it preferably in Python.
2. Why the class drivers cannot be used for system tests?
3. What is the difference between stubs and drivers and why are they valuable for the software development?
4. What is the motivation behind the TDD instruction to produce the driver before doing any change in the code? Why is it valuable?

16

Interface tier design

Key topics in this chapter

- The Interaction Flow Modeling Language (IFML)
- View components
- Web page patterns
- Operations in IFML

16.1 Introduction to interface tier design

The interface tier design of a system depends fundamentally on the detailed use cases or system sequence diagrams because the interface must allow a user to follow all use case flows. Design class diagrams and contracts may be very useful as well.

During interface design, the nonfunctional requirements that were annotated with the use cases should be revised again, because they may contain indications on how to design the use case interface.

The Interaction Flow Modeling Language (IFML) is an OMG standard[1] for modeling user interfaces compatible to UML. It was inspired in the language WebML (Ceri et al., 2003). A Web IFML editor is available in https://editor.ifmledit.org/ (Accessed 21 August 2023).

This chapter intends to present the most fundamental concepts of IFML and its modeling potential. It is important to remark that this standard does not deal with interface appearance (colors, position, and size of components), but only with the sequential flow of user operations from one interface element to the others. If you are interested in knowing and using a free design system that was built with concerns of user experience and user interface, you can try using the **Bold** Design System, developed by the Bridge Lab team to improve and standardize our products. The **Bold** design system is available at https://bold.bridge.ufsc.br/ (Accessed 30 August 2023).

16.2 View containers

View Containers are the interface elements that are effectively accessed by the user, such as a Web page or a smartphone screen. Typically, a view container may contain other view containers as well as view components that, as is seen below, are the elements of an interface that interacts with the user.

For example, Fig. 16−1 presents a view container that contains two view containers.

---

[1] Object Management Group. Available at https://www.omg.org/spec/IFML/1.0/PDF. (Accessed 21 August 2023).

Object-Oriented Analysis and Design for Information Systems. DOI: https://doi.org/10.1016/B978-0-443-13739-6.00013-7

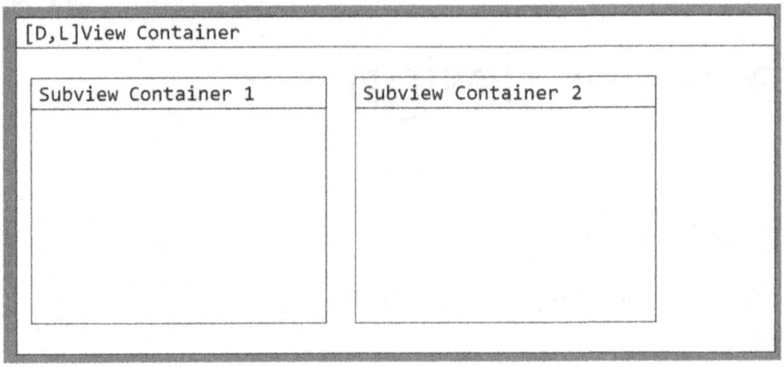

FIGURE 16–1 View containers.

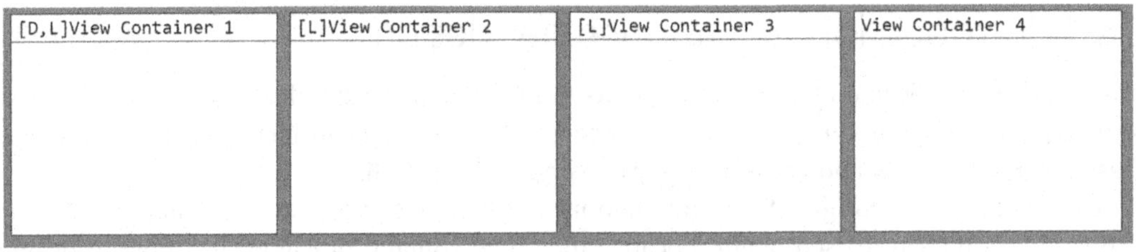

FIGURE 16–2 Default and landmark view containers.

Also, in Fig. 16–1, the main container shows special properties indicated by the label "D" and "L":

- [D] indicates the *default* view container of an application. When a user enters this application, the only page marked with [D] (there can be only one) will be accessed by default.
- [L] represents a *landmark* page or area. This means that the page or area is directly accessible from any other page included in the same area. Thus it avoids the need to create lots of flows to pages that must be accessed from many places.

In Fig. 16–2, we see an application with four pages. View container 1 is the default page. View containers 1–3 are landmark pages, and therefore, they are directly accessed from any page in this application. View container 4 would only be accessible by a direct link from another page because it is not landmark. In practice, for each page in this application, an upper menu will be rendered with links to view containers 1–3.

Other stereotypes that can be used with containers are:

- ≪ *Window* ≫: a view container that is rendered as a window.
- ≪ *Modal* ≫: a view container that is rendered as a window that prevents interaction with any other element of the interface, except for the modal.
- ≪ *Modeless* ≫: a view container that is rendered as a window that allows interaction with other windows in the screen.

16.3 View components

View components are the most basic elements in an IFML specification. They represent the interface elements that accept input from the user and that present information to the user. View components may be directly associated to design classes in the domain model and allow viewing data about instances of these classes.

In respect to view components, IFML is extensible. Initially, a small number of options is provided, but they can be extended and refined to support many kinds of interfaces. The three options originally defined with the standard are:

- *Details*: Displays information about a single object.
- *List*: Displays information about multiple instances of a class in the form of a list.
- *Form*: Allows form-based data entry and presentation.

There are other view components and new ones may be defined. This chapter presents details on the most fundamental ones. For each kind of view component, an UML stereotype is presented.

16.3.1 Details

The *details* view component presents information about a single object of a given class. It is defined by the following properties:

- A *name*, which is chosen by the designer.
- An *entity* or *source of data*, which is usually a class from the design class diagram.

Additionally, some implementations of the standard define the property *display attributes*, which is a list of attributes from the class to be displayed when the details view is rendered.

Most view components such as *details* also allow for the definition of one or more *conditional expressions* that work like selectors or filters over the set of instances to be shown. Usually, those conditions are used in conjunction with *parameter bindings*, which are associated to the navigation flows between components and may carry one or more values to serve as arguments in order to filter the set of instances and show only the desired one.

For all IFML examples beyond this point, the domain model shown in Fig. 12−1 is used as reference.

Fig. 16−3 presents a details view component intended to show data about a proposal in SISMOB. The component is still isolated from any data flow, but there is already a data binding that says that it will be filled with instances of class *Proposal*.

Fig. 16−4 shows a possible Web rendering for the details view component.

The final rendered page may vary, because it is possible to add style definitions so that interfaces with different designs and appearance may be produced.

16.3.2 List

The view component *list* presents one or more attributes of a set of instances of a class in the form of a list. A list and its variations are used when a view like a menu is necessary for

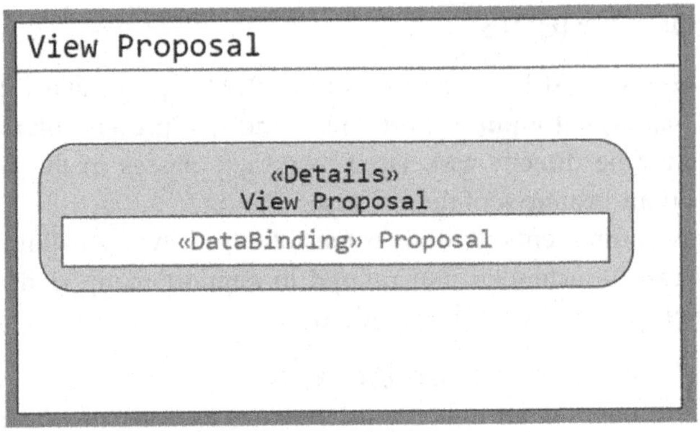

FIGURE 16–3 A details component.

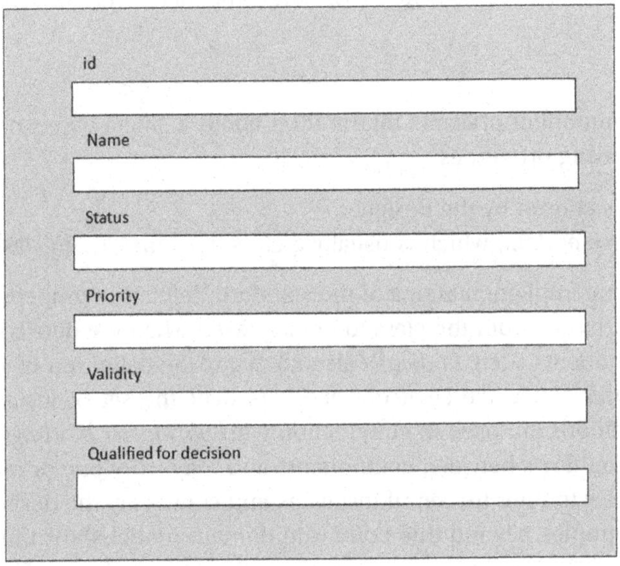

FIGURE 16–4 A possible rendering of Fig. 16–3.

the user to select one or more elements and perform actions with them. The properties of lists are the same as those of the details view component.

It is possible, for example, to define list for selecting proposals, as shown in Fig. 16–5.

Observe that again the data binding is the class *Proposal*, meaning that data about instances of it may be shown in the lines of the list. Although not seen in the image, a list may also define which fields (attributes) will be shown, and it can have filters to select which instances will be included in the list. Fig. 16–6 shows an example of a still unpopulated list for *Proposal* showing the attributes *name, status*, and *priority*.

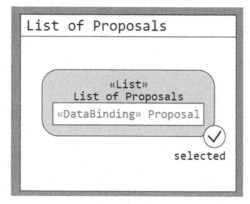

FIGURE 16–5 A list view component.

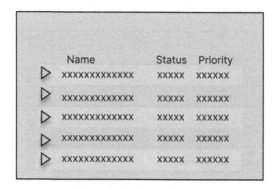

FIGURE 16–6 A renderization of a list view component.

The triangles in the figure indicate that the list may be clicked, and when it happens, the default event *selected* (see Fig. 16–5) will be triggered.

16.3.3 Form

A *form* is used for data input. It is very useful for creating new instances and for providing parameters for searches, queries, and commands.

A form is composed of a set of *fields*. Each field holds an alphanumeric value. There are text fields, selection fields, and multiselecting fields, and others may be defined.

A form may or may not be associated to a class. If it is associated to a class, then its fields are associated to the attributes of that class. Otherwise, the fields are not associated to any class, as in the case of Fig. 16–7, which presents a form with two fields (unseen in the figure) for *username* and *password*.

Forms that are used to collect parameters for a query or command usually do not need to be associated to classes. Fig. 16–8 presents its rendering.

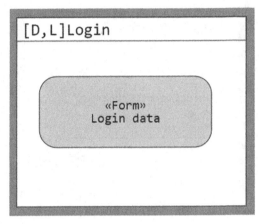

FIGURE 16–7 A form view component.

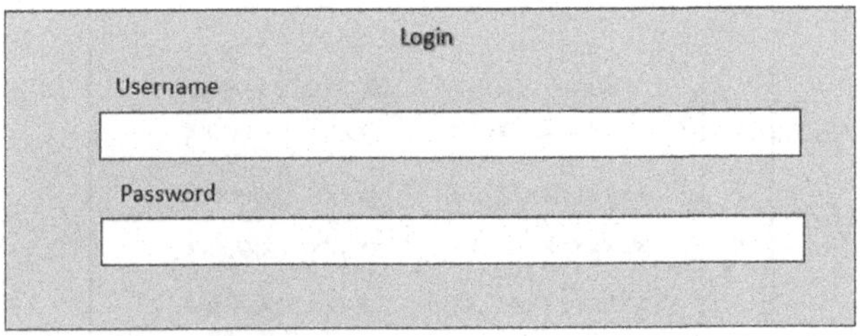

FIGURE 16–8 A possible renderization for a *form*.

16.4 Flows

A *flow* is an oriented connection between two view containers or view components. Flows may be used not only to define navigation possibilities between pages, but also to define data dependencies. For example, selecting an element in a list view component may cause information about the element to appear in a details view component. This can be accomplished by defining a flow from the list to the details. Fig. 16–9 shows a flow that starts at the event "*selected*" in the list of proposals. This event is attached to a flow that sends control to the details view component. The effect of this interaction is that the proposal selected from the list will be shown in the details area of the interface. As both view components are inside the same container, they both will be seen in the same page.

16.4.1 Navigation flow

Navigation flows are a type of flow that is rendered as a clickable link in its origin page or view component. When the link is clicked, it navigates to the destination view container or view component. The navigation flow is represented by an arrow.

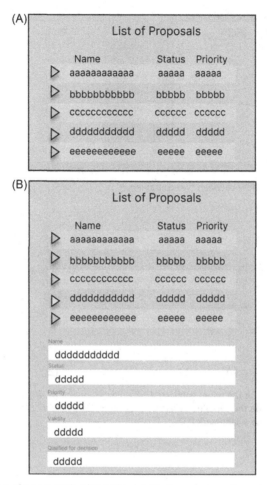

FIGURE 16–9 A renderization of a page with a list and a details view components, and a flow between them. (A) Before selecting line "d." (B) After selecting line "d."

Fig. 16–10 shows an example of a navigation flow between two containers. The resulting rendering of the origin page contains a link to the other page, as shown in Fig. 16–11.

If the flow had its origin at the list view component, as in Fig. 16–12, then each line in the list would have an individual link to the *details* page.

16.4.2 Data flow

Data flows are a kind of flow that is not rendered but that defines data dependency between view components. Dashed arrows represent data flows.

Data flows do not define navigation between view components. They are used to get values from one component without navigating to/from it. They are particularly useful when

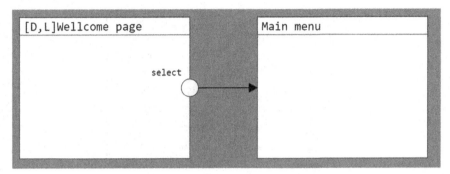

FIGURE 16–10 A navigational flow between two containers.

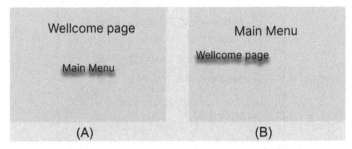

FIGURE 16–11 A renderization of the pages connected by a navigational flow. (A) before clicking in "*Main Menu*," a link defined by the user inside the container. (B) after clicking in "*Main Menu*"; the link returning to *Welcome page* appears because this page is landmark [L].

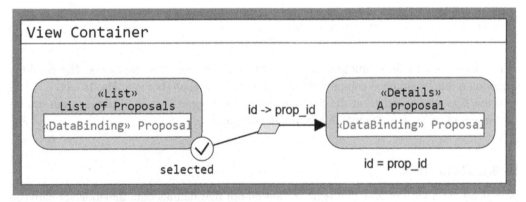

FIGURE 16–12 A data binding between two views.

a component needs data from more than one component. The following sections present examples of data flows that get data from different sources.

16.4.3 Parameter binding

A *parameter binding* is a piece of information that is transmitted from the origin to the destination of a flow. A parameter binding has a *name* and a *value*. The name and value are sent by the origin element, and they are matched to one of the attributes (usually a key) of the class in the destination element.

A flow may have a multiple parameter binding, passing a set of values instead of one.

Usually, object keys or attribute values are passed by parameter bindings. By default, a flow from a view component binds the key of the selected object at the origin component and takes it to the destination, where it can be used, for example, by a conditional expression.

With flows and parameter binding, it is possible to use a view component to define which elements are shown in another view component.

The IFML diagram shown in Fig. 16−12 shows a list of proposals with a flow to a details view component. The details view has a key attribute *id*. As the *id* key of the selected book at the list is bound to the flow by *prop_id* that goes to the details view, only a proposal in which *id* is identical to *prop_id* is shown when the details view is rendered.

When the user selects a proposal in the list, by clicking the respective link, the details view presents information about the proposal.

Parameter binding may also be used to associate a form to another view component. For example, the form may provide a search field, and a list would present only the elements that satisfy some search criteria.

Fig. 16−13 shows an example where a search field is used to find the proposal of a given municipal manager. The user may type the proposal's name or part of it in the search field, and the results are shown in the *Proposals* list.

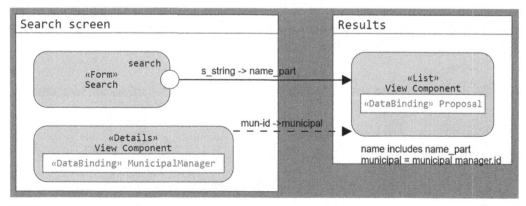

FIGURE 16–13 A view that takes keys from two different views.

Initially, the focus is on the form in *Search Screen*. When the event *search* is triggered, the flow goes to the list view in *Results*. This list view has two binding conditions: the text entered in the form must be included in the name of the proposal, and the id of the municipal manager taken from the details in *Search Screen* must coincide with the id of the municipal manager linked to the *Proposal*.

16.5 Web interface patterns

Most web interface patterns presented in this section are adapted from Ceri et al. (2003) and Tidwell (2005).

16.5.1 Cascade index

A *cascade index* is a sequence of menus based on lists that eventually reaches a details view. For example, a user could begin by selecting a *Proposal*. Then, the user could select a list of *Sending* from a selected proposal, then access a list of proposal's assessments, and finally one assessment individually. Fig. 16–14 illustrates that pattern.

In the diagram of Fig. 16–14, as the parameter bindings are default, the flows carry the id's of the selected elements. Those id's may be used by the conditional expressions at the destination view component to define which element(s) is(are) to be shown. As the id is the default data carried by a parameter binding, it is not usually shown in the diagram.

One variant of this pattern consists of showing some data from the object selected in one of the intermediary lists. Fig. 16–15 illustrates that situation.

There, when a proposal is selected, the interface shows the proposal's details and a list of sendings for further selection.

16.5.2 Filtered index

In some cases, it may be necessary to show a list with selected elements. For example, the SISMOB has in average 20–40 thousand proposals being analyzed and executed at the same time; in this case it would not be feasible for a user to simply browse for a proposal in that list. A filtered list could be used instead, for example, asking the user to provide a keyword to show a reduced list of proposals.

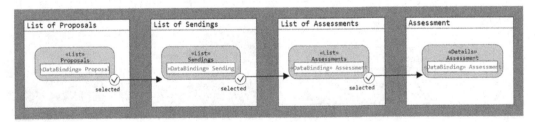

FIGURE 16–14 A cascade index.

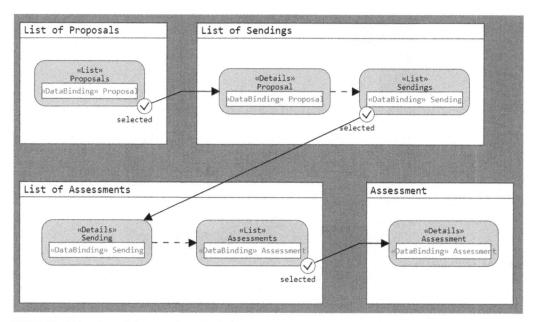

FIGURE 16–15 A variant of the cascade index that shows details of the intermediary objects.

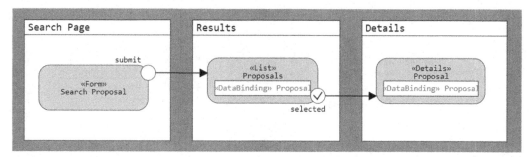

FIGURE 16–16 A filtered index.

This pattern is accomplished by a connection between a form, a list, and a details component, as shown in Fig. 16–16.

A maximum number of results may be defined for this list so that unnecessarily large lists are not presented.

16.5.3 Guided tour

A *guided tour* is a pattern that allows one to visualize details of a set of objects one at a time by using scroll operations. It is implemented by using two or more events that will be rendered as buttons, as seen in Fig. 16–17.

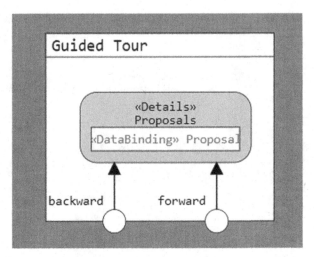

FIGURE 16–17 A guided tour.

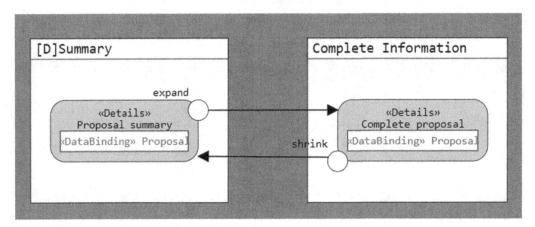

FIGURE 16–18 Viewpoints.

16.5.4 Viewpoints

Sometimes, it may be interesting to present different faces of certain objects in different moments. For example, summarized data about a proposal may be presented by default, but that data may be expanded or contracted again at the user's will.

In order to implement the viewpoints pattern, two or more details components may be defined for the same class, with different sets of attributes. Flows may be defined between the different components to allow the user to change from one view to another, as shown in Fig. 16–18.

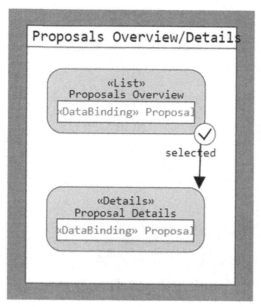

FIGURE 16–19 Overview plus detail.

16.5.5 Overview plus detail

The *overview plus detail* pattern is very common in applications such as email browsers, but it can be applied to a variety of other situations. The idea is to have in the same page a scrolling list of elements and the details view of one selected element in a region next to the list.

Fig. 16−19 shows an IFML definition that uses this pattern with a list and a details view component linked to it by a flow. They are rendered in the same window.

16.5.6 Top-level navigation

Top-level navigation is a frequent pattern in Web pages where a top-level menu allows access to different areas of the site. The example in Fig. 16−20 illustrates top-level navigation being defined by a set of landmark areas, each containing one or more pages, which would be rendered as submenu selected options.

16.6 Connecting the IFML model with system operations

IFML allows operations to be modeled by using *actions* (Fig. 16−21) that are executed after some interface events (menu selection, button pressed, etc.) happen. These components perform all the operational logic of the system that is fruit of the detailed use cases and/or system sequence diagrams.

The operation components do not hold or render information; they just *process* information. Therefore they are represented graphically outside the containers.

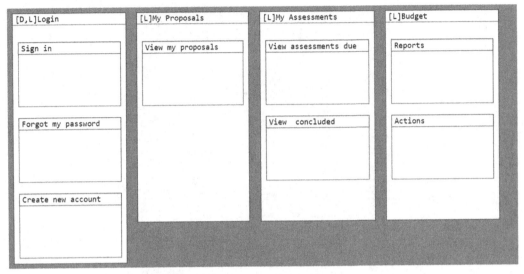

FIGURE 16–20 Top-level navigation being defined by a set of landmark areas.

FIGURE 16–21 An action component calling a system operation.

Every operation component should have at least one input flow. Sometimes all the information the operation needs is obtained from a single view component, but sometimes more than one view component may be necessary to supply all the data needed by an operation. In this case, the operation must receive one navigation flow and a set of data flows.

Operation components have special output flows:

- *OK flow*, which defines where the focus goes when the operation is successfully performed for every object.
- *Fail flow*, which defines where the focus goes when the operation fails for at least one of the objects affected by it.

16.6.1 IFML models for CRUDL operations

This section shows how to implement a CRUDL-style interface for managing information about publishers using IFML view components and system operations.

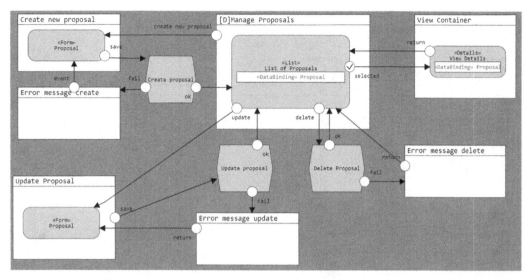

FIGURE 16–22 A simplified model for the CRUDL pattern.

The CRUDL main page, *Manage Proposals*, presents a list of existing proposals (associated to that specific municipal manager). The creation of a new proposal is initiated by clicking on a button on the main page that gives access to a form container where the data about the proposal will be filled. If the creation of a new proposal is successful, control returns to the main list, and the new proposal will appear in that list. If there is an error, control goes to an error page, from which it is possible to return to the main page (Fig. 16−22).

The second operation of a CRUD, *retrieve*, is represented by the flow that navigates from the list to the details page.

The third operation, *update*, allows a publisher to be selected in the main list, and the attributes of the selected proposal are used to fill the fields of a container form with *Proposal* as the source class. There the nonimmutable ones can be edited by the user and saved, with the flow returning to the main list.

Finally, the operation for deleting a proposal is added. A delete operation may be accessed from the main list. If it succeeds, the flow returns to the main list. Otherwise, an error message is shown.

16.6.2 Use case interface modeling with IFML

Working with interfaces is possible at this time because use cases have already been explored and the team has a deeper understanding about the interface structure and the user needs, which allow them to design an acceptable interface.

In this section, we will revisit the sequence diagram of Figure 7−8, now reproduced as Fig. 16−23 and using it as an example on how to design the user interaction with the interface:

Fig. 16−24 shows a possible IFML diagram to model the interaction of the user with the interface of this system.

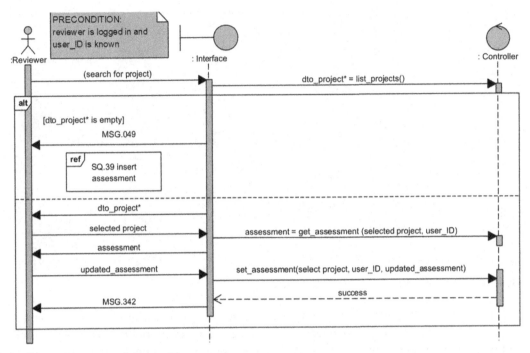

FIGURE 16–23 Sequence diagram used as example.

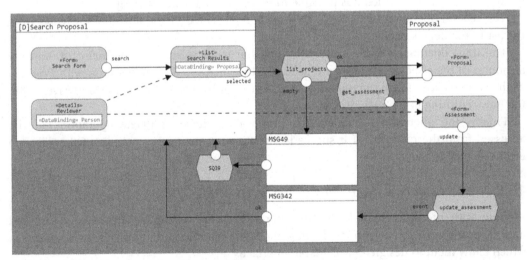

FIGURE 16–24 IFML diagram for updating assessment. *IFML*, Interaction Flow Modeling Language.

In order to prepare an interface design based on that sequence diagram, the team should look at the system operations, including their parameters and results:

- Any system operation, be it a command or query, must be activated somewhere in the interface. The activation event can be obtained by clicking a button or a link, by selecting an item from a list, etc. Sometimes the same event may activate more than one system operation: if two or more system operations happen just after a system event (left side of the sequence diagram), then they are possibly activated by the same user action.
- Any parameter a system operation has must be obtained somewhere. Some parameters could be obtained from external sources (such as a clock), but most parameters would be obtained in the interface. Thus for most parameters there will be an interface view component that allows the user to introduce the necessary data.
- Any result obtained by a system query must be presented somewhere. Some results may be hidden from the user in some cases, but usually they are presented. View components such as lists, details, and others may be used to show system query results.

Questions

1. Why IFML notation needs dataflows that are not navigable?
2. Construct an IFML model that uses filtered index and viewpoints simultaneously.
3. Look at Fig. 16–16 and make explicit the parameter bindings necessary for this model.

17 ∷

Data persistence

Key topics in this chapter

- Object-relational Mapping (ORM)
- Virtual Proxy
- Brokers
- Virtual Caches

17.1 Introduction to data persistence

The availability of persistence mechanisms for commercial languages[1] has made database design much easier for many projects. With adequate tools, it is possible to automatically generate the persistence tier for a great number of information systems. For some critical and legacy systems, however, database adjustments may be still necessary to accommodate special features or to satisfy performance or security requirements.

Usually, object-oriented systems are implemented in object-oriented languages, but persistent[2] data storage is accomplished with *relational databases*. Although other techniques such as object-oriented databases (Won, 1990) and XML databases (Bourret, 2010) are also options for implementing permanent storage of data, the pattern *ORM, object-relational mapping*, is still the preferred approach.

The goal of this chapter is to explain what happens inside the persistence tier of a system when a persistence mechanism based on ORM is used. First, a good persistence mechanism requires domain and data storage to be separated into different tiers within the application. Remember that the interface tier may be modeled with use cases and IFML, and the domain tier may be designed using class diagrams and contracts as its basis. None of the aforementioned tiers addresses data storage or persistence. Persistence should be designed as a separate concern: a background system that will keep data securely and permanently in its place without interfering on the domain or interface logic.

The persistence mechanism should assure that the objects are saved in a permanent memory device, and that they are loaded from there when necessary. Domain and interface logic should not be polluted by persistence concerns.

Object-oriented design provides lots of good concepts such as encapsulation, responsibility, and delegation that help designers deal with the complexities of the logic for accessing

---

[1] See, for example: http://www.hibernate.org/. (Accessed 31 August 2023).

[2] *Persistent* in this context is the opposite of *transient*, that is, persistent information is information that must be kept until some user explicitly deletes it. Transient information is kept only during a session of use of the system.

Object-Oriented Analysis and Design for Information Systems. DOI: https://doi.org/10.1016/B978-0-443-13739-6.00009-5

and transforming information. But when data must be stored in a more permanent way—disks and tapes, for example—the relational database is a good option because it is very efficient in terms of time usage and there are lots of optimization techniques to improve relational database operations. Thus if the team wants to work in the best of two worlds (object and relational), the mapping between them must be understood.

The literature refers to the problem of *object-relational impedance mismatch* (Ireland et al., 2009), because most of the good features obtained by object-oriented design are lost when a flat relational database is used.

The implementation of a persistence mechanism minimizes that problem by using a set of predefined classes not belonging to the domain tier that take care of all logic involving domain objects being saved and retrieved from a relational database.

17.2 Object-relational mapping

A complete and detailed design class diagram (DCD) allows for the automatic generation of a relational database structure that reflects in secondary memory[3] the information that the objects represent in main memory. The following sections present some equivalence rules that should be observed when using ORM and if the team wants to minimize the object-relational impedance mismatch.

17.2.1 Classes and attributes

The first set of rules addresses classes and their attributes. Each persistent class of the DCD corresponds to a *relational table*. Each attribute is a *column* of the table, and each instance is a *line* or *record* of the table.

The stereotypes of some attributes such as «*unique*», «*opt*», and «*imm*» affect the properties of the columns of the relational tables. Some of the features described here may not be implemented by some commercial database management systems. In that case, adjustments might be necessary to provide a safe implementation free from the object-relational impedance mismatch.

Attributes stereotyped with «*unique*» are represented as columns marked as *unique*, which cannot repeat values. However, even objects with no unique attribute have an *identity* that distinguishes them from other objects. Even objects with the same value for every single attribute may be differentiated by their identity. In the case of relational tables, this is accomplished by defining a *primary key* to each relational table. A primary key, just like a unique column, should not repeat elements. An element in a primary key column should also not be null. Primary keys

---

[3] *Secondary memory* is usually slower than *main memory*. However, it is also much cheaper, and thus, it is widely used to store large quantities of data that do not fit in the more expensive main memory. Usually, secondary memory consists of media such as magnetic or optical disks, tapes, or solid-state drivers. Data stored in secondary memory usually cannot be processed directly by the computer unless it is loaded into main memory. Main memory is also known as *RAM* (*random access memory*), and physically, it is usually implemented by nonpersistent electronic integrated circuits.

usually are simply sequential numbers generated automatically by the application in such a way that the same number is never generated twice for the same table. *Primary keys do not correspond to any of the attributes of an object*: they correspond to the object identity.

Fig. 17–1 shows the class that is the basis for the following examples, and Table 17–1 shows the equivalent relational table with three instances of that class represented.

Although other formats could be used to specify the constraints on the columns, here they are presented as acronyms for quick reference:

- *unique*, means that the column cannot repeat values.
- *imm*, or *immutable*, means that the value in the column cannot be updated.
- *nn*, or *not null*, means that the column does not admit the null value. It is exactly the opposite of the ≪*opt*≫ or ≪*optional*≫ stereotype used for design classes. It is used here because *not null* is a more common constraint implemented in databases than *optional*.
- *pk*, or *primary key*, means that the column is the primary key of the table. Primary key columns in the examples of this chapter are painted in gray. If one or more columns compose the *pk*, all columns are necessarily *immutable* and *not null*. If only a *single column* is *pk*, then it must be *unique* as well. However, if the *PK* is composite, spreading over more than one column, then each individual column may or may not be unique, but the combination of all columns is unique.

The first column in Table 17–1 is *pk_book*. Notice that it does not correspond to any attribute of the reference class. Its value is artificially generated by a *number sequence generator* so

```
Book
<<imm>> <<unique>> +isbn : ISBN
<<imm>> +title : String
<<imm>> +authors_name : String
+price : Money
<<imm>> +page_count : Natural
+ / publisher_name : String
<<opt>> +cover_image : Image
+quantity_in_stock : Natural = 0
```

FIGURE 17–1 A class used in examples.

Table 17–1 Relational table equivalent to the class in Fig. 17–1.

Table: Book

pk,unique, imm,nn pk_book	unique, imm,nn isbn	imm,nn title	imm,nn authors_name	nn price	imm,nn page_count	cover_image	nn quantity_in_stock
10001	0553286587	Rama II	Arthur C. Clarke and Gentry Lee	6.99	466		2
10002	0553293370	Foundation and Empire	Isaac Asimov	5.99	282		3
10003	0671742515	The Long Dark Tea-Time of the Soul	Douglas N. Adams	6.99	307		21

that it is unique for the whole application or at least for that table. Some authors refer to it as a *surrogate key*, that is, a value that has no semantic meaning and is unique systemwide, never reused, system generated, and not handled by users or application.

The other columns correspond to the nonderived attributes of the reference class:

- *isbn* is a unique, immutable, and not null attribute. Therefore the equivalent column is *unique*, *imm*, and *nn*.
- *title*, *authors_name*, and *page_count* are nonderived attributes that are immutable and not null. Therefore the equivalent column for each one is *imm* and *nn*, but not *unique*.
- *price* and *quantity_in_stock* are nonderived attributes that may change but cannot be null. Therefore the equivalent column for each is *nn* only.
- *cover_image* is an optional attribute that may be updated. Therefore the respective column has no constraint: it may be updated and may be null.
- *publisher_name* is a derived attribute. Therefore it is not represented in the relational table.

17.2.1.1 Number sequence generator

Most database management systems provide number sequence generators that generate numbers that never repeat. This is necessary to provide values for primary keys, especially when multiple users are producing new records at the same time. The number sequence generator must assure that different users would not produce the same number at the same time.

Number sequence generators may be associated directly to the column of the table that contains primary keys. Every time a new record is inserted in the table, a new number in the sequence is created.

The database designer may choose an initial value for the sequence as well as an increment. For example, beginning with 500 with an increment of 5, the sequence generated would be 500, 505, 510, 515, etc.

17.2.1.2 Index selection

By default, a relational table is just a set of records. Finding a given object at a table would require iterating over all elements until the desired element is found. For example, looking for a book given its ISBN would require an exhaustive search that in average looks at half the table.

Databases usually provide, however, the possibility of indexing columns. An *indexed column* has an auxiliary table that allows specific records to be found in almost constant time. For example, if the *isbn* column of the table is indexed, then when a book is searched based on its ISBN, no iteration is performed over the set of all records: the system simply would translate the value of the ISBN into a position in memory by using a hash function and retrieve the element from that position. If that is not the desired element, then it looks for the next, and so on until finding it. If the hash function is well implemented and the hash table has enough space to avoid collisions (two values being translated to the same hash value), then usually the desired element is really in the first place searched, or very close to it at least.

The use of indices improves query speed. However, it slows database updating because every time a record is updated, inserted, or deleted, the auxiliary table must be updated as well (Choenni et al., 1993). Furthermore, indices also require more storage space for accommodating the auxiliary tables.

A primary key is indexed by default. Other columns may be indexed if the designer chooses to do that. Given the restrictions mentioned before, creating other indices may be an advantage in the case of an attribute that is used as internal qualifier. In that case, finding the objects quickly may be crucial for the application's performance. Otherwise, indices should be avoided. For example, columns that are rarely used for searching purposes (e.g., a book's page count) should not be indexed.

17.2.2 Associations

Generally, associations between classes correspond to *associative tables* in the relational model, that is, tables with a primary key composed of the primary keys values of the tables that represent the participating classes. In this case, each column of the primary key is said to be composed of foreign keys (*fk*) that are primary keys for other tables.

In this case, the primary key of the associative table is in fact composed of two (or more) columns. Each column may repeat values individually depending on the association multiplicity; but the pair (or tuple) of values that compound the primary key can never be repeated.

Depending on the multiplicity of the association roles, some rules must be observed. Many-to-many associations will have no individual unique restrictions. However, one-to-may associations require a unique restriction in one of the columns that form the primary key and one-to-one require a unique restriction in both columns that form the primary key. This is explained in further details in the following subsections.

17.2.2.1 Many-to-many associations

If the association is many-to-many with both role multiplicities defined as *, then there is no restriction on the columns that compose the primary key of the associative table. Fig. 17−2 shows an example. The relational table for class *Book* is already represented in Table 17−1, and the relational representation of class *Person* is represented in Table 17−2.

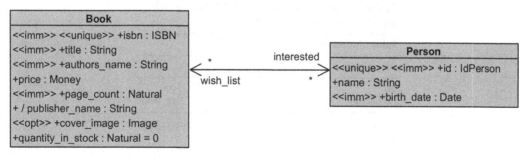

FIGURE 17–2 A bidirectional many-to-many association.

Notice that in Table 17–2 a customer has two unique columns: *pk_person* and *id*. The *pk_person* is a code generated internally to the system and unknown to the user. This column is also the primary key for this table. The other unique column is *id*, which may be some number that identifies this person and is known outside the system, such as the social security number.

Now, the many-to-many association of Fig. 17–2 can be represented as in Table 17–3 with a primary key composed of the *fk* of *Book* and *Person*. The unique restriction applies to both columns at once but not to them individually, and the *not null* restriction applies to each column individually.

Table 17–3 shows an associative relational table that represents the links between some people and some books. Notice that the *pk* spreads over two columns now. Each column contains a *fk*, that is, a value that corresponds to the primary key of another table.

In the associative table *interested/wish_list*, the columns *fk_person* and *fk_book* together form the *composite primary key*. Each one cannot be null individually, and pairs of *fk_person*/*fk_book* cannot be repeated. However, as the association is many-to-many, each individual column may repeat values, as seen in Table 17–3.

Table 17–3 shows that Abe (person 20001) desires the books "Rama II" (10001) and "The Long Dark Tea-Time of the Soul" (10003), Beth (person 20002) only desires "Rama II" (10001), and Charles (person 20003) has no wishes.

Instead of naming the associative table with the names of the classes (*Person/Book*), it is preferable to name it with the names of the roles (*interested/wish_list*), because more than one association may exist between two classes, and this way they will have different names.

Table 17–2   Relational table for class *Person*.

Table: Person

pk,unique,imm,nn pk_person	unique,imm,nn id	nn name	imm,nn birth_date
20001	987–65-4320	Abe	01/04/1970
20002	987–65-4329	Beth	02/23/1982
20003	987–65-4325	Charles	12/05/1979

Table 17–3   Associative table representing a many-to-many association.

Table: interested/wish_list

pk, unique

nn fk_person	nn fk_book
20001	10001
20002	10001
20001	10003

If the association is mandatory in one direction or both directions, then special considerations must be observed:

- If the association is mandatory on *one* side, then all primary keys from the *other* side must appear at least once in the associative table. *If* the role *interested* was mandatory (1..*) in the example of Fig. 17–2, then each book should have at least one associated person as interested. Then, each primary key value from the *Book* table should appear in the *interested/wish_list* table at least once.
- If the association is mandatory on *both* sides, then all instances from both classes should appear at least once in the associative table. If in the example of Fig. 17–2, both roles were mandatory (1..*), then each book from the *Book* table and each person from the *Person* table should appear at least once in the associative table.

More generally speaking, considering that *A* has an association to *B*, and that the lower bound of the *B* role is *n* while the upper bound is *m* (multiplicity is *n..m*), the number of times that each instance of *A* must appear in the associative table is at least *n*, and no more than *m*. For example, if the multiplicity of role *B* is 2.5, then each instance of *A* must appear in the associative table at least twice and no more than five times.

17.2.2.2 One-to-many associations
When the association is one-to-many, then the column on the *many* side must have a *unique* constraint. This means that the column may not repeat elements individually while the other column in the composed primary key may repeat elements. The elements that cannot be repeated in the associative table therefore can be linked to a single element of the other table; this constraint assures that the association is one-to-many. Fig. 17–3 shows an example of a one-to-many association.

Table 17–4 shows an associative table for the one-to-many association represented in Fig. 17–3. Notice that the *unique* constraint in the right column prevents the table from associating a book to more than one publisher.

As seen in Table 17–4, publisher 30001 has one book (10002) and publisher 30002 has two books (10001 and 10003). As books cannot be repeated in this table, no book can be associated to more than one publisher.

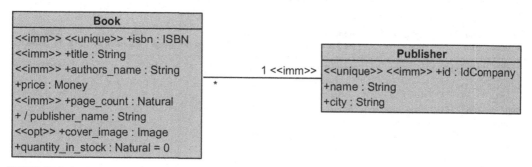

FIGURE 17–3 One-to-many association.

It is also possible to represent associations from many to one as *fk* in the table that represents the class at the *many* side of the association. For example, as each book may have only one publisher, then the association between book and publisher could be implemented as in Table 17–5.

The foreign key *fk_publisher* is a direct reference to the primary key of the *Publisher* table. If the association is straight to 1, then the foreign key column must not be null. If the association is to 0.0.1, then the foreign key column should not have that constraint.

Although this approach is not as homogeneous as associative tables, it is usually preferred by designers because it avoids the need to implement a new table. One disadvantage is that in this case, many-to-many associations are implemented as associative tables and many-to-one associations are implemented inside one of the original tables. Also, if the association is not mandatory (if its multiplicity is 0.1), and relatively few elements are associated, there would be lots of null values in the foreign key column, wasting storage space and degrading performance. However, if the association is straight to 1, this disadvantage does not apply.

Table 17–4   Associative table representing a one-to-many association.

Table: publisher/book

pk	
imm, nn fk_publisher	unique, nn fk_book
30002	10001
30001	10002
30002	10003

Table 17–5   An association being modeled as a single foreign key.

Table: Book

pk, unique, imm, nn pk_book	unique, imm, nn isbn	imm, nn title	imm, nn authors_name	nn price	imm, nn page_count	cover_image	nn quantity_in_stock	imm, nn fk_publisher
10001	0553286587	Rama II	Arthur C. Clarke and Gentry Lee	6.99	466		2	30002
10002	0553293370	Foundation and Empire	Isaac Asimov	5.99	282		3	30001
10003	0671742515	The Long Dark Tea-Time of the Soul	Douglas N. Adams	6.99	307		21	30002

17.2.2.3 One-to-one associations

One-to-one associations, mandatory or optional, require that the associative table have a *unique* constraint in both columns of the composed primary key to prevent any element on both sides from appearing more than once in the associative table. Fig. 17−4 shows an example of one-to-one association that is mandatory on one side and optional on the other.

Table 17−6 shows the relational table that implements the one-to-one association of Fig. 17−4.

As the role is mandatory for payments, all instances of *Payment* must appear in the associative table, but not all instances of *Order* must appear, because the role is not mandatory for them.

As in the case of many-to-one associations, one-to-one associations may also be implemented as *fk* in one of the original tables. The foreign key column must necessarily be unique in that case. If the association role is also mandatory, then the foreign key column should not be null.

17.2.2.4 Ordered associations

An association with an ordered role (*sequence* or *ordered set*) may be implemented as an associative table with an extra column to represent the order of the element in the role's collection of elements. Fig. 17−5 shows an example with two situations: ordered set and sequence (a list in which elements may be repeated).

FIGURE 17–4 A one-to-one association that is mandatory on one side and optional on the other.

Table 17–6   Associative table representing a one-to-one association.

Table: order/payment	
pk	
imm, uniq, nn **fk_order**	**uniq, nn** **fk_payment**
50001	60001
50003	60002
50005	60003
50011	60004
50016	60005
50021	60006
50030	60007

The difference between the relational implementation of an ordered set and a sequence is that in the case of the ordered set, the *order* column must not be included in the composed primary key, as shown in Table 17–7.

However, in the case of a sequence (elements may be repeated), the *order* column must be part of the composed primary key, which in this case is composed of three columns (Table 17–8).

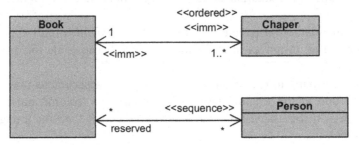

FIGURE 17–5 Ordered set and sequence.

Table 17–7   Relational table representing an ordered set.

Table: book/chapter

Pk		
im,nn fk_book	im,unique, nn fk_chapter	nn order
10001	130001	1
10001	130002	2
10001	130003	3
10002	130004	1
10002	130005	2
10003	130006	1
10003	130007	2

Table 17–8   Relational table representing a sequence.

Table: book/customer

pk		
nn fk_book	nn fk_customer	nn order
10001	20001	1
10001	20003	2
10001	20002	3
10001	20001	4
10002	20003	1
10003	20001	1
10003	20002	2

In Table 17–8, the fact that the *order* column is included in the primary key allows the same person to reserve the same book more than once (e.g., 20001, Abe, has two reservations for book 10001, Rama II, in the first and fourth positions on the reservation list). A repetition like this would not be possible in Table 17–7, because the primary key does not include the *order* column: the same pair *fk_book/fk_chapter* cannot appear more than once in the table, regardless of its position.

In both cases, to prevent a given position to be occupied more than once, a *unique* constraint spreading over the origin class and the position should be defined. In the case of Tables 17–7 and 17–8, the pair *fk_book/order* should be unique.

17.2.2.5 Associations representing bags

In the case of *bags*, in which elements may be repeated but have no position, the usual solution is to add an extra column to the associative table with a counter for the number of times a given pair participates in the association. Fig. 17–6 shows an example of this kind of association.

Table 17–9 shows the implementation of the associative table for the example in Fig. 17–6.

Table 17–9 specifies that Abe (20001) has viewed the book "Foundation and Empire" (10002) six times. Beth (20002) viewed "Rama II" (10001) twice, "Foundation and Empire" (10002) once, and "The Long Dark Tea-Time of the Soul" (10003) once. It is not necessary to represent in the table any pair whose quantity is zero; this is why Charles (20003) does not appear in the table: he has never viewed any book.

17.2.2.6 Qualified associations

In the case of a qualified association defined as a map (multiplicity in destiny 1 or 0.1) with an internal qualifier (the qualifier is an attribute of the qualified class), it is sufficient to

FIGURE 17–6 A bag.

Table 17–9 Associative table representing a bag.

Table: book/viewer		
pk		
nn **fk_book**	**nn** **fk_customer**	**nn** **quantity**
10002	20002	1
10001	20002	2
10002	20001	6
10003	20002	1

implement the association as a regular one-to-many or many-to-many association depending on the multiplicity on the side of the qualifier, as explained in previous sections.

The only special care that the database designer must take in that case is to ensure that the column of the qualifier attribute is *unique* and *immutable*. It may be indexed if quick access to the records is necessary.

However, when the qualifier is *external*, it is necessary to add a third column to the associative table to allow for the representation of the qualifier. Fig. 17−7 shows an example of that situation.

Table 17−10 shows the implementation for the map defined in Fig. 17−7. The associative table has a primary key that is composed only of the origin class primary key and the qualifier. The destination class is left out of the primary key. However, it must be marked as *unique* because, in the example, each phone has a single type.

If the external qualifier defines a partition (multiplicity *), as shown in Fig. 17−8, it is implemented as shown in Table 17−10. But in the case of a partition with an external qualifier, the primary key must have three parts, including the origin and destination *fk* as well as the qualifier. Also, as the origin role multiplicity is 1, the destination class column must be marked with *unique*. In the example shown in Table 17−11, this means that a book may not have more than one genre.

If the role multiplicity at the origin were * (defining a relation where a book could have more than one genre), the implementation would basically be the same. The only difference is that the *unique* constraint in the destination column (*fk_book*) should not exist.

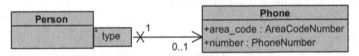

FIGURE 17−7 Association with external qualifier.

Table 17−10   Associative table representing a map with external qualifier.

Table: customer/phone		
pk		
nn	**nn**	**uniq, nn**
fk_person	**type**	**fk_phone**
20001	Home	70001
20001	Cellphone	70002
20002	Home	70003

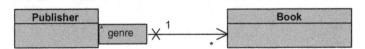

FIGURE 17−8 A partition.

17.2.2.7 Association classes

An association with an association class is represented in two parts: a relational table for the association class with its attributes, and an associative table for the association with a reference to the association class table. Fig. 17−9 shows an association class, and Tables 17−12 and 17−13 implement its relational equivalent.

Thus one way to represent associations with association classes is to use a table to represent the association class (Table 17−12), and an associative table (Table 17−13) with three columns: the primary keys of the participating classes (which form the composite primary key of the association) and the primary key of the association class, which is not part of the composite primary key of the association, but must be immutable and unique in that table.

Table 17–11   Associative table representing a partition with external qualifier.

Table: publisher/book

pk		
nn fk_publisher	nn genre	unique, nn fk_book
60001	sci-fi	10001
60001	sci-fi	10002
60002	humor	10003

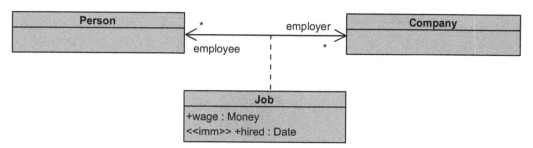

FIGURE 17–9 An association class.

Table 17–12   Relational representation of an association with association class part one: the association class.

Table: Job

pk, nn, imm, unique pk_job	nn wage	nn, imm hired
80001	1500.00	02/15/2008
80002	1200.00	03/01/1999
80003	2000.00	04/16/2005
80004	900.00	01/17/2001

A further constraint is that all values for *pk_job* in the *Job* table must appear in the *fk_job* column of the *employee/employer* table.

17.2.2.8 n-ary associations

In the case of associations among three or more classes (*n*-ary), an associative table is defined in which the primary key is formed by the primary keys of all participating classes. Fig. 17–10 shows an example of a ternary association, and Table 17–14 shows its relational representation.

Table 17–13 Relational representation of an association with association class part two: the association.

Table: employee/employer

pk		
nn	nn	nn, imm, unique
fk_person	fk_company	fk_job
20001	70001	80001
20001	70005	80002
20002	70001	80003
20003	70002	80004

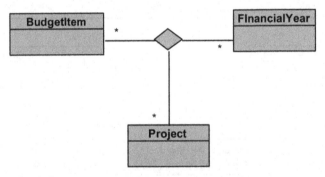

FIGURE 17–10 A ternary association.

Table 17–14 Relational equivalent of a ternary association.

Table: BudgetItem/FinantialYear/Project

pk		
nn	nn	nn
fk_budget_item	fk_financial_year	fk_project
90001	100001	110001
90001	100002	110002
90002	100001	110003

In Table 17−14, pairs such as *fk_budget_item/fk_project* may repeat elements (90001/100001, for instance). But a triple such as *fk_budget_item/fk_financial_year/fk_project* should never repeat.

17.2.2.9 Façade *controller associations*

Some of the associations from the façade controller do not need to persist. Associations from the controller to all instances of a class, which are mandatory for the instances, do not need to be transformed into association tables, because, as the controller is also a singleton, they always repeat the same value for the controller column and have all the elements on the other side. That information is already available in the primary key column of the table representing the conceptual class, and, therefore, that association table would be redundant. For example, in Fig. 17−11, the association between the controller and *Person* via *customer* is mandatory for all people. Thus an associative table for representing that association would a primary key to the controller in one column and all primary keys of *Person* in the other column. As that information is already represented in the *Person* table, simply repeating them in a different table is unnecessary.

However, this observation is valid only if the association role is strictly 1 on the controller side. If the controller side has multiplicity 0.1, then the association should be represented separately. In Fig. 17−11, the *premium_customer* association must be represented somewhere because not every customer belongs to it. There are at least two choices for representing nonmandatory associations from the controller, for example, premium customers: adding a Boolean field to the *Person* table indicating which people are premium, or creating a single column table that contains the primary keys of premium customers.

The premium customer table does not have to include a column that represents the primary key of the controller because the controller is not an entity (and therefore it has no primary key), and because the controller is a singleton and even if a primary key is assigned to it, repeating the same value in all rows of the table would be unnecessary.

Table 17−15 shows a possible implementation for this optional association.

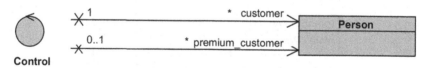

FIGURE 17–11 A mandatory and optional associations from the controller façade.

Table 17–15 Implementation of an optional association from the façade controller.

Table: controller/premium
pk
nn, unique fk_customer
20001 20002

According to Table 17−15, only Abe (20001) and Bea (20002) are premium customers, and Charles (20003) is not.

17.2.3 Inheritance

Relational databases do not support inheritance directly. Mapping inheritance relations to relational databases is an issue that demands attention. There are many different approaches, and this section discusses some of them. All examples in the following subsections are based on Fig. 17−12.

17.2.3.1 Implementing the entire hierarchy in a single table

One solution for representing inheritance that sounds straightforward at first glance is to implement the entire hierarchy in a single table. This table contains all the attributes of all classes in the hierarchy. It also has to identify which instantiated class is being represented in each record; this can be accomplished by adding a *type* column, as in Table 17−16.

Only attributes that belong to the class at the top of the hierarchy may not be null, because all other attributes could be null when the record belongs to one subclass and the attribute to another subclass. For example, if the type of the record is *PromptPayment*, then *start_date* and *nr_of_installments* must necessarily be null. If it is assumed that an object cannot change its class after instantiation, then the column *type* should be immutable.

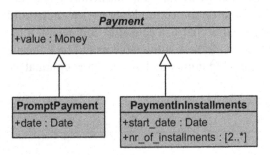

FIGURE 17−12 An example of inheritance.

Table 17−16 Implementation of inheritance in a single table with a *type* field.

Table: Payment

pk, nn, unique, imm pk_payment	nn,imm type	nn value	date	start_date	number_of_installments
200001	PromptPayment	$300.00	04/09/2024		
200002	PromptPayment	$251.00	07/02/2024		
200003	PaymentInInstallments	$1890.00		12/09/2024	12

Table 17–17   Implementation of inheritance using one table for each concrete class part 1: *PromptPayment*.

Table: PromptPayment

pk, nn, unique, imm pk_prompt_payment	nn value	nn date
200001	300.00	04/09/2024
200002	251.00	07/02/2024

Table 17–18   Implementation of inheritance using a table for each concrete class part 2: *PaymentInInstallments*.

Table: PaymentInInstallments

pk, nn, unique, imm pk_payment	nn value	nn start_date	nn nr_of_installments
200003	1890.00	12/09/2013	12

If multiple inheritance is used (e.g., if a payment could be prompt and installments at the same time),[4] then the *type* column should be replaced by a set of Boolean columns: *is_prompt_payment* and *is_payment_in_installments*. In this case, a payment could be prompt, in installments, or both (or neither, if they could also be instances of *Payment*, which in the present example cannot occur because *Payment* is an abstract class).

This approach has some disadvantages. It is hard to manage consistency between subclasses because all data are stored in the same place. Managing it adequately would require various complex control mechanisms. Also, lots of fields in the table would be null all the time, and the big table would be a very sparse one, especially if a big and complex hierarchy is being represented.

17.2.3.2 Each concrete class as a single table

Another approach to deal with inheritance is to represent each concrete class as a separate table. Each table would contain the attributes of the concrete class and the attributes of all its superclasses. Tables 17−17 and 17−18 show a possible implementation using that approach.

If only attributes are inherited, this approach may work. However, if superclasses define their own associations that must be inherited, then managing this becomes a headache because either an associative table should fill in data from different tables in a single column, or a single associative table should be implemented for each subclass that inherits the association.

---

[4] Of course, this cannot be true. It's just a supposition for the sake of the example.

17.2.3.3 Each class in a single table

A better choice for implementing inheritance given the aforementioned problems is to define one table for each class of the hierarchy, even the abstract ones. That way, attributes and association inheritance may be easily implemented. The main disadvantage is that for instantiating an object, a number of tables equal to the number of its superclasses plus one should be accessed. Tables 17−19 to 17−21 show how to implement this approach. There must be references from the subclasses' tables to each immediate superclass table.

17.3 Saving and loading objects

The equivalence between object-oriented design and the relational database is just part of the compatibility issues between these two paradigms. It is necessary also to decide how and when objects will be loaded and saved to the database. Some designers prefer to determine themselves the moment when such operations should be performed. However, that

Table 17–19 Implementation of inheritance using a table for each class, part 1: *Payment*.

Table: Payment

pk, nn, unique, imm pk_prompt_payment	nn value	nn date
200001	300.00	04/09/2024
200002	251.00	07/02/2024

Table 17–20 Implementation of inheritance using a table for each class, part 2: *PromptPayment*.

Table: PromptPayment

pk, nn, unique, imm pk_prompt_payment	nn, unique, imm fk_payment	nn date
300001	200001	04/09/2024
300002	200002	07/02/2024

Table 17–21 Implementation of inheritance using a table for each class, part 3: *PaymentInInstallments*.

Table: PaymentInInstallments

pk, nn, unique, imm pk_payment_in_installments	nn, unique, imm fk_payment	nn start_date	nn nr_of_installments
400001	200003	12/09/2023	12

handcrafted approach for saving and loading objects is subject to logic errors and usually may pollute the domain-level code.

In addition, if the decision when to save and load objects is taken manually, sometimes those operations can be performed without necessity (e.g., loading objects that are already in memory and saving objects that were not changed). Controlling these issues case by case is not the most agile way to develop software.

It is possible to implement the processes for saving and loading objects with automatic mechanisms. In this case, the designer should only decide which classes, attributes, and associations are persistent, and a whole set of methods and data structures will be automatically created to allow those elements to be loaded and saved at the appropriate moments. Initially, this section presents the basic or naïve implementation of this mechanism. Later, the limitations of the technique are explained, and possible solutions drafted.

17.3.1 Virtual proxy

In order to implement an automatic mechanism for saving and loading objects, we can use a design pattern called *virtual proxy* (Gamma et al., 1995). A virtual proxy is a very simple object that implements only two responsibilities:

- It must know the value of the primary key of the real object it represents.
- It must redirect to the real object all messages it receives in its name.

Below is a draft of the way a virtual proxy works:

```
from broker import *

class VirtualProxy:
    def __init__(self, an_real_object_pk):
        self.real_object_pk = an_real_object_pk

    def __getattr__(self, name):
        real_object = BrokerManager.get_real_object(real_object_pk)

        def method(*args, **kwargs):
            if hasattr(self.real_object, name):
                return getattr(self.real_object, name)(*args, **kwargs)
            else:
                return self.execute(name, self.real_object, args, kwargs)
```

The logic behind the virtual proxy is that one of its instances will intercept any message sent to another object through an association link. The proxy will call, then, a broker that may be one for a system or one per class, in order to locate the real object and send it back to the proxy. If the broker finds that the object is in main memory (inside one of the caches), then it will simply send to the proxy a link to the real object. If the object is not in memory, then the broker will locate it in the database and load it to a clean cache. Finally, if the object has this message implemented, then it is executed. Otherwise, an exception will be raised.

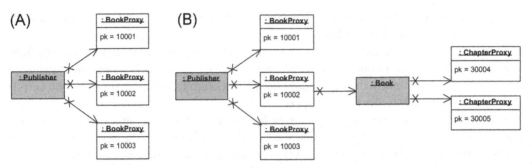

FIGURE 17–13 Two instances, (A) before and (B) after calling an object that is not in memory.

Later, in the following sections, the way the *BrokerManager* works is gradually explained.

Thus the design with virtual proxies requires that instead of associating domain objects directly with other domain objects, they must be associated to their proxies. In this way, it is possible to bring into memory an instance of *Publisher* without loading all instances of *Book* that are linked to it. The instance of *Publisher* is associated to the *proxies of books*, which are very simple objects. The proxies are created in main memory and require much less space than the instances of the real class, such as those of *Book*. An instance of *Book* is loaded only if necessary, that is, only if a message is sent to it through its proxy. This economic way of using memory is called *lazy load*, and it is very efficient in terms of time and main memory in some situations.

To prevent the designer from worrying about when the objects must be loaded, the virtual proxy mechanism must be interposed to all persistent links in main memory. Real objects send messages to each other as if the proxies did not exist. But proxies intercept every message. The proxies ensure that the real object will be loaded if it is not in memory.

Fig. 17–13 is an example of the *lazy load* mechanism. Initially (A), only one instance of *Publisher* is in main memory. It is associated to three books. However, instead of having the books in memory, only their proxies are there. If the instance of *Publisher* must send a message to one of the books, it simply sends the message through the link; the message is intercepted by the proxy that calls the *BrokerManager*, which ensures that the book is loaded into the memory (B). As the book is associated to some chapters, only the chapters' proxies are created in memory, not the real objects.

If one of the chapters receives a message from the book, then only that chapter would be brought into memory.

17.3.1.1 Virtual data structures

The implementation of virtual proxies for each object may be inefficient when an object has many links; for example, a publisher with 50,000 registered books would demand the instantiation of 50,000 proxies to be associated to it when it is brought into memory. Fortunately, there is a way to avoid instantiating large quantities of proxies, which is the implementation of virtual data structures to physically replace the implementation of the associations in main memory.

Thus an instance *Publisher* would not have 50,000 links to 50,000 proxies of *Book*, but a single link to a *VirtualSet* structure with 50,000 PKs to books. The *VirtualSet* implements usual operations to add, remove, update, and query objects: the same operations that a normal set implements. The only difference is that it does not store the real objects, but only their primary keys. The virtual set does not bring objects into memory; it brings only their primary key numbers. The *VirtualSet* and its counterparts, *VirtualSequence*, *VirtualOrderedSet*, *VirtualBag*, *VirtualMap*, etc., use the *BrokerManager* to load real objects when necessary, instead of holding all the real objects.

A virtual data structure may be implemented with the following principles:

- Instead of a physical representation of a collection of objects, it is a physical representation of a collection of the primary key values of the real objects.
- The method that adds an object to the collection must only add the primary key of the real object to the physical representation.
- The method that removes an object from the collection must only remove the primary key of the real object from the physical representation.
- Any method that performs a query on the data structure to return one or more objects receives the real object(s), which are requested from the broker manager.

Thus adding and removing links between objects may be performed without having the real objects in memory (at least from one side of the link). An object is only brought into memory when information about it becomes necessary, that is, when it receives a message.

17.3.1.2 Lazy load

Lazy load is useful because it only brings into memory objects that are going to receive a message. For example, if an instance of *Publisher* is in main memory and one of its books is going to be updated, then it is not necessary to load all instances of *Book* linked to the publisher, but only one.

On the other hand, if the instance of *Publisher* must search its books to find the most expensive of them, then all instances of *Book* that are linked to it must be loaded into main memory. This is the drawback of the technique. Performing all operations on objects in main memory can be an extraordinary waste of time. Imagine loading 50,000 instances of books to main memory just to discover which one of them has the highest price.

One possible solution would be modifying the *virtual proxy* class to allow it to bring into memory not only the primary key of the object, but a subset of its attributes as well. In order to find the highest priced book, a virtual set would contain pair of primary keys and price. Thus the higher price can be found without loading any complete book into main memory.

Virtual proxies work well when relatively few objects are brought into memory for each user operation. For example, a user searching for books to buy will only view a relatively small quantity of books in the list. That user would operate over just a single shopping cart and order. Those kinds of operations over small sets of objects are perfectly handled automatically by virtual proxies. However, when queries or commands involve iterating over large collections of objects, such as increasing the price of all books in the store, then using virtual proxies should be avoided, unless wasted processing time is not a problem; but that usually is not the case.

Thus for performing queries or commands over large collections of objects, if the query or command uses just a few attributes of the objects, it would be advisable to consider replacing the virtual proxy mechanism in that specific case by a query or command directly performed over the database. Therefore some messages, when they reach specific objects, would be redirected to a specific encapsulated implementation that performs the necessary actions in the database and returns the results as necessary, rather than being redirected to a proxy.

17.3.2 Brokers and materialization

The process of loading an object from the database into main memory is called *materialization*. Materialization is usually requested by a proxy to a *broker manager*, which may in turn delegate materialization to a *specialized broker*. The broker manager looks if the requested object is in main memory. If it is not, then the broker manager activates the specialized broker to materialize the object.

Each class may have its own specialized broker. However, a single broker may also be implemented to serve all classes. A specialized broker must implement a method called *materialize* that does the following:

1. It creates in main memory an instance of the persistent class.
2. It initializes the values of the attributes of the new instance with values taken from the respective line and columns in the database.
3. It loads and initializes the virtual data structures that implement the associations of the object with the primary keys of the respective linked objects.

In order to obtain the values for the primary keys of the linked objects, the specialized broker must know what associations are attached to the object being loaded; then it searches the occurrences of the primary key of the object in the associative tables that implement those associations. The primary keys of other objects associated to the primary key of the object being materialized are added into the virtual data structure, which has the responsibility of holding the respective association.

For example, an implementation of a broker for the class *Book*, *Broker4Book* should materialize instances of *Book*, as defined in Fig. 17−14.

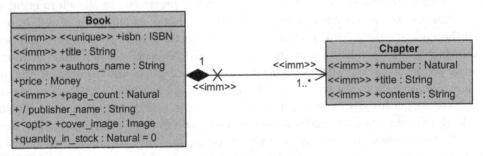

FIGURE 17–14 A conceptual model for books and their chapters.

According to this conceptual model, *Broker4Book* must implement the *materialize* method by performing the following operations:

1. Create an instance of *Book*.
2. Fill in the *isbn, title, authors_name, price, page_count, cover_image*, and *quantity_in_stock* attributes of the new instance with the values stored in the respective columns of the *Book* column in the database.
3. Search the *book_chapter* table for occurrences of the primary key of the book in the *fk_book* column. For every occurrence, add the corresponding value found in the *fk_chapter* column to the virtual set *chapters* of the new instance of *Book*, which implements the association role for the book.

The materialization performed by the specialized broker must not be confused with the creation of a new instance as defined by the system operation contracts. In the contracts, the creation of an instance refers to the insertion of new information in the system, independent of the physical storage (main memory or secondary memory). The materialization performed by the *broker* only refers to the operation of bringing into the main memory an existing object that is not there physically yet. Materialization is, therefore, an operation that belongs exclusively to the persistence tier; it has nothing to do with the business tier.

17.3.3 Caches

Objects in main memory may be classified as follows regarding their state related to the database:

- *Clean* or *dirty*, depending on whether they are consistent with the version stored in the database.
- *Old* or *new*, depending on whether they already exist in the database or not.
- *Deleted* or *kept*, depending on whether they have been deleted in main memory but not yet deleted in the database.

A *cache* is a data structure similar to a *map* or *dictionary* that associates primary key values to the real objects they represent.

Although there are eight possible combinations for the features defined above, in practice only four combinations are sufficient to manage objects in main memory:

- *Old clean cache*: Keeps objects that are in main memory and consistent with the database.
- *Old dirty cache*: Keeps objects that are in main memory and in the database, but that have been updated only in main memory and, therefore, are inconsistent with the database.
- *New cache*: Keeps objects that have been created in main memory, but which are not yet in the database.
- *Delete cache*: Keeps objects that were deleted in memory, but still exist in the database.

The broker manager verifies that an object is in main memory by performing a query on the existing caches, asking for the primary key of the object being requested. If the broker manager finds a reference to that object in one of the caches, it returns the reference to the proxy that asked for it. On the other hand, if the broker manager does not find any reference to the requested object in any cache, then it asks a specialized broker (as, e.g., *Broker4Book*) to materialize the object. The object is then materialized and inserted into the *old clean cache*.

If, after that, the object is updated in main memory, it must be moved to the *old dirty cache*.

The persistence mechanism must have ways to assure that every time the inner state of an object in the old clean cache is changed, it is moved to the old dirty cache. This could be accomplished, for example, by adding a special command such as *BrokerManager.become_-dirty(self)* to any method that changes the object. If the object originally is in the old clean cache, that method will move it to the old dirty cache.

Objects that were created in memory as a result of a contract postcondition are stored into the *new cache*. An object that is in the new cache may not be moved to the old dirty cache, even if its attributes are changed. It stays in the new cache until a *commit* is performed. After the commit, it is moved to an old clean cache.

When an object is deleted from main memory, the result will depend on which cache the object came from. If it was in the old clean cache or in the old dirty cache, then it is moved to the *delete cache*. However, if it was in the new cache, then it may be simply deleted from main memory.

17.3.3.1 Commit and rollback

The *commit* and *rollback* operations are usually activated by the interface tier to indicate that a transaction was successful and confirmed, or that it was canceled, respectively. These operations are implemented by the broker manager. In the case of a commit, the broker manager should do the following:

1. Perform an *update* in the database for every object in the old dirty cache and move those objects to the old clean cache.
2. Perform an *insert* in the database for every object in the new cache and move those objects to the old clean cache.
3. Perform a *remove* in the database for every object in the delete cache and delete those objects from main memory.

In the case of a *rollback*, the broker manager must simply remove all objects from all caches, except those in the old clean cache.

As the old clean cache may grow indefinitely, it is necessary to implement some mechanism to remove the oldest objects from it every time its size reaches some previously established threshold.

The other caches only grow up-to-the-moment a commit or rollback is performed. At that moment, they are emptied.

17.3.3.2 Cache control in a multiuser server

If more than one user connects to the system, it is necessary to determine how to share objects among different users. Assuming we have a client/server architecture with interface, domain, and persistence tiers, at least two approaches are possible:

- *The three tiers are executed in the client.* There is no main memory share in the server, only the database. The client is heavy, and the server is used only to access or store data after a commit is performed. In this case, what travels in the network is data in the form of relational table records and SQL[5] instructions. Information travels only when an object must be materialized or committed. The disadvantage of this design is that the client node is overloaded. However, client applications have recently become richer and more complex. Not depending on a server to process the logic of the application may be the best option.
- *The domain and persistence tiers are implemented in the server, and only the interface tier is implemented in the client.* In this case, the objects will exist in main memory *only in the server*, and what travels through the network are the parameters of the system operations and the returns from queries, usually in the form of DTOs. The advantage is that clients are lighter, and usually it may be cheaper to upgrade a server than upgrading thousands of clients. However, for some applications that require fast processing of the data, waiting for a busy server may not be viable.

If the objects are physically in the server only, there are still more possibilities. One that must be ruled out is to allow all users share the four caches. It has the disadvantage that a user could have access to objects that are being modified, created, or deleted but have not yet been committed by another user. This option seems to be unadvisable for most applications.

The other option is to share only the objects in the old clean cache among the users. There should be multiple instances of other three caches that are private to each user. If an object is in a private cache of one user, then the other users cannot access it. They must wait for a commit or rollback from the first user. Thus the persistence mechanism for multiuser access could be implemented like this:

- An old clean cache is shared by all users.
- Each user has a private old dirty cache, delete cache, and new cache.

By doing this, it is possible to ensure that no user would have access to objects that are being modified by other users. Therefore it is possible to use the caches to implement a *lock* mechanism, that is, when a user is updating an object, the other users cannot access it. Only when the user that has the object performs a commit or rollback, and the object is moved to the old clean cache or cleaned from main memory, can the other users gain access to it again.

---

[5] *Structured Query Language,* the dominant language for defining, accessing, and updating relational databases (Date, 1982).

An advantage of this method is the optimized usage of main memory. All users share the objects in the old clean cache, which is the only one that grows indefinitely. The other four caches, which are specific for each user, only grow during a transaction. When a commit or rollback happens, those caches are emptied.

However, this may negatively affect scalability, because some users could be stuck while others are dealing with some objects. It is possible to implement a more sophisticated control mechanism based on *optimistic merges*: two or more users may edit the same object as long as they do not update the same attribute or association.

This must be used with care, however. Concurrency issues may be rather complicated concerns, and many decisions may depend on business rules. For example, may the price of a book be updated while a user is finishing an order?

Some applications could even require a more pessimistic locking strategy: if a user is browsing an object, no other user may even have access to view it. This is the case for banking applications, for example, which require maximum data security.

Questions

1. What kind of associative table should be used to represent an association that is ordered in both directions? How do you represent it in the case of two ordered sets, or two sequences, or one ordered set and one sequence?
2. What kind of association table should be used to represent an association with an association class that is marked with {*bag*} on one side?

Bibliography

References

Adams, D.N., 1979. The Hitchhiker's Guide to the Galaxy. Completely Unexpected Productions Ltd.

Albrecht, A.J., 1979. Measuring application development productivity. Proceedings of the Joint SHARE/GUIDE and IBM Application Development Symposium, Chicago. pp. 83–92.

Albrecht, A.J., Gaffney, J.E., 1983. Software function, Source lines of code, and development effort prediction: a software science validation. IEEE Trans. Softw. Eng. 9 (6), 639–648.

Alford, M., 1991. Requirements-Driven Software Design. McGraw-Hill.

Ambler, S.W., 2000. Web services programming tips and tricks: modeling essential use cases. Available at: <http://www.ibm.com/developerworks/library/ws-tip-essentialuse/index.html>.

Ambler, S.W., 2004. The Object Primer: Agile Model-Driven Development with UML 2.0, third ed. Cambridge University Press, Cambridge University Press.

Anderson, D.J., 2010. Kanban: Successful Evolutionary Change for Your Technology Business. Blue Hole Press, Germany.

Beck, K., 1989. Simple Smalltalk testing with patterns. Available at: <http://www.xprogramming.com/test-fram.htm> (accessed 31.08.13).

Beck, K., 2003. Test-Driven Development by Example. Addison-Wesley.

Beck, K., Andres, C., 2004. Extreme Programming Explained: Embrace Change, second ed. Addison-Wesley.

Beizer, B., 1990. Software Testing Techniques, second ed. Van Nostrand Reinhold.

Bloch, A., 1980. Murphy's Law, and Other Reasons Why Things Go Wrong. Price/Stern/Sloan Publishers, Inc, Los Angeles.

Boehm, B.W., 2000. Software Cost Estimation with COCOMO II. Prentice-Hall.

Booch, G., Maksimchuk, R.A., Engle, M.W., Young, B.J., Conallen, J., Houston, K.A., 2007. Object-Oriented Analysis and Design with Applications, third ed. Addison-Wesley Professional.

Bourret, R., 2010. XML database products. Available at, <http://www.rpbourret.com/xml/XMLDatabaseProds.htm> (accessed 11.09.13).

Burnstein, I., 2003. Practical Software Testing. Springer-Verlag.

Cabot, J., 2007. From declarative to imperative UML/OCL operation specifications. Lect. Notes Comput. Sci. 198–213.

Ceri, S., Fraternali, P., Bongio, A., Brambilla, M., Comai, S., Matera, M., 2003. Designing Data-Intensive Web Applications. Morgan Kaufmann.

Choenni, S., Blanken, H., Chang, T., 1993. Index selection in relational databases. Proc. Int. Conf. Comput. Inf. 491–496.

Cockburn, A., 2001. Writing Effective Use Cases. Addison-Wesley.

Date, C.J., 1982. An Introduction to Database Systems. Addison-Wesley.

English, A.V., 2007. Business modeling with UML: understanding the similarities and differences between business use cases and system use cases. <http://www.ibm.com/developerworks/rational/library/apr07/english/>. (Retrieved 14.11.12).

Fowler, M., 2003. Patterns of Enterprise Application Architecture. Addison-Wesley.

Gamma, E., Helm, R., Johnson, R., Vlissides, J., 1995. Design Patterns: Elements of Reusable Object-Oriented Software. Addison-Wesley.

Gause, D.C., Weinberg, G.M., 1989. Exploring Requirements: Quality before Design. Dorset House Pub.

Goldberg, A., Robson, D., 1989. Smalltalk 80: The Language. Addison-Wesley.

Grady, R., 1992. Practical Software Metrics for Project Management and Process Improvement. Prentice-Hall.

Ireland, C., Keynes, M. Bowers, D., Newton, M., Waugh, K., 2009. A classification of object-relational impedance mismatch. Advanced Databases and Knowledge Management, DBKDA '09, Gosier pp. 36–43.

Jacobson, I., 1994. The Object Advantage: Business Process Reengineering with Object Technology. Addison-Wesley.

Jacobson, I., Christenson, M., Jonsson, P., Övergaard, G., 1992. Object-Oriented Software Engineering: A Use Case Driven Approach. Addison-Wesley.

Karner, G., 1993. Use case points: resource estimation for objectory projects. Objective Systems.

Kroll, P., Kruchten, P., 2003. The Rational Unified Process Made Easy: A Practicioner's Guide to RUP. Addison-Wesley.

Kruchten, P., 2003. The Rational Unified Process: An Introduction, third ed. Addison-Wesley.

Larman, C., 2004. Applying UML and Patterns: An Introduction to Object-Oriented Analysis and Design and the Unified Process, third ed. Prentice-Hall.

Lieberherr, K., I. Holland, 1989. Assuring good style for object-oriented programs. IEEE Software.

Liskov, B., 1974. Programming with abstract data types, in Proceedings of the ACM SIGPLAN Symposium on Very High Level Languages (pp. 50–59), Santa Monica, California.

Meszaros, G., 2007. xUnit Test Patterns: Refactoring Test Code. Addison-Wesley.

Meyer, B., 1988. Object-Oriented Software Construction. Prentice Hall.

Miles, R., Hamilton, K., 2006. Learning UML 2.0. O'Reilly.

Miquirice, S., Wazlawick, R.S., 2018. Relationship Between Cohesion and Coupling Metrics for Object-Oriented Systems. In: 24th International Conference on Information and Software Technologies (ICIST 2018), Vilnius, Lithuania. Springer Verlag CCIS Series: Communications in Computer and Information Science, v. 920. pp. 1–13.

Molyneaux, I., 2009. The Art of Application Performance Testing: Help for Programmers and Quality Assurance. O'Reilly Media.

Myers, G.J., Sandler, C., Badgett, T., Thomas, T.M., 2004. The Art of Software Testing, second ed. John Wiley & Sons, New Jersey.

Nelson, W.B., 2004. Accelerated Testing: Statistical Models, Test Plans, and Data Analysis. John Wiley & Sons.

Nielsen, J., Usability Engineering. Academic Press, 1994.

Object Management Group, 2010. OCL 2.3.1 Specification. OMG.

Object Management Group, 2011. OMG Unified Modeling LanguageTM (OMG UML), Superstructure, Version 2.4.1. OMG.

Pressman, R.S., 2008. Web Engineering: A Practicioner's Approach. McGraw Hill.

Pressman, R.S., 2010. Software Engineering: A Praticioner's Approach. McGraw Hill.

Probasco, L., 2001. What makes a good use case name?. Rational Edge.

Ribu, K., 2001. Estimating Object-Oriented Software Projects With Use Cases. (Master of Science thesis), University of Oslo, Department of Informatics.

Royce, W.W., 1970. Managing the development of large software systems. Proceedings of the IEEE WESCON. IEEE, Los Angeles.

Santos, C.C., 2007. Automatic Generation of Communication Diagrams From OCL Contracts (Masters dissertation), UFSC, Florianópolis.

Satzinger, J.W., Jackson, R.B., Burd, D.S., 2011. Systems Analysis and Design in a Changing World, sixth ed. Course Technology.

Shapiro, R., White, S.S., Bock, C., Palmer, N., Muehlen, M., Gagné, D., 2012. BPMN 2.0 Handbook, 2nd ed. Future Strategies Inc, Light House Point, Fl.

Tidwell, J., 2005. Designing Interfaces: Patterns for Effective Interaction Design. O'Reilly Media.

Warmer, J., Keppe, A., 1998. The Object Constraint Language: Precise Modeling with UML. Addison-Wesley.

Won, K., 1990. Introduction to Object-Oriented Databases. The MIT Press.

Woolf, B., 1998. Null object In: Martin, R., Riehle, D., Buschmann, F. (Eds.), Pattern Languages of Program Design, 3. Addison-Wesley.

Index

Note: Page numbers followed by "*f*" and "*t*" refer to figures and tables, respectively

Printed in the United States
by Baker & Taylor Publisher Services